MELOPOIESIS

APPROACHES TO THE STUDY OF
LITERATURE AND MUSIC

MELOPOIESIS

APPROACHES TO THE STUDY OF
LITERATURE AND MUSIC

JEAN-PIERRE BARRICELLI

WITH A FOREWORD BY
CALVIN S. BROWN

NEW YORK UNIVERSITY PRESS
New York and London

Library of Congress Cataloging-in-Publication Data

Barricelli, Jean Pierre.
Melopoiesis : approaches to the study of
literature and music.

Bibliography: p.
Includes index.
1. Music and literature.   I. Title.
ML3849.B27   1988   780'.08   87-22063
ISBN 0-8147-1099-9

Book design by Ken Venezio

Poema docet musica,
vitam carmen.

To the Dantes and Beethovens of history, and to those like
Norma, my wife, and Marco, Laura, Franca, my children,
who hold them in the highest esteem.

CONTENTS

FOREWORD

Professor Barricelli is one of the relatively small group of scholars competent in both literature and music who, during the past few decades, have been exploring the relationships between these two arts. In this volume he conveniently brings together a group of his studies which originally appeared over a number of years in diverse periodicals and an equal number which appear here for the first time. Thus, this collection is only in part what a painter would call a retrospective exhibition of his interdisciplinary scholarship.

Any outsider who thinks that the interrelations between two arts must be a narrow field of study will be surprised by the variety of subjects treated here. Altogether, they illustrate most of the common types of interdisciplinary investigation, including biographical study, comparisons of individual works, terms common to both arts, literary and musical movements, malicious parody, methodological theory, and various other things. Even more striking than the variety is the overlapping of these categories. This is simply evidence of the nature of the field: the relations between music and literature are not only various; they are also complex. It is a truism—but nonetheless true—that a study of any problem at any depth usually raises more questions than it answers. Furthermore, these problems are typically interconnected, so that they cannot be shoved into individual pigeonholes and isolated there.

What Conrad Aiken once called "the miracle of interconnectedness" produces the striking richness of these essays. Things not directly implied by the subject at hand keep cropping up because their bearing on that subject needs to be explored. In the essay on "Romantic Writers and Music: The Case of Mazzini," for example, the first pages set the stage by giving an excellent short account of the role of music in Romanticism before the specific subject, Mazzini, appears. The essay comparing Proust and Balzac contains some valuable observations on the differences between the equipment a writer requires in order to deal with painting and that which he needs to deal with music; and an excursus on D'Annunzio helps to nail down some of the points made about Proust and Balzac. Somewhat similarly, at the end of the essay on Sibelius and the *Kalevala*, Richard Strauss is introduced to help explain, by contrast, what Barricelli means by his insistence on the "inwardness" of Sibelius's music.

Even the notes contribute to the breadth and interest of the discussions. In the study of the fauns of Mallarmé and Debussy, a fine truculent note points out the irrelevance of most semiotic theory to aesthetic criticism. This is not the only instance of a necessary negative judgment. After a detailed study of the treatment of Beethoven's Ninth Symphony in Alejo Carpentier's *Los pasos perdidos* and Anthony Burgess's A *Clockwork Orange*, Barricelli raises the question of *why* these writers deliberately set out to demean this symphony, not with witty parody or amusing persiflage, but simply with an unexplained and virulent hatred. I suspect that the phenomenon is like China's "Great Leap Forward." Those who have the illusion that they are creating a brave new world regularly want to destroy the past, which they view—correctly—as an obstacle to their schemes.

Obviously, one can profit from these studies without necessasrily having to agree with everything in them. For example, I find the suggestions as to what musical form (if any) *Le Neveu de Rameau* follows unconvincing, but in the course of exploring this question Barricelli makes a number of useful and interesting points about various other aspects of Diderot's problematical essay. Or one may want to go beyond the conclusions of some of the studies. "Romantic Irony in Music" shows that this concept, already vague and loose as a literary term, is even more elusive when it is applied to music. I hope that this essay may help to keep Romantic irony as a term of musical criticism from going the way of leitmotif in literary criticism and becoming merely a meaningless fashionable buzzword used by those who are temperamentally inclined towards the display of fancy terms. Speaking of temperaments, the demonstration that Tchaikowsky did a sorry job of his musical treatments of Pushkin's *Eugene Onegin* and *The Queen of Spades* because he did not appreciate, or even comprehend, Pushkin's irony, is conclusive. This case shows that, in the arts, the creator's inherent temperameant sets limits that no amount of technique, enthusiasm, or inspiration can overcome.

These studies all exemplify the mild skepticism necessary in work of this kind. Barricelli does not casually assume (as some enthusiasts do) that great artists are, by definition, omniscient. One cannot count on a composer who deals with literary works to have, automatically, a high degree of literary sensitivity or even of comprehension. Nor does a writer who puts music into his works necessarily have any real grasp of it. In studying the growth of Balzac's interest in Beethoven, Barricelli clearly distinguishes between what Balzac could and did appreciate in the composer and those things which were out of his range either musically or temperamentally. To evaluate the accomplishment of Liszt's programmatic *Dante Symphony*, he must (and does) show that the composer had a detailed knowledge and understanding of the *Commedia*. Any musical version of the Faust legend which wants to be taken seriously must go beyond background music, settings of songs, and other such selective and ornamental undertakings and come to grips with the story's philosophical kernel: the problem of evil. And Barricelli awards the palms to Boïto and Busoni because they did this, not just in their words, but in their music.

All together, these essays offer their readers a good look at the world of interdiscplinary scholarship, a number of discussions of basic ideas having to do with the two temporal arts, and a great deal of interesting discussion of individual practitioners of both arts and of their creations.

Sanibel, Florida   Calvin S. Brown
November, 1986

Mozart manuscript fragments: "Se al labbro,"
K295, and letter to his father from Mannheim,
Feb. "30," 1778.

Art by Franca Barricelli.

PREFACE

More years ago than I care to remember, my Harvard mentor, Professor Jean Seznec, guided me in the specialized yet generalist direction of literature and music. "I work with letters and the visual arts," said the author of *The Survival of the Pagan Gods*, "and you, a musician and comparatist, should work analogously in the direction of letters and music." The encouragement of Renato Poggioli and Harry Levin will always be gratefully remembered; but to Jean Seznec's repeated query upon all encounters at literary conferences—"Et la musique?"—I owe my conscience of the current volume.

Half of these pieces (dated by year) were first published as articles in learned journals, but in good Montaignean fashion I know of none that is not unpretentiously and in the strictest sense of the word an essay. I should be foolish to seek the reader's agreement with any of them, particularly with those which are the most speculative. His interest is all I hope to receive. The remaining half (undated) of these essays is of recent, unpublished vintage, readied especially because of the flattering courtesy of the New York University Press to collect into one volume my past and present efforts in this interart relationship.

I have been fortunate in this understaking to benefit from the expertise of several colleagues: Harry Zohn, Terri Frongia, and Cynthia Maldonado, with each of whom I have co-authored an essay. Indeed, I feel that in these instances I have followed their lead and worked my essays around their ideas. To them, therefore, I am deeply indebted for the development of the topics on Zweig, Otello, and Mann, respectively. I am grateful, too, to Alain Veylit for his fine translation into English of my piece on Gambara. All other translations in this volume are by the author(s), unless otherwise indicated.

I also owe an expression of appreciation to the editors of journals containing my previously published essays, who have graciously allowed a reprinting of my work in this volume:

The Bucknell Review and Associated University Presses, for "Liszt's Journey Through Dante's Hereafter" [XXVI, 2, 1982]

The Comparatist and Wayne State University Press, for "The Ambiguous Fauns of Mallarmé and Debussy" [IX, May 1985]

Criticism, for "Music and the Structure of Diderot's 'Le Neveu de Rameau' [V, 2, Spring 1963]

Fantasy Studies, for "Music and Fantasy" [I, 1, expected 1988]

The International Comparative Literature Association, for "Romantic Irony in Music" [in *Romantic Irony*, F. Garber, ed., expected 1988]

Italian Quarterly, for "Revisiting the *Canti Carnascialeschi*" [XI, 43, 1967]

Journal of European Studies and Alpha Academic, for "Faust and the Music of Evil" [XIII, 1983]

Modern Language Quarterly, for "Balzac and Beethoven: The Growth of a Concept" [XXV, December 1964]

Studies in Romanticism, for "Romantic Writers and Music: The Case of Mazzini" [XIV, 2, Spring 1975]. Courtesy of the Trustees of Boston Univeristy.

"A Case of Literary Diplomacy: Balzac and Meyerbeer" was originally published in *L'Année balzacienne 1967*, and "Explorations in a Non-Western Context" first appeared in *Neohelicon*, X, 1, 1983. "Percept and Concept: On Hugo's *Hernani* and Verdi's *Ernani*" is to form part of the Proceedings of the Eleventh Congress of the International Comparative Literature Association (Paris: Sorbonne, 1985). *The Juilliard Review*, which published "Music in Zweig's Last Years: Some Unpublished Letters" [III, 2, Spring 1956], and *Science/Technology and the Humanities*, which published "Critical Limitations in Musico-Literary Study" [I, 2, Spring 1978], have ceased publication.

The University of California has generously supported my endeavors over the years, and of its faith in this, my scholarly life's true focus, I am humbly cognizant.

INTRODUCTION

CRITICAL LIMITATIONS
IN MUSICO-LITERARY STUDY

In the burgeoning field of interdisciplinary study and, for me particularly, of the interrelations of literature, we find ourselves becoming necessarily more and more concerned with methodological inquiries, lest we allow the interests of fashion to encourage dilettantism by the untutored. A description of the financial background of Honoré de Balzac's novels does not qualify the study as interdisciplinary unless the focus is changed, unless there is a veritable "foreground" analysis of the economic history and realities out of which the novels grew. Similarly, a few remarks relating Freudian psychology to a passage in Alberto Moravia may pass as psychoanalytic criticism but hardly justify the claim of interdisciplinary investigation. The point I am making, to echo a judicious observation by Henry H. H. Remak, is that to be genuinely interdisciplinary the analysis of, say, literature and economics or literature and psychology must be done in such a way as to make a contribution, not only to the field of literature, but to that of economics, or that of psychology, as well.

Such analysis involves professional competence in more than one discipline. And in an era of specialization—often exaggerated specialization that in the humanistic disciplines has amounted to intellectual constriction—the unidisciplinary vision has been deemed the only respectable posture for a scholar. The urge to multiply the optic has invited instinctively, from the threatened, myopic class, the charge of dilettantism, meaning a rejection of the pluralistic intellect as something undignifiable with serious consideration. Yet knowledge must grow into learning, and learning alone adumbrates wisdom. In the humanities, knowledge limited to one discipline (sometimes even to a single concealed fold in one discipline) surely has its place; but so does expanded, multidisciplinary learning. In comparative literature, one cannot expect to know Romanticism by reducing it to its original German stirrings; nor can one know the Renaissance by limiting it to its original Italian impetus. And one knows these better when other branches of learning are invited to inform the original interliterary core. Now, literature is by its very nature interdisciplinary, a centrifugal rather than a centripetal force in society, civilization, and culture. It relates to *all* fields of endeavor. Therefore, the true interdisciplinary scholar should contribute as much to the initial as to the related discipline. And whereas not all topics or approaches demand a complete, dual expertise, to make his binary contribution he should still be equally conversant, ideally, in both fields—or, indeed, in all the fields he is attempting to merge.

In my opinion, the most difficult interrelationship for the *literato,* whether author or critic, involves music. It is perhaps not surprising that thus far we have been favored by but one classic written on the theory and practice of the correlation: Calvin S. Brown's pioneering yet still fundamental and sound *Music and Literature: A Comparison of the Arts* (1948),[1] an indispensable and enlightening volume for anyone attempting to engage the field. This correlation harbors critical limitations of a special nature owing to the technical knowledge implicit in the undertaking, a knowledge that does not inform the investigations made by those who merely detect surface correspondences or who find an initial guideline, and not more, in the notion that of all the basic fine arts only music and literature unfold on the axis of time. My experience has been that, to understand a political period with somewhere near the competence of a political scientist's understanding of it—or to know what to look for in a painting with an eye trained almost like a painter's—ultimately requires less exposure and less education in the other discipline than to know the science of music, to appreciate what goes on in a four-part fugue, in the development section of a movement in a symphony, in a inverted cancrizan or a passacaglia. Our eye trains more easily than our ear, and our mind is more immediately disposed to the concrete than to the abstract. Because music becomes so seriously a matter for technical training in abstract aural perceptions, the danger of superficiality looms more heavily in interrelating it than in interrelating most other arts.

To be sure, the musico-literary scholar has a number of safe grounds on which to tread, grounds he may cultivate without a *thorough* knowledge of the *science* of music. His subject may be historical, such as the relationship between politics and the arts at given periods, or the bonds between text and

tones as they develop during a certain era or beyond Western culture; or it
may be biographical, such as the manner in which a composer invades a
writer's consciousness or the importance music itself acquires in the spiritual
life of a noted individual. But other grounds require, in varying degrees, a
more technical knowledge of the art of sounds, for the subject matter may
be philosophical or aesthetic, such as the way in which music "means," or
the way writers react intellectually to music or composers use it ironically,
or indeed the way it can acquire significance, thanks to its grounding in
fantasy, even in today's science fiction. Or the grounds may shift more in a
psychological direction, showing the way folly relates to genius or the way
music acts as a psychic stimulus for remembrance, love, and dream. The
more technically equipped scholar may find special rewards in the structural
approach when a literary work adopts a musical form (here terminological
questions become important) or when a musical idea is employed thematically in literature or shapes the text architecturally through devices that are
strictly musical. Or when a literary heritage is gainfully exploited by a composer. When drama moves to opera, the adaptational re-creation of an already famous text may invite a fruitful interrelationship, something that is
true also when an opera assumes literary qualities or when the literary qualities gain conceptually through the modifications of music. There exists, of
course, the negative side of the equation as well, when the operatic composer, for instance, violates the integrity of the dramatic text.

The danger of a pitfall occurs in those studies based on close structural
analogy, though by the same token this is the area in which the scholar may
reap even higher rewards. But here, where an attempt is made to establish
a one-to-one relationship between two arts expressed in two different artistic
idioms, the approach demands a truly professional competence in both media. And successful illustrations of such a unique blending are bound to be
few. More often than not, we have called to our attention false or inappro-
priate correlations. Take, for example, the idea of Beethoven's last quartets
and T. S. Eliot's *Four Quartets* (which the poet may not have intended,
though he certainly intended the musical construction), or, reversing the
order of the arts, the interpretation of Dante by Tchaikowsky in the Overture
to *Francesca da Rimini* (which the composer did not necessarily expect to
invite, though his known literary knowledge has invited many to find parallels with the fifth canto of the *Inferno*). The dire critical limitation we
should be aware of here is the dilettante's comparison which relies on infer-

ence rather than analysis. Analogy is important in the cognitive and comparative process, but analogy fashioned inferentially and not analytically is rootless and constitutes a grievous methodological error, since neither discipline gains anything in the process. The word *melopoiesis*, which fuses the concepts of music and poetry as once they were inseparable in ancient Greece, or for that matter in ancient China, best indicates the interpenetrating unity of the dual inquiry at hand.

Let me attempt, now, to be more specific by introducing four examples, two drawn from the relationship which transposes musical structure into the work of literature, and two from the reverse direction, the musical interpretation of a work of literature. I have already mentioned one of them, because it is a common example: T. S. Eliot's *Four Quartets* and music, or even the *Quartets* and specifically Beethoven's String Quartet in A Minor, opus 132 (which has five movements). An interdisciplinary analysis of this relationship should suggest that Eliot did not know much about music, or as much as he should have to lead the reader (and critic) on as indeed he does. We all know, and perhaps have been misguided by, Eliot's allusions to Beethoven, his probable acquaintance with J. W. N. Sullivan's book on the composer's spiritual development, and the words in his often quoted essay "The Music of Poetry" of 1942, in which he refers to the relationship between poetic and musical structure, though he admits he has no "technical knowledge" of music:

The use of recurrent themes is as natural to poetry as to music. There are possibilities for verse which bear some analogy to the development of a theme by different groups of instruments; there are possibilities of transitions in a poem comparable to the different movements of a symphony or a quartet; there are possibilities of contrapuntal arrangement of subject-matter.

This statement has led many critics to view the *Quartets* in relation to specific musical models, particularly Beethoven's late quartets where, says one critic, "the music is beyond music."[2] Supposedly, the Beethoven blueprint lay before the poet, who then organized his poetic material in five divisions which reflect a musical composition's sequence of movements, and further both stated and modulated his themes the way they are stated and modulated in a musical movement. According to this kind of "analysis," Eliot's work begins with the statement of some philosophical idea: let us say an insight into the nature of time as a form of consciousness and our subsequent liberation from time by expansion into new dimensions growing out of it. The would-be musical counterstatement of this idea—and counterstatement is admittedly important in the development of a musical idea—is a poetic restatement from a different angle and expressed in a different style. Eliot's opening words on the reality or nonreality of "what might have been"— a rather dryly set forth philosophical statement—is echoed more poetically by modulating (good musical word!) from the dry:

> Time present and time past
> Are both perhaps present in time future,
> And time future contained in time present . . .

to the more symbolic repetition:

> Footfalls echo in the memory
> Down the passage which we did not take.
> Toward the door we never opened
> Into the rose-garden . . .

Supposedly, this represents counterstatement, a contrast between two stylistic levels. But in music counterstatement drives the composition forward; in Eliot, it merely echoes. In music it counters with another statement; it does not restate or repeat. Yet, despite his rather naïve knowledge of musical idiom, in his essay Eliot invites us to read quite a bit into what he sees as "the development of a theme by different groups of instruments" and the contrastive effect of a "contrapuntal arrangement of the subject matter." Eliot does not seem to realize, nor do the critics who take his clues, that instruments that echo merely echo—they do not "develop"—and that the relationship between "time present . . . and past" and echoing "footfalls . . . in memory" is in no way contrapuntal. If anything, it is simply "canon" in music, and not even that; it is not counterpoint, which can occur only when two ideas are sounded simultaneously—something which can happen only with great tour de force in literature. This may sound like nitpicking, but I will still stand on it, since it has traduced many a critic into uttering banalities with reference to the musico-literary correlation in Eliot.

Eliot continues, in "The Music of Poetry":

In a poem of any length, there must be transitions between passages of greater and less intensity, to give a rhythm of fluctuating emotion essential to the musical structure of the whole; and the passages of less intensity will be, in relation to the level on which the total poem operates, prosaic—so that, in the sense implied by the context, it may be said that no poet can write a poem of amplitude unless he is a master of the prosaic.

And by this, we are supposed to appreciate antithetical effects, often obtained in the *Quartets* by the alternation of highly poetic with rather prosaic passages, as musical. It seems to me that all that is involved here is the sense of good writing, good composition, which Dante and Shakespeare had as well as did Michelangelo and Mozart, and that there is nothing to the aesthetics of antithetical effects which makes them peculiarly musical.

Along these same lines, we should recall how often, in speaking of the musical dimension of the *Quartets*, critics have referred to the recurring image, the image reiterated in the variations of different contexts (the fire symbol in Eliot's poem); or, writes C. A. Bodelsen, "the resumption on phrases, or whole lines, so as to call up the memory of the contexts in which they have previously appeared, and thus link up the poems with one another." Thus, a verse in "Burnt Norton" is repeated in "Little Gidding," or similar experiences in "Little Gidding" relate "Burnt Norton" to "The Dry Salvages" or to "East Coker," and "themes from all the Quartets form a sort of coda in the last lines of the last quartet."[3] But, again, is this not simply the mark of good writing or, to include the other arts, of good composition? Did Tolstoy do anything different in *War and Peace* or Manzoni in *I promessi sposi* or Proust in *A la recherche du temps perdu* or Dante in the *Commedia?* Granted, repetition is a central musical necessity and recall is a central device, but both repetition and recall unify all artistic expression, from architecture and painting to music and literature, and we should be as justified saying that *Four Quartets* are pictorial or architectural as that they are musical. And finally, to associate the *Quartets* with Beethoven's late quartets, using Sullivan's classic study of Beethoven's highly spiritualized final years' expression and mood as a guiding thought, constitutes a form of gratuitous analogy by inference which I cannot accept. Nor, perhaps, would Beethoven.

To this kind of inferential and inaccurate use of musical analogy I would oppose Thomas Mann's use of the leitmotif, particularly in its Wagnerian manner, in *Tonio Kröger*, which he then developed less obviously in subsequent writings and finally applied most subtly in *Der Zauberberg*. As employed by Wagner, a leitmotif is usually a short musical formula connecting the music to an extramusical referent, serving descriptively as a reminder of an idea, primarily a psychological quality or historical situation. Conveying an idea without expressing it fully is one of the miracles made possible by the abstractness of the musical idiom. An author so deeply conscious of music as Mann was—who knew the real meaning of contrapuntal arrangements and orchestral developments—must be believed without reservation when he writes of *Tonio Kröger* (in 1936 in the Preface to *Stories of Three Decades*):

Here probably I first learned to employ music as a shaping influence in my art. The conception of epic prose-composition as a weaving of themes, as a musical complex of associations, I later employed largely in *Der Zauberberg*. Except that there the verbal leitmotif is no longer, as in *Buddenbrooks*, employed in the representation of form alone, but has taken on a less mechanical, more musical character, and tries to mirror the emotion and idea.

Indeed, the transposition here of one art onto another, while of course not literal (since we are dealing, after all—and happily—with two different arts with different modes of expression), is close enough aesthetically to justify an analysis and leave aside all reliance on inference. The recurrence of the description of Tonio's father, "a tall, carefully dressed man with thoughtful blue eyes, who always wore a wild flower in his buttonhole," or of the phrase "We are not gypsies in green carts, but substantial people," constitutes perhaps the most obvious and even crude parallel with leitmotif in Mann's prose; it is as heavy and deliberate as the overall sonata form of the story (the two themes of Hans and Inge in the exposition, the significant conversations with Lisabeta in the development, the journey in the recapitulation, the letter to Lisabeta in the coda—restated all together in the summarizing four paragraphs).[4] But, then, what he does with a more Wagnerian (and ultimately expanded) use of a leitmotif—that is, with a mere color (white) or a known historical period (the Middle Ages) or a common concept (the Devil), that recalls experiences, thus drawing into an essential unity an array of seemingly disparate ideas, and how he allows these motifs in turn to spawn other motifs—deserves to be considered under the nearly literal heading of contrapuntal arrangement and orchestral development. After all, a short set of ideas or sequence of words held together by their inner grammar, as it were, but reaching in meaning beyond their immediate context, is little different from a group of notes held together by their inherent melodic line and relating a past reality or idea to the immediate context. This is particularly true in *Der Zauberberg*, and unfortunately for the analyst the novel represents the kind of structure which must be experienced by the reader who hears psychomusically (the counterpart of the listener who reads purely rationally), for in having it analyzed and thus eviscerated we lose all sense of its organic unity. Apart from this consideration, the fact remains that *Der Zauberberg* is a musical work and that *Four Quartets*, despite the title and the genre, is not. The former may be analyzed, albeit with some difficulty and never completely, in musical terms; the latter's musical dimension can only be inferred.

If now we turn our attention to musical interpretations of works of literature, purposely discarding opera where word complements music, and focusing, say, on the symphonic poem, we find ourselves on even more dangerous terrain. While literature can imitate something of the musical process through its own powers of nuance, association, varied repetition, and recall, music lacks literature's specificity and cannot really shape itself into a concrete and unique statement. Its expressive power, which is far greater than that of the finest in literature, namely poetry, is not verbal. Therefore, to approach something like Dukas's *L'Apprenti sorcier* or Strauss's *Don Quixote* with the tools of a literary critic is to invite vapid dilettantism and the worst kind of commentary by inference.

Take, for example, the danger of reading Dante into Tchaikowsky's Overture to *Francesca da Rimini*. If we are guided by the title, we can listen for the sounds of the windstorm; the pathetic voice of Francesca in the solo clarinet; and the general pathos of a nostalgic love story, passionate and serene as it was at different moments. But if we are not so guided, the Overture might just as easily suggest anything from a day at the races to a restless child finally making it to bed. The point is that there is nothing particularly Dantean about the composition.

Now, we all know this; we all know about these easy inferential pitfalls, and belaboring the point would be redundant. But the question does come up—and justifiably—namely, is it ever possible to do a literary analysis of a piece of music on a one-to-one basis in such a way as to avoid superficiality and make a contribution to both arts? The answer is yes, but such interrelations are extremely rare. In fact, there may not be more than a dozen of them in all musico-literary history, and for this reason the desire to find exact interart correspondences should be pursued diffidently and limited only to concrete instances of unmistakable relationship. Such instances would include the Debussy-Mallarmé *Après-midi d'un faune*, certain poems by

Conrad Aiken, the Carpentier-Beethoven *El acoso*, and Anthony Burgess's *Napoleon Symphony*, among very few others, and less so A. Huxley's *Point Counterpoint* and De Quincey's "Dream Fugue." I might add, too, in the dramatic context, Benjamin Britten's *A Midsummer Night's Dream*, Igor Stravinsky's *Oedipus Rex*, and Claude Debussy's *Pelléas et Mélisande*. But the clearest and cleanest example, to my way of thinking, is Liszt's symphonic poem of 1885 based on Dante's *Divina Commedia*. Here the composer becomes a remarkable literary interpreter. If we just take the first movement, the "Inferno," we see how many musical devices, which singly do not permit us to venture beyond the music itself, in the aggregate shape a vision that makes the music say with notes much of what the poem said with words. I am not simply relying on the obvious clue provided by Liszt when he wrote certain verses from the *Commedia* right into the score above the appropriate instruments. I am referring more to the expressive and compositional devices used in the music itself to depict not just Hell but Dante's Hell: the infernally devised orchestration, the rapid rhythmic pattern of triplets and chromatics, the downward movement of melodic lines whose gravity does not permit the pleasure of an uplifting statement, the total lack of modulations lest smooth transitions belie the jagged nature of this underworld, the leitmotif of hopelessness, the Devils' grotesque march and their mockery of the appoggiatura sighs of the sinners (a masterpiece of literary interpretation through music), the single voice of Francesca and the implied presence (through thirds and sixths) of Paolo, the defiance of the infernal rebels like Capaneus and Vanni Fucci, and the flat open-fifth mechanicalness of Lucifer. The music tells a story, interprets it, in most ways *is* that story, and yet it can stand on its own, without the external referent of Dante's work, and make sense musically. We cannot say this with reference to Tchaikowsky's music about Francesca, which is merely *generally* descriptive of a literary text; Liszt, through his theory of the "transposition of art" (using one art to do what the other had done), makes his composition *specifically* descriptive. While the former at best makes us "react to" by inferring, the latter "tells" us to interpret in a way that is accessible to both literary and musical analysis.

Unless, then, we can establish specific structural interrelationships between literature and music, as in the case of Thomas Mann, or between music and literature, as in the case of Franz Liszt, musico-literary study will produce too many painful efforts based on vague analogy to remain intellectually respectable. The area is fraught with critical limitations, and we must guard against the directing voice of poets like T. S. Eliot as well as against the eager identifications of bemused listeners. Melopoiesis must always stand out as a solidly multidisciplined, formal construct.

(1978)

[I]

LITERATURE AND MUSIC

1

MUSIC IN ZWEIG'S LAST YEARS: SOME UNPUBLISHED LETTERS[1]

Two fundamental aspects of the life and work of the Austrian writer Stefan Zweig are poignantly revealed in two sets of hitherto unpublished letters to the musicologists Alfred Einstein and Madame Gisella Selden-Goth. The first is the vital part that music and the collection of music manuscripts played in the last decade of his life; the second, his reaction to a rapidly disintegrating Europe, the growing feeling of exile and homelessness which culminated in his final tragedy. The period covered by this correspondence may be termed the "twilight of a great European." The menacing course of world events in the mid-1930s led the Austrian writer to abandon his beautiful Salzburg home where he had lived since shortly after the end of World War I. It was an ever growing sense of doom that caused him to give up many of his old pleasures, such as manuscript collecting, along with many of his old associations, and to travel about restlessly (even though he had become a British subject and England could be considered his domicile during most of this period).

The correspondence with Alfred Einstein comprises fifty letters and cards dating from December 1930 to September 1941.[2] It would be possible to offer many reasons why Zweig was drawn closely to Einstein, but foremost, undoubtedly, was the kinship he felt to a person who was steeped in Mozart, to an expert whose wide-ranging Mozart activities included many fine editions and keen critical studies, not to mention what Zweig considered Einstein's magnum opus, his revision of the Köchel-Verzeichnis.

Zweig considered Mme Selden-Goth another kindred spirit. His correspondence with her includes sixty-three letters and cards[3] ranging in time from June 1935 to Christmas 1941, just two months before his suicide. She was an impassioned music collector, historian, and editor who lived in Florence prior to World War II, spent the war years in the United States, and subsequently returned to Italy. Her friendship with Zweig, as with Einstein, had been of long standing; the Austrian writer considered her a widely traveled and cultured "good European" and fellow collector. What makes the letters to these two correspondents alive, both humanly and dramatically, are on the one hand his reactions to the world situation, notably his increasing perturbation and pessimism, and on the other his profound knowledge of, and abiding interest in, music and musicians. These two aspects face each other, as it were, like forces of good and evil, one seeking to deject and destroy, the other to encourage and edify that sensitive entity that was the soul of Stefan Zweig.

It has been justly remarked that Zweig's ultimate tragedy might have been averted if he had been able to maintain his musical interests during his final crisis. The truth of this hypothesis becomes quite evident when one examines the musical references pervading these letters: the dominating figure of Arturo Toscanini, the author's eagerness to mediate in musical matters even after he had abandoned his world-famous manuscript collection, his helpful personal interest in Einstein's Mozart studies, and his frequent initiative in developing musical projects. His very last letters contain almost no such references, nor do they indicate even the physical possibility of pursuing any such interests. Instead, we read with sorrow of his progressive disillusionment with the world.

As has already been indicated, it was probably Mozart who brought Einstein and Zweig close together. The former's scholarly stature, for Zweig, was symbolized by his edition of the Köchel-Verzeichnis, published in Leipzig in 1937, an accomplishment to which he referred on May 24 of that year as "a work that, I feel for certain and without rancor, will survive the whole pack of mine." But long before this his desire to bring Mozartiana to his friend's attention is quite clear. In September 1931, he called his attention to a thirty-page diary of Mozart's son, which was on sale; in March 1932, he told him of an unknown Mozart piece he had seen in the possession of Schumann's grandson—a possible inclusion in Einstein's forthcoming bibliography; in April 1935 he asked him to stop to see a Mozart archive in Vienna; in March 1935 he called his attention to a Mozart aria in his autograph catalogues and induced him to work at his Salzburg home, presumably to pursue the completion of that very magnum opus, the Köchel; a one-page sketch of Mozart's Horn Concerto, offered for sale by someone in

Paris, and bought by pianist Alfred Cortot, was the subject of a letter in November 1936, in which he also directed the musicologist's attention to the Glasgow Mozart collection. Even after the publication of the Köchel, similar references keep appearing: in a letter of August 1937, he made mention of all his Mozart manuscripts that were being sold by the Viennese dealer Heinrich Hinterberger,[4] but even this sudden and, one assumes, painful separation from his cherished autographs did not prevent him, some time after November 1938, from relating with a fair measure of excitement how in Philadelphia he had discovered an unknown little sketch by Mozart along with two letters of the composer's sister, one of which included a poem the former had written for her marriage. And what overtones of admiration one hears in December 1939, even while disillusionment continues to set in, when he read the negative notation in the catalogue of the firm of Breslauer which proved the stature of his friend as a Mozart scholar: "unknown to Einstein"!

The two men were always on the alert to do each other favors. The story of a very special publication is a good illustration of this. Einstein once introduced Zweig to the writer and collector Speyer,[5] a contact which led to Zweig's acquisition in the summer of 1935 of the original manuscript of the Mozart-Goethe song "Das Veilchen." He thereupon prevailed upon his publisher, Herbert Reichner, to issue it in a limited facsimile edition, which delighted many bibliophiles.[6] What enhanced the desirability of the edition was that he asked Einstein to write a historico-critical introduction. This particular manuscript always remained especially close to Zweig's heart; it was one of the few pieces he kept after the dissolution of his famous collection. No better memento of his earlier interests and association with his friend could he have retained than this one. After his death, and until recently, it remained in the possession of Zweig's first wife, Friderike.

The story of the "Veilchen" is an example of Zweig's eagerness to develop projects, to spark musical activities, and of his desire to collaborate in them personally. Once he bespoke Einstein's interest in an international publishing project in several languages: three volumes that would present the creative process in art and would show "on the basis of well-organized biographical, autobiographical, epistolary and illustrative material how the various musicians really composed, the artists painted, and the poets wrote." To be sure, Zweig foresaw the negative conclusion that there are no laws for the creative process, but he considered the project in itself both interesting and worthwhile. He would write a comprehensive introduction for all three tomes; Einstein would be responsible for putting together the book on music. Zweig was quite certain that the work would be definitive for decades, and his careful selection of great composers—among them Gluck, Verdi, Wagner, Mozart, and Beethoven—would make it internationally acceptable. He went so far as to caution Einstein, who agreed to the project, against presenting too many canonized Germans, and advised him to include some extremist—Schönberg, for instance—instead of Brahms. Even though nothing came of this grand project, it is revealing to learn how earnestly Zweig wanted to associate himself with the musical field and to immortalize, as it were, his unquenchable passion for music by promoting something on an international level that would have a universal appeal. In one letter he stated quite unmistakably that even if immediate responses to music are not so plentiful, good musical works have greater permanence than literary works (Honoré de Balzac, Anthony Burgess, and Richard Strauss would not have disagreed).

Zweig again showed his eagerness to promote musical projects when, in the late 1930s, he became one of the editors and advisers of *Forum-Bücher*, a paperbound series of German books published jointly by the houses of Bermann-Fischer, Querido, and Allert de Lange in Stockholm and Amsterdam. At that time, he suggested that Einstein compile a volume of letters of German composers accompanied by an introduction and a commentary. This time the plan materialized, and the volume appeared under the title *Briefe deutscher Musiker*.

On November 28, 1936 (his birthday), Zweig was presented the opportunity of becoming directly involved in a musical publication: Mme Selden-Goth suggested that they collaborate on a little book about Beethoven. The reaction was most enthusiastic, for it was no secret that for years he had planned somehow to interpret Beethoven the man. Unfortunately, this particular desire was never realized. Thus, Zweig's only direct contributions to music literature remained on the modest, however deserving, side: a preface to Paul Stefan's book on Toscanini; several short essays on friends like Ferruccio Busoni and Bruno Walter; the long poems "The Conductor" (a poetic portrait of Gustav Mahler) and "The Singer" (inspired by Madame Cahier); and sketches of a pageant entitled *The Origin of Music*. It should be mentioned also that, after the death of Hugo von Hofmannsthal, Zweig became Richard Strauss's librettist, putting the finishing touches on *Arabella* and writing for him *Die Schweigsame Frau* (adapted from Ben Jonson).[7]

However unsuccessful, Zweig's goodwill and altruism made him a very active mediator, almost a manager, whose interest it was to introduce Einstein to his own publishers. He frequently spoke to Newman Flower of Cassell's in London, Ben Huebsch of the Viking Press in New York, and Herbert Reichner in Vienna about his musicologist friend. He tried to persuade them to publish Einstein's book on madrigals, for example, a difficult enterprise for any publisher; he took it upon himself to introduce the musicologist to Julien Cain, director of the Bibliothèque Nationale of Paris; he made an effort to get Mr. Flower interested in Einstein's history of music. In short, the agent-mediator did everything in his power to promote works of music and music criticism which he deemed in any way meritorious, as if he grew in self-realization every time he came into contact with this particular art. That the "Veilchen" was the only Einstein item printed by Zweig's publishers is irrelevant; what is impressive is the attitude of the Austrian man of letters toward the art for which he evidently felt the greatest affinity. His beloved manuscript collection bears ample witness to this, especially when one notices the predominance of musical manuscripts during the later years of the collection. And even after he had disposed of it, Zweig kept up his interest in manuscripts and actually acquired a few—by Mozart, Wagner, Weber, and Debussy. Above all, he took a vicarious pleasure in Gisella Selden-Goth's collection. In many of his letters he advised her on the acquisition of choice items, repeatedly acting here too as mediator and exchanging little collector's joys with her. Congratulating her on the purchase of a Haydn manuscript, Zweig wrote in August 1935: "In these items one must not begrudge oneself such little joys now and then, because one cannot have the big joy, the 'high C,' anymore." Also in his letters to Einstein he keeps mentioning musical manuscripts—by Gluck, Beethoven, Handel, and others—which he thought would be of interest to his friend. The dissolution of his own collection notwithstanding, Zweig was unable to resist a bargain, especially one in the field of music.

One cannot hope to appreciate the meaning that music held for Stefan Zweig without being aware of the role played by Arturo Toscanini. The writer's great love and admiration for him are touchingly reflected in his correspondence to fellow admirers of the fascinating maestro. To him, Tos-

canini was the symbol of his beloved, vanishing "world of yesterday," a
world made worth living in by the uplifting and fraternalizing powers of
music. Referring to his last year is Salzburg, Zweig wrote to Mme Selden-
Goth on July 7, 1936: "This past year it was a mysterious heightening of
enjoyment to me to feel that the Toscanini world is functioning freely for
the last time." It is not unusual, then, that on the occasion of the maestro's
seventieth birthday in 1937, Zweig, still the literary, musical, and personal
mediator and arouser of appreciations, sought to arrange a fitting birthday
salute for him. In an undated letter from this period he wrote to Mme
Selden-Goth: "The nicest thing would have been to raise enough money for
a Toscanini Foundation—a sort of Nobel Prize for music, which could be
conferred by him during his lifetime and by a committee afterwards. But to
collect funds would take time and the genius of a [Bronislaw] Hubermann."
Mme Selden-Goth's comment after Zweig's death is impressive: "Stefan Zweig
comprehended as no one else Toscanini's loyalty to musical and ethical
greatness. Toscanini the man revealed his soul to him more closely than he
would have to a mere musician."[8] There is no doubt, therefore, that the
Austrian eagerly welcomed every opportunity to see and hear the Italian,
and his letters to both correspondents mention concerts and personal meetings in Milan, London, and New York—experiences which allowed him to
sense perfection in an imperfect world. How symptomatic is that letter to
Einstein of May 24, 1937, in which he tells of an unforgettable rehearsal
he had attended, one in which he had taken a "Toscanini bath" that cleansed
his soul from daily cares!

    In some respects, the disintegration of his "world of yesterday," of his
"Toscanini world," manifested itself in unfavorable reactions, expressed in
no uncertain terms, to the famous music festivals of his own Salzburg. Once,
in a letter to Mme Selden-Goth dated March 3, 1938, the writer criticized
the maestro for withdrawing from the Salzburg Festival, but rejoiced at having cut his own ties with his erstwhile home:

Toscanini's cancellation was well-meant but premature, and a tactical blunder. He
shouldn't have abandoned Austria while it still resists; the only result is going to be
that Furtwängler and [Richard] Strauss will turn Salzburg into a German festival
town already this year. Fortunately, I detached myself long ago from that city. A god
or devil has granted me clear vision and saved me from being turned into a fool by
those closest to me.

The music lover Zweig's attitude toward the Salzburg festivals was ambivalent. In happier days they had occasioned reunions with admired friends like Toscanini and Bruno Walter, but in later years he came to resent the commercialization of these art festivals and their disturbance of his own work, and sought to absent himself from the city while they were in progress. Again to Mme Selden-Goth he wrote from Marienbad on August 19, 1935:

As for Salzburg, I am sorry to have missed two or three musical events and four or five people, but I am happy to have evaded all the hustle and bustle. Trying to force down in one gulp just about all the people we know in Europe would certainly have given us mental indigestion.

And on May 21, 1937, he wrote to the same correspondent:

I can understand very well that after a Florence Music Festival you have no desire for a Salzburg one. Nothing is more dangerous than the festive becoming a regular institution, the formerly extraordinary becoming a scheduled annual event, with Mozart as the fixed summer menu.

But a far more devastating symptom of Zweig's moral sickness and disillusionment with the world had come in 1935 when, moving to London, he decided to dissolve his world-renowned manuscript collection.[9] In a letter to Mme Selden-Goth from London dated April 18, 1936, he gives his reasons for this surprising action:

I had a number of reasons for dissolving my collection. The first is the reorganization of my life. Here in my London flat I should not have the possibility of putting up the whole collection. There isn't even room for Beethoven's writing desk. Secondly, I really lack the time to keep on collecting in my old style. Thirdly, the collecting of literary and musical documents with the idea of historical completeness no longer seems the proper thing to me. So I have limited myself to some few items to which I really have a personal relationship; each of these pieces, such as Mozart's "The Violet" and a sheet from the manuscript of "Faust," represents a genre at its finest. Added to this were considerations which grew in importance with the years; I mean the problem of what was to be done with my collection after my death. Originally I thought of bequeathing it to some museum with the stipulation that it be continued. But I have certainly lost all desire to give anything to a German museum or to German interests generally. So I put behind me this collection as well as my house and many other things of my past, and have felt freer ever since. Seldom before have I had as strong a feeling that I have done the right thing as after this decision.

Whatever his rationalizations, however, it seems that this incident had deeper psychological connotations: it was an act of frustration, of self-negation, closely paralleling the many tragedies that a disintegrating world made manifest to his eyes. In a way, this action too, even if self-imposed, contributed to the disappointment which engendered that feeling of homelessness and pessimism so prevalent in Zweig's later years. "We have lost more than Austria herself," he wrote to Einstein on May 7, 1938, after the Nazi aggression, "but with her our entire effectiveness." Furthermore, the indignities to which creative people were subjected—not finding publishers, being hounded, and the like—were a final blow to the fine sensibility of the generous writer. These were foul conditions under which work was an impossibility; these were evils that encroached upon the world of beauty whose essence is peace and purity. When Einstein was compiling his volume of music letters in 1938, his friend wrote to him on August 27: "In spite of your embitterment, I should advise you not to include anything aggressive in your introduction. Let us at least keep the world of music pure and free from this cacophony of politics." Unfortunately, Zweig himself never found it possible to achieve such peace and purity; on the contrary, tragedy and evil marked a crescendo of frustration and disillusionment in his final years. For this reason, Mme Selden-Goth expressed the belief that more music in his last days could have saved Stefan Zweig. "A chamber music ensemble playing in his home, or the opportunity to listen now and then to an orchestra led by one of his master-conductor friends, might have eased the tension of his racked brain, constantly brooding over a bleak personal future and a vision of humanity in agony."[10] But this was not to be; the forces of despair slowly blotted out those of encouragement.

Such, then, is the secret human drama behind Zweig's correspondence with Alfred Einstein and Mme Gisella Selden-Goth. Through it, these letters acquire lasting significance and become a not unworthy memorial to Stefan Zweig the "musician," for they illustrate clearly the integral part of his life that was music, and suggest by extension what it might be for mankind.

(1956)

2

BALZAC AND BEETHOVEN:
THE GROWTH OF A CONCEPT

Ludwig van Beethoven's acceptance by the French public was slow, dubious, and far from complete even by the end of Balzac's life. If a few connoisseurs recognized the transcendent power of the composer's symphonies, many more expressed dislike for them; and his chamber works, according to Romain Rolland, made no impact upon French musical consciousness until well after his death and that of Balzac (1850). Outwardly, events seemed to belie this fact. Conductor François Antoine Habeneck's genial baton, from 1828 onward, shook many Frenchmen from their torpor. By March 1831 all nine symphonies had been performed in Paris. The Société des Concerts du Conservatoire's little hall was filled to capacity with cheering audiences; tickets had to be purchased months in advance, the famous soprano Malibran swooned the first time she heard the Fifth Symphony; Vigny began an unfinished poem in an epical mood entitled "Beethoven"; and, beginning in 1834, *La Gazette musicale* consistently praised the master from Bonn. In addition, there were the literary interpretations of Beethoven by d'Ortigue; the determination of Castil-Blaze to reconcile the German's scores with Romantic trends; the crusading zeal of Berlioz; Liszt's piano transcriptions of the symphonies; and the audible praises of Hugo, Sand, Nerval, Lamennais, and Deschamps.

All these plaudits, not to speak of the earlier panegyrics of E. T. A. Hoffmann, reached Balzac in the middle of his long-standing and fervent adherence to Rossinian music. We cannot say, however, that his attraction to Beethoven followed the common matter of a fad, or that what he heard about the composer represented anything like a fad. The stirs that Habeneck's concerts provoked resembled little more than ripples in the wider pool of uncertainty and animosity which characterized French reaction. If a chronicler in an 1837 issue of *L'Artiste* congratulated the Société because "now we want to hear Beethoven's symphonies every evening," whereas about a decade before people had declared that "Beethoven was a maniac" and that "his symphonies were booed by our audiences,"[1] we should not overlook Berlioz's lament of that same year:

Many people are beginning to speak only with disdain about these immortal compositions. Well, gentlemen, truthfully, when you see every day, without surprise, the fiftieth performance of some dramatic platitude, are we really abusing your patience if we offer you, with such discreet persistency, masterpieces of such magnitude?[2]

The cultural mood of the country, dominated by Italian or Italianate music (a rubric which included Mozart and Haydn), tended to oppose the incursion of the German school. Mme de Staël herself, in her Teutonic-minded *De l'Allemagne*, had not mentioned Beethoven, and Chateaubriand had found only one brief moment to refer to him, in *Mémoires d'outre-tombe*. Stendhal clearly preferred Rossini; Lamartine, although lured by the dreamy exercise of the imagination which Beethoven occasioned in him, indicated in his *Entretien* on Mozart that he would like to be the Salzburger or Rossini; Chopin expressed himself with cautious disapproval; and Adam, in adopting Rossini's style for *La Muette de Portici*, showed that he conferred the honor of primacy upon the Italian composer.

The larger public agreed with Adam and with reactionary critics like Paul Scudo, or with musical historians like François Joseph Fétis, who might grant that Beethoven was a philosopher and thinker but refused to acknowledge him as an artist and musician: "if he is probably a man of genius, even of immense genius, he is not a man of taste."[3] The uncertainty needed many more years to dissipate, and while the process began during Balzac's lifetime, four years after his death readers of *La Revue des deux mondes* could still find the usually perspicacious Eugène Delacroix stating reservations, accusing Beethoven of want of "correction" and of lack of "rigorous proportions," but concluding: "I'll give him the benefit of the doubt against my very feelings."[4]

Balzac did not oscillate. The earliest documented encounter between him and Beethoven's music is recorded in an article of 1831 which refers to "a piece by Beethoven, a score with as much charm as brilliance."[5] In January 1834, in Geneva, he heard a selection from the Sixth Symphony. Then— again in terms of the record we have—he heard the Fifth, one of Habeneck's brilliant performances which brought the entire audience simulta-neously to its feet.[6] The novelist was thunderstruck. We cannot, however, determine exactly how many works by the master he heard during the course of his musical evenings; if we accept his own account, we are left with a disarming statistic. "You understand," he wrote to his Polish friend and future wife Eve Hanska toward the end of 1837, "that I still know only the Symphony in C Minor and the little excerpt of the *Pastoral* Symphony we went together to hear scraped in Geneva, on some third floor?"[7]

But it is difficult to accept his declaration at face value, because for a year Balzac had attempted in his correspondence to dispell Mme Hanska's sus-picions about his overly active private life with allusions to hard work and to an uneventful social and cultural existence.[8] As one of Liszt's favorite listeners since the beginning of their friendship around a half decade before, he certainly had heard, along with sonatas he grew to appreciate like "Les Adieux," at least the piano transcriptions of the symphonies—definitely the *Eroica*. The evenings at the homes of Fétis, Erard, and Apponyi, which he sometimes attended, featured many works by Beethoven, not to mention the Concerts du Conservatoire. This is the background which permitted him to refer to the Seventh Symphony in *Ursule Mirouët* and to compare the Fifth with its "brilliant sisters" in *César Birotteau*.

Balzac's response to Rossini's music was one of immediate enthusiasm, whereas Beethoven's music, impressive but enigmatic, occasioned in him the growth of a concept which, for all its attractiveness, he could never express meaningfully in words. His earliest reference to the composer appears insignificantly in 1829 in *La Physiologie du mariage*. Then in 1831, in the description of an orgy in *La Peau de chagrin*, we come across an insecure allusion to the occasional lulls in the party's movement: "Those alternations of silence and sound have a vague resemblance with a Beethoven sym-phony." Balzac missed completely the charged pathos of such silences which, as Rousseau had prophesied, come within the orbit of musical descriptive-ness. After a few pages of the autobiographical novel, he abandons objective analogy in favor of subjective meaning: "I exhaled my unhappiness in mel-odies. Beethoven or Mozart were often my discreet confidants."[9] In *Louis Lambert* in 1832, he was content to place Beethoven's name in music alongside the names of those who represent the summits of achievement in other fields: Columbus, Raphael, Napoleon, and Laplace.

Two years later the concept began to mature; Balzac mentions the Fifth

Symphony with reverence: "After that supreme musical poem, we have
nothing left to say; we can only lower our hands and meditate."[10] Then in
La Recherche de l'Absolu Beethoven becomes a great figure who is misunderstood and whose simplicity of means alienates the intricacy-minded public: "The public generally prefers abnormal force that overflows to equal
force that persists. The public has neither time nor patience to detect the
immense power concealed under a uniform appearance." That same year,
after hearing a performance of the Fifth Symphony—his sole distraction, he
claims—between April 28 and May 10, the theme of jealousy, a tangible
indication of his fascination, enters his correspondence in a letter to Mme
Hanska: "I am jealous only of the illustrious dead: Beethoven, Michelangelo, Raphael, Poussin, Milton" (*Lettres*, 1: 156–57); in 1835, in *Séraphita*,
his emotional agitation continues before the composer's "palace of harmony" which he can compare only with one of his most respected literary
figures, Dante. Here he attempts to formulate an appropriate, analogical
vocabulary to describe his feelings, relying on visual images like "a river of
light" and "waves of flames" to express what he views as the unseizable
immensity of the two artists: "In them you roll in endless whirlpools, where
your mind cannot always sustain you. It is surely necessary to possess a
powerful intelligence to emerge safe and sound."

One senses a crescendo in Balzac's reaction and an increasing fondness
for the music. He delights, in March 1835, in "the Beethoven performed at
the Conservatory as you will never hear it anywhere" (*Lettres*, 1: 245). As
the term "metaphysical genius," with which Beethoven was frequently described by admirers as well as by some uneasy detractors, acquired its in-
nuendoes of magnitude, Balzac focused more and more on the spirit of the
composer's music, on the mystical beauties it revealed and the gigantic ideas
it inspired, ideas so gigantic that they defied definition. A French musician
around 1840 said retrospectively: "Beethoven taught us the poetry of music
. . . the dignity of our profession, and after having partly grasped him, we
soon recognized the duty, entrusted to us, of becoming the promulgators of
his idea."[11] Unable to seize the "idea," Balzac turned to conquer the "poetry." His was a Romantic reaction, to be sure, one which transported the
composer into a remote sphere from which he threatened all who approached and which enabled him to achieve forbidding aloofness. Those to
whom Beethoven spoke could not speak of him in turn except with a vocabulary of awe.

Berlioz above all referred to him as a poet-superman and fired his comments with poetical images: Beethoven is "like those eagles of the Andes who wing through space at heights below which other creatures would find nothing but asphyxiation and death," or a movement seemed "as if it had been sadly murmured by the Archangel Michael on some day when, overcome by a feeling of melancholy, he contemplated the universe from the threshold of the empyrean." [12] D'Ortigue's descriptions of the Fifth Symphony were thoroughly "unmusical" and just as literary as those of Berlioz in *Le Rénovateur*. [13] Balzac, in turn, gravitated analogously and conveniently toward the sense of poetry which wafted from the idea rather than toward the idea itself which he felt incapable of transmitting. He cloaked his inability under Romantic images that longed for remote regions of ecstasy and that compelled the soul to gaze steadily into the infinite. For the esoteric elite which felt drawn to the great symphonies, the word "infinite" solved the enigma of Beethoven.

Beginning with *Le Lys dans la vallée* of 1835–36, a lyrical novel pervaded by a fragrance of country blossoms, Balzac's references to Beethoven acquire poetic hues. One thing which struck him about the Fifth Symphony was the way in which the last movement recalls rhythmically the first and transforms melodically and harmonically the opening theme. About the bouquets gathered for his platonic mistress, Mme de Mortsauf, the narrator Félix de Vandenesse writes that they resembled "floral symphonies, through which my deceived desire made me deploy efforts that Beethoven deployed with his notes—a profound doubling back onto itself, prodigious flights toward the heavens." As Mme de Mortsauf looked at them intensely and fondly and "nourished herself by them," their lovely presence instilled in her the very feelings Félix had while picking them, reverting the flowers back, as it were, into "all the thoughts that I had placed into them." In a letter to Mme Hanska, dated May 10, 1836, Balzac speaks of "the feeling that a beautiful Beethoven passage gives you, presenting you, in its purest form, a whole feeling, a whole nature." He points up the loftiness of this feeling, adding that "in Heaven, all is infinite" (*Lettres*, 1: 311–12).

When the theme of jealousy returns in another letter one year later, Michelangelo, Raphael, Poussin, and Milton have been superseded by the "illustrious" personality of the composer alone: "Beethoven is the only man who makes me know jealousy." There is no doubt of his ascendancy in Balzac's mind when we read the next sentence: "I should rather have wanted to be Beethoven than Rossini and Mozart." The apogee has been reached. Even his friend from Pesaro must step down to acknowledge the master from Bonn, for "there is a divine power in that man." And with this, the novelist plunges into a flowery description of the finale of the Fifth Symphony, referring to "an enchanter," "beautiful palaces," "marvels," the Florentine Baptistry, "beauties of an unknown kind," "fairies . . . that swirl with the beauties of woman and the variegated wings of angels," and to a "superior air . . . which, according to Swedenborg, sings and spreads perfumes, has color and feeling, abounds and beatifies you"! Then Balzac asserts the supremacy of music over literature and terminates the letter with a brief allusion to his correspondent's city in Ukraine "where you can't hear a Beethoven symphony" (*Lettres*, 1: 443, 447).

While working in November and December 1837 to meet the publication deadline for *Histoire de la grandeur et de la décadence de César Birotteau*, he inserted into the novel a similar but longer and more ecstatic description of the finale of the Fifth Symphony. Again Balzac listens to his "ideal" music through the earphones of literary images. The finale represents by analogy what the ball of Birotteau, celebrating his new apartment decorated by Grindot and his own decoration with the star of the Legion of Honor, represents in his life. His long-cherished ambition realized, the pious and virtuous perfumer has reached a culminating moment of grandeur. The first part of the novel ends with a recollection of the symphony's final allegro. The author speaks of "a fantasy, large as a poem"; of the composer as a "sublime magician" and of his "dazzling theme toward which all the musical forces have converged"; of a "radiant fairy"; of angels and the golden doors of the Baptistry; of a "marvelous palace" and incense and an "altar of happiness"; of superhuman beings "dressed in white tunics bordered with blue"; of Loves "spreading the flames of their torches"; of love, harmony, happiness, and ambrosia; and of sudden "cold realities" from which the composer removes you "when he has whetted your appetite for his divine melodies and makes your soul shout: More!"

If this lavish and languorous description suits M. Birotteau's euphoric mood, it does not suit Beethoven's compelling and energetic mettle. Instead of being overwhelmed by the almost martial pounding of the finale's rhythm, the protagonist is lifted on dreamy wings to a beatific fairyland of houris and harems. In this singular failure, Balzac outdoes descriptively the literary habits of his contemporary melophiles. His optical orgy forsakes the permissible language of lyrical emotion which leaves the image fugacious and transparent, and he becomes absorbed in an idiom of relief and color. By using a rich brush, he fails to subordinate the elements of his description to the logic of the musical form and to intellectual clarity. Too much observation strangles the dream he wishes to communicate, and the auditive impression becomes visual ludicrousness.

Balzac's poetic debauch nonetheless has its psychological interest. That he abandoned himself to such an ungermane cascade of visions betrays a lack of control over the subject matter and a resultant dramatic struggle with himself, with his inability to match verbally the music's beauty. We are touched and moved to smiling sympathy. Balzac confessed his apprehension that same year: "No, the mind of the writer does not give similar pleasures, because what we depict is finite, determined, and what Beethoven throws at you is infinite" (*Lettres*, 1: 443). So he released his copious images in the hope that their sheer number would constitute a form of tribute to the source which inspired them.

In the long novel, Birotteau's ball represents but an instant of attainment; the fateful knocks on the door by his dishonestly motivated subaltern, Crevel, announce a sad dénouement. The finale is also a finale of the "grandeur," a commencement of the "decadence." The Fifth Symphony makes a second appearance at the end of *César Birotteau* when the merchant, almost on his deathbed, emerges from ruin after an epic struggle of honesty and smiles at the rehabilitation of his finances. Here Balzac's characterization of the music is more exact. He speaks of the "heroic movement of the finale of the great symphony," which to the perfumer rang like a "grand finale," or of "that ideal music [that] made the clarions sound." In retrospect, the suggestive language used to describe the music at the ball served to convey merely an impression of grandeur; now the more precise vocabulary asserts its realization. Berlioz found the key to the finale's prodigious effect not only in its dynamic swelling, but also in its modulation from minor to major.[14] Something similar occurs in Balzac's novel as it moves from the major of the "grandeur" to the minor of the "decadence" and back to the major of the triumphant restoration.

In this respect, Balzac may have emulated the structure of Beethoven's symphony. There is no doubt that the impressiveness of the musical insertions in the novel lies, not in what the descriptions say, but in what they do. An epic sweep of events, climaxed by two dramatic musical appearances, bespeaks an architectural purpose which, in this case, is highly successful. The finale is evoked not merely to compare two moments in the merchant's life;[15] it serves a powerful structural function, the second evocation acting like another "profound doubling back onto itself" which unifies the novel through its cyclic force.

While Balzac was writing *César Birotteau*, he was also at work on *Gambara*. In the latter novel we find the first and only technical attempt to understand musical method. Although its theme centers around an analysis of a Meyerbeer opera and an explication of one of the protagonist's own, many clues point to the presence of Beethoven in the background of the whole tale. To begin with, it expounds theses which come more within the orbit of symphonic than of operatic music. There is what Balzac considered a Germanic sense of harmony in Gambara's aesthetics and in his consciousness of instruments, qualities which the novelist associated with Beethoven. Gambara himself, the composer of new music, is a misunderstood artist. He compares his music with Beethoven's and begins the overture of his opera in the key of the Fifth Symphony, Balzac's favorite. Then there is also a subtle implication: we know that Gambara's music had met with no success in Italy, and we are forced to make a telling association when he exclaims: "Give the Italians some Beethoven, they won't follow you." Furthermore, one of the characters—the conductor Gigelmi, "one of the greatest of musical celebrities," who makes perceptive remarks about his art—is deaf. And finally, there are many and obsessive references to Beethoven, including an association with a "prodigious doubling back of the whole opera onto itself."

One exchange in particular between the conductor and Count Andrea Marcosini arrests our attention. Gigelmi's comments still bear the poetical imprint: though deprived of his auditory sense, he hears—or sees—the music of the Symphony in C Minor because "music exists independently of its performance." He speaks of "the world of Fantasy," of "the golden wings of the *G natural* theme," of "a whole nature," of lights and clouds and divine hymns. In contrast, the count's comments are surprisingly exact:

His works are remarkable above all because of their structural simplicity, and because of how this structure is implemented. With most composers, wild and disorganized orchestral passages come together only to produce a momentary effect; they do not always blend with the number through the regularity of their development. With Beethoven, these effects are, so to speak, distributed ahead of time. Similar to various regiments that contribute, through their regular advance, to battlefield advantage, the sections of Beethoven's symphonic orchestra follow orders given in the general interest, and are subordinated to admirably conceived plans. . . . The [theme] that is farthest from the action comes and joins, at a certain moment, the development by means of threads woven into the fabric [of the composition].[16]

Alfred Einstein pointed out that, characteristically, the Romantics misunderstood Beethoven; they admired the symphonies, not for the clarity of their form, but for the manifold possibilities of interpreting them.[17] Hence the encouragement to talk of "poetry" for those who felt that the composer was especially "deep" because they did not quite understand him or could not comprehend purely instrumental music in general. With or without the help of his obscure music teacher of the late 1830s, Jacques Strunz, Balzac shows by his approach and by the accuracy of his observation that this time he may have succeeded in glimpsing, however briefly, "beauties of an unknown kind." His analogy with the instrumental order of battle, recalling the implication in *César Birotteau* of the "musical powers" which converge, indicates his growing awareness of pure music and of the abstract calculations upon which much of the moving power of music depends. To be able to sense—I do not wish to say distinguish—the organized forces of a score is to require a listening attitude different from the one needed to appreciate program music. The analyses of Meyerbeer's and the protagonist's operas notwithstanding, *Gambara* represents a protest on behalf of instrumental music against the existing supremacy of opera. And it was Beethoven who, while initiating Balzac into the vaporous sphere of the infinite, also offered him a first key to the citadel of symphonic music.

The year 1837 marks neither the end nor the beginning of Balzac's admiration for Beethoven.[18] It marks, rather, a culmination, after which a dénouement takes place. In the period after 1837, Balzac endeavored to put the composer of the Fifth Symphony and the composer of *Mosè in Egitto* into perspective. Not even a "divine power" could usurp the prominent position which Rossini had held for so many years. The heroine of *Massimilla Doni* (1839), rejoicing in "triumphant Italy," has faith that some day Rossini will be ranked among the "Homers of music"; Beethoven and the other *tedeschi* are made to genuflect. Elsewhere in the tale, however, Beethoven is treated with reverence. After that, he reappears in novels and correspondence in sentimental settings—in *Béatrix* (1839) as a favorite author to whose works Félicité des Touches returns with affection after a venturesome episode, and as an inspiring symphonist in a letter to Mme Desbordes-Valmore (1840), whose finely written messages Balzac likened to "the most beautiful passages in a Beethoven symphony."[19]

Ursule Mirouët (1841) portrays another heroine who confides in the composer, this time in his Seventh Symphony, which she plays at the piano and which Balzac undoubtedly imagined in the form of one of Liszt's accomplished transcriptions. Aware of the technical difficulties involved, the novelist wished to enhance Ursule's talent, which had been brought to perfection by her teacher, Schmucke. Always amazed by Liszt and by the digital intricacies of Beethoven's music when performed on the keyboard, Balzac could not help exclaiming once to Mme Hanska about her pianist daughter: "Tell me how old is Anna who understands Beethoven!" (*Lettres*, 2: 27). The very tone of the last word in this exclamation registers awe. His music is "grandiose," and the Seventh Symphony "must be studied to be understood." If Gambara was correct, therefore, when he stated that such great music can invite the attention of genial listeners only, then Ursule may well use it as a device with which to rid her home of unwelcome, boorish visitors who have nothing in common with grandeur.

Yet Rossini was not forgotten. A letter to his Polish friend in 1845 shows that Balzac's esteem had not waned: "yesterday I went to hear the *Desert Symphony* [by Félicien David] and I was totally stunned as a result. Nothing better of its kind has been written, since Beethoven, Rossini excepted" (*Lettres*, 3: 26). Indeed, when the name of the German composer is absent, Rossini enjoys the enduring devotion of a man whose heart, Pascal would say, has its own reasons. But when Rossini's name is absent and that of Beethoven stands magically alone, then Balzac's reason pays tribute to an artist to whom he could apply only the adjective "sublime": "the sublime productions," "a sublime symphony," "the sublime magician," "that sublime musical poem," and, at the end of 1845, the ecstatic declaration: "Beethoven's genius, it's sublime!"[20]

For while Beethoven did not cause a change in his musical evolution but rather entered it as an addition, Balzac in the long run remained convinced of his ultimate and absolute greatness: "He hasn't been understood yet," he wrote in *Gambara*, "how could be be superseded?" Self-confession, historical truth, and admiration make these words a welcome shift from those of less perceptive, Stendhalian intellects, Balzac's contemporaries, who remained eternally mistrustful of the message from across the Rhine, not to speak of those who even later maltreated Beethoven, the various Tolstoys in their ascetic detestation of superiority. Beethoven's music, as Hoffmann had said of the Fifth Symphony, confirmed the alliance of genius and art in the highest degree, and his art embodied an important Balzacian principle: that of passing, as Gambara put it, "from sensation to idea."

But what "ideas" did Balzac grasp—the sense of the infinite which emerges from Beethoven's developments which, however concise, leave us with a ring of endless possibilities? The suggestive power of the orchestration, its discursive thoughts and harmonic implications which prompt bright or dark dispositions toward life and nature? Romantically, the Faustian dimensions of the composer's independence and originality "[which] nourishes itself from the outflowings and the sap of universal life . . . to capture infinite Nature, or more precisely to communicate with it, to lose itself in it"?[21] Aesthetically, did Balzac understand how Beethoven's pure form incarnates such abstract ideas or how, in the Schopenhauerian manner, a serious and complex thought like the expression of man in the highest powers can remain essentially symphonic? We must answer no. Between Balzac's reaction to Beethoven and his expression of it, *Gambara* notwithstanding, lay an unbridged gap across which the living energy of meaning did not pass.

Yet my negative observation should not sound categorical. For Balzac recognized that instrumental music could be more than the marvelous divertissement and ornamental art which the symphonies of Mozart and Haydn represented for so many listeners. He realized the difference between the open quality of seductiveness of Rossini's manner and the more intimate quality of poetic sensibility of Beethoven's. He felt a presence, something he could not verbalize. something which left sensation behind and, through its incalculable force of sounds, shaped his concept of Beethoven. And his was a reaction as genuine as it was legitimate, for Beethoven, more than anyone else, had fused great thoughts—liberty, equality, heroism, and struggle—as well as the more personal experiences of life, with musical expression. Quite naturally, Balzac shaped his concept by using attributes he admired, bestowed upon some of his favorite characters, and liked to ascribe to himself: temerity, power, excellence in mastery of the art, overtones of Promethean pride, perhaps some immoderateness and a capacity for a frenzy of feelings—in short, the concept of Titanism, the source of Tolstoy's grievances against the German composer.

Heroic will stirred Balzac, even in a modest creature like César Birotteau, and this attraction was the first step toward his understanding of Beethoven. Therefore, I agree with Thérèse Marix-Spire that, if Balzac had lived longer, Beethoven in time would have held his exclusive esteem.[22] Although he continued to be a rhapsodist for Rossini, he presents himself also as a psalmodist for Beethoven and, ultimately, is secretly persuaded by him. He opts for the master from Bonn. A fundamental affinity existed, approaching but not attaining revelation. Did he not—unwittingly?—envisage a famous scene from *Fidelio* as early as 1833, one which curiously sums up his own situation: "I am like a prisoner who, from the depth of his cell, hears a wonderful feminine voice from afar. He bears his whole soul in the fragile and powerful perceptions of that voice . . ."?[23]

(1964)

[3]

REVISITING THE
CANTI CARNASCIALESCHI

Music and poetry, the sister arts by which we come to identify much that was admirable in Italian Renaissance life, found simultaneous expression in Florence under the aegis of Lorenzo il Magnifico. While cooperation between the two arts was a matter of ancient tradition, the fresh impetus this collaboration received during the carnivals is all too frequently glossed over even by leading scholars like Burckhardt, Symonds, and Pater. We read about the poems, like the "Trionfo di Bacco e Arianna," but not enough about their composite purpose, and rarely about the musical tradition which gave them life. Indeed, Italian music would seem to originate with opera in the seventeenth century, or perhaps according to Victor Hugo with Palestrina in the sixteenth, but the splendid flowering that took place in the fifteenth remains a matter of relative neglect among our literati, especially when it comes to the *canti carnascialeschi*.

The reasons are fairly clear. Not without justification, cultural historians maintain that music inevitably lags behind the other arts until it absorbs the educative influences of literature and painting. More immediately, there is the problem of inaccessibility of the secular music of Lorenzo de' Medici's Florence, and that of deciphering an obsolete notation. And finally, I must mention the difficulty today of responding intellectually and emotionally to the unfamiliar idiom. Still, if we think of the poetry of the *canti*, we are not entitled to leave aside the music, nor are we entitled to leave aside its performance. Poet, composer, and performer did not enjoy separate existences in the minds of the people of the Quattrocento.

The fact that a Tuscan Benedictine monk, Guido d'Arezzo, founded our modern system of notation bespeaks a deep-rooted musical awareness in Florentine culture at least as far back as the tenth century. But, apart from the products of speculative and artistic talents dedicated primarily to the expression of the religious cult, Florence had for centuries a rich tradition of secular or popular music. Two hundred years before Lorenzo, Folgore da San Gemignano had reflected the festive, musical life of his city:

> Il lunedì per capo di semana,
>   con istormenti matinata fare,
>   et amorose donzelle danzare . . .

> (Monday at head of the week
>   makes morning song with instruments
>   and loving damsels dance . . .)

Folgore's happy spontaneity, like that of the many open-air *feste* on farms and in vineyards, or the *stornelli* sung by peasants working in the fields, or the dances on the *aja* after the wheat threshing or vintage seasons, is a discernible antecedent of the jolly spontaneity of the *canti carnascialeschi*. Even laud singing had become so popular during the thirteenth century that most parishes had organized a *compagnia dei laudesi* (the earliest in Florence, the "Compagnia dei Laudesi della Beata Vergine Maria," dating from 1183). In short, "every spectacle was a feast, and everything became a spectacle, a tableau to be seen in the stall of the painter, betrothals, marriages, the vestiture of monks and nuns, a priest's first mass, the 'mystery of some death,' the assembly at parliament, the election of magistrates, the taking of office of magistrates, the departure or arrival of armies, the arrival or departure of foreign dignitaries."[1]

Music and poetry became closely allied spiritually with the advent of the Dolce Stil Nuovo. The appearance of this style of lyric poetry at a time of pronounced interest in music and singing is not coincidental. We all know of how Dante begged Casella to sing in Purgatory and, on the other hand, of how Pietro Alighieri, Dante's son, complained that his father's musical efforts had never met with the success they supposedly deserved.[2] We also know that, before and after the Dolce Stil, Folgore, Cavalcanti, Lapo Gianni, Compagni, Sacchetti, Petrarch, and others were set to music by any number of contemporary composers.[3]

In his lively portrait of Florentine life, *Paradiso degli Alberti*, Giovanni da Prato says of the composer Francesco Landino: "He sang his love songs so sweetly that there was no one to compare with him for the sweetness of his most sweet harmonies."[4] Landino's three characteristic forms link poetically with the *canti*: the *ballata*, the *madrigale*, and the *caccia*. Most interesting was the latter, with its spirited verses describing country life and the hunt, and musically set for two voices and a bass instrument. As we might expect, the feeling of chase was rendered by the two voices in canon form. Carducci suggests that the *caccie*, of true Florentine origin, were the first rhymed examples of peasant language and customs, and adds that they were dramatized "as later the *Canti Carnascialeschi*, sung either by choruses or by a single person accompanied by chorus, with the gestures or with the tools of hunting or fishing."[5]

The amorous and elegant madrigals of the Trecento (not to be confused with those, quite different, of the Cinquecento) also prefigure the *canti* of Lorenzo's Quattrocento. Whether bucolic or political, allegorical or sensuous, the collaboration between poet and composer—if Sacchetti and Jacopo di Bologna may serve as examples—was immediate. Similarly, the popular *ballate* appear as forerunners of the *canti*, with their portrayals of many scenes of life underscored by dramatic or sentimental motifs.

At this point, it is important to remember the first great landmark in Italian musical history after Gregorian Chant: the *ars nova*, which, though expounded theoretically in France by Philippe de Vitry early in the fourteenth century, was the product of Italian influences. And for about one hundred years, up to 1450, Florence was the center of the new art, with which the music of the *canti* is circuitously bound. For while we may follow Carducci in linking the poetic forms of the songs directly with a recognizable Florentine ancestry, their musical style, being the reimportation of a domestic product turned slightly Gothic, bears only an indirect relation with the earlier Renaissance school.

De Vitry and his contemporary Marchetto di Padova determined that the simultaneous rendering of several vocal parts required that music be measured and that the monophonic Plainsong, based neither on regular beats nor on bars but on upbeat (anacrusis) and downbeat (thesis) movement, could not serve the purpose. Previous attempts by the *ars antiqua* to combine two voices (organums), they thought, had produced dreary progressions of fourths and fifths, and the sole recognition of time values—by threes—had contributed to the monotony. Recognizing duple time, they fixed measure and wrote three-part songs, made freer use of chromatic intervals, and through their instinctive dislike for the diminished fifth B–F approached the modern idea of the leading tone by making the B♭ or the F♯ —all of which helped lay the foundations of harmony and counterpoint. The enthusiastic group of Italian composers which followed in the wake of these innovations gave Tuscan musical life considerable vigor, as the illuminated Squarcialupi Codex of the Laurentian Library, discovered in 1913, suggests. It contains 149 songs to fit most occasions, along with the names of some of the four-teenth-century composers: Giovanni de Cascia, Ghirlandellus di Firenze, Jacopo di Bologna, Lorenzo di Firenze, Donato, Monaco Benedettino, Abate Riminese, Niccolò Pontificio, Francesco Landino, Vincenzo Fiorentino, among others.

But these innovations found more fertile ground for development beyond the Alps before they reappeared in the music of the *canti carnascialeschi*. They were richly cultivated by John Dunstable in England, and in the Netherlands, especially at the court of Philip of Burgundy, by his pupils Gilles Binchois and Guillaume Dufay. The transfer of the papacy to Avignon naturally attracted French and Dutch musicians south, and with the return of the pope to Rome in 1377, many of these musicians, Dufay among them, filtered into northern and central Italy, thus giving the Florentine music of the Quattrocento a robust Gothic quality.

New forms tended to supersede the older ones: the three-voice *canzone*, the *mottetto*, and the *falso bordone*. Actually, the *caccia* returned disguised as the four-part *villota*,[6] the canon being pursued by three voices over an instrumental bass. And as it evolved, it acquired the *nio*, the danced portion of the composition, and it also absorbed the French *chanson*. Together with liturgical music, all these forms—the *falso bordone* in particular, like the later *frottola* of the North Italian courts—formed the homophonic structures on which the *canti* were patterned. They reveal an accomplished virtuosity of treatment—the piling up of various voices with often unexpected curves in the melodic lines running polyphonically, organic developments under a strangely wandering soprano—not unlike the play of lines and masses in Gothic cathedrals.

Yet the fusion of the Netherlandish musical elements with those poetic forms which had remained purely Italian from the Trecento produced something uniquely Renaissance in spirit. The "new" musical culture took place in direct relation, not only to secular poetic expression, but indeed to the artistic demands of national life: hence, the fresh impetus given to the traditional collaboration between music and poetry. More important, if the

modern idea of music as an art is based on the recognition of the significance of the individual and on personal expression, one might claim that
this basic aesthetic point of view dawns with the *canti* under Lorenzo. The
evolution comes about more naturally in the context of secular than of church
music, and one might be justified in thinking that it took place when Lorenzo decided to turn the celebration of the *carnovale*, which seemed dull
to him, into a veritable *spettacolo*.

Lorenzo de' Medici did not have to develop a special awareness of music
to pursue his goal. We know him as a poet; we do not always know him as
one who cultivated music as a natural asset. One critic notes the latter point
well: "At first, it abetted his fervid poetic instinct and his precocious worldly
diversions, like a form of relief from the austerity of his studies; then, in
accordance with his maturity and administrative work, it became strongly
bound to his concept of life, a lavishing of joy that was going to invite the
most factious interpretations by historians and moralists."[7] From an early
age, the colorful musical activities of the Florentines, the enterprising *liete
brigate*, the triumphs, masquerades, dances, and songs which stretched from,
say, the Calendimaggio to San Giovanni, had woven themselves into the
fabric of his existence, as had undoubtedly the carols and songs his own
mother, Lucrezia Tornabuoni, used to write.

When the rising tide of humanism engulfed him, he found philosophical
support in ancient Greek thought for the love he felt by now for music.
That is, he culled what he wanted from Greek thought: Plato's definition of
rhythm as "order in movement," along with Plato's and Pythagoras's claim
for a place for music in all education, and the definition offered of music
by so many other philosophers as "the speech of the soul." He closed at
least one eye to their dialectical distinctions involving moral values whereby
music could serve to betray the finer instincts by playing up to emotions
ungoverned by reason. For some humanists, and for the Church, which
looked askance at the increasing popularity of the secular art, music could
be dangerous. But for Lorenzo, the force was too compelling and too bound
with *bel viver* to be bogged down in dialectical palavers. On the one hand,
he spoke platonically about music, dividing it into *parlare, armonia*, and
ritmo (rima) and elaborating in his *Comento* on some of his poems:

Music is common to all things—which would not be without some form of consonance—and logically they must move along through music, just the way we note

that by tuning two string instruments to a single tone, and placing one alongside the other, when one sounds, the strings of the other also vibrate because of their tonal conformity and similarity of sound.

On the other hand, however, he showed he did not content himself with theory alone, or with alleged dangers, when he gave such full-bodied encouragement to the rollicking inclination of his people through the *canti carnascialeschi*.

Lorenzo's enthusiasm for this musico-poetic form and the new and dramatic vigor he brought to the pageantry itself has made many credit him erroneously with originating this method of celebration. Certainly the splendor it acquired under Lorenzo has remained legendary. The legend dates from Vasari's account, who wrote of the *trionfi* and *carri*:

They took place normally at night, as if this were the best time to hide the defects of execution and so to stress more the spectator's visual illusion. It was a very beautiful thing to see in the afternoon and lasting until 3 or 4 A.M. into the night, twenty-five or thirty pairs of richly equipped horses, running through the city, with their masters disguised and masked according to the topic invented and each unit with six or eight footmen, donning the same livery, torches in hand, at times numbering over four-hundred, setting the night aglow like day with such a beautiful, delightful, and superb spectacle.[8]

May we see here the beginnings of the musical theater?: richly decorated floats representing classical or popular allegory, splendidly idealistic or sumptuously obscene, a distinct sense of characterization portraying the artisanry and the varied works of the guilds, all combined with instruments, verses, lights, dancing, costumes, singing, props, and carpentry? In this form of musical humanism, individual talent collaborated with popular instinct, tradition, and the secrets of noble crafts; artisans and artists blended visions in the context of a figurative and audio-oral art which fused its formulas while addressing itself to the eyes and ears, the mind and heart.

The example of Lorenzo sufficed to inspire other poets to bend their talents in the direction of the *canti*. It did not matter that poetically the *canti* were little more than the popular *ballate* molded to the type of feast at hand; what mattered was the graceful spirit which Lorenzo injected into the poems, thereby converting the themes of the people into fine poetry. The first general collection of this poetry was published in 1559; the authors mentioned are mainly Florentine: Lorenzo, Bientina, Giambullari, G. B. dell'Ottonaio.

The *canzone a ballo,* developed by Sacchetti and later by Giustiniani, found in Lorenzo and in Angiolo Poliziano its highest expression. It was like a *canto* in its motifs: the invitation to a moment's pleasure and scorn for its slanderers, a *carpe diem* intoxication of joy and love, framed in jocund ironies or in obscene allegories, and cast in short seven- or eight-syllable lines which lent themselves to rapid musical setting, to both dynamic rhythms and fluid movement. With their refrains and echoes, the *canti* marked the streets of Florence seasonally with a variety of different but convergent cadences. Lorenzo's descriptive realism and sensual courtesies tinged with irony complemented Poliziano's discursive verses, rich with popular locutions and learned stylizations of them, and always unpredictably malicious or charming. The latter, as we all know, was the greater poet, but it was the former who formulated the symbolic maxim of his time and city:

> Quant'è bella giovinezza,
>   Che si fugge tuttavia!
>   Chi vuol esser lieto, sia:
>   Di doman non c'è certezza.

> (How beautiful is youth,
>   That nonetheless does flee!
>   Let him find happiness who seeks,
>   For there's no certainty tomorrow.)

De Sanctis's description of such *ballate scherzose* as Boccaccio's cynicism transferred to the public square and hailed in triumph is not an overstatement. It was exactly this mood of melancholy carefreeness and extravagance which attracted the best poets, whether Poliziano or Agnolo Divizio da Bibbiena. And it was this same mood which elicited the responses of many musicians: Johannes, Alexander, Bartholomeus the organist, Alexander Coppinus, Pintellus, Bernardo Pisano, Prete Michele (Pesenti), Philippus de Lurano, Fogliano, Tromboncino, Cara—and the most famous, Antonio Squarcialupi, Heinrich Isaak (Arrigo Tedesco), and Alexander Agricola.

For many years the leading musician in Lorenzo's court, Squarcialupi was a friend of Dufay and, as a close associate of Cosimo and Piero de' Medici, had had a distinct role in shaping Lorenzo's musical sensitivity. Though the greatest organist of his day (he was appointed to Santa Maria del Fiore), a singer, a lute player, and a recognized composer, nothing of his has come down to us. He put at least two *canti* to music and urged that others do the same: he asked Dufay, for example, to write the music for Lorenzo's "Amor ch'ai visto ciascun mio pensiero."[9] To him we owe the collection of songs found in the codex bearing his name, and to him his colleagues owed a large measure of the intellectual liberalism and formal sensitivity which characterized Renaissance music in Italy: the need for the composer to create in an atmosphere which was not subject to religious directive.[10]

After Squarcialupi's death, Lorenzo called the celebrated Dutch musician, Heinrich Isaak, to Florence. While he brought with him an unsurpassed knowledge of the art of polyphony,[11] which he applied to solemn sacred music, he was also drawn to the less pretentious *ballate* and became one of Lorenzo's chief collaborators for the carnivals. In fact, he wrote the music for Lorenzo's first *canto*, about the "Venditori di bernicocoli e confortini." Because of his stylistic refinement, gay musical wit, and inventive versatility which permitted him to compose freely for the varied poetic meters of the *canti*, Isaak remained for years the major musical influence in Florence and the close personal friend of Lorenzo.[12]

On the other hand, another Dutch musician, Alexander Agricola (surnamed "de Alemania") was perhaps the most bizarre composer at the Medicean court. His style, mostly polyphonic but subtle and technically obscure, revealed more than that of any other composer of the *canti* a strong Flemish background. Agricola was less able than Isaak to absorb and reproduce a different mode of sensibility; his compositions stand out for their marked differences with the musical modes of other composers. The peculiar complications of his idiom joined to a quasi-ecclesiastic character of some impressiveness, appealed to many, so that his Gothic strains perplexed only few of his listeners.

Not many of the *canti carnascialeschi* have come down to us in their musical forms, certainly not as many as we should like. But there are enough of them to give us a sense of the entire production. Most may be found in the Codici della Biblioteca Nazionale and in the Codici della Biblioteca del Conservatorio Musicale of Florence and Perugia. A fine group of twenty has been deciphered and published by Masson.[13]

It is clear that the *canti* evolved over the years from simpler to more complex textures. The first were sung in three voices, like the *canzoni a ballo*; they were written vertically, very unpretentiously, note against note, and for performance required anyone with a good ear whose voice projected

well, even from behind a large mask. But just as the festivities became more
elaborate under Lorenzo, and the poetry developed from a popular genre to
a conscious literary expression, so did the music become more involved,
ascending from three to as many as sixteen voices and attaining the complicated structure of later madrigals. Without doubt, there were many dou-
blings of the soprano voice carrying the melody, and of the basses moving
solidly in fourths and fifths. In fact, one of the important changes taking
place in music during this period concerned the gradual transference of the
main theme from the tenor line, where it characteristically resided during
the Middle Ages, to the soprano. Yet the swelling of the vocal score did not
disturb the essential vertical frame of the compositions. Rhythm and stresses
remained clear, and the listener was involved in an experience of intense
expressiveness, energetic colors and contrasts, and ordered, gay vehemence.
The solemn or thin qualities he was accustomed to—in church or in the
fields—gave way to a rich theatrical imagination. We generally refer to
Monteverdi as the composer who gave musical expression to the kind of
human love found in the verses of Petrarch, Ronsard, or Shakespeare. With
the *canti*, we confront a quite different mood of human love, a more fren-
zied passion, the Dionysian dance rather than the Apollonian. It is not
surprising, then, to come across a broken line which oscillates between a
would-be recitative and a lyrical melody. But the musical expression, harmoniously wedded to the poetic, is concise, and the shortness of the piece
guarantees automatically against emphasis.

In the Masson collection, we may note some songs called *Canti dei Lanzi*.
These were special carnival songs, parodies of the obnoxious *lanzichenecchi*
(foreign mercenaries who descended into Italy at the end of the fifteenth
century), whose vandalism and vulgarity contrasted with the decorum of the
lanzi, the infantry of Maximilian I. Here the music more than the poetry
modified the original intent. While the poetry did indeed temper its critical
thrust by yielding to spirited descriptions of the different groups of soldiers
(*alabardieri, picchieri, columbrinieri, giocatori di spada, scoppettieri*), the
virtuosity of the music seems to have been the real focal point of attention.
Musically, these songs resembled the *todesche*, which were close to the Nea-
politan *villanelle*. The reason these special songs are interesting lies in the
fact that they constitute a slight departure from the usual practice of the
composer, which was to emphasize the words. In imitation of the Greeks,
the humanistic ideal, especially in Florence, stressed the Platonic premise

that music should enrich the poetic text. The *Canti dei Lanzi* stand out, therefore, as instances in which the notion that the function of music was to bring out the full emotional possibility of the word so that the poetic line could have its greatest effect upon the listener, tended to be reversed.

Instruments were coordinated in relation to the different voices, and their families blended more or less in the same logical combinations of sonority we have today. The bright colors of the floats and costumes, and the new sensuous art, encouraged invention and the fabrication of all kinds of string and wind instruments. We should be justified in imagining the use of trumpets, lyres, lutes, and viols, along with harps, pipes, cembali, drums, and trombones.[14] If we go by the fact that the *concerti dei pifferi*, as combinations of woods and brasses, flourished in Lorenzo's Florence, then we might envision the kind of small orchestra which supported the singing and the dancers' rhythms of the carnival songs. We might also surmise that instruments quite unknown today, or heard today only in isolated contexts, punctuated the festivities: the *piva* (more the shawm than the pipe), the *botazzus* (a cylindrical wooden bottle), the *zampogna* (bagpipe), the *rubeba* (rebeck), the *ciramella* (or *cennamella*: a clarinetlike, double-piped reed), and others.

According to one common interpretation of the purpose of the *canti carnascialeschi*, Lorenzo encouraged them for their diversionary value, in an attempt to muffle the spirit of Tuscan liberty. To license the merry and libidinous pageantry meant to turn the minds of the populace away from public affairs. Not only Savonarola but Carducci, too, shared this view, which would not be out of place on a page of Machiavelli or La Rochefoucauld. It is not essentially different from the view of the ancient Chinese, whose Orpheus had fixed the rules of music in order to establish and maintain harmony among the civil servants. Rossi, on the other hand, is more generous:[15] Lorenzo's was not a sinister and picturesque deception of the unsuspecting masses in the name of art but, rather, was a spontaneous yielding to an innate passion of the Florentines, whose love for color, pageantry, and the fine arts has never been open to question. This view approximates my own. Aristotle's definition of music according to effect included three categories: the moral, the active, and the enthusiastic—and this last category aptly suits the *canti*. I should like to side with those who suggest that their fundamental motivation rests primarily on a psychosociological rather than on an intellectual or political basis.[16] They did not grow so much from an intellectual impulse or from an ulterior political motive as from a need and a desire to meet increasing demands for a full worldly life. The cathartic value of enthusiasm is central to this psychosociology.

The catharsis is both individual and collective, though more individual than collective—for, in the long run, the intimate union of poetry and music in the *canti carnascialeschi* constituted in the reality of performance both an associative and a dissociative force. It was associative in that the individuals identified their collective needs and desires with the group: singers, acrobats, fellow citizens, and all. This was made all the more possible by the fact that poet and composer alike, however artistically self-conscious, yielded his personality to the *canti*, as it were, so that conceivably the people as a group ended by sensing themselves as the veritable creators of the feast.

It was even more dissociative in that each individual—above all, the participating individual (indeed, anyone could participate)—with visible independence no longer experienced the usual, conventional suppression of his instincts. Then as now, during a carnival, each man had a right to his grimace and howling song. The lyrics and the allegories and the floats, seen and heard in a context of happy anarchy and agreement, meant that he could revert to his uninhibited self by shedding the trappings of heritage and civilized tradition. As astute a ruler as Lorenzo surely could sense the value of the image and the propensity of his people to find satisfaction in the image—an alter ego—where genuine or social self-realization was all too often lacking. There was compensation in it, as there was for the ancient slave during the Saturnalia who was given liberty to sing, jump, and get drunk, as if he had been free or master. What happened was that he saw himself more fittingly in the role of freeman, as the humble *pescivendolo* of the Quattrocento probably saw himself more effectively as a greater *mercante*, than for what he really was. In a setting of even truculent merrymaking, the fiction was healthy. As Valéry claimed, speaking in an analogous frame of reference: "So it is that simulation, the capacity to show yourself other than you are, appears to us as a property of a sane man, of a normal being, almost a criterion, a necessity."[17] In addition, we must remember that the fiction of the carnival was contained in that it was a self-sufficing action, not inconclusively open-ended like so many of life's actions. It was renewable in a year, and he who participated in it did so because he had the chance, within a prescribed period of time, to release a self which otherwise lived silently under the conventional mask of daily existence. In this sense, one might argue, the mask of his fiction was more real than the mask of his reality. This is the kind of human paradox that man has always relished, Florentines in particular, and the opportunity to express it with music could only have spelled release and signified health.

In a *carnovale*, everyone chose his head mask, his costume, the self that he often dreamed about. And he chose his songs. In its élans and enthusiasms, the music enabled him, as Nietzsche would have said, to rise above our crude and chaotic world into a transfigured one expressive of our desires and hopes. But there was nothing necessarily sophisticated or transcendent about the transfiguration; the songs related to earthly love, earthly abandon, and earthly happiness. The hidden tonality, however, being fixed on the need for health and desire for release, was one of freedom. This enfranchisement, albeit illusory, may well be the secret reason for the enormous success of the *canti carnscialeschi* during the later Quattrocento, a success which brought together the leading artists of the time, related all the arts, and revealed a kind of natural unity among them, creating a mood of free affirmation of existence. "Fanciulle e cicale," "I cialdonai," "I romiti," "Galanti di Valenza," "Canzone dei sette pianeti," "Canzone delle cicale" tell us more than they seem to say. To see in them only an escape (which, in part, they possibly were), or an interlude of peace (which, somehow, they may have been), or a political scheme (which, at some time, surely crossed Lorenzo's mind), is to stress ancillary possibilities and demean the *canti* with views which are perhaps too limited and pragmatic. Artistic expressions, whether refined or ribald, are never so simplistic. The *canti* appear as profound cultural expressions of an artistic people; a kind of popular *epos*; a synthesis of sounds, images, and thoughts, with a recognizable psychosociological dimension and a pronounced musico-poetic self-consciousness.

(1967)

[4]

THE EVOLUTION OF TEXT AND
TONE IN THE RENAISSANCE

More than a political, economic, and social phenomenon, which it assuredly was, the Renaissance represented a cultural phenomenon involving
words, tones, and colors: cultural, in the truest sense of the term, as distinguished from simply civilizational, which includes scientific discoveries, en-
gineering improvements, medical advancements, and the like, none of which
is as enduring as the work of art, in Horatian terms, *aere perennius*. But,
even in the context presented by our history books, the cultural explosion
involved literature and the plastic arts, the *Orlando furioso*, the *Bartolomeo
Colleoni*, Santa Maria del Fiore, and *The Birth of Venus*. Much less attention is devoted to music, for which only musicologists make the case.

These musicologists have asked themselves the question, then, of whether
Renaissance music, Orlando di Lasso and Giovanni Gabrieli notwithstanding, was consistent with the Renaissance spirit, and they have disagreed,
adducing historical or philosophical (aesthetic) arguments: the Gothic nature
of the polyphonic style or the medievally derived madrigal did not fit with
the Italian sense of *rinascimento*. This is possible, as is the argument that
unlike literature and the visual arts, music could not point to ancient Greek
or Roman models for the new style. Besides, it had been too inextricably
bound to the traditions and practices of Christianity and the Church to find
much leeway in other directions. I doubt, however, that the "secondary
citizenship" of music related to the greater possibility offered by the other
arts to immortalize with fame and glory the munificent patrons.[1] All the arts
depended on patronage, but their dependency was never bondage. As one
critic observes, music did have its share in the new attitudes, though with
some differences, even if "the notorious difficulty of verbally describing musical qualities left the connection between Renaissance ideals and musical

practice rather loose."[2] It was Friedrich Blume who put many of the theories in harmonized perspective and stressed the notion of an *ars nova* by highlighting the new aesthetic attitudes of Johannes Tinctoris and Franchino Gafori. Blume points to Tinctoris's treatises, *De Natura et Proprietate Tonorum* (1476) and *De Arte Contrapuncti* (1477), and to the mingling of *varietas*, a Nordic, Netherlandish skill in setting, and *suavitas*, a Southern, Italian beauty of sound. A friend of most contemporary composers, Tinctoris deemed it feasible to define music as an independent art, subject to itself, and procuring a special order of pleasure: "Nearly all the works of these men exhale such sweetness that in my opinion they are to be considered most suitable, not only for men and heroes, but even for the immortal gods. Indeed, I never hear them, I never examine them, without coming away happier and more enlightened."[3]

Though more keenly aware of the medieval tradition, Gafori too saw music in terms of the humanist—his *Pratica Musicae* (1496) and *De Harmonia* (1500/1518) attest to this—and he, too, knew most of the composers of his day. There were other theoreticians as well, of course, like Ramos de Pareja (*Musica Pratica*, 1482) and Johannes Gallicus (*Ritus Canendi Vetustissimus et Novus*, 1458–1464), the former stressing the new age, the latter more aware of the continuum between tradition and the new. Still, it was Tinctoris who, consistent with the spirit of *rinascimento*, akin to Marsilio Ficino's sense of rebirth from the "lacuna" of the *medio evo*, as a historian looked to music's autonomy, liberated from confining medieval theorems. If Marchetto di Padova had analysed *harmonia* as a "numerical ratio of high and low tones," Tinctoris adduced rather the concept of *euphonia*, or what the *ear*, not the theory, tells us: hence the demise of the music of the spheres in favor of music played and sung, or the passage from *musica teorica* to *musica practica*—an *ars perfecta*.

After Tinctoris, the importance in this process of Nicola Vicentino, during the middle of the sixteenth century, cannot be minimized. His *L'antica musica ridotta alla moderna prattica* (1555) argued strongly in favor of modern superiority; fullness (*perfectus* means "full") in harmony through a "piling up of consonances," which is what the ear feeds upon—agreeable sound and satisfaction—this was the empirical principle of his theory.[4] We must remember throughout all this that music meant the sounds produced by the singing voice, usually accompanied by instruments. And the singing voice meant the presence of words. The textual part of the musical legacy remained unshaken throughout the period of rebirth, even though, in the context of the new freedom and autonomy, instrumental music began—but only began—to develop along its own lines. Language, as we know, tends to abet class consciousness, and it is not surprising to see theories formulated about music for the refined taste of gentlemen and music for the daily needs of the plebs. Vicentino speaks clearly of chromatic and enharmonic music, reserved for the refined ears of the upper class, and diatonic (public) music, sung for the use of vulgar ears. By extension, the "reborn" music related to the refined occasions of court as contrasted with the plebeian occasions of popular festivals. Thus, *musica moderna* became *musica riservata* for polite society, the latter leading in time to (vocal) chamber music and, eventually, to (instrumental) chamber music as we know it.

As Vicentino theorized, a composer derives impetus for his music from the *concetto* and its *passione* which words stimulate; *musica riservata*, then, as if following the Platonic path whereby tones must draw their meaning from the text, gave priority to the words. In similar fashion, the socialization of musical expression through text contirbuted, in Vicentino, to a distinction between music to be sung in church and music for the *camera*—a further theoretical refinement away from common or "vulgar" music and resulting in a separation of simple and solemn expression guided by the Latin language for liturgy from the gentle and varied expression supported by the cultivated Italian language of gentility, and also from the rougher and colorful expression shaped by the popular Italian language of buffoons. The stratification leaves no doubt as to the increased self-consciousness of the composer who was contributing to a new aesthetic and "unmedieval" age for his art, now an independent idiom on the same level as literature, painting, sculpture, and architecture. Because of this, it became clear that, as for every true art, understanding required the cultivation of sophisticated appreciation, what Baldassare Castiglione was to call "trained ears" (*orecchie esercitate*).

The "Magna Carta" of music in the Renaissance, "its conclusive, encyclopedic self-portrait . . . announcing a turning point"[5] not only toward overall generic autonomy but also toward the autonomy of purely instrumental ensembles, was Gioseffo Zarlino's *Istitutioni Harmoniche* (1558). By alluding to Aristotle's "free play of the spirit," he set the stage for the art's infinite developments, including the fantasies of virtuosity. Still, the dominance of words, even if absent, in musical expression remained a fact of cultural life, and even Zarlino saw in the ability of tone and rhythm to "imitate words," like an *imitatio naturae*, the accomplishment of music's highest objective.

This continued insistence on the text, coupled with the art's new expressiveness, gave music a new vitality. Zarlino's overtures notwithstanding, music without words was still too unpracticed to expand to large-scale use. In fact, the prohibitions against the "free play of the spirit" that stemmed from the Aristotelian dictum and even more from the flowering Platonic tradition (music in the *Republic* is strictly controlled to build moral character as opposed to anarchic fantasies) would have paradoxically hindered truly creative innovations without the protection, as it were, of the words. The relatively unchanging or stable nature of the texts allowed for the imaginative changes taking place underneath them in the accompaniments to go undetected. Thus, the historical alliance of text and music cannot be considered inhibiting to the latter; quite to the contrary, I might argue that music as a developing art was strengthened by it.

There was definitely a musical *risorgimento*, therefore; there was a Renaissance spirit in music comparable to the spirit in the plastic arts and literature, and the phenomenon may be traced historically through its most outstanding practitioners and styles. A brief run-down suffices. Significantly, they all speak to the evolution of tone and text.

In the fifteenth century, John Dunstable's elegantly flowing vocal effects, including contrapuntal polytextuality, gave his sacred music a distinctive aesthetic that abandoned the more angular medieval style and that, by "paraphrasing," created new melodies on preexisting chants. Passing beyond the *ars nova* and smoothing out the Dunstable dissonances, however controlled, Guillaume Dufay used the Italian *ballata* style to interrelate texture, text, and tone in a form of imitative writing (each entering voice imitates the previous voice), thereby overstepping the separate function the *ars nova* attributed to each voice. The text registered better—something Gilles Binchois recognized when he transferred the technique to secular songs. Dufay's use of secular tunes as *cantus firmus* in his sacred music, his weaving lay motifs into liturgical polyphony—a century later the Council of Trent was to censor this practice—and his integrating the "unrelated" textual movements of the Mass into an aesthetic whole represented a great musical innovation made possible under the protective coating of the words. An ingenious craftsman like Johannes Ockeghem then capitalized on these innovations with even greater imaginativeness and technical virtuosity, bringing together two, two-voice canons, or "vocalizing" all (even instrumental) parts, or engaging in asymmetrical phrases.

Among them, the Northern composers refined polyphony, while in the South a variant culture—the improvisatory song of poet-musicians—showed a preference for formulaic chord patterns and *fioriture,* both of which pointed to more clearly declaimed texts. The princes, like Lorenzo de' Medici, imported Northern composers (Lorenzo's composers—among them Heinrich Isaak, Alexander Agricola, Alessandro Coppini, Bartolomeo degli Organi, and Ser Giovanni Serragli—served the rich tradition of the *canti carnascialeschi,* with its cars, floats, masked musicians, dancers, signers, and torches, and the fine contributing poets like Poliziano and Lorenzo himself) who delighted in setting Italian verses to music. Among these were, for example, Petrarch's "Vergine bella" (set by Dufay) and Giustiniani's "O rosa bella" (set by Dunstable). The poet-musicians varied and embellished the often bare outlines of these verses with their seven-stringed lira da braccio. Toward the end of the fifteenth century particularly—through the welter of popular forms like the *strambotti, capitoli,* and *ballate,* alongside the more literarily sophisticated *canzoni*—emerged the influential *frottole,* musical aids to the courtier and suitable to all occasions of amorous and courtly life without disregarding moralistic concerns. In Isabella d'Este's Mantuan court, composers Bartolomeo Tromboncino and Marchetto Cara stressed the concept of fine poetry for music, and hence a chordal orientation, really a principal melody with inner voices filling the texture, in lieu of a polyphonic one, came about. Their charm became more intellectually demanding as the *frottola* incorporated poetic texts of lofty merit; and, regardless of subject matter, as it gained in aesthetic stature it paved the way for the madrigal, the most significant musico-poetical art form of the period, an interpenetration of Italian harmonic structures in the *canti carnascialeschi* and Franco-Netherlandish polyphony.

In the sixteenth century, the French *chanson,* in which musical rhythm was determined by prosody, or the text's rhythm in a union of tone and text in which the poetry dominated, further strengthened the bond between the two arts. It is hard to separate that French music from the verbal element. The poet Pierre de Ronsard did not find instrumental music agreeable without the human voice—an attitude that in France lasted indeed until the nineteenth century. Clément Janequin went so far as to supplement the voice with extramusical effects; in "La Guerre" (the battle of Marignano of 1515) we hear bird calls, hunt calls, street cries, and female chatter, all of which makes tone subservient to text. Josquin des Prez stressed the *vocal* quality of the musical line, constructing tonal phrases that intimately blended music and words through natural stress as well as meaning (e.g., with the word "rise" the phrase rises; with "jealousy" it slithers around; with "sad" it descends; with "doubt" it hesitates). Hence, innovation inspired by the text stimulated music's evolutionary process, not by way of artificial devices that ultimately remain outside of musical expression, but by way of a structural integration of, say, the birdcalls into the very fabric of the composition.

During the period of the Pléïade in France, Jean-Antoine de Baïf and Ronsard wrote poetry primarily with the musical concept in mind, envisaging a verse form chanted in the ancient Greek manner: the *vers mesurés*, which demanded a very studied music. This was primarily Baïf's aesthetic application of Humanism, though metrical verse forced language into an arbitrarily chosen rhythm and the *chansonniers*, therefore, looked down on such a contrived, restricting idea. Ronsard, who liked polyphony and whose sonnets were put to music by Janequin (among others), was sensible enough to imitate the Italian more natural blending of sound and syllable. When the influence of the Italian madrigal made itself felt, the *chanson* under Claude Le Jeune became perhaps more intellectually staid, but by the same token it may be considered an ancestor of the nineteenth-century art song.

During the late Renaissance, richly in Venice and flourishingly in England, the madrigal dominated the musical scene with profusion. Originally as an Italian poem set to Northern—Flemish or Franco-Flemish—music, using *cantus firmus* and contrapuntal parts, it differed from its fourteenth-century parent and ennobled the *frottola*. We need only think of Adriaan Willaert. But it did more. It illustrated musical Humanism at its best, a perfected and perfect fusion of text and tone, with the latter carefully reflecting the former, homophonically and polyphonically, and with the former essential to the latter, lest the unverbalized musical changes in tempo and mood appear meaningless. The fluidity of free verse aided the musical principle as each voice enjoyed its own distinctiveness. More than John Dowland, who liked the song medium, madrigal honors in England went to such composers as Thomas Morley, Thomas Weelkes, Orlando Gibbons, and John Ward, and, of course, to William Byrd who, though better known for his church music, skillfully fused his sense of textual importance with the "human" requirements of tone, of the ear, in adroit polyphonic contexts. Before long, the madrigal flattened social contrasts in music, given its democratic popularity that extended from London to Naples.

By now, musical experiments and innovations had advanced the cause of the art's individuality among its Renaissance sisters so much that the Counter Reformation, with its strict rules aimed at removing aesthetic distractions and any semblance of worldly association, had only a theoretical effect. Cristóbal de Morales and Tomás Luis de Victoria wrote sophisticated music to sacred texts; Juan del Encina did the same to secular texts (recall the *villancico*); continuing the tradition of the Minnesänger, the biblically inspired Meistersinger wrote new music for existing melodies and vice versa, while on the secular side, the polyphonic *Lied* took definite shape. Again, the symbiotic interrelation of tone and text obtained, without which even the monophonic hymnal creations of Martin Luther very likely would not have come into being.

Orlando di Lasso stands out as a towering figure during this period. His psalms and motets culminated the initial orientations of Dunstable and Dufay. The music is exquisitely wrought, encompassing everything from serenity to humor. And the Church could not object, for his fine literary sensibility, especially in his masses, gave unusual prominence to the words of the poet or of the liturgy. But it was Giovanni Pierluigi da Palestrina— whose pure melodic lines bestowed dignity on the words and whose harmonic and contrapuntal structures eschewed all dissonance—who set aside many of the new directions by absorbing them (above all the advances made by the madrigal) yet bleaching their excessive vigors and enthusiasms. In his meditative spirituality and aesthetic equanimity, he fashioned a quintessential blend of syllable and sound, paralleling the perfect blend of harmony and melody. And this constitutes as much a *rinascimento* in music that prepared Baroque expression as a culmination of the text-and-tone conjunction that prepared the birth of opera and the consequent beauties of Claudio Monteverdi.

5

"HOW SOUR SWEET MUSIC . . .
WHEN TIME IS BROKE"

"How sour sweet music is / When time is broke and no proportion kept!"[1] The lines occur in William Shakespeare's *Richard II*, spoken by King Richard himself, just before he is lamentably killed in prison at the very end of the play. Not that this monarch is a model of wisdom. After having impoverished England with his extravagances, surrounded himself with flatterers and boon companions, lost the good will of his people who welcomed Bolingbroke whose lands he had seized to wage his Irish wars, and been abandoned by his soldiers, he humbly submits to imprisonment, giving up his crown to Bolingbroke, that is, to Henry IV. For him, who could not maintain his kingly office through mind and sword, history has come unhinged, his royal destiny has collapsed, the balanced proportion has been lost, and the logical flow of time has cracked. To use Yeats's "Second Coming" metaphor, things have fallen apart because the center has not held. All this, of course, from Richard's own perception of things. Alone in the dungeon of Pomfret Castle, he hears music and comments that now this normally sweet music is sour, thereby suggesting for us some relationship between history and the art of sounds, as perceived by the individual psyche.

Richard implies that music is sweet by nature; sweetness, we must infer, becomes an objective attribute, independent of our private act of perception—of the quality *we* impose upon what we hear, of that subjective manner of perceiving and understanding we now refer to under the pompous heading of phenomenology. He also says that "when time is broke," off center, out of joint, as it was for his cousin-character Hamlet—when history indulges in violence and destruction while seeking to pursue its course rather than in discourse and compromise—this thing, music, which by nature is "sweet," becomes "sour" the moment we inject it with our own unhappiness, our own suffering, and what it is objectively may be something totally different from what we make it become subjectively. The old dichotomy of relativity versus absolutism comes to mind, or, let us say, of Romanticism versus Classicism. But more about this later. "This music mads me," continues Richard; "let it sound no more."

We are here at the juncture of psychoaesthetics and philosophy. Therefore, since we are talking about an aesthetic matter, let us become psychophilosophers for a brief moment. Let us recognize that what we learn from Richard's ambivalence is judgmental relativity. When Richard implies that music is sweet, this is like our claiming that poetry is beautiful or that high waterfalls are grandiose. In a world full of meanness and ugliness, we like to feel that our views are nourished by some absolute, by some objective and eternal value that informs our aesthetic experience. If by sweetness Richard means beauty—which he does—then beauty is the objective attribute of music. That is what, in a different context, Leonard Meyer calls "a tendency toward Platonic idealism. . . . , embedded in the way in which we ordinarily talk about and conceive the world."[2]

But Richard, Meyer would say, is also Aristotelian. Sweetness may be an essential quality of the music, but it is made to sound in an existential context, and when this existential context is history out of proportion and broken, fallen apart, the interaction between Richard and his context turns the music sour. The Platonic absolute yields to the Aristotelian relative, let alone the Spenglerian disintegration.

All of this might suggest, then, a strong—meaning influential—connection between music and history, both in the manner in which music is perceived and in the manner in which it is composed. And if, even in rapid flight, we spread our wings over the past 2,500 years, we note repeated instances of the interrelationship. We notice how in ancient Greece music was a handmaid of politics, something which made Plato in the *Republic* label it dangerous. A tradition had it that music should be strictly controlled, much as it is in the Soviet Union today, since, particularly in times of historical crises, music could promote good citizenship and loyalty, and thereby strengthen the State. Conversely, if not controlled—that is, if traduced by the spirit of change and innovation—music leads to upheaval, to social modification and revolution, to events considered nefarious at that time. It was noted that after the physically exhausting and spiritually debilitating war between the Greeks and Persians, or between the city-states, traditional musical forms dissolved. This is what Yeats underscored when, to his famous verse, he added: "Mere anarchy is loosed upon the world."[3] Aristophanes complained about new music without sanity, experimental, and infectious for the entire State. Wordless music especially could lead astray. And in the *Politics*, Aristotle followed suit.

Rome was not much different in its views, if Quintilian was any example, for music, by sapping the Empire's strength if "misused," would destroy it. Later on, Boethius prescribed that music ennobles and degrades and that it should remain consonant with nature and not undergo unnatural innovations that would lead to revolt against authority. Boethius provides the compendial statement of antiquity. And we know that Charlemagne tried to standardize music for his own political ends. Music and the logical flow of history, of national destiny, go hand in hand.

With such a background joining history to the art of sounds, nationalism, a few centuries later, could easily color musical expression with a wide gamut of political tints. Mozart occasionally, and Beethoven frequently, as in the freedom songs, relate music to political ideology. But I should rather point to wordless music: to that of Chopin, who relates to Polish nationalism; that of Liszt, to the working class; that of Wagner, to his desire to rejuvenate the German State; that of Verdi, to the insurrection that led to Italian liberation from foreign domination; that of Smetana, to his desire to make music a historical document for Bohemia; and that of Glinka, to Russian autonomy through patriotic legend. In a follow-up of this activity, Sibelius will later speak through his music of his oppressed Finnish fatherland, Richard Strauss will accept (though not necessarily ideologically)[4] to be linked to the glories of the Third Reich, and Shostakovitch and Prokofiev will infuse their compositions with patriotic pride. Those among these composers who made the politicians uneasy were innovators in the musical idiom, and just as the Austrians feared Verdi the Soviets feared Sibelius sufficiently to ban his music, and their own Prokofiev sufficiently to attempt to silence his innovating atonalism and "futurism," as it were, lest he become another rabble-rousing, traditionally nonconforming Stravinsky. And, in a different context, if we read *The Music of Revolution* (1978) by Hans Eisler, a composer and student of Schönberg and Brecht, we are informed today of actual Marxist music and of a Marxist musical aesthetic.

Now, that music can be perceived and composed in certain ways and be associated with historical events and political ideologies opens the door to the fundamental consideration, adumbrated by Richard II, of *meaning* in music. For the fact remains inalienable that music itself, wordless or worded, program or pure, is an abstract art (in the common use of the adjective), by nature indifferent to concrete conceptualization. In whatever context, meaning may be defined as anything which relates to something beyond itself, let us say to something similar to itself in kind like a dominant chord that refers to a tonic chord sounded sometime after it (or before it), or to something different from itself in kind like a literary work or an emotion that the musical composition attempts to transcribe by analogy. Meaning arises when we become aware, affectively or intellectually, of what is going on internally in the composition (for which I use the word "intrinsic") or of what is being related to externally (for which I use the word "extrinsic"). In other words, in the *intrinsic* sense music points to itself, to its notes as notes and to its sounds as sounds. The intrinsic quality, free from extramusical considerations, is the basic and natural condition of music, the root of its superior autonomousness among the arts. This music—Bach's fugues, Mozart's concertos, Beethoven's quartets, Schubert's symphonies, those of Charles Ives, Poulenc's improvisations, even Scott Joplin's ragtime tunes—has a long and distinguished lineage and is impervious to the hammerings of history, of historical crises and political insurrections. The apocalyptic Four Horsemen cannot contaminate it. And it perpetuates itself organically from within. There is what Gerald Abraham describes as "an autonomous process of self-evaluation" that takes place, "proceeding by successive exhaustion of techniques and styles and their replacement by new ones."[5] The apogee of counterpoint with Palestrina coexisted with the first stirrings of tonal harmony and expressive melody which slowly gained prominence with Monteverdi, just as the heavily textured baroque of Bach and Buxtehude dissolved as the thinly lined sonatas of Vivaldi, Mozart, and Haydn gained prominence. While one thing is going on, something else is starting. The process is ongoing and evolutionary. About intrinsically oriented music, where sounds are simply themselves and not vehicles for nonmusical thoughts and feelings, we make predictions as we listen to it (even if our anticipations are often incorrect: for example, our experience with the failure of a Haydn rondo-finale to return as expected to the main theme); since the notes imply one another, point to one another, they are related through an internal coherence that makes predicting possible. And music thrives on the satisfaction of predictability as well as on the surprise of the unpredicted. This quality provides the common ground that links a Berg violin concerto to a Handel sonata, or a Corelli concerto grosso to a Schönberg orchestral essay. Theirs is music whose ingredients relate to something similar to themselves in kind.

In the *extrinsic* sense, music must still retain its intrinsic quality but additionally it points to something beyond the notes, beyond what they say by themselves, toward something that another factor, like a literary work, makes them say, or toward something, like love, sorrow, serenity, death, jest, or anger (or sourness in broken times), *we* make them say. Hence Beethoven's *Pastoral* Symphony, or Liszt's *Dante Symphony* or Debussy's *L'Après-midi d'un faune* Prelude or even Mahler's First Symphony (with all of its extra-musical allusions) fall within this category, not to speak of the whole range of music set to a text, from masses and oratorios to operas and art songs.

At this point one may observe that suddenly I am alluding to composers associated with the Romantic tradition, whereas up until now my examples were chosen mainly from the opposing traditions. The observation is important. In my opinion, the passage from a primarily intrinsic consciousness in (wordless) music to a primarily extrinsic consciousness occurred, as in so many other aspects of culture, with the French Revolution, that bloody atrocity that nonetheless reoriented the West. It heralded Romanticism. At this historical juncture, the arts, notably music among them, began acting often as vehicles for personal or social and political purposes. In so doing, music deliberately or subtly pointed beyond itself, to literature or landscape or historical event explicitly in the overtures of Tchaikowsky (like *1812*) or Mendelssohn (like *Fingal's Cave*) or the tone poems of Liszt, or it pointed to private creeds and emotions implicitly in the Catholic symphonies of Bruckner or the nationalistic and otherwise descriptive piano works of Chopin, not to mention the lightheartedly carefree waltzes of Johann Strauss. The insinuation (and insinuations) of folk motifs into (and in) the musical compositions certainly aided in the process. (Again, I leave out worded music which, as we might gather, developed enormously at this time, particularly opera from Weber, Rossini, and Berlioz to Wagner, Verdi, Puccini, and Richard Strauss, and the art song under Schubert, Schumann, Wolf, Chausson, and Debussy—a development which would not have occurred with such richness without the prompting and encouragement of the extrinsic consciousness.) When music was its own end, as it was commonly in the seventeenth and eighteenth centuries, we find ourselves perceiving music intrinsically, reacting to notes as they point to themselves. When it was put to the service of something else, or at least when a nonmusical factor dominated the composer's mood, as in the nineteenth century, we find ourselves reacting to the extrinsic, say descriptive, quality. Put differently, Romantic music usually contains a *message*—even in a Brahms or a Tchaikowsky symphony—which a Mozart symphony or a Tartini sonata does not contain. I would say that a Mozart symphony has *character:* we *go to it* because it is intrinsically self-contained; in contrast, a Brahms symphony has *suggestion:* it *comes to us* because it is extrinsically oriented. I would add that this is going to be true anytime the composition invites an emotional participation instead of an intellectual involvement (if I am allowed to skirt such nice refinements as the concept of an intellectual emotion). Suggestion embraces emotion—the message, whereas intellect embraces character—the thing itself.

For this reason, I must conclude that music can reflect or need not reflect political events or historical crises. I am not talking about styles. Styles derive from the cultural orientations of given historical periods; they constitute "the universe of discourse within which musical meanings arise."[6] But music—the notes themselves, their "musical" meaning independent of style—depends on our mode of perception. Less abstract than music, painting (at least up until the twentieth century) and literature have lent themselves more naturally to the events of history (one thinks of Picasso's *Guernica* or of E. E. Cummings's "Thanksgiving 1956" as examples). The composer so suggested it, and the listener had to receive the message that way, from Beethoven's Sixth Symphony to Richard Strauss's *Ein Heldenleben.* Otherwise, at other times, music has remained aloof.

Yet, to repeat, *any* music can be made to sound an extrinsic message, depending on our perception, on the meaning *we* impose upon it which in itself it does not or may not have. We are all aware of how Bach was polyphony for Schumann but of how Bach became a Romantic deity for Albert Schweitzer. Their performances of him were totally different, the first sounding mathematical, the second exultational. Similarly, we are aware of how music is sweet by nature but of how it is sour for Richard II. But that music itself is ultimately an intrinsic construct, regardless of historical disproportions, unholding centers, or breakages in time, his creator knew well, for Shakespeare wisely contradicts Richard in one of his sonnets, as if this time to say: "let it sound some more." Let the sounds be themselves, not vehicles for inviting all the vagaries of human feelings. Busoni suggested that it is not the function of music to excite the passions—I might add, to shape itself in the molds and caldrons of history—but to produce rationalized tonal combinations and stylized forms.[7] The great English Bard put it more elegantly in Sonnet 8:

> Music to hear, why hear'st thou music sadly?
> Sweets with sweets war not, joy delights in joy.[8]

6

EXPLORATIONS IN
A NON-WESTERN CONTEXT

The field of the interrelations of literature and music in the West is growing slowly but steadily, even as it is more than usually frought with dangers to specialist and dilettante alike, dangers that stem from methodologies that reflect analogical thinking by inference rather than through analysis when comparisons are made on the basis of structure. Within the Western context, the possibilities of significant analytical studies on the level of structural correspondences (e.g., theme and variation, sonata or symphonic form, fugue, rondo, passacaglia, leitmotif, counterpoint) remain fruitful because of the frequent musical aspirations of writers like Denis Diderot, Thomas De Quincey, Gabriele D'Annunzio, or Alejo Carpentier. The situation is different in the non-Western tradition, where the style of music, as frequently its purpose, is not the same, and where many of the aforementioned structural elements do not obtain. I have tried to arrive at a few exploratory conjectures, in the hope of attracting to the subject scholars with better credentials than mine in non-Western studies, and the first thing I noticed in so trying is that non-Western writers have not been lured consciously into verbalizing music, just as composers have not set forth a strict musicalization of a literary text except in the context of accompanying poetry, drama, or dance.[1]

The most logical area to begin the exploration of musico-literary affinities outside of the Western tradition would seem to be in that which centers around poetic expression. "Music without poetry is not music," said the ancient Chinese. And the reverse also held true. There was never a time in those days that the one art did not serve as handmaiden to the other.[2] Unfortunately, most of ancient Chinese lyric and dramatic poetry has been lost, and even for the extant poetry—for example, Confucius's *Shih Ching* collection of 305 poems—we do not have the music. We must wait until the twelfth century to find some record of the melodies; yet music was always there, and the two arts have parted company only during the last two centuries.

What fascinates the investigator in the case of China is that Chinese is a tone language, and the spoken inflections make for a complex relation with music. It is fair to say that in the West most words may be individualized by meaning; even a centrifugal word in Attic Greek like *areté*, which may spin off into a half-dozen meanings, remains individualized, and while it does depend on context it does not, like a Chinese vocable, lose meaning without that context, and, in addition, without the written symbol. Inflection, furthermore, extends variety. Now, if language is music in its simplest form, then a successive arrangement of inflections is not very different from the movement of sounds which forms the essence of melody. In other words, music is inherent in the Chinese language itself (as in African tribal idioms), and the poet did not have to reshape syntax, vocabulary, and semantics in order to musicalize his language in the manner of Western poets who pursued the musical aesthetic, like Carl Bellman, Clemens Brentano, D'Annunzio, Edgar Allan Poe, Paul Verlaine, Ernst Jandl, and others.

Before the eighth century, traditional Chinese poetry—say, *shih*—did not enjoy a harmonization of music with the spoken inflections; but with the advent of *tz'u*—that form of poetry conditioned by the inflections of language—the situation changed. With T'ang poets like Li Po and Tu Fu, poetry, through a harmonized coexistence with music, became less rigid and acquired greater freedom. The period that lends itself most logically to a musico-literary inquiry is that of the Sung Dynasty from the tenth to the thirteenth centuries when *tz'u* enjoyed its greatest development. Not only would the production of the popular Liu Yung bear investigation, but indeed the altercation between one of the greatest of Chinese poets, Su Tung-po, and one of the greatest women in Chinese literature, Li Chin-chao, who criticized Su because, unlike her own *tz'u*, his did not harmonize with "musical" expression. There was, too, the effort of Chou Pang-yen, the poet and musician of the Imperial Court, to bring together the poetry of *tz'u* and its music. The nature of this form makes almost natural the existence of a multiple talent, something which in the West one tends to regard with special wonder, particularly in the musico-literary association, not so much on the conceptual level of a Thomas Mann or a George Bernard Shaw or a

Romain Rolland, as on the level of practiced crafts: E. T. A. Hoffmann, for example, or Jean-Jacques Rousseau, Richard Wagner, or Arrigo Boïto. In China during this period, there is, besides Chou, Chiang K'uei, both poet and musician, who even compiled an extant book on the subject. In all instances, focus should always be on the possibility of analyzing the inter-relationship through questions like the choice the poet makes, the aesthetic value coupled with the necessity of semantics, the treatment and develop-ment of the verbal and melodic materials, and the resulting integrated tex-ture.[3]

Ch'u, the third major type of Chinese poetry, basically the song that led to opera, developed several centuries before the Ming Dynasty (fourteenth to seventeenth centuries). Eventually, it became a song drama integrated with instruments; in fact, the later (Ching Dynasty) little dramas known as *k'un ch'u* may be considered early opera. During the preceding Yüan Dy-nasty, an instructional manual appeared, *Cho Keng Lu*, directing the singer how to perform *ch'u* in six categories: tone production, rhythm and singing, monosyllabic singing, single-verse singing, types of song, and breathing. It would seem from this categorization that research would be well served by consulting the techniques of tone production in relation to the text and by comparing the Chinese way of approaching the problem with the various Western ways that involve styles like bel canto, lyric, dramatic, art song, and many more, given the wealth of singing manuals in the West—always bearing in mind the central question of how music and text are made to interrelate (e.g., Giulio Caccini, *Le nuove musiche*; Nicola Porpora, through the works of his students Domenico Corri and Isaac Nathan; Charles Bur-ney, *The Present State of Music in France and Italy*; Auguste Matthieu Panseron, *Méthode de vocalisation pour soprano et ténor*; Manuel García, *Traité complet de l'art du chant*, among others). An interesting phenome-non occurred during Ming: that of slipping extraneous words into the text, even if the words had no meaning. Were the additions both demanded and conditioned by melodic needs? The phenomenon occurs in African music, too.

Manchu oppressiveness did much to drain *ch'u* of the vitality it had gained during Yüan and Ming, but the operatic tradition continued, albeit less sophisticated, based on the *pang t'u* song—a high voice over wood-block rhythm patterns. The ensuing operative form, like *P'i Huang*, complete with two score instruments (percussion, trumpets, flutes), made successful ap-

pearances in Europe and the United States in 1929.[4] In a technique analogous if not actually parallel to that of slipping extraneous words into the
text, the execution of the complex vocal lines was left to the performer. In
the West, too, during the seventeenth and eighteenth centuries, we wit-
nessed the decoration of written notes by the singer's own ornamental additions—the *agréments*, as they came to be known in France after Lully, who
had returned to originally Italian devices. Here again, one would have to
ask how and to what extent the Chinese *"agréments"* were conditioned by
the inflection of the words themselves, assuming that the problem of locat-
ing the actual notations could be solved. And there is always the matter of
semantics to contend with. In the West, where the focus in songs or arias is
all too frequently the music at the expense of the text, which has therefore
a tendency to suffer keenly from banality, the semantic question is not as
sharp as in the East. It is not coincidental that in Chinese the two characters
symbolizing music, *yin* and *yueh*, define it, not only as tone and rhythm
(*yin*), but also, along with pleasure, psychological meaning (*yueh*). The
potentially difficult question of meaning through inflection in conjuction
with melodic movement is eased considerably by the fact that Chinese is a
monosyllabic language, which suggests that musico-literary expression is given
more to monosyllabic melody than to melismatic melody. Indeed, Confucius himself had established a distinction between the two: the latter (*su
yueh*) is more common and appeals only to the ear, whereas the former (*ya
yueh*) is refined and appeals to the mind and soul.

Therefore, Chinese poetry, particularly *tz'u* and *ch'u*, offers an attractive
possibility for comparison with the West within the context of the musico-
literary interrelation. More than a dilettantish affinity may result in analyzing much parallelisms, for the same reason that the attitudes and pronouncements of that rhapsodic third-century group of philosopher-poets, the
Seven Sages of Bamboo Grove, with their intense appreciation of nature,
wine, and music, may justifiably be studied in relation to the European
Romantic psyche.

It is quite well known that in Japan the fine arts find their basic orientation in the written word, a situation which encourages study of the interrelationship with literature. As in earlier China, poetry and music formed
inseparable bonds, though, if we look back at the Nara period of the sixth
to seventh centuries, we find that music was not indigenous but imported
from China, Korea, and India. None of the four thousand poems of the

Manyōshū anthology could be heard without music. In later periods, with the modification of foreign influences which climax with the total isolation during Tokugawa or Edo (seventeenth to nineteenth centuries), Japanese music became more and more indigenous and was put to broader use: theater, for instance (as distinguished from opera). But if Lady Murasaki's *Genji Monogatari* during the Heian period (eighth to twelfth centuries) is an example, music had long before become a pervasive presence in upper-class social life: lute lessons, the sound of the *koto*, the need to learn music, the measure of characters and of life through music throughout the novel. Then, during Kamakura (twelfth to seventeenth centuries), had come the growth of theatrical arts and lute sagas, like the *Heike* story, which could not be recited without the accompaniment of the *biwa* (lute).

In all of this, the basic question for me remains the interrelationship. The problems are different from those involving an inflected language like Chinese; they center around matters less of texture as such than of mutual correspondence, around exactly how the instrument accompanied the voice. Since the Japanese music I am speaking of was conceived as ancillary to literature or, say, as a vehicle for words, the point of investigation remains the manner in which this dominant position of *vocal* music was implemented. Whether or not imported, instruments—that is, music—accompanied the human voice or provided the interludes between verses or songs. Given this orientation, the parallel growth of Japanese music history with music for the theater does not come as a surprise, particularly during the Edo period.

The classical *Nohgaku* of this and the previous periods, or *Noh* drama, is a *Gesamtkunstwerk* in the best sense, uniting harmoniously all theatrical elements: dance, setting, costume, mask, and, of course, poetry and music.[5] Much has been written about the structure of a *noh*, its performance, its texts, its instruments, but, confirms Rikutaro Fukuda, not on the interactions of music and words, which seem to me to be as important as the interaction that takes place between performer and audience. In fact, the latter interaction must necessarily be induced by the former. The accompanying *kyogen* comedy came generally without music, but the *noh* lived by it, as it were, from the introductory music in the first *dan* (unit), in the *jo* section and ensuing *shidai* (music representing a supporting actor), right through to the final *dan*, the fifth, in the *kyu* section, where the highlight focuses on the *mai* dance and where the music depends on the character of the actor. In between—in the second, third, and fourth *dan* of the *ha* section—we hear the main actor's first song, the *issei*; the *michiyuki* movement; the recitative and chorus; the highest musical point of emotional tension, the *kuri*; the *kuse* or dance center of the play; and the musical ending, the *rongi*, which is usually followed by the *nakairi* interlude.

With music depending on the personality of the actor and on the text, which portrays the main character fully, there should be room for close analyses of the musico-literary interrelation. Since the music has a literary orientation, the text is the clue for understanding the music; in turn, the music adapts itself to the necessities of the words. What are the melodic rules that govern this kind of symbiotic accompaniment? At what point does the melody start, and why? What and how are notes stressed, and where do they end? Despite the literariness of *noh*, there are styles which stress melody, just as there are those which stress words. If we study these in terms of the two manners, the lyric and the strong, we might gain useful insights into the musico-literary relationship, just as we might from a study of the instruments used: not just the drum section of *kotsuzumi*, *otsuzumi*, and *taiko*, but especially the all-important flute. In fact, are there times when the flute is used "literarily"? Elastic rhythm, indefinite pitch, restricted melodic movement, singing based on poetry, and music alert to every emotional change in the words: all these factors are to be recalled when approaching the interrelation and might prove especially interesting in the case of the theoretical discussions recorded by that multiple talent of the fifteenth century, Zeami Motokiyo, who wrote both text and music to his *noh* plays, and now, with his father, transformed shrine ritual music (known as monkey music: *sarugaku*) and folk-dance music *(dengaku)* into a subtle art form. In Zeami's *Atsumori* we hear: "the songs of woodsmen and the flute-playing of herdsmen . . . through poets' verses are known to all the world . . . bamboo-flute . . . Guide us on our passage through this sad world . . . reaper's flute . . . Korean flute."[6]

Even more exciting from my point of view might be a study of the interrelation of Kabuki drama, which evolved during the Edo period and used the services of music in a more integrated way. For in this noncourtly, popular theater, plot is often propelled, not just by narration (the *chobo*, in itself like a Greek chorus), but indeed by the music. In a play like *Geppo and His Daughter Tsuji* of 1773, it is the music that carries the action forward and, as in other plays, comes to acquire symbolic meaning. The introduction of the *shamisen* a century earlier, with its versality of suggestion, standardized regular musical accompaniment *(nagauta)* by the ensemble known as *debayashi* and provided interpretative sounds which relayed meaning to the audience. Musicians were on stage as well as off; their music identified specific places, animals, geographical landmarks, atmospheric conditions—and if the music in itself did not, the types of instruments did. None of this use of music or instruments (court flutes, bamboo flutes, many drums) in their melodic and percussive combinations could be called realistic. Rather, one accepts the sounds on the level of abstraction, as in the case of the wind pattern heard on a quiet night when a thief is prowling around, since, one critic comments, a chill wind is like the cold eye of a robber.[7] The possibilities for musico-literary analysis here at the heart of such a sophisticated aesthetics are rich. They become even richer when we realize that, in order to appreciate the drama, the audience must have a foreknowledge of the identifying patterns—which is another way of saying that we are in the presence of the leitmotif a century and a half before Wagner. Even if the instruments are blocks and bells, they are musically conceived in their sounds and they live a special relationship with the text.

The famous drama *Momiji Gari* should provide a particularly fertile source for investigation, since the text is supported by two kinds of music written by two different people, the onstage music and the offstage *geza-ongaku* melodic and percussive strains. Changes in action are supported by stylistic switches and by the introduction of special instruments over the pervasive phrases of the *shamisen*, to all of which—orchestral tone color and the psychological timing of musical effects like leitmotifs propelling the text—the audience contributes personally and imaginatively. If this music were not passed on by rote but were notated, and if what exists in *geza* notation could be pried loose today from the *geza* guilds, the researcher would experience only normal obstacles in pursuing his goal. Unfortunately, however, such research as I am proposing would demand a combination of patience, insight, and diplomacy. Perhaps these days more and more, as Western music continues its evolution on Japanese soil alongside the varied and unique *hogaku* (just as Arabic music might—against many odds, to be sure—filter gradually southward into Black African expression), there will be increased attempts to set down workable notations of benefit to the westerner.

The westerner comes to Indian music with fewer hesitations than he is likely to have when he faces Chinese and Japanese music, but he is in for a surprise caused by any number of aesthetic complexities that emerge, and attempting to evolve a musico-literary concept requires taking many subtle factors into account. Indian monody and its relation to the *raga* (see below) is a succession of concordant, rather than related, notes, and this—coupled with the fantasies of time measure and the absence of a universal system of notation—creates special problems when we look into the matter of coherence between tone and text. While the mood, once established by the *raga*, is fixed, time and tune work with emotions to create and promote the melodic line. As is the case with the other countries I am exploring here, the notion of Western harmony was foreign to the musical concept in India; note clusters, therefore, do not identify the melodic line, whereas salient notes do, and this saliency is unalterable because it is deeply rooted in tradition. And finally, *grace-gamakas* (sound curves), microtones, and time measures notwithstanding, the real difficulty for the westerner is to learn to appreciate execution and accuracy above tone and timbre, especially with the singing of words.

Sanskrit, the language of the *Vedas*, not to mention the *Mahabārata*, the *Rāmāyana*, and the *Puranas*, retained a close connection with music at all times; the verses were changed in set musical patterns. Even today, if we look at South India, Brahmin families devote their lives to proper chanting.[8] It is important to remember, however, that as in Japan music was traditionally associated with literature or the written word until recent times, so in India has music been traditionally associated with the dance. Music accompanied poetry for religious purposes, but prominence was exerted by the dance. The *Mahabārata*'s mightly warrior Arjun was an expert musician and dancer; he had received the *Bhagavad-Gītā*—or sacred song—from Vishnu's incarnation Krishna, a flute player, and taught these arts to Princess Uttara. Clearly, then, apart from the added factor of dance, the musico-literary connection is culturally strong.[9]

India can boast of having possessed the first musicologists—Narada, for example, around the turn of the millennium, whose *Bhārata Natya Shastra* not only explored the relation between sacred and secular music or between *shabdams* (danced songs) and *padams* (danced love lyrics) but also provided a coherent aesthetic, typically Hindu in its belief in the unity of diversity, whereby all Art (music, dance, painting, drama, criticism) is One. Assuming the focus on dance, and with music and vocal music central, he discusses that sophisticated modal system conceived to evoke particular moods or emotions, the *rasa*. This concept, which addresses love, pathos, humor, anger, terror, heroism, disgust, and wonder, among other qualities—each associated with a particular deity and color—becomes important for the musico-literary researcher, for, again, it bespeaks a veritable intimacy and interdependence between the two arts. And this remained true even after regional languages, the *desa-bhasa*, challenged Sanskrit in the sixth century and when, because of the new languages, compositional styles had to be altered. A simple comparison of the ensuing styles—the regional variations with the original one—should reveal any number of facts concerning the interrelation and point to variances in inspiration and temperament.

To be consulted would be the first modern book on Indian music, Sarangadeva's eighteenth-century treatise *Sangīta-ratnākara*, where the art's relationship with the texts is inherent in the presentation that does not deal with instruments but, rather, discusses northern Muslim and southern Hindu music, or what later became known as the Karnatic and the Hindustani styles. Another question that might be raised pertains to the realm of *ragas* and *talas* and how the texts are influenced by the manner in which these organize melody and rhythm, respectively (Sarangadeva's work contains 264 *ragas*). As microtonal scales—with octaves divided into twenty-two intervals and with the sound sequences used according to traditional regulations and melodic turns identifiable in improvisation—the *ragas* are of central interest. One historian says that they have always been associated with religious practices, that even in secular form they have retained deep spiritual qualities, and that as they developed over the centuries they are today India's main "cultural export."[10] Indeed, a wealth of referential material exists; I am thinking in particular of all those critics of the time like Natanga (the first to discuss *raga*, in the eleventh century, in his *Brihaddesi*), Durgashakti, Banbhatta, Tastika, and Kashyapa, or more recent ones like Krishnadhan Banerji or Vishnu Narayan Bhatkhande. And if the musico-literary interrelation elicits a desire to study the multiple talent, like Chou Pang-yen or Zeami Motokiyo, one might turn to the poet-musician of the fifteenth century, Vidyapati, and his variety of *keertan*, or sung prayers. Furthermore, in the realm of songs, the *dhrupads* of the fifteenth to sixteenth centuries invite investigation, especially those that were written for the anti-*dhrupad* movement of that same period, when more technical brilliance and imaginativeness were called for (the style known as *khayal*, or imagination). Then, too, interesting stylistic phenomena, in both text and music, appear with the Hindu-Muslim compact in the arts at this very time; *Lahjat-é-*

Sikandar Shaki is the first book on Indian music written in Persian and based on Sanskrit sources. In line with this, that other multiple talent, Sultan Ibrahim Adil Shah II (fifteenth century) composed songs praising Hindu gods and issued them in a Muslim publication. All of this, together with Thyagaraja's two thousand religious songs, or *kritis* (eighteenth and nineteenth centuries), with their excellent blends of music and words in the form of poetic prose, should greatly kindle our curiosity.[11]

Finally, no student of the musico-literary interrelation can afford not to consider the work of the great Hindu artist Rabindranath Tagore, poet, musician, ballet master, actor, and director. He experimented with folk melodies and created a new melodic genre, *Rabindra-sangeet*, and his plays are lyrical dramas, spotted with song and bathed in a musical atmosphere. Tagore was especially conscious of the intimate correspondence between sound and word, not on the simple level of the former acting as accompaniment to the other, but indeed on the more complex level of creating veritable textures in combination. While he is now remembered primarily as a poet, one cannot discount his musical insistence while practicing the poet's craft, for, in his words, "music is the purest form of art, the direct expression of beauty."

In this assertion he echoed a vital metaphysical concern of Indian culture, where music is central in the creation of the universe. Shiva, as Lord of the Dance, danced creation into existence after having played the drum; in fact, the god of destruction and reproduction holds the drum in the right hand as a symbol of creation. Sound, therefore, lies at origin. And if creation sprang as a drama, then dramatic art becomes the basic cosmic form, which blends in a *Gesamtkunstwerk* of its own music, dance, costumes, and poetry, among other arts. This was as much the case with Sanskrit drama (really dance operas) as it is today with folk drama: all parts assume equal importance. It would be valuable, therefore, for the researcher to look into early Hindu plays, say those of the famous fourth-century author Kalidāsā, and analyze the nature of the problems, the practices, the verses's reliance on harmonic effect, and the aesthetic results of the interrelation comparatively with *ch'u* and *noh* or *kabuki*. For, up until the nineteenth century, versification was based on the alternation of long and short syllables, so that in a way stricter than in the West one can thereby speak of an inner form of rhythm and timbre, with consonants as well as vowels affecting rhyme, not to speak of the sheer repetition of consonants for musical effect and of fragmentation of sounds as in musical development—let alone, finally, how the whole then sounds in combination with actual music. The field would seem to be quite open.

The centuries of musical tradition in the West which led to that apparently purely Western, sophisticated, and abstract interrelation with literature on the basis of structure also led to the conventionalized search for signs in the abstraction of sounds: the sign for joy in the major key and for sorrow in the minor. Yet the West could just as easily have been trained the other way around. But music in China, Japan, India, and especially Africa (by which I mean Black Africa), aided as it is by microtones, does not imply preconceptions. It is less the pure art form as Mann or Shaw accept it, inviting listening for its own hedonistic sake, than an expression of life in all its aspects. Indeed, Japanese use of the *ko-tsuzumi* or the *ekiro* in direct imitation of nature, or African use of the bull roarer *(ngwe)* in direct imitation of a panther, represents a practice that critical Western taste tends to frown upon in high-flown settings, since even "impure" program or descriptive music is admitted with discomfort in some circles, beginning with Ottorino Respighi's use of an actual nightingale in *I pini di Roma*. But in the outdoor settings of Africa, nature-imitated sounds are incorporated directly into the music, thus making it a kind of "concrete" music, which at times may sound quite cacophonous. Here again, the words do not just stand by but become part and parcel of the presentation, which then becomes transformed into a genuine experience. Music in Africa is a utility, a necessary and vital function of life, an outward manifestation of a profound—call it religious—teleology.[12] When we pass from the Orient and South Asia to Africa, we pass from art as such to ethnography or cultural anthropology, that is, from the writer-musician as a self-conscious artist to the individual or group spontaneously expressing itself for a social or religious purpose.

The scholar of the musico-literary interrelation will soon realize that in Africa music is always coupled with poetry and dance, but a fundamental problem faces him: he must get used to the peculiar notes and scales, to the rudimentary instruments, and to the strange tonalities which sound much more unmelodious to the westerner than do the microscale modalities of China, Japan, and India. Nonetheless, exceptional talents—all multiple talents in this part of the world—exist, professional musicians who perform important roles in society, like *griots* who invoke the supernatural or the *mvet* (harp or zither) players who stem from the oral tradition, dance and tell stories, chant and declaim, combining music and epic poetry. No two performances can be alike, since this music, like Arabic music, is not the creative kind of the self-conscious artist but the natural kind of the player for whom, as one commentator observes, absence of technique does not mean absence of artistry.[13] A special relation between music and words exists automatically because of the performer's total instinct for rhythm.

African music is really the intonation and rhythm of speech; an instrument is tuned so that it is "linguistically" comprehensible; and in certain languages especially, like the Duala of the Bantus, a contradiction between melody and the spoken word is inconceivable.[14] Nothing is easier than to glide from speech into song, as the *mvet* players do. It is said that, without African languages, no African music would exist. And this we might understand, inasmuch as the languages do not have a tonic accent as they have in the West; they are, not unlike Chinese, tonal, but in the sense that a word or phrase may be a series of notes tied over at one- to three-degree intervals. (Chinese, we may remember, is monosyllabic and is therefore less accommodating to melismatic expression.)

This does not mean to imply that speech is sung (or music is spoken) in unison when groups express themselves. Pygmies, for example, whose every social activity is built around "worded" music, enjoy such a developed sense of rhythm and form that their multileveled singing may be heard polyphonically, as it were, above the clapping of hands and the beating of sticks. But more often than not, in other areas of the continent, unison appears frequently, whether in the form of yodeling, humming, falsettos, whisperings, vibratos, or tongue flutters.

The point is that the overlap between music and speech—or text, if all this were recorded—is exploited with many variations. The Yoruba have developed four major chants (*rara, iwe, ifa,* and *ijah*) with alternating voices or spoken-sung alternations, according to the demands of the story, and the narrator may be interrupted by the audience, which may in turn contribute whatever the plot or the theme or the mood seems to require, though often the contributions are conceptually unrelated. The "text," like the music, is subject to improvisation. And within this otherwise strict framework, even if the verbo-musical relation could not be more intimate, the improvisational possibility exists to lengthen the words in order to fit the musical phrase's time span by extension through nonsense syllables or prolonged filler vowels—something resembling what happened on occasion to *ch'u* during the

Ming Dynasty in China. In both China (I am thinking also of *tz'u*) and Africa, after all, the melodic organization or contour must wed the intonation of the text, because distortions create aesthetic and semantic difficulties. Song in Africa exists basically for communication; it is the welder of social experience and a guide in life, from cradle songs to reflective or historical songs, whether in Ruanda, the Cameroons, Congo, Gabon, Dahomey, or among the Ibo of Nigeria.

The binding quality of the interrelation always prevails, even if we might read that at times, when songs are used for recreation or work or war or rites, the words guide the choice of musical themes. In a sense, this is unavoidable; where the set of cultures regards music as a social activity, the text necessarily gains a certain emphasis. But the basic fact remains that the music gives the songs coherence, and through the coherence comes the meaning. If the text provides changes of mood, the music defines the occasion. And, of course, the dance forms part of the whole, for the three arts interlock. As in India, bodily response takes its cue from the instruments, voices, and words.

I speak freely about an African musical tradition despite the number of nations and tribal cultures that make up the Black Continent, because this tradition seems to have a geographical consistency and constancy (leaving apart Bushmen, Pygmies, Saharan boundary people, and the Ethiopian Church). Styles overlap, as do traditions, and similar features relating to the musico-literary nexus may be observed. As Arabic influence seeps downward—and the Arabs lean more toward vocal than instrumental music—musical common denominators among black peoples may modify, but if the European experience is any example, perhaps the modifications will be minimal. Rather than synthesize the traditions, colonization tended to polarize them; African and European music lived apart. Will the Arabic and the Christian (church) practices today fare more influentially? Whatever the case, to understand the musico-literary question in Black Africa today or yesterday, the primary requirement is to know the social context.

I am convinced by my readings in Wiant, Malm, Massey, Bebey, and others, and by my personal contacts with specialists, that much research of a comparative nature is to be done in the interdisciplinary area of musico-literary interrelations in China, Japan, India, and Africa. Knowledge of the languages involved, or at the very least the accurate service of translators and specialists in the arts in question is, of course, fundamental. Bringing

Western musico-literary study in contact with non-Western examples is essential, if only to heighten our awareness not just of the interdiscipline itself but also of the human experience throughout the world. For as Hsi K'ang, one of the Seven Sages of Bamboo Grove, said, "Music is the voice of nature," and as we all know, literature is the conscience of society.

(1983)

[7]

ROMANTIC WRITERS AND MUSIC:
THE CASE OF MAZZINI

*Music is . . . the sole idiom common to all nations, the only one
to transmit explicitly a presentiment of humanity . . . , a harmony of creation . . . , a note in the divine chord that the whole
universe will be called upon some day to express.*

(Mazzini)

The paradoxical Romantic mind harbored divergent attitudes—no doubt the
basic reason that Romanticism may be defined only by its undefinability.
Besides, to define it in any other way would be to make it Classical. The
word "Romantic" is a variable. But, if the attitudes diverged, we should be
wrong in assuming that the cause of the divergence was a confusion of
values. Along with an unimpaired expression of release from Classical au-
thoritarianism, Romanticism bespoke a need to embrace totality in all its
contradictions, the sense that exploded from Goethe's near Promethean exclamation: *Hinaus, ins Freie!* ["Outdoors, in open freedom!"]. His Faust did
not find what he wanted in the disciplined pursuits of philosophy, theology,
astrology, or any other formalized intellectual endeavor, and his pact with
the Devil acquired a symbolic significance which profoundly influenced the
Romantic psyche and Romantic art. It reflected a need greater than itself.

This urge for totality, which encompassed the farthest boundaries of emotion and the imagination together with the stricter confines of reason, directed the Romantic mind inevitably and primarily to a consideration of
music—the art of emotion at its purest, founded on the mystery of a seemingly mathematical logic, capable of both stretching to and exploring infinity—and through music to the sense of unity inherent in every ultimate
notion of totality. Some poets treated music casually, but to many more it
was clear that the most intimate workings of their poetry responded to mu-

sic's spiritual (some said religious) foundations, so that music became, recognized as such or not, the Romantic art par excellence, the art that enabled man to transcend himself and sense entirety, the chief vehicle, not only of poetic, but also of moral inspiration. E. T. A. Hoffmann's words come to mind: "Music is the most Romantic of all the arts—one might almost say, the only genuinely Romantic one—for its sole subject is the infinite,"[1] or indeed Beethoven's credo: "music provides the only incorporeal entry into a world superior to that of conscience—that world which embraces man, but which man by himself could not embrace."[2]

Beethoven's dictum appears an extension of Goethe's expression of freedom. And any philosophy—or, more simply, any attitude which pursues freedom in opposition to restriction—will necessarily engage in paradoxes, even cultivate them. But paradoxes are not contradictions.[3] Of all the arts, music suggested to the Romantic mind the idea of a living organism, constantly changing like Romanticism itself (the final chorus of Rossini's *Guglielmo Tell* echoes Goethe as it exclaims: "About us all changes and grows. / Fresh the air!"), yet paradoxically, though not contradictorily, remaining the same organism. It was "something that lives!"—to adopt Georg Büchner's often repeated phrase. As the Romantic conceived it, then, music possessed an eternal essence that lived through the ages and bound the ancient Greek lyrist to the modern composer in a closer, albeit mystical, kinship than bound their respective counterparts in the other arts. If diverseness was its condition, eternity was its substance. Its deepest meaning, for the philosopher, novelist, or poet, would probably never change and would always remain intangible, and this sense of the stability of eternity endowed music, through its permanence, with a quality of objectivity. Simultaneously, someone like, say, Hegel, Stendhal, or Keats was keenly sensitive to the subjective responses elicited by the movement of diverseness, that is, by the different individual reactions, physiological and mental, of persons facing a highly abstract art which communicates through one composer various meanings to various listeners, personal meanings that cannot be stated in any medium other than music.

Such observations concerning unity and paradox or object and subject encouraged and justified in many idealistic Romantic minds the notion that in the cross-cultural language of music resided a special potential for binding mankind in a universal confraternity. The associative leap seemed short and logical, for music explored, not only the objective infinity of creation, but also the subjective infinity (in Pascal's sense) of man. While the nature of the art was aesthetic, its role was humanitarian and its mission social. Liszt, for example, like Beethoven and Berlioz before him, discarded his earlier conception of art for art's sake and espoused the theory of music as an interpreter of life and benefactor of it. No differently did Balzac muse about the socially regenerating forces concealed in the art of sounds. Better than words, lines, or shapes, music can penetrate the farthest in both suggesting and interpreting the flux and dream of man because, by addressing the heart directly and by persuading before convincing, it possesses a power of contagion capable of stirring individuals and masses alike. In this sense, a patriotic anthem and a dynamic symphony are not dissimilar. Not only the utopian descendants of Claude-Henri de Saint-Simon held this view, but indeed most Romantics during the last quarter of the eighteenth and the first half of the nineteenth centuries.

It is not surprising, then, to discover that Romantic fascination with music led to a virtual mania for writing about music. In the 1770s, Rousseau's voice was among the first to be heard in this context. Before him, since the Renaissance, writings about music had been by and for musicians; after him, writers wrote about music and involved themselves musically. Superficial or profound listeners, all Romantics wanted to have their say. Recognized authors collaborated with musicians, not alone for opera librettos but for other purposes: Herder worked with J. C. F. Bach to translate the texts of Handel's *Messiah* and *Alexander's Feast;* Goethe wrote texts for Singspiele; and George Sand encouraged and actively promoted Chopin. By the time Berlioz looked to Byron, Liszt to Goethe and Dante, and Verdi to Shakespeare, a pattern of reciprocity had been established between music and poetry, the pattern magnificently set by Beethoven's look to Schiller in the Ninth Symphony's "Ode to Joy." In addition, Stendhal turned music critic and wrote biographies of Mozart, Haydn, and Rossini. Burns collected lyrics and music, wrote prefaces, and enlisted the help of composers in editing *The Scots Musical Museum.* Byron collaborated with Isaac Nathan, who wrote musical settings for the *Hebrew Melodies.* Byronism, in fact, inspired many musical works from Berlioz to Tchaikowsky. Shelley wrote lyrics for music destined to be sung by Sophia Stacey. And it became right for writers to honor composers in their prose or poetry. Thus, Musset praised Schubert; Gautier praised Berlioz and Chopin; Hugo and Coleridge praised Palestrina; Shelley praised Mozart; Balzac praised Beethoven and Rossini;

and Byron, too, praised Rossini, to the disgust of Leigh Hunt, who prided himself on his musical knowledge.

Furthermore, and most important, music received heightened consideration in literature itself, as a literary effect and as subject matter. In Goethe's novel *Werther* as in Balzac's *Modeste Mignon*, where a piano score is printed with the prose, Lotte's and Modeste's expressive playing form an integral part of the two plots. Composers became literary figures: Kreisler, for example, in Hoffmann's stories, and Gambara by, again, Balzac. Shelley, passionately fond of the art, made music a pervasive theme of his poetry; Heine's *Hildegarde von Hohenthal* contains a plot in which music and life intermingle in a series of discussions of composers from Palestrina to Gluck; Diderot, who published a *Traité d'harmonie*, wrote a dialogue around Rameau's nephew reminding us of various musical forms.[4] Like so many other writer-melomaniacs, Wackenroder, through his fictional musician Berglinger, and also Jean-Paul Richter, endowed music with the quality of a drug or balm. Therefore, when later Poe and Verlaine spoke of music in terms that made the art central to literary expression, they merely joined a tradition vaunting a distinguished lineage. And through all this, we should not omit the impressive attempt of Clemens Brentano, whose poetry strives to attain the quality of unearthly music—that is, poetry whose significance resides in the sounds of its words alone, in a sense a verbal music or melic metapoetry which extends beyond the boundary of the meaning of words.

While Romantic literature is echoed through the music of the period, the influence of Romantic writers on composers is greater than that of composers on writers. In fact—and quite apart from the fact that many composers like Berlioz, Wagner, Weber, and Schumann were either significant literary figures in their own right or enjoyed a good competence as writers—it almost seemed that the writers were aiming to direct the course of music through the welter of values that characterized the paradoxical Romantic period, values that clashed in their conflicting stresses on opera or symphony, melody or harmony, Italian music or German music, descriptive music or pure music, virtuosity or simplicity, music with words or music without words, the human voice or the string instrument. The polemics were fought with partisan intensity but without acrimony (except, perhaps, when Berlioz entered the arena), for behind the polemics resided the realization that music expressed a total phenomenon, a universe—or, as Coleridge put it, telescoping the universal down to the individual mind, "Music converses with the *life* of my mind, as if it were itself the Mind of my life."[5]

Romantic philosophers joined hands with creative writers in thinking of music as possessing the key to the hidden meanings of life. They stressed the notion of movement and diversity, of the living organism which has an evolution (the German *Entwickelung*), the same notion of development which in music led Beethoven to fashion a new form of the sonata. Fichte, Hegel, Schelling, and Schopenhauer saw the new aesthetic in dynamic terms, a moving, energetic change from previous history, not in the Classical manner as something static that was at worst a play of sounds to delight the ears of drawing room clientèle, or at best an exhaustive statement of a single idea, but rather, in the new manner, as a dialectic conflict that reflected the composer's personal impressions and experiences, often deeply philosophical in character,[6] like Beethoven's last quartets, or even the symphonies of Brahms.

The ancient philosophy of Sophists and Epicureans had questioned the idea that music stood in causal relationship with specific determinate feelings. Subsequent history then repeated the view that the feelings elicited by music are too complex for verbalization and too extensive for conceptual identification. Hence the phrase common to all Romantic utterance: "Music begins where the word ends." For the rationalist eighteenth century, what the Romantics referred to as the ineffable and sublime in music often represented a defect—particularly with reference to purely instrumental music, because without words, the intention of its expression seemed unclear. But the Romantics claimed this to be music's true virtue: its sublime conceptual obscurity, a rarefied and yet probing aesthetic stimulation which sent a universe of emotions flowing through every sensitive mind and heart, and elevated man above the mortal sphere to a point where he approached contact with creation, or the Absolute. These were the thoughts of Wackenroder, Tieck, Novalis, and Hoffmann, of Byron, Lamartine, and Foscolo, and were well summarized by Keats in *Lamia* where he described music as the mainstay of the soul, the force that plays on the inner ear in moments of supreme artistic creativity. Differently worded, these were the thoughts, too, of the philosophers.

But philosophers, it has been said, are rational animals, less concerned with aesthetic experience than with ethical results. With rare exceptions, all philosophers claimed that music's value lay in its effects. The thrust of the art, then, was not to convey pleasing sounds (which would make music simply an opiate for idle pleasure) but to mold "good" people and lead them to "right" action. Plato began the process of attributing moral values to music when he constructed a musical aesthetics based on the morality of the Greek modes. Superior to architecture, painting, and sculpture, he thought, music—through the facts of rhythm and harmony which affect the inner soul more than the other arts do—must be used to improve man, that is, improve his behavior, character, and intellect. Aristotle and Plotinus echoed Plato's recommendation of music as a preparation for philosophic study, and so did St. Augustine and Boethius. Descartes, too, with his stress on mathematical factors, attributed moral values to rhythms, and Leibniz held that music is a manifestation of universal rhythm based on number and relation—a position easily absorbed by Rousseau, who believed that, if man were exposed to the proper musical rhythms, he could learn to live in accordance with natural law and become one with nature.[7] Kant, too, recognized the power of music to influence the soul; for purposes of meaning, he stressed music with words over purely instrumental music, and followed in the Platonic tradition by declaring that, though music has less worth than the other arts because it is "rather enjoyment than culture," it nonetheless "moves the mind in a greater variety of ways and more intensely."[8]

Contrary to some Romantic thinkers, Hegel denied music objective qualities, particularly the external objectivity enjoyed by painting and sculpture, but because of this separation of the art from the listener he was led to assert that music "penetrates into the very core of the soul and is one with its subjectivity,"[9] Therefore, it affects the human being directly.

While there were aestheticians and philosophers, notably Herbart and Hanslick, who refused to view music as a facet, in some cases a central facet, of a general metaphysics and to ascribe actual "meaning" to the art ("Music is *music*", wrote Herbart, "and to be beautiful need mean nothing."[10]), the basic Romantic attitude, philosophically speaking, was expressed by those who informed music with metaphysical reality. Schelling, for instance, declared music to be "nothing more than the original rhythm of nature and of the universe itself."[11] Schopenhauer went even further. While he agreed with Hanslick that music possessed a world of its own, Schopenhauer made music fundamental in his construct of the will, that is, of the life force; he considered music as *direct* an objectification and copy of the whole *will* as the world itself, nay, even as the ideas, whose multiplied manifestation constitutes the world of individual things. . . . [Music is] *the copy of the will itself,* whose objectivity the ideas are. This is why the effect of music is so much more powerful and penetrating than that of the other arts, for they speak only of shadow, but it speaks of the thing itself.[12]

Through music, the crowning achievement of all the arts and sum total of all artistic expression, nature reveals her inner secrets and motives, in a way accessible only to feeling. Leibniz was wrong, he claimed: music does not represent an unconscious counting of numbers but an unconscious philosophizing. Music being the expression of the will, words are of subordinate value; yet, through them, not only do we perceive music's inherent sense of expressing every movement of the will and every feeling, but in addition we receive "the objects of these feelings, the motives which occasion them."[13] Hence, music encourages a transition from will to vision and from desire to contemplation.

Finally, and later, Nietzsche, like Schopenhauer, exalted melody above all else ("Melody is . . . primary and universal."[14]) and endowed music with a profound, all-pervasive power:

The poems of the lyrist can express nothing which did not already lie hidden in the vast universality and absoluteness of the music which compelled him to figurative speech. Language can never render the cosmic symbolism of music, because music stands in symbolic relation to the primoridal contradiction and primoridal pain in the heart of the Primal Unity, and therefore symbolizes a sphere which is beyond and before all phenomena. Rather are all phenomena, compared with it, merely symbols: hence *Language*, as the organ and symbol of phenomena, can never, by any means, disclose the innermost heart of music; language, in its attempt to imitate it, can only be in superficial contact with music.[15]

Through music, therefore, man can improve his existence.[16]

Supported by philosophical thought, then, Romantic writers paid special attention to the two elements which the ancient Pythagoreans had singled out as fundamental principles: harmony and number—harmony as reconciliation of opposites; number as a principle of distinction and multiplicity. They found this focus attractive because both principles lie at the base of the universe and make of the cosmos, however characterized by multiplicity, a unitarian concept: unity in diversity. In this sense, music became the symbolic image of the universe: its strange but eternal and identifiable math-

ematics and its constant movement of change within a context of order and
balance. The Romantic mind easily transferred these values onto the human
plane, thereby making music everything that is harmonious and propor-
tioned in human institutions. What a thinker like Schopenhauer saw in
music philosophically—that is, the essence of the universe—a writer like
Mazzini saw metaphorically—that is, a metaphysico-symbolic conception of
ethical as well as aesthetic worth.[17]

Giuseppe Mazzini, the essayist, political writer, sociologist, patriot, re-
publican revolutionary, and idealist, published his *Filosofia della musica* in
1836, during the height of the Romantic movement, when Schopenhauer's
influence was still years from being felt, Wagner had only recently left his
teens, and Nietzsche was not yet born. The eighty-page treatise is a remarkable document in many ways. If one removes its occasional patriotic utterances in favor of Italian manifest destiny, the bulk of the publication stands
as a synthesis of personal and highly sensitive, acute, and cultivated perceptions on the meaning of music; its debasement by misguided Romantic affections; its potential for regeneration; and its cosmopolitan, humanitarian
mission. In spirit he was Romantic, in the "musical" tradition of Wackenroder and Rousseau, a younger contemporary of Wordsworth and Balzac,
Byron and Tieck, a precursor of Wagner and Nietzsche. But in aesthetics
he was anti-Romantic in that he severely condemned Romantic superficiality in musical taste and practice. The paradox of Romanticism exercised
itself brilliantly in him.

In his Introduction to an edition of Mazzini's work, Adriano Lualdi, while
at times patronizing with patriotic tones, made a number of insightful comments to which I am indebted, and which invite elaboration. For among
all those who have discussed Mazzini's works—including Andeina Biondi,
Edyth Hinkley, and Giovanni Cattani—Lualdi is the only one, through his
Introduction, to have signaled the importance of the *Filosofia della musica*.[18]

This is largely because, despite the countless allusions to music penned
by Romantic writers, Mazzini was among the first to assess the art philosophically, and to do so by addressing himself, not to "teachers and traffick-
ers in notes," but to "the few who feel the ministry of the art and understand
the immense influence that through it could be exercised on society, if
pedantry and venality had not reduced it to a servile mechanism, a plaything
for the idle rich."[19] Mazzini wanted to "go back to the philosophical origins

of the musical problem"—which no one had done. With characteristic Romantic fervor he asked:

Who has ever thought that the fundamental problem of music might be one with the progressive concept of the terrestrial universe, that the secret of its development might be found in the development of the general synthesis of the period, that the strongest reason for our current decline into our predominant materialism might be found in the lack of a social faith, and that the path of resurrection and reemergence of this faith might be found in an association with the destinies of literature and philosophy?

The hallmark of all Mazzini's writings was its "sociality," its persistent, idealistic social consciousness and sense of duty and responsibility. Even purely artistic or aesthetic matters were subjected by him to the test of his noble ethics—and music was no exception—in fact, music was not a pleasure but a "sacred mission."

In 1836 Mazzini had just emerged from a period of spiritual depression and suffering, crisis and doubt, over the destiny of Italian political unification and freedom, after which he arrived at a definition of life as a mission. Music too, then, had a mission, since it is the vital impulse of life, "the image of beauty and of eternal harmony," "the fragrance of the universe," "an echo of the invisible world." Mazzini sensed that he was witnessing the end of a historical and artistic period in which the "vital concept" that had developed was now "irrevocably exhausted," and he wished to inaugurate a new one—in music and through music in man and in European society. Romanticism had given the individual the certainty of his own ego, but what was needed now was a religious, unifying concept, lest anarchy atomize human existence.

Music possessed this centralizing potential, but while most of his contemporaries loved the pleasant pastime music had become—the formless excesses of melodrama; the extravagances of virtuosity, rhetoric, and artifice; or, as he put it, "the combination of sounds without intent, unity, or moral concept"—Mazzini decried it. When he spoke of the needed progress, he meant evolution and, more candidly, revolution, the "regenerating concept" in technique, taste, and the whole spiritual and social atmosphere which art either foresees or reflects.[20] Keats, too, spoke in terms of the regenerative influence of the worship of beauty. But for Mazzini this kind of progress— that of regeneration—could occur only when the two forces rending society, indeed polarizing it, were fused. Individualism and collectivism—that is,

analysis and synthesis—excluded and ignored each other and counterpro-
ductively occasioned their own ruin, since the former, according to Mazzini, degenerates into materialism and the latter loses itself in an inert mysticism.

Now, in Mazzini's eyes, these two principles were metaphorically symbolized in music, in melody and harmony, respectively, the first being represented by the Italian school, the second by the German school. Italian
music was individualistic, impulsively lyrical, inspired, supremely artistic
but not religious. It was Art for Art's sake, and therefore it lacked unity, said
Mazzini, and moved along in a "fractional, disconnected, and interrupted"
manner. Rossini generally summarized the best qualities of Italian music.
He rebelled against the authority of accepted mode and expected conven-
tion, affirming the principle of musical independence; but great as he was,
he opened no doors to the future. "Where is the new element?" Mazzini
asked, "where is there a single concept . . . to harmonize into an epic the
whole chain of his composition? [Yes, his *Mosè*, the third act of *Otello*, and
large parts of *Semiramide* and *Guglielmo Tell* are sublime,] but I speak of
the genre, of the dominant concept, not of one scene or one act but of the
works of Rossini." He was a summarizer (*compendiatore*) and imitator, not
an initiator, and Mazzini admonished the young, to whom he addressed
himself in his *Filosofia della musica*, to emancipate themselves from the
musical era Rossini represented. For if Rossini innovated, he did so more
in form than in idea, more in ways to develop than in principle. As a genius
of liberty rather than synthesis, Rossini wrote limpid music characterized by
"free, unbridled, brilliant . . . melodies"—excellent but limited qualities,
which revealed powers that were not, as Lualdi states, harmonized into a
supreme law or consecrated by an eternal faith.[21] Through him, who synthesized the Italian school, Italian music revealed "man without God."

But music must be absorbed into, and identified with, "the progressive
motion of the universe." To do this, it must glow with a religious aura.
German music, as opposed to Italian music, was harmonic, social, idealistic, and mystical;[22] but for Mazzini it lacked that energetic spark which
commanded or attracted large followings and catalyzed its listeners.

It represents social thought, the general concept, the idea, but without that individuality which translates thought into action, which develops the concept through its
various applications, which elaborates and symbolizes the idea. The ego is gone.

. . . As in a dream world, . . . where all images float in a kind of infinite, German music lulls the instincts, the power of matter, while it elevates the spirit.

It possessed, in Mazzini's metaphor, the temple, the religion and altar and incense, but it lacked the worshiper, the high priest of the faith. In other words, "there is God there without man." It was "elegiac," the "music of remebrances, desires, melancholy hopes, and sorrow that cannot receive comfort from human lips, the music of angels that have lost heaven and wander around it. Its home is the infinite, and in it it drowns." Its melody was brief, timid, and elusive, leaving the listener with the need to recompose it. And, while German music was endowed with the necessary religious sense, the religion had no symbol or human coefficient, so that faith was not activated by fact.

Continuing on the heel of the nationalistic-aesthetic battle fought on French soil between the followers of Piccinni and Gluck, the Romantics debated heavily the relative merits of the Italian and German schools; the polemics even reached the surprising point of finding Mozart, Meyerbeer, and Chopin listed among composers in the Italian style and Berlioz and Liszt among composers in the German. Mazzini transcended the inherent paradoxes of the debate by taking an overview of the quarrel, just as, Italian patriot though he was who expected Italy to produce the luminary of the new music, he took an overview of the European continent, argued for a united, federated Europe as seriously as for a European musical style, and converted his national patriotism into supranational humanitarianism. Mazzini summarized:

Italian music lacks the concept which sanctifies all undertakings, the moral thought which guides the forces of the intellect, the baptism of a mission. German music lacks the energy to accomplish it, the material instrument for the conquest; it lacks not sentiment but the formula of the mission. Italian music sterilizes itself in materialism. German music consumes itself uselessly in mysticism. . . . The music we believe in we will not have until the two [schools], fused into one, will orient themselves toward a social purpose, . . . a conscience of unity, until the two elements which today constitute two [rival] worlds unite to animate but one . . . ; then musical expression will take up again its two basic aims: individuality and the notion of the universe.

The two forms of musical energy must be mingled, not to perpetuate traditions, but to create a new European school organically evolved from the past. Romanticism tore down better than it built; "it had no organic concept."[23] Music, wrote Mazzini, does not move in a circle or step on ground already tread, but advances from period to period, expanding its own sphere, rising to a higher concept when the previous one becomes fully developed, rebaptizing itself into life with the introduction of a new principle, after all the consequences of the older one have been deduced and applied.

Mazzini's desire for total artistic synthesis,[24] expanding to all the arts Friedrich Schlegel's wish to unify again the separated poetic genres,[25] suggested, not that an art form represented a cultural era or that a cultural era might be discerned and understood through one of its art forms, but that all the arts together evoked the spiritual image of a given historical moment. Music, the last of the arts to develop formally in time, but the first by nature and most immediately capable of influencing man, was, for Mazzini, the most ardent manifestation of the human spirit. The last cause became the first cause. The Marseillaise, for example, to which Mazzini alluded indirectly, caused an internationally felt revolutionary upheaval in the sense that it passionately expressed a will, creating itself as the artistic refraction of an action it helped to perform. The question was not whether the French Revolution would have taken place without the anthem but exactly to what extent it would have done what it did without the spiritual power of music behind it—a power with which food, ammunition, manpower, and even orations cannot really be compared. This was what Mazzini meant when he wrote: "A hymn of a couple of measures has created in recent times a victory."

But Mazzini's work did not focus on national anthems. He spoke indirectly of symphonic, and directly and explicitly of operatic music, the form most discussed in his day. Romanticism encouraged lyrical drama with enthusiastic accolades whose excesses, defended by mottoes of freedom, in turn promoted questionable aesthetic practices. Lyrical drama became grand scale melodrama in the hands of potpourri artists and facile imitators. The exhilarating Rossini aria or the older and severe Frescobaldi fugue were worked over and emulated, but even so came out as neither Rossini nor Frescobaldi. Mazzini realized that, in the long run, there were two kinds of masterpieces: those that opened the gates to the future and those that summarized and perfected the past. The latter enjoy immediate success because they promote tradition; the former have to struggle to win a place in the sun. Beethoven had met with reluctant ears outside his native Germany;

Berlioz was boycotted in his own Paris. But, after Rossini, Meyerbeer was idolized everywhere: his sense of the total and grand appealed to the Romantic mind. Mazzini himself joined in the praise—surprising to us today, perhaps, but in 1836, with *Les Huguenots* succeeding *L'Étoile du nord* and *Robert le Diable*, at least Meyerbeer pointed in new directions and thus attempted to enact ideas Mazzini appreciated, such as an encompassing, synthetic production utilizing the chorus, and an awareness of local color, which opera paid no attention to at that time and which meant, not that kind of historical accuracy resulting from documentation or direct observation, but—as in Rossini's *Guglielmo Tell* of 1829 or in Verdi's *Aïda* forty years later, notes Lualdi—the subordination of direct observation and documentation to intuition.[26] Gluck's proposed reforms needed a century to take effect in the framework of Verdian and Wagnerian opera. Meanwhile, nothing was happening in operatic music, while much was happening in the other arts, though frequently it was not encouraging. Even so, music lagged behind. Like Canova in sculpture and Monti in literature, Cherubini and Spontini in operatic music had lived out their Classical heritage; Rossini, however genially, summarized; Bellini (according to Mazzini), gifted though he was, lacked power and variety and, like Metastasio's and Lamartine's poetry, tended more toward "debilitating" our energies than "invigorating" them; and Donizetti—the only progressive genius around in the field of opera, because he was more capable of technical mastery and of advanced harmony, counterpoint, and orchestration—exhibited excellent "regenerative" qualities in *La favorita* and *Don Pasquale* but, on the whole, followed too closely "the Rossinian system."

The message from other fields of endeavor was not one to arouse enthusiasm either: the critique of Kant and the idealistic aestheticism of Friedrich Schelling mingled in the Romantic pessimism of Schopenhauer; painting was becoming the slave of landscapes; in literature, only Manzoni wrote with equanimity; otherwise, the main preoccupation seemed to be that of man desperately seeking out himself, while Heine sneered on the banks of the Seine, and Leopardi lamented his lost youth in Recanati. But, at least something was taking place. Opera, on the other hand (and I speak primarily of musical drama rather than of comic opera, which, through Pergolesi, Mozart, and others had progressed more successfully than drama), had developed into a simple—and ingenuous—Romantic pastime in a sumptuous house where singers vocalized with bravura while vain spectators talked freely among themselves or even retired to play whist in the rear, and where the abused recitative vied in boredom with a prolonged tonal uniformity.

Listen to Mazzini's invective:

An opera can be defined [today] only by an enumeration of parts—a series of cavatinas, choruses, duets, short numbers, and finales—interrupted, not bound together, by any kind of recitative that no one listens to: it's a mosaic, a gallery, a jungle, more often a clash of thoughts that are different, independent, disconnected, thoughts that swirl like ghosts in a magic circle inside certain boundaries; it's a tumult, an eddying of motifs and phrases and little musical concepts. . . . One would say a Saturday dance. —One would say a fantastic race over various moors and meadows, the kind described in a ballad by Bürger, with the infernal horse bearing Leonora and a corpse on its back—that is, music and the public—and dragging them furiously from slope to slope at the sound of that monotonous cadenza: *the dead travel fast.* Hurrah! Hurrah! Where are we going? What does this music want? Where does it lead? Where is the unity, and why not stop at that point? Why break this idea with that other idea? For what purpose? Because of what predominant concept? Hurrah! Hurrah! The hour is almost over. It's after midnight. The public wants its due: that certain number of tunes for the *prima donna.* The hour has struck—one applauds and leaves. The young man who had deluded himself by thinking he would find comfort in music, or who imagined he would return home with an idea, with one more affection, withdraws slowly and mutely, his head weary, grieved, with a ring in his ears and an emptiness in his heart, and with Fontenelle's *"music, what do you want of me?"* on his lips. Music today has descended to this level.

This is a remarkable page, written at the height of musical Romanticism, when opera houses attracted overflowing crowds and each new production generated clamorous excitement. Even stylistically, this page displays special qualities: like a broad cadenza, it rises, crescendo, and rounds itself out, as it were, through its keen dramatic intuitions, then breaks itself up into pieces, like the fragmentariness of the music it describes, into a staccato of questions which have no valid answers, and then collapses into a disconsolate and discouraged conclusion.

The engaging, indeed compelling tone of the *Filosofia della musica* stems not only from the idealistic tension that gives it a lofty distinction but also from the feelings and insights which suggest themselves between the lines and which invest the ideas expressed with passionate conviction. Alfred Einstein finds it worthy to devote three paragraphs to it in the section on philosophy in his study of Romanticism and music but shows his misunderstanding bewilderment when he describes it as "one of the strangest

publications in the world."[27] Mazzini's work has all the earmarks of a spontaneous piece, written romantically with impulsiveness and with no view to
a preestablished order of presentation. But its very fluidity allows for connotations and innuendos that go far beyond the year in which it was written.

Mazzini complained that music had removed itself from civic life, despite
the large audiences in concert halls and opera houses, and had "limited
itself to a sphere of eccentric, individual motion." It denied itself all intent
save that of "momentary sensations and a pleasure that disappears with the
sounds," where it should have appeared like that form of "unity directly
connected with the great social unity." Contradicting writers like Stendhal
and Novalis, he saw it as the diversion of a corrupt and sensual generation
and, in this view, anticipated Liszt's *Letters by a Bachelor of Music* by several years. We should not forget that, at this time, Balzac, George Sand,
and Musset, among others, were reveling in the voluptuous satisfactions of
music, as they liked to phrase it, while Hoffmann's writings about bizarre
musicians possessed by demons found multitudes of receptive readers.

Composers heeded the demands of a frivolous public which got its little
titillations and delighted in the little effects the musician thought up or
improvised. In a society bent on distraction and which had no true listeners,
the notion of a total effect was a foreign concept, and Mazzini decried this
fact while recalling that in ancient Greece music was the nation's universal
language—a kind of "sacred vehicle of history, philosophy, law, and moral
education." Coleridge, who had no technical knowledge of music, though
he openly declared he wished he had, made a point of the fact that "the
best sort of music is what it should be—sacred."[28] Similarly, Mazzini argued that what was needed was for music to become "spiritualized," and to
do this he offered a number of farsighted suggestions that anticipated Wagner (to say nothing of Verdi) more clearly than Balzac in his Hoffmannian
tale of *Gambara*. Again I must note a remarkable page, in which we see
that Mazzini's concern with the philosophical or ethical dimension of music
did not leave aside the art's formal or aesthetic aspects, since through them
the lofty, socializing, and humanizing goals of music may be attained. Since
opera represented total art, he spoke in terms of musical drama:

Every man, every character has his own tendency and style, a concept that he develops during his lifetime. Why not represent that concept in a musical expression
that belongs to that individual alone and not to others? Why not take advantage of
the orchestration to symbolize the characters in its accompaniments—that is, that

tumult of affections, instincts, and material and moral tendencies that most often affect his soul and spur his will? Why not have a musical phrase, several fundamental and pointed notes, recur at intervals . . . ? Why can't the chorus, which in Greek drama stood for unity of impression and moral judgment or the majority's conscience . . . , be more broadly developed in modern musical drama, by having the secondary passive level to which it is assigned today stand for the solemn and complete representation of the popular element? . . . Why can't the chorus, as the collective individuality, be like the people, of which it is the born interpreter, and attain an independent and spontaneous life of its own? . . . Why should it not constitute an element off contrast [vis-à-vis the characters] . . . , be interwoven with more melodies, musical phrases that intersect, combine, and are harmonized . . . , at first unifying two voices, then three, then four, and so on in a series of ascendent intonations [for instance], something like what Haydn did [instrumentally] in the Creation Symphony . . . ? Why could not the obbligato recitative . . . assume greater importance in future compositions, given the flexibility of which it is capable? Why does not one employ a manner of development that is consistent with the best dramatic effects . . . [something that] arias cannot do . . . ? [Why not suppress] the insipid cavatinas, the inevitable Da Capos, the monotony of the eternal and vulgar cadenzas . . . , [why not] prohibit embellishments, vocal flourishes, and trimmings? . . . Why not, after economizing on all the useless (and there is much of it), amplify the proportions of tempos, where the historical reason and the aesthetics of the concept . . . require it?

After reading this page, ideas relating to leitmotif (beyond Berlioz's *idée fixe*), infinite melody, choral prominence, rhythmic variation, and coherent development clearly come to mind, welded in a unified composition, something like the musical counterpart of the dramas of the "divine" Schiller, whom Mazzini respected so highly. Keats's notion of the "wandering melody" of poetry also comes to mind. But with reference to the future, it is the *Niebelungenlied* and *Falstaff* that seem just around the corner.

The impact of Mazzini's words, however, remained Romantic through their philosophical insistence that music was a reflection of humanity or, in the word of Senancour, an "emanation." In this view, an Augustinian note was sounded, for the domain of Calliope extended not just to instrument and song but indeed to poetry, dance, theater, history, and astronomy. As Augustine put it, "Music is *in* everything, a hymn emanated from the world." It is in the individual as it is in society: hence Mazzini's analogy with respect to melody and harmony. It would be easy, as has been done, to look upon his equation as simplistic, metaphysically unacceptable qua music and technically erroneous.[29] One could say that no difference exists between melody and harmony, that any melody generates from a harmonic presupposition which is not less substantial for being unstated, and that any sequence of harmonies contains inherent sonorous elements capable of being expressed melodically. One could go on to say that only when one becomes academically technical can melody or harmony be isolated, taken apart for purposes of anatomical analysis, and that Mazzini's dream of uniting Italian melody and Germany harmony even in the abstract cultural and psychic sense of Thomas Mann's *Tonio Kröger* or *Der Tod in Venedig* existed only in a void.

But to do this is to misunderstand both Mazzini and the Romantic mind. Mazzini was dominated by the need for some form of organic arrangement whereby everything corresponded—even in the later synesthetic or Baudelairian sense of the word—to the universal order of nature. Shelley had expressed it in terms of a bird's song in his poem "To a Skylark." Like Schopenhauer, Mazzini intuited that, if we must speak anatomically, the fibers and the muscles of the universal system ramify from the same ganglion or nerve center. Music is this ganglion, an organic essence of intimate unity, not only in the context of will, but also in terms of a metaphor of totality, particularly with reference to its universal humanity. The Pythagorean concept of harmony and number obtained, in a philosophical sense— the harmony of reconciliation, and the number, through individual melodies, of multiplicity. Though many of his ideas have an aesthetic thrust, Mazzini did not speak of music academically, but philosophically, as the title of his work indicates. While what he wrote was largely anti-Romantic with reference to current musical practice, his perspective for a new music of the future was Romantic. Paradoxically, but in Hegelian fashion, he patriotically stressed Italian eminence over the virtues of other nations, but only to blend all merits internationally into the superior synthesis of a European music—in itself an analogy of totality. He knew that, in strictly musical terms, he spoke as a layman—and here, too, he was Romantic, for the Romantics were great verbalizers about the art of music but were in fact also poorly tutored in that same art, as the cases of Stendhal and Coleridge typify, Hoffmann being a notable exception. The Romantics loved music in a spiritual sense as profoundly as they ignored it in a technical sense. This was perhaps the greatest paradox of Romanticism—and, again paradoxically, it occurred with reference to the one art the movement considered its own, or its essential expression par excellence.

But to me Mazzini stands out as the rare writer who, while using music as a metaphor, still, in the process, arrived at telling insights concerning music qua music. It was not that, in this case, he was un-Romantic but that he illustrated, like Balzac, the enormous imaginative range of which the Romantic mind was capable in arriving at a truthful vision. For music is the very soul of loveliness, and, like Keats, Mazzini could never feel certain of any truth but for a clear perception of its Beauty.

At this point, I might return to Schopenhauer and Nietzsche to put Mazzini's thought into greater relief and wider perspective. Schopenhauer offers us a convenient point of view through which to approach Mazzini's aesthetic and metaphoric orientation. In seeking a balance between the means music uses and the end it attains, Schopenhauer was aware of how all representation—of concrete form or of abstract emotion—acquired greater meaning and intensity through music, whose tones initiate us to a more secret, intimate, and otherwise inexpressible sense of scenes, events, situations, and passions—particularly as these are presented in the theater. What happens is that music reveals, beyond the manifestation of the senses, the inner will that arouses them. Melodies, then, act in relation to particular phenomena which they express musically somewhat the way universals or concepts act in relation to individual objects—with one sole difference: concepts only contain the forms initially abstracted by perception, a little like an external rind or bark detached from things, and therefore they remain abstractions and nothing but abstractions, whereas music gives off the inner gem or force from which all reality develops—in other words, the heart or essence of things themselves. Concepts are *universalia post rem*, while music gives us *universalia ante rem* and, in addition, a reality which is *universalia in re*.[30] Similarly, Mazzini spoke of the great revelatory intensity of music, particularly in its operatic dimension, and of the seminal, germinating virtue of melody, through whose harmonic elaborations we may glimpse both antecedent and immanent universals, the "presentiment of humanity" along with the "balm of the modern world."

We might also call upon Nietzsche, who appeared later on the scene, and who, like Mazzini before him and echoing Goethe's famous definition, denounced Romanticism as decadent or sick, yet devised an aesthetic that coincided as much with Romantic though as Schopenhauer's. While Mazzini wanted to elevate poetry, or the word, to a level befitting the loftiness of the music that gives it form ("Poetry, today a slave, will be . . . music's sister . . . [and together] they will direct themselves toward a social purpose"), and Nietzsche opposed this view by calling melody "primary and universal" over the text,[31] the latter did regard music as possessing a "cosmic symbolism."[32] In Nietzsche's view, all phenomena themselves are merely symbols when compared with music. Therefore, through music, man can revalue his values and transform this crude world into a more highly imaginative and better place to live.[33] The musician can at least partially redeem corrupt society, transport us into more rarefied regions of physical and emotional as well as conceptual existence, and so help bring harmony and order into our chaotic lives by rising to a sphere which is expressive of our desires and hopes. Thirty-six years after the *Filosofia della musica*, and with a different vocabulary, Nietzsche echoed Mazzini's sense of music as a cosmogonical metaphor—Mazzini's "harmony of creation"—while orienting his thought with human concern in the missionary direction of social and spiritual reevaluation.

At the end of his little treatise, Mazzini felt it fitting to set his Romantic imagination free to roam lyrically through the skies of the music of the future. His was not Wordsworth's "still sad music of humanity" but, if music realized its mission, the future joyful music of humanity. Music

will rise to unexplored heavens, it will draw from Art secrets hitherto unknown, it will diffuse over Raphaelesque melodies and through an uninterrupted harmony a shadow of that Infinite which is the yearning of our souls . . . and, placing before itself the social concept (and this is the mission reserved for music), it will elevate it onto the level of a faith . . . , and change cold and inactive beliefs into enthusiasm . . . on a scale of sublime harmonies, where every instrument is an emotion, every melody an action, every chord a synthesis of the soul, rising from the mud of blind sensations, from the tumult of material instincts, to the heavens of the angels foreseen by Weber, Mozart, and Beethoven—a heaven of pure quiet, of serene conscience where the soul retempers itself with love . . . , holy and eternal.

There was no more lyrical way to embrace totality through music's ethical and aesthetic ability to both reflect and structure the universe. And there was no more moving way to reconcile the paradox and embrace the dual representation of music, that is, the pattern of the cosmos, or the stability of eternity, its objectivity, and the phenomenon of expression and communication of the movement of diverseness, its subjectivity.

Mazzini's words, so totally idealistic, make us think of Jacques Barzun's statement about Romanticism: "Granted that it failed to win the world, it was the right kind of failure."[34] Mazzini went "out of bounds," as it were—

but music was going at least to tear down the Classical and Baroque major-minor key system of tonality and replace it with something that might be characterized—consistent with Goethe's expression of freedom and complete with the paradoxes that invariably permeate it—as a spirit, as distinguished from a style. Ultimately, the Romantic philosophy of music related more to a spiritual force than to a mode of expression. And Mazzini's demand for "spiritualization" was realized, and the failure to grasp totality produced many smaller successes along the way—not less real for being small by comparison with totality. Mazzini advises experimentalism—"a series of experiments which at first will invite derision by many, then study, and will finally be considered a real advancement [over past efforts]"—and new rhythms, a coloristic use of harmony and instrumental timbres, a relaxation of formal canons, and a veneration of many practices previously considered misuses. This was the way "foreseen" by Beethoven, the way implied by Mazzini's support of a virile and religious music, combining the power of Byron and the faith of Schiller.

Romanticism saw everything as a function of art, which annihilates the antinomies of life, as Schlegel claimed, and "potentializes" it through the total idea. In this sense, it operates beyond the phenomenon, in what Keats called a suspension beyond the limits, what Vigny called the interior songs of thoughts, or what Leopardi called the infinite. Mazzini used music as a metaphor and expressed it, ultimately, in the terms of Faust: "I have flown over the entire universe." In many ways, Mazzini's work was like that of many Romantic poets who wrote "poetic symphonies" through a desire to see a life in organic relationship with the beyond: hence the religious character of much Romantic musical appreciation, Mazzini's included, so that, while music reaches the beyond, it also permeates the One. While it "begins where the word ends," it also infuses the individual, and "individuality is holy" and "will always have to constitute the point from which any music moves forth." The objective validates the subjective. Music enables us to face our consciences with humanity as a referent—to look at the world, not merely "through the dusk of a beautiful dream," as Wackenroder put it,[35] but with the sense of "SACRIFICE" required by any true faith.[36] For this reason, Beethoven's music, to which Mazzini, like Balzac, Coleridge, and Hoffmann paid tribute, will come to symbolize for many later Romantics the desired tendency toward a religious and limitless universality. "When I open my eyes," Beethoven had written, speaking of so much of the music that surrounded him, "I am forced to sigh, because what I see is contrary to my religion, and I must despise those who do not feel that music is the highest revelation of the world."[37] Almost verbatim, these were the words Mazzini was to utter, adding to them an awareness of the mathematical mysteries that relate music to number, for music, he wrote, is "the algebra of the soul of which humanity lives"—a thought not much different from Novalis's statement: "In music, mathematics appears as a revelation of creative idealism."[38] This is what in our day Albert Einstein meant when he said that, if one wants to understand the universe, one should listen to Bach's Fantasia and Fugue in G Minor.[39] This is what in his day Mazzini meant when, by stating that music is a liberating and humanizing divine force, "a note in the divine chord that the whole universe will be called upon some day to express,"[40] he implied what many a Romantic mind had sensed: music's Promethean spirit which breaks the chains of our narrow (and, for some, corrupt) terrestrial experiences and proclaims its Faustian impulse to listen to the bells of Easter.

(1975)

MUSIC IN LITERATURE

A CASE OF LITERARY DIPLOMACY: BALZAC AND MEYERBEER[1]

Because he allegedly vaunted *Robert le Diable* in *Gambara*, Balzac was labeled a passionate admirer of Meyerbeer's opera. Rémy Montaléc speaks of "sparkling pages which are a masterpiece of musical criticism,"[2] and Mme Maurice-Amor, accusing the novelist of following the fashion of popular adulation, merely talks about "his enthusiasm for *Robert le Diable*."[3] Others still, like Gaston Guichard, question Balzac's good taste for having placed that composer on a par with Beethoven and Weber,[4] while Mme Marix-Spire sees in *Gambara* a genuine exaltation of that opera.[5]

   Yet, we must take into account the severe criticisms of Meyerbeer contained in his discussion in *Gambara*. Should we fail to recognize their importance, we might miss the interesting possibility—in my opinion very real—of what we might call a case of literary diplomacy. Did not Balzac promise Meyerbeer at one time to make one of the composer's works the dominant theme of one of his novels,[6] a promise made via the intermediary of the editor of *La Gazette musicale* (Maurice Schlesinger, who had published *Robert le Diable* and *Les Huguenots*[7]) in which *Gambara* first appeared? Newly and deeply impressed by Beethoven's genius, besides being one of Rossini's long-standing friends, Balzac could not write that vibrant eulogy of a composer he admired but nevertheless deemed inferior to the German and Italian masters. Thus, when he asked Schlesinger to send him the best pieces of favorable and unfavorable criticism he had on hand in his office files, he did so indeed to confirm the authority of his own judgment, but also to find a means of evading the embarrassment of not being able to fulfill a promise that he no longer felt could be fulfilled wholeheartedly. The matter demanded tact. He had to convey an overall favorable impression of the work while in fact textually manipulating strong reservations. His adroitly ambig-

uous handling of historical prototypes as represented in the characters of
Béatrix (Conti: Liszt, Sandeau; Félicité: Marie d'Agoult, George Sand, and
others) is ample proof of his ability for this kind of jugglery.[8]

The enormous success of *Robert le Diable* in Paris and in Europe is well
known and did not leave Balzac indifferent. He wrote *Gambara* and chose
the opera partly in order to present the German side of the quarrel that raged
on the subject of German versus Italian music, even though this meant, at
the same time, having to balance his position with a description of Rossini's
Mosè in Egitto in *Massimilla Doni* to expound the Italian point of view.[9]
His Romantic predilection for descriptive music and dramatic situations, of
which Meyerbeer's opera is a peerless example, is also well known. Nevertheless, we should not overlook the fact that it is the Hoffmannian com-
poser-critic-theoretician Gambara, rather than Meyerbeer, who represents
the German point of view; that he ends up denouncing the opera; and that
Count Marcosini initiates the debate with an ostensive attack meant to pro-
voke some reaction on his part. Marcosini's arguments are far too precise,
to be sure, to be considered a mere exercise in rhetoric. He condemns the
French librettists both for transmuting an otherwise interesting story into a
fable and for elaborating a "true dramatic nightmare which oppresses the
spectators without arousing in them any strong emotions." From a musical
perspective, he criticizes the way in which melody and voice frequently
drown in the orchestral harmony, thus destroying the unity and credibility
of the music. Moreover, even though he grants that Meyerbeer does not
lack sensibility, he labels him a "skillful harvester [*vendangeur*] of notes"
with a somewhat exaggerated tendency toward plagal cadences. If indeed
Gambara declares to his interlocutor that he has failed to understand "this
immense musical drama," he does so "casually," and in the next sentence
he refers to the musical score as the "work of a note-mounter [*sertisseur*]."

Gambara delivers his speech when "deep into one of those semi-slumbers
common to drinkers." This description is most significant, since Balzac uses
drunkenness as the most convenient means of manipulating his dual intention. This fact has not been appreciated as much as it deserves. Gambara
indeed is fond of the bottle, and when under the influence of alcohol he
appears to be readier to expound his musical criticism to those around him
than when he is sober and involved with those disconcerting avant-garde
experimentations despised by everyone. Balzac himself cares to make clear
that his hero's good sense seemed to be in inverse proportion to his degree

of sobriety. Would Meyerbeer have felt any reassurance because of this about Balzac's good intentions?

It has been deduced that Gambara's real genius found expression only in moments of intoxication or that, as Marcosini proclaims, "only drunkenness saves him." Hunt's comments are typical in this respect: "when Gambara is drunk, he is sufficiently alive to sensation and emotion, as being the essential elements of music, to produce ravishing melodies and harmonies."[10]

Yet paradoxically, during such moments, he produces cavatinas that are wonderful only to the ears of a pedestrian audience and not the great, dramatic music that, according to him, was inspired by the feeling of a universe in harmony with what he calls the concert of angels. The other music, his true music, one that expresses ideas rather than sensations, "can only have an audience endowed with genius," and Gambara celebrates it to adopt it as his own, to renounce the holy bottle, to reject popularity and remain "faithful to the IDEAL" that others have killed.

Consequently, if Gambara, to please the crowd, lowers himself to the level of each and every one when he composes music in a state of inebriation, it logically ensues that in a deep state of drunkenness he will manifest a similar tendency in his interpretation of music—in this case, that of *Robert le Diable*. True, it is while indulging that he has praised Marcosini's eulogy of Beethoven and that he had discoursed intelligently about idealism and sensualism. On that occasion, however, he was far from a semicomatose condition and was not yet under the influence of the systematic wine treatment administered by his friends. It seems that here Balzac deftly avoids giving us a definition of intoxication. But, if we read between the lines, we note that being in a state of stupor and being simply "very animated" by the effect of wine (a condition which, according to Hoffmann, accelerates the flow of ideas) represent two quite different dispositions. Thus, Balzac lets his composer discuss Beethoven and the music of the future while sober or merely "animated"; he reserves Meyerbeer for those moments when his anesthetized sensibility reduces to insignificance the narrow gap between the rational and the irrational, whereby judgment becomes ambiguous—hence the mixture of sagacity and unfounded praise peppered with exaggerations. Indeed, at a given moment, Gambara associates *Don Giovanni* with *Robert le Diable*, in a whimsical fit of which Balzac, who considered Mozart's work the perfect opera, was wholly aware. And the ensuing remarks that describe *Robert le Diable* as more "abundant" than *Don Giovanni*, whose harmonic and melodic proportions are "exact," lead us to doubt seriously the value of the supposedly competing composition.[11]

In his introduction to the main section of his "panegyric," Balzac has Gambara pronounce two evasive statements—on purpose, we might think, as if to undermine what he seems to be saying. One of these statements, uttered upon downing a full glass of Giro wine, says little in its own context and even less in a Balzacian context: "such music is made neither for the incredulous nor for those who do not love." In other words, such music has value only for those who have already had a thorough experience of religion and of love. Yet the role played by music in *La Comédie humaine* demonstrates precisely the opposite, for the magic virtue of music consists in the power to heighten and purify one's sentiments and ideas. Thus, the atheist will convert at the tones of the organ, and many a young hero and heroine wake up to love the moment they hear a beautiful melody.

The ambiguity of the other statement is spicy enough: "it is a music *chosen* with love, but within the *treasures* of a rich and fertile imagination in which knowledge has *pressed* the ideas so as to *distill* their musical essence."[12] Otherwise put, and all (intentional?) gibberish aside, Meyerbeer borrows well; the word "imagination," kept in the singular, preserves the ambiguity of such a statement in his favor. The basic tone set, Balzac may embark on a scene-by-scene analysis of the opera without too much risk of exaggerating his "tribute."

The selections and arias he praises are numerous, such as the Bacchanal of the Overture, "Tu ne sauras" (Act I); "Si je le permets" (Act II); then "Valse infernale," "Quand j'ai quitté la Normandie," and "Nonnes qui reposez sous cette froide pierre" (Act III); the cavatina "Grâce à toi" (Act IV), and the prayer "Gloire à la Providence" (Act V). Only once does he allow himself a direct criticism; it happens, significantly, when dealing with an important section of the work: the end. Gambara declares: "here the music has weakened," because he was not allowed to hear either what he wanted to hear (the "concert of happy angels") or what he felt ("a hope in his heart"). Obviously, Rossini was a better composer: "I needed another Mosè's prayer."

In most cases, however, the criticism is kept indirect. He presents us with a literary rather than a musical analysis of some scenes (the Bertram-Alice section in Act III; the beginning of Act IV); or he does not mention some arias the critics had praised ("Je lui dus la victoire" [Act I]; Bertram's exhortation to Robert to provide him with the magic bough [Act III]). Balzac admired Beethoven too much to join the chorus of voices that lauded "Des chevaliers de ma patrie," an imitation of the Finale of the Fifth Symphony.

His criticism is most subtle when his enthusiasm hides a barbed thrust. The Overture of our "note-harvester" reminds us of Mozart; the Finale is reminiscent of *Don Giovanni*; the recitatives in Act I make Gluck spring to mind. While deliberately dodging the prolixity of Act II, he insinuates in his discussion that he has his own home-grown ideas on the subject, prolix and perhaps intentionally disconcerting ideas: "That beginning overwhelms with grief all those who develop the themes at the bottom of their heart by endowing them with all the extended breadth that the composer required them to communicate"! And finally, after talking about an act that includes dances, choruses, marches, knights preparing for a tournament, fanfares, a love duet, Moorish motives, Spanish rhythms, a Siciliana, "the daisies of a French comic opera," the whole topped by Isabelle's voice singing scales, he praises (this has to be deadpan humor) an act in which "everything is homogeneous" and thanks to which "you have caught a glimpse of human life in its sole and unique expression . . ."!

Balzac uses a variant of the same method when the music reaches a climax in Act III with the Bacchanal in D Minor that concludes it. Gambara encourages the music to go forward (which is plainly impossible, since the movement is interrupted by a procession of nuns and by three short ballets—whose intrusion in an opera he hates), and just as if he found Meyerbeer's handling of the thing neither satisfying nor sufficient, "he developed the bacchanal on his own by improvising imaginative variations on it."

His eulogy once finished, the dry manner in which Gambara attacks the opera (with "a most open countenance") the next day when he is sober cannot really be considered a contradiction of what he had celebrated the previous evening. We are reminded here of Schiller's Karl von Moor's exclamation: "May I be cursed for having said that! But I was drowned in the vapors of wine, and my heart did not hear what my tongue was saying."[13] Gambara now talks about

a miserable opera . . . [which] remains music made by ordinary means . . . , heaps of notes, *verba et voces* . . . chopped up phrases whose sources I recognized. The number *Gloire à la Providence* resembles too much a piece by Handel, the chorus of the knights going to battle is akin to the Scottish air in *La Dame blanche*.

He terminates his assessment with this offensive remark: "In the long run, if the opera is such a success, it is because the music belongs to everybody, and so it's got to be popular." Gambara avenges Marcosini's initial position. The real judgment on Meyerbeer is rendered at that moment; and with it, too, Balzac's own verdict.[14] Therefore, we would be right in thinking that the novelist did not say what he seemed ostensibly to be saying. Like Vergil in the *Aeneid* (another work whose "diplomatic" dimension has been traditionally neglected), the veil of praise conceals a genuine criticism.

Because of his tacit or overt objections, then, Balzac may not be the fervent panegyrist of *Robert le Diable* that he appears to be at first reading, the panegyrist he might have been had he let himself be influenced by the fashion of his time. The so-called action-symphony of Meyerbeer cannot be compared with the analytical symphony of Beethoven. On various occasions the novelist tells us that he does not favor endless roulades or too many ballets or gratuitous pieces of virtuosity that are there only to please the egos of prima donnas—in brief, all elements that Meyerbeer made lavish use of in his opera. If, on the one hand, he could confess to fully enjoying the barbaric "poetry" of that supershow, on the other, his reverence for the "divine Rossini" belonged to another kind of enjoyment and, to an even greater degree, his cult of the "sublime Beethoven." The name of the composer of *Robert le Diable*, as a matter of fact, rarely appears in his other works or in his correspondence, in comparison with the number of times he mentions the names of the authors of *Mosè in Egitto* and the Fifth Symphony. And nothing in this context allows us to think that Meyerbeer was one of his truly favorite composers.

In stark contrast with the enthusiasm that reflects the excitement that characterizes his contemporaries, Balzac, in his corner, seems to give us in this case a proof of diplomatic detachment. It may be that, as a result, he was a finer musical critic than is usually admitted and that he foresaw that for posterity the idol of Paris in time would flounder as a *magni nominis umbra*.

(1967)

9

MUSIC AND THE STRUCTURE OF DIDEROT'S *LÈ NEVEU DE RAMEAU*

"cette admirable satire de moeurs, dans laquelle il faudra toujours aller chercher son dernier mot sur la musique." [1]

The Horatian epithet of the "beautiful disorder" has often been conferred upon Diderot's seemingly disheveled and erratic masterpiece, *Le Neveu de Rameau*. Although it gives a reasonable impression of the work's virtuosity, the epithet lacks accuracy. The more we familiarize ourselves with *Le Neveu de Rameau*, the more the feeling of versatility gives way to a sense of organic structure, chiefly, I believe, because of a balanced variety of formal relationships which can best be described as musical. Rhythmic patterns, thematic developments, modulations, dynamic effects, tonalities—all share in unifying the opus and in evolving a superaesthetic. The satire thus becomes a concordant whole and not a discordant plurality of features. Implying that *Le Neveu de Rameau* is primarily an aesthetic creation, I am focusing purely on musical form. In isolating one element of the author's method, I propose to indicate the possibility of a musical purpose and not to discuss the controversial topic of the work's meaning, even if, in any great work, form and content, if distinguishable, are ultimately inseparable.

If Herbert Dieckmann's suggestion is correct that the dialogue's lack of influence in the realm of philosophy was due possibly to the author's capricious playing with bold and radical ideas without generally committing himself outright to them,[2] then I may be justified in centering on the artistic motivation rather than on the philosophical commitment. Structure does not serve here, as it did in the masterpieces of ancient dialogue, as the handmaiden of psychological and didactic purposes. *Le Neveu de Rameau* can be seen, organically, as a musical composition in which all parts are harmoniously arranged. Structure, in this case, means that special aesthetic coherence of elements, that totality of analogous relationships, which surmount the logic of literal meaning. The work does not invite just the broad musical comparison which associated the *Divine Comedy*'s many levels of meaning with "polyphony" or Sancho Panza's relation to Don Quijote with "counterpoint." Such analogies, whatever their worth, hardly warrant labeling Dante's or Cervantes's creation as musical. In contrast, Diderot's creation, because so many of its structural devices are suggestive of music, does merit the label, even though, strictly speaking, my analysis aims more to speculate than to prove.

Satire and portrait have been stressed as the dominant elements in the dialogue, alongside which the digressions on musical topics should seem only extraneous. Indeed, for Rudolf Schlösser, who demands that all matters treated be strictly subservient to the purpose of the satire, the long discussion on contemporary music and French and Italian opera constitutes the worst flaw in the work, being both episodic and expressive of Diderot's, not Rameau's, musical theories.[3] The explanations generally given for its presence—namely, that accuracy in the portrait of a musician or that relief from the protagonist's perverse ethics demanded it—do little to dispel Schlösser's concern. The key to the work being aesthetic, his concern cannot be alleviated on purely substantive grounds.

A French translator of Goethe attributes to the German master the opinion that the musical annotations and digressions in *Le Neveu de Rameau* are not an "hors-d'oeuvre" but, on the contrary, the "principal force of the work, the one that puts all parts into play . . . , the underpinning of this piece; everything else relates to it."[4] That the quotation seems to be a figment of the translator's imagination does not detract from the truth of the statement, or, for that matter, from the spirit of Goethe's remarks on Diderot. For the dialogue is truly an interplay of parts. Recounting a colorful philosophical debate in a café, Diderot symphonizes his contradictory ethics in a spirited thirty-minute exposé which compels our admiration largely because of the way he orchestrates his ideas. "In none other of his writings, with the possible exception of *Jacques the Fatalist*, are the symphonics of a complicated, polyphonal structure so carefully worked out, narration, satire, philosophy, pantomime intertwining and balancing each other."[5] Were it not for this variously harnessed, artistic arrangement, not only would the

contents scatter pyrotechnically far afield, but the personalities of the inter-
locutors would lose their fascination, and the opus might well become as
unpalatable as *Le Fils naturel*. It is hardly a coincidence that Diderot worked
longer on *Le Neveu de Rameau* than on anything else he wrote, the actual
composition encompassing from fifteen to seventeen years.

Despite the *Principes généraux d'acoustique* and the three monographs on
the science of music in *Cinq mémoires sur différents sujets de mathéma-
tiques*, Diderot's knowledge of music was guided more by artistic than by
technical interests. True, the Abbé Raynal—according to Melchior Grimm—
did consider him capable of explaining the theories of Jean-Philippe Rameau;[6] Boyer and Bemetzrieder did solicit his aid to further their musical
ideas;[7] and composers and theoreticians (Duni, Grétry, La Borde, Cahusac)
did accept him as an authority, whether or not they agreed with his stand
during the "Querelle des Bouffons." True also, like Balzac with Jacques
Strunz, he did have many conversations with Rameau and Philidor and
Blainville designed to enhance his musical education technically, and he
did greatly impress the traveling Charles Burney, who reported "that among
all the sciences which his extensive genius and learning had investigated,
there is no one that he interests himself more about than music."[8] But in
the strict sense of the word, his musical formation remained inferior to that
of some of his contemporaries like Rousseau. The admission is quite clear
in the dialogue: LUI [HE] "You are not a musician?" MOI [I] "No." That
Diderot, however, had enough knowledge of musical composition as an art
to cast a prose piece into what may be regarded as a musical form is unden-
iable. The *Leçons de clavecin* prove this abundantly. Besides, as with Balzac, we must not overlook the resourcefulness and the enthusiasm of his
imagination, for which he often settled as an adequate substitute for knowledge, and which of themselves made him, broadly speaking, a musician.
We are reminded of his own definition in the *Troisième entretien sur Le
Fils naturel:* "When I say *musician*, I mean the man who possesses the
genius of his art; he is different from the one who only knows how to string
modulations together and put notes together."[9] In the long run, technical
learning is of marginal relevance for a man who has supplanted it with an
aesthetic vision.

In attempting to extract the various ingredients of musical structure, it
would be prejudicial to my speculative purpose to apply the sharp magnify-
ing lens of the analyst who seeks the concise, logical, and linear juxtaposi-

tion of parts characteristic of a Mozart symphony. To do so would mean to undo the work's greatest aesthetic asset: its suggestiveness. Diderot's intention was not to transcribe in prose closely modeled on the musical process the forms of opera, symphony, or theme and variations. It was, I could argue, meant to create a pervading musical impression substantiated partially by Jean-François Rameau's musical heritage, discussions, and interludes, but primarily and more subtly, by an overall architecture relying for cohesiveness on musical analogy. We read in Paul Meyer's essay that the dialogue resembles a construction neither symmetrical nor rational in the strictest sense, but one governed by obscure forces which determine the psychological laws that regulate the association of ideas.[10] And Leo Spitzer notes that the extravagant wanderings of the nephew's mind bring to the surface features latent in the workings of the human mind.[11] Both of these statements, in reality, point to a fundamental facet of musical, even more intimately than of poetical, aesthetics: the art of subtle associations.

For *Le Neveu de Rameau* progresses musically by relations, that is, by oblique and affinitive communications. Quite obviously, any one musical element, isolated from the total context, would seem merely adventitious. The fact that emotions intensify as the satire progresses and thus produce a clear crescendo effect does not distinguish the work from any other well-constructed piece of literature. But the sheer accumulation of indications of patterns and devices common in music not only suggests a whole but also awakens our musical sensibility and sharpens our aesthetic receptivity. Diderot's process was one of recomposing, as only elusive, momentarily tangible clues can recompose by weaving a sense of illusion. In a way, it was a transubstantiation. At the bottom of *Le Neveu de Rameau* lies his variously stated, empirical belief that beauty is the perception of relations and that the sense of beauty is a form of experience. "I call beauty . . . everything that contains in itself something to awaken the notion of relationships in my understanding."[12] Diderot's contemporary J. B. La Borde held firmly that his friend's musical appreciation derived from the perception of relationships.[13] Though not necessarily representative of the author's final view on aesthetics, the statements apply. The dialogue occasions a musical experience in the reader. Doubly effective by virtue of its musical affinities, the technique of literary suggestion was never so appropriately handled, because our experience is not impaired by any kind of awareness of the author's possible foreplanning. At best, there was broad intention; there was no spe-

cific, deliberate, detailed plan. In no other way can the work's lifelike spontaneity and musiclike fluidity be explained. Its illusion and strong musical
suggestiveness are directly related to Diderot's unerring sense for associations
(he displayed this in his *Salons*) and should be looked upon as the instinctive
outcome of his singleness of purpose.

Jean Fabre remarked perceptively:

> To begin with, you will note how artfully the four great pantomimes which serve as
> intermissions are distributed and graduated: you begin with a solo violin recital, then
> follows one on an imaginary clavichord, and the illusion is already created: "Surely
> the chords resounded in his ears and in mine." Then there is a fugue sketched out
> in a cappella by a Protean chorister, beginning with the "vivat Mascarillus," in the
> manner of a conclusion, but of a transition as well, since not too long afterward it
> is a whole opera that is unleashed: singers, orchestra, the very hall—all roles played
> simultaneously by a single man, in an extraordinary swelling of music and poetry.
> Finally, the series is crowned by the beggars' pantomime or the earth's great shaking,
> when the spectacle is no longer on the stage, nor in the hall, but extends into a mad
> vision of the world regulated like a gigantic ballet. Such a progression, by virtue of
> its very lack of measure, reveals a profound sense of measure, whether you accept
> the term in its musical sense or whether you give it its full aesthetic and literary
> value.[14]

One could begin more fundamentally than Fabre, without incurring the
risk of a Procrustean analysis which would distort the satire's secret direction. Among the first impressions we receive in reading *Le Neveu de Rameau* is the manner in which various musical forms are suggested to us,
while in effect they are being simultaneously blended and re-created to express a transcending design. Often we are reminded of an opera, the stage
set to represent the Café de la Régence in 1760 with Paris behind it. Diderot
is idling when the curtain rises on the chess players at the café. "The setting
of *Le Neveu de Rameau* is probably the most successful and complete of all
those painted by the philosopher. . . . The Café de la Régence . . . is
captured in a few lines. . . . That Café . . . we see it. In its discrete way,
it lives and reacts, from one end of the dialogue to the other."[15] Not un-
usually for Diderot, the "possible theatrical effect"[16] provides the first key to
his aesthetic. As an overture, the several narrative pages of introduction, by
presenting the protagonist, foreshadow his moods, arguments, ironies, and
actions, especially the passage which sarcastically describes an opera by Rameau senior or a conventional libretto: "there are harmonies, bits of songs,
loose ideas, noise, thefts, triumphs, lances, glories, murmurs, breathless vic-

tories, dance airs." The tempo of Diderot's piece will obviously be lively. The ballets and pantomimes, twelve in number, performed and enjoyed so haggardly by the bohemian as they offer momentary respite from an otherwise unrelieved conversation ("Sometimes dance delights, calms your bile"[17]), are reminiscent of the interludes which were common in the Baroque operatic tradition. But Diderot uses them differently, in accordance with the views of various Encyclopedists and of Louis de Cahusac,[18] who claimed that the ballet, as it was employed, presented both antiquated routines and a series of disconnected scenes. His interest in the dance form reached a high point in the episode of the two young peasants in the *Troisième entretien* of 1757, when, after the elder Rameau's creation of the opera-ballet, he clamored for revitalizing innovations which would transmute the old *ballet de cour* into a *ballet d'action*. "Pantomime [must] be closely tied to dramatic action; . . . dance be made out in the form of a veritable poem."[19] *Le Neveu de Rameau*'s pantomime-ballets are not disconnected from the dramatic action of the dialogue. They distill the essence from the previous discussions while developing them physically, thereby giving them the kind of visual reality denied to words. By being integrated into the very fabric of the suggested opera, they serve their proper function: to demonstrate the emotional crises. And because their lengths vary, we automatically give more prominence to the longer and less to the shorter ones, so that they appear to divide the whole satire into acts and scenes.

The long speeches, too, represent climaxes characteristic of operatic writing. Not only as lyrical effluences, but also as interpretations of the key scenes during which the individual soliloquizes, they function as veritable arias. If "the aria is a kind of speech,"[20] then in this context the reverse is also true. Used with reserve, as Grimm had cautioned, "the aria is almost always the scene's peroration." Rameau's various tales and monologues highlight the discussion. His taunting monologue on Virtue—almost like a precursor of Rossini's "Calunnia" aria in *Il barbiere di Siviglia*—appears as the first peroration. Another is the account of the "little priest," the cause of his disaster; still another, the story of the "opulent and wasteful" Jew. These are sometimes coupled with outbursts of pantomime for maximum effect in culminating a scene (the Virtue "aria," for example, with the subsequent demonstration of the hypochondriac, or the story of the renegade followed by the Vivat Mascarillus "fugue song," which, as Fabre noted, is both a conclusion and a transition).

Given the operatic context, the remaining dialogue automatically becomes recitative, although solely by an extension analogous to what Diderot himself described elsewhere as "paced steps and measured pantomime" which act as "the dance's recitative."[21] The brisk exchanges of the dialogue provide the pivots for rapid changes of direction in thought and constitute, as it were, a *recitativo secco*.

Finally, the suggestion of a finale balances neatly the suggestion of an overture. The principle of pantomime, which permeates the work as a mood in the manner of a basso continuo and through Rameau's performances in the manner of a Wagnerian leitmotif, is ultimately conceptualized—"pantomimes of the human species"—gathering unto itself the converged meanings of all anteceding discussions and providing certainly the emotional but also the intellectual climax with which good operas should terminate. The final scene of Verdi's *Falstaff* is no more crowning.

It is what Diderot suggests symphonically that invites our musical attention still more closely. The polyphonic structure, involving four principal themes—narration, philosophy, satire, pantomime—comes immediately into evidence with the introductory descriptive pages, followed by a section generally serious in tone during which Diderot carries the bulk of a conversation revolving about the nature of genius. This, in turn, gives way to a third section, largely Rameau's mockeries of his parasitic existence, and finally to his mimetic performances on a violin and a harpsichord. The rest of the dialogue is only deceptively unrestrained. Many are the attendant subjects of elements, like sundry limbs of the themes of genius and parasite, which spur the conversation adventurously onward: pride, vanity, virtue, music, money, misery, luxury, immorality, hunger, evil, falseness, and people generally. In reality, however, the discussion divides itself symmetrically into three developments, each pitting themes and subjects against one another in an unexampled variety of juxtapositions, and each followed by a bridging interlude, by some of the same pantomimes which would divide the opera into acts: the hypochondriac, the fugue, and the dejected and proud man. Ultimately, all the themes along with the most prominent subjects (misery, hunger, people, pride, and luxury) flow synthetically into a recapitulatory coda (the opera's Finale), a deft feat of orchestration, distinguished, as I said before, by the summing disclosure of the satirical philosophy of universal pantomime.

Diderot makes the greatest possible literary use of what delights us repeatedly in music: our recognition of phrases and harmonies in ever-changing relationship. When he abandons a subject and later resumes it, frequently with variants, he gives us a true musical illusion by multiplying our subconscious processes of association. Themes and subjects are fundamentally more important for what they do, in music, than for what they say. Once enunciated, they make themselves felt in other contexts and touch them with a significance beyond their own. So it is, in *Le Neveu de Rameau*, that a statement like "let us extend our sight onto the coming centuries" is recalled many pages later when we are told about the course that music should follow: "Lyrical poetry still awaits birth," and still later: "[There is] nothing so flat than a series of perfect chords. You need something that prods, that loosens up the light sheaf and scatters its rays," to extract but a few references to a future aesthetic. So it is, also, with the subject of misery, from the early description of Rameau "lean and wan," through the many allusions to his deprivation and that of others, to the eventual incarnation of the evil itself, "crouched, mouth wide open, in order to receive a few drops of the ice water escaping from the Danaides's keg." The subject of pride is even more sustained in its development, as it expands subtly from dignity to self-respect: first the Nephew says he cannot humble himself and crawl at someone else's orders; then he is loath to submit to an inferior; in the end, he contemptuously scorns the ugliness of necessity which forces him to assume a pose. The portrait of Rameau discloses more than just "the professional man steeped in music";[22] it functions itself as a theme of dominant proportion, recurring regularly and growing commensurately, from Introduction to Coda. One of its more specific developments concerns his gnawing sense of personal failure: his lack of success as a composer early in the dialogue ("yes, yes, I am mediocre") is rationalized philosophically in the middle ("we are of no consequence") and reappears in the end in terms of his inefficacy as a husband ("No, no, I'll never get over it"). While avoiding the dangers, then, of plotting planned, linear relationships, we can say that, through numerous subject or thematic developments, we discern an almost measurable calculation of forces, a coherence made audible and cast into a musical mold.

As the first or sonata form movement of a symphony derives its power and character from the opposition of two central themes, thereby making it essentially a psychological and dramatic form, so the contrast between Moi and Lui is responsible for *Le Neveu de Rameau*'s motivity. The narrator's "soul agitated by two opposite movements" reflects more than just the state of mind of Diderot or his predilection for the expressionistic form of the soliloquy in which Moi is divided with himself. Basically, the movements are psychological but also ideological, confronting the bohemian's sincere moral and physical rascality with his friend's confused indignation: the former's parasitical ethics produces in the latter a series of reactions (amused curiosity, pity mingled with scorn, attraction, repulsion) leading inexorably to a moral crisis. What matters here is that "the Moi and the Lui come away from this confrontation better confirmed in their essence."[23] Fabre put it this way: "Moi becomes that other, and Lui is enhanced by what is most secret in Moi."[24] The symphony's opposing themes do find each other's harmonies.

This dialectic is effectively sustained by an extreme play of sound components, the alternating or contrasting of the conversation's dynamic levels. Note how often the person who describes himself as a "bottomless bag of impertinences" elicits his listener's agreement ("I'm on the brink of agreeing with you" or "There is some truth in all you have just said"), and how, conversely, the Nephew yields, if only momentarily, to the narrator's point of view ("That's correct"; "You're right"). Subjects not only contrast with each other, but, borrowing the symphonic device of intrathematic juxtaposition, oppose themselves every time Moi is attracted to Lui's view and vice versa. The result is that our musical impressions are vastly broadened, for we find that the original thematic arrangement of narration-philosophy-satire-pantomime is paralleled by four additional elements, the multiple subjects of Moi and Lui, each of which is subdivided into two, a *pro se* and a *contra se*. Outlandish escapades and materialist's quandaries, righteous commentaries and signal ideals, weave an involved polyphony not dissimilar to the author's own complex personality. And the marvelous unity which binds the whole together, like the world view which draws all sections of a Beethoven symphony into the same emotional mold, finds its expression in the satire in the fact that at bottom both Moi and Lui are the same person, Denis Diderot.

In its widest outline, *Le Neveu de Rameau* may further connote "a kind of rondo, with the theme of music itself as the refrain between variations."[25] More specifically, the impression is one of the theme and variations proper to a passacaglia. Not only is the passacaglia, or chaconne, historically a dance form, capriciously evoked by Rameau's capers, but more seriously by

the strong suggestion of a ground bass and by the same expansion and intensification of themes and subjects alluded to before. There are the nuclear
pessimistic ideas, lurking behind every exchange in the dialogue, of man's
inconsequence and of his pantomime—including that of Rameau himself,
who, while accusing others of hypocrisy, shows that he has mimed his own
life instead of living it. There are also the intercalations of the author, sincere, profound, and moving intercalations which do their best to dull the
sharpness of his friend's bedeviled paradoxes and "constitute a kind of basso
continuo for the whole piece."[26] Equally indicative is the manner in which
each would-be variation of a subject, differently presented, combines with
others, gathering the kind of cumulative momentum that makes the final
pages as psychologically satisfying as those of Bach's great organ Passacaglia
in C Minor. Genius, misery, greatness, pride, and hunger, converging in a
whirling finish, may produce a "vile pantomime"—but an attractive one
nonetheless. In still another way, the sensation communicates itself by the
progressively intensified growth of Rameau as a character, from an unexcep-
tional individual likeness to an inimitable literary type, and by the increased
virtuosity of his antics, from the mimicking of a violin modulating to the
simultaneous demonstration of an entire orchestra supporting a whole operatic performance. The Nephew's orchestral skill is matched only by Diderot's dexterity in orchestrating his work.

Various other modulations contribute to the crescendo effect, adding a
calculated dramatic dimension to *Le Neveu de Rameau*. We follow the
mounting indignation of the sentimentally moral MOI as LUI's eccentric
philosophy unfolds and the gulf separating them widens steadily. From a
modest "wretch," Rameau becomes a "madman, a stark-madman"; is accused of "turpitude"; and at the very end is belabored with epithets of "slug-
gard, glutton, coward, mean soul." For while the beginning exchanges were
narrowly circumscribed as to target, LUI ended by questioning all the consecrated canons of human conduct. Yet, despite the narrator's vexation, a
corollary process is at work by which his friend's frankness, consistency, and
disarming perspicacity invite admiration and transform the failure of genius
into the genius of failure.[27] Rameau transmutes his mental and physical
acrobatics into dreams; Diderot converts his dialogue into something resembling counterpoint.

Diderot practically defined modulation when, two years before beginning
Le Neveu de Rameau, he remarked on his technique of seemingly disjointed

dialogues: "to go from one thing to another through the medium of a common quality." [28] Without the transitional notes, as it were, the conversation would fragment into a diversity of non sequiturs. In *Le Neveu de Rameau*, there are what may be called pivotal tones, such as LUI's reference to "dissonances in social harmony," which invites MOI's "By that comparison, you bring me back from custom to music, from which I had wandered off despite myself." Elsewhere, he abandons a topic in order to talk about music: "Let's leave that . . . , you will inform me more easily of the things I ignore and of what you know about music. Let's talk music, dear Rameau." And still elsewhere, the views expressed on practicing musicians pivot to a consideration of teachers, then of professional men, then of the provocative theory of "professional idioms" (the word *idiotismes* is also associated with "idiocies") by which Rameau disparages a person's genuine qualifications, and this in turn literally swells into a discussion of relativity, vanity, honesty, and virtue. Or there are broader pivotal tonalities, the many musical interludes, such as the Nephew's antics as a violinist and harpsichordist which lead to an exchange on whether a man exercising a profession really has to know the skill he practices. The importance of not stepping out of role ("Everything in this world has its own worth") changes hue when the Nephew twists it to praise evil, his own included ("I congratulate myself"), providing one does it well, so that the ensuing story of the renegade and the Jew terminates in his startling self-acceptance for being "quaint in my debasement." These transitions represent more than the normal process of well-connected literary composition. Too frequent to be taken for granted, they suggest, in their musical context, a musical behavior. Each note is in place. "You must now how to prepare and place these major, peremptory tones," says Rameau.

Written in a tempo which might be described as an allegro vivace, the dialogue is buoyant with witty sallies and scintillating repartee. It argues the aesthetic value of dissonance by pointing up the characteristic and unique, the trivial and bizarre, the irregular and jarring, rather than the classical qualities of consonance, order, clarity, and proportion. And it does so with disordered opulence, defying the tidy definitions of harmony. Indeed, as Jean-Philippe Rameau had pointed out, while consonance automatically supposes a tonality, dissonance does not and can be integrated only through overabundance. Unity and, in the broadest sense, harmony come—again, according to the author of *Traité de l'harmonie réduite à ses principes na-*

turels—through the attraction to consonance inherent in all dissonance.[29] The theory corresponds to psychological realities. Analogously, the Nephew's personality is overabundant, excessive; "[it] cuts into [that of] others." Diderot finds attractive his linguistic and social anomalies which "relieve that annoying uniformity that our education, our social conventions, our proper practices have introduced," simply because, in being off-key, they disclose a higher tonality of truth. "This is when the man with good common sense listens, and unravels his world." If only for this reason, Diderot leaves the Nephew as he leaves his own mind (or as a composer likes to leave his theme) "master to pursue the first wise or crazy idea that comes."

Style relates directly to the dithyrambic nature of the dialogue. Since this subject has been explored, only some brief comments which bear on a larger, organic, musical process are of relevance here. Otto Engelmayer remarks:

It is not by chance that Diderot lets the nature of language and linguistic expression be developed in the spirit of music through the genial musician Rameau. The expressive principle of language is the same as music's. We do not mean this in the sense of the ideal of harmony of the classics, or in the acoustic sense of Chateaubriand's euphony or Hugo's verses. For this, Diderot well lacked the lyrical qualities, despite his intimate relationship with music. He always thinks of a "musicalizing" of language in the sense of raising its expressive capacity and flexibility. This language, however, is not the spiritually rich language of pronouncements and madrigals. It is a language which, like music, is totally spontaneous reaction and appeals to the finest psychic movements and, like music, is directed exclusively by the rhythm and dynamics of psychic movement, not by reflection and theoretical rules.[30]

Four stylistic techniques are alternated and juxtaposed, very much like the themes and subjects which arrange themselves contrapuntally throughout *Le Neveu de Rameau*. Diderot heaps phrase upon phrase or word upon word (accumulation: "there he is a priest, king, tyrant, he threatens, commands, gets carried away; he is a slave, he obeys. He calms down, he gets desperate, he complains, he laughs"); or he proceeds by short phrase sequences (*coupé*: "Diogenes mocked needs—But one must be dressed—No. He went around completely naked—Sometimes it was cold in Athens—Not as much as here— People ate there—Probably—At whose expense?—Nature's"); or he rounds a sentence rhetorically (period: "If it does not displease the sublime minister you quoted to me, I believe that if a lie can be useful for one moment, it necessarily damages in the long run, and that, conversely, truth is necessarily useful in the long run, though it can happen that at a certain moment it is damaging"); or he allows for rises and falls or for conversational pauses (dynamics and statics: "And what the devil do you want me to use my money for, unless it's for a good meal, good company, good wines, beautiful women," and so on, followed by the more tranquil "But let's get back to Racine"). At no time is any one of these four devices so overemployed as to overshadow the others and control the movement of the whole scene. Note the few pages which follow the last pantomime, where the satire ends with real precipitation: a vivacissimo recitative is artfully restrained for a moment while Rameau reminisces about his wife, then gathers momentum again as it rushes to its laughing conclusion. The alternation or combination of techniques of this kind establishes what may be regarded as rhythm by pattern, a skillful manipulation, itself a form of orchestration, like the distribution of tonal color among the various families of instruments. Such relations, which underlie all rhythmic structures, provide the work with something akin to a texture of chords, or to a harmonic underpinning, as opposed to the horizontal motion of themes or melodies.

Two modes quite naturally render the "psychic movement" of the "tragedy-farce," as Carlyle called the satire: the minor and the major, depending on whether the conversation drifts into a pessimistic or an optimistic frame. As the fundamentally immoral character of all human society is repeatedly reviewed, the governing mode bears a minor impress. Yet the elevation of tone which the author achieves by making Rameau's farce attain the heights of tragedy and his tragedy express ironically the anguish of his farce suggests a kind of abstract melody, a prolonged overtone with positive resonance which assumes its own basically optimistic significance. Ostensibly pessimistic, *Le Neveu de Rameau* rises to transcendent assurances via music. There is an element of catharsis involved. It ramifies into the three directions of Lui, Moi, and the reader. In the first instance, it is consummated physically, for the process of physical exhaustion brings Rameau's complexes to consciousness. It affords them expression, and, while not eliminating them in the psychoanalytic sense, still enables him to experience, and us to sense, that stir of superior existence which his materialism, unrelieved, would have stifled. In the second instance, the consummation is intellectual. As the narrator discovers that Lui's views concern not only society but the very unconstrained, natural order of things, his catharsis comes about in the Aristotelian sense which would make the Nephew serve as a deterrent to humanity. This, despite Moi's granting a number of premises he had pas-

sionately refused to accept. In the third instance, that of the reader, apart
from whatever moral experience he may share with MOI (including the sympathy he is bound to feel for LUI, not out of any sense of complicity with
his dubious ethics, but rather out of a fuller understanding of an ultimately
more pitiful than shameful individual), the catharsis is of an entirely different order: it is aesthetic. It relates to the purification or purgation, again in
the Aristotelian sense, of the spectator who can eventually illuminate and
polarize the erratic debate; see it in terms of which neither interlocutor is
aware; and transcend it musically, shaping it into a significant musical experience. In more ways than one, Art alone survives the debacle of values
and is exalted. The gross materialistic premises in the aggregate contribute
more to a work of art than to one of philosophy. As in Greek tragedy, the
spectator's catharsis results from an experience of formal perfection, which,
by implication, represents order, unity, and consonance.

In *Le Neveu de Rameau* more than ever before, Diderot implemented his
statement of 1757: "The story will transport me beyond the scene,"[31] by
outstripping the often too confining logic of the novelist's construction and
by giving it a superior coherence. The freedom with which the dialogue
develops builds up, in my opinion, a most striking series of musical correspondences and comes as close as anything has come to belying Coleridge's
assertion that speech cannot present two ideas concurrently. I would speculate that Diderot's train of vision is too far-reaching and too orchestral to be
pursued in the ordinary ways of standard literary forms. He appears to wish
to create in the reader's mind a willing suspension, sufficient just to convey
overtones of music.[32] The structure of his piece, therefore, is musical *ana-
logically*. He subtly applies his musical devices, it would seem, in measured
dosages—enough to fuse opera, symphony, and theme and variations, the
three most practiced musical forms of his day—into something literarily
transcendent. Not that the idea of correlation between the arts was new; it
was not. In fact, Diderot did not favor confusing the arts, at least at the
expense of literature. But confusing the arts, and arriving at a higher form
of expression are two different things. If "Music is a language . . . , the
clavier is the alphabet, the keys are the letters [and] with these letters one
forms syllables; with these syllables, words; with these words, phrases; with
these phrases, a speech . . . ,"[33] then, as was the case with the *air-dis-
cours*, the converse is conceivable. For me, the satire stands out exactly and
primarily because it is a superb example of how much Diderot did to mul-

tiply artistic relations, thereby elevating the aesthetic level through which art becomes a joint creation of author and reader. With this as *Le Neveu de Rameau's* secret premise and ranking achievement, Diderot, I would argue, attained a veritable superaesthetic. And with this in mind, I look back and exclaim with Moi: "That was masterfully executed."

(*1963*)

10

FROM THE SUBLIME TO THE SUBLIMINAL: THE PROUST-BALZAC MUSICAL CONNECTION

La musique, c'est l'âme.
—Balzac

La musique, c'est l'âme devenue sonore.
—Proust

The musical presence in the works of Honoré de Balzac and Marcel Proust is clearly strong, though much less has been written about it in *La Comédie humaine*[1] as compared with *A la recherche du temps perdu*. We know both authors as astute observers of social mores and, above all, of the undercurrents or forces that shaped the profiles of their cultures, one hundred years apart, during the first part of the nineteenth century and the first part of the twentieth. But, as we also know, their sensibilities diverged. On the surface, the Romantic visionary and the psychological Impressionist would not seem to share too much ground, despite their common concern with society, and since the affective powers of music attack the psyche before they reveal themselves through social responses, critics, who—mistakenly—have become accustomed to reading Balzac only as a sociologist, have found it more natural to explore the intricacies of Proust's awareness of the art than Balzac's.

Both authors, however, had some kind of a grounding in music—not much, to be sure—that found its way into various significant events and moods of their works. A knowledge of music may not be acquired by dint of listening as easily as a knowledge of painting may be absorbed through observing. A painting can be described to the untutored; a sonata must be analyzed. Balzac and Proust had no mentors under whose tutelage they wrote their exquisite pages on the visual arts, whatever their familiarity with the thoughts of art historians. But each required a mentor for music, for insights into the way music hangs together or signifies. We live in a visual rather than auditory civilization: the palette is more immediate than an orchestration. Hence, Balzac needed his Jacques Strunz, who introduced the author of *Gambara* to the science of music, and Proust, regardless of his childhood lessons at the piano,[2] had his Reynaldo Hahn in later life to suggest to him the possibilities of musical development. More often than not, Balzac's orientation leaned outward displaying his pseudotechnical knowledge of the art and imbuing it with religious, indeed mystical, meaning, while Proust's leaned inward, superficially fascinated by technical questions, but really more concerned with undertaking a journey into the inner recesses of memory and the revelation of arcane paths to self-discovery, of recapturing one's own special dimension in time. Balzac's manner is inevitably more involuted, being guided spiritually by rounding out the notion of temporality into the concept of sublimity, of our essential aspiration from the hither to the timeless yon, to the ideal. Proust's, on the other hand, is more convoluted, as in a godless world it twists and turns sinuously onto itself and spreads throughout the fabric of our existential coming and going and its appurtenant emotional modes. And this manner produces a tonality, which Balzac's does not, thanks to a persistent use of musical images and metaphors that reminds me of Alejo Carpentier.

Yet the outer sublime and the inner subliminal ultimately meet. Balzac did not simply adumbrate Proust; he prefigured him. I am tempted to say that even their musical affinity for language might have hinted as much. We do not think readily of Balzac in this melo-linguistic context, but, as philologist Mario Roques said during the "Journées balzaciennes" at the University of Paris in 1950, anyone who can create a title as assonantly beautiful as *Le Lys dans la vallée* must perforce be a musician. Proust, on the other hand, does not surprise us when he creates that mellifluous title, *A l'ombre des jeunes filles en fleur.*

So much in Proust reminds the reader of Balzac because the latter, too, approached music on the level of the human psyche, of subconscious motivations that end by coloring our recessed feelings, restoring us to ourselves. Except for the matter of style, it could have been Proust jotting down these thoughts from *Massimilla Doni:* "In the language of music, to paint is to

awaken in our hearts through sounds certain memories or certain images of
our intelligence, and these memories and images have their colors; they are
sad or gay. . . . Each instrument has its mission and addresses itself to
certain ideas the way each color relates to certain feelings we have in us."
If melody captures the imagination and harmony the soul, as the protagonist
of *Gambara* likes to remind us, then their combined effect can arouse voluptuous or hyperphysical hallucinations. Says the good Schmucke about
his friend Pons in *Le Cousin Pons:* "Listening to him one became hallucin-
ated with whirls of images, tipsy with heady perfumes; one descended into
the supreme enchantments of music."

This amounts to a Proustian psychomusical credo composed of three in-
tertwined elements: dream, remembrance, and love. Balzac's correspondence with Mme Eve Hanska contains many references to their interrelation. Indeed, it has been pointed out that he might easily have defined good
music as that which intoxicates with love, cradles reverie, and stimulates
remembrance.[3] Such an attitude, to be sure, was in spirit not untypical of
that of the Romantic generation as a whole, beginning with E. T. A. Hoffmann. We need only think of Stendhal. But, as I have suggested over the
years, with Balzac the attitude acquired deep roots and modulated into conviction, and the conviction permeated all his work as it did Proust's. "To
listen to music means to love better . . . ; good remembrances get hold of
me when I hear good music . . . ; Religion, love, and music comprise the
triple expression of the same fact . . . ; to love and to find once more the
movements of my heart rendered well by the musician's phrases . . . ; there
is only music to express love."[4] In one way or another, many events are
shaped by the musical presence: in *Mémoires de deux jeunes mariées* (the
preservation of love through music), *La Femme de trente ans* (using music
to win a lover from a rival), *Un Drame au bord de la mer* (music and pure
affection), *Le Bal de Sceaux* and *Les Illusions perdues* (music as an instrument of transference of thoughts and feelings), *La Peau de chagrin* and
Modeste Mignon (music as confidant), *Béatrix* (music as catalyst in both
love's flowering and disillusion), *Ursule Mirouët* (music as the sole art whose
power "speaks to thought through thought itself, without the aid of words,
colors, or form," and where, as in *Melmoth réconcilié*, its mystical force
binds humans together, transporting them "to the very summits where faith
encounters its divine object, the Eternal"[5]), *Le Cousin Pons* (music used
therapeutically for the dying Pons)—and the enumeration could lengthen.

Reminiscences and expectations intermingle in *La Duchesse de Langeais*, particularly after the heroine retires to a Carmelite nunnery and her former lover, General de Montriveau, experiences, like Swann, "the vague recall of a wonderfully melancholy air" of yesteryear; "Terrible sensation!" expands Balzac, "to hope for the resurrection of a lost love, to find it still lost, to sense it mysteriously, after five years." As the situation unfolds and the religious tonalities increase, the author shows commensurate subtlety in expressing the fleeting intangibles of meaning that dart like brief flashes of understanding from the sound centers of music. The General's remembrance is effortless, like the involuntary memory stimulated by Vinteuil's *petite phrase* in the section entitled "Un amour de Swann," a psychological process to be encountered also in *Facino Cane* as a barcarolle theme conjured up instinctively the mysterious protagonist's recollection of his native Venice.

In *Massimilla Doni*, Balzac probes the psychopathological and the psychophysiological question; the work is, in his words, his *sujet psychique*. Tenor Genovese's turbulent infatuation with soprano Tinti, like Emilio's spellbound attraction to Massimilla, runs so deep that it obliterates the proper functioning of the muscles and the senses. In her absence, his bel canto rings superbly; in her presence, he becomes "a braying ass." The "inner keys," or nerve centers, are adversely affected. Balzac describes the eternal antithesis between passion and art: "When an artist is so unfortunate as to be full of the passion he wishes to express, he cannot depict it, for he becomes the thing itself instead of being its image." Latent in the subconscious, promptings of purity (for the spiritual Massimilla) and the secrets of sex (for the carnal Tinti) surface and disturb the relationships until their friends manage by subterfuge to restore nature's balance. In the course of things, as when Massimilla hears the first notes of the Overture to Rossini's *Mosè in Egitto* and feels a "convulsive movement" in relation to her secret suffering, the introspective power of music manifests itself by attributing to a given selection, whatever its merit, certain qualities of a most personal nature. We are reminded again of the Vinteuil phrase, this time as experienced by Marcel the narrator in the context of Albertine. Massimilla confesses: "The situation has become so much part of me that this too gay passage is filled with sadness for me." When listening to music, it is not always music we hear but, Marcel discovered, ourselves—hence, for Balzac, its "divine power," its association with the sublime. It flails destructively if passion tips the balance at the expense of art, but it sublimates if the balance is fixed. "This power over our internal being is one of music's greatnesses"; it lives by dream, remembrance, and love, absorbing them into a transcendent ideal.

This idealism becomes the underlying philosophical theme of *Gambara*, whose Hoffmannian mad genius of a composer anticipates elements of musical aesthetics (i.e., atonality) that were to be experimented with during Proust's generation. Again the principle of involuntary memory emerges: "Does not [music] awaken remembrances by now torpid? Take a thousand people in a hall: a motif comes forth . . . ; the phrase . . . that enters all those people develops in them as many different poems: one sees a woman dreamed over a long time . . . ; some woman recalls the thousand feelings that tortured her during a jealous hour; another one . . . depicts herself as an ideal being with the rich colors of dream," and so on. But through Gambara, Balzac reaches beyond the earthy boundaries of the human toward the superhuman sphere of creation; when drunk, his music establishes human contact, but when sober, sitting at the total instrument of his invention, the fantastic Panharmonicon, he performs his "idea-music," sounds that exist only for him in his overheated imagination and that sever his ties with his dismayed listeners. "That man's intelligence has two windows: one is closed to the world, the other is open to the heavens." Unfortunately, too great an idea strangles that very idea; Gambara was not a god who could create from nothingness, for, like Frenhofer the painter in *Le Chef-d'oeuvre inconnu*, he lacked the secret of that coercive force discussed in *La recherche de l'Absolu* which would have granted him infinite realizations. He was only a man; his will could follow only physically determined laws and their limited progressions. But by the same token he could dream, and in so doing, remain faithful to "the IDEAL."

A heavenly fervor inbued this ideal. In his outward extension of the powers of music, Balzac equated it with religion, with the sublime so spiritually expressed in *Séraphîta*. Influenced by mystics like Swedenborg and Saint-Martin,[6] it is not difficult to see his basic awareness of music, which was psychological, nourished by the Swede's mystical utterances on "musicalia et cantica," whereby music and love, the harmonies of sounds and the harmonies of colors and visual things, happiness and the spiritual world, are conjoined in a transcendent idealization. Synesthesia and the theory of correspondences shape the universe. Balzac was of no mind to refuse the visionary opportunity. For him, the sublime of "divine music" ultimately guides the human psyche.

For Proust, on the other hand, music functions subliminally, exclusively below the threshold of consciousness or apprehension. If, as for Balzac too, it involves stimuli that become effective subconsciously before becoming so consciously, for Proust their ultimate (though not immediate) effectiveness relies on repetition, and through repetition the substantiation of memory. What Balzac elevated, Proust deepened, pulling music down from its "divine world." What the former heard and analyzed with his heart, the latter did with his brain, though he spoke as if from the heart. One found space in music; the other—thanks to repetition—time. Balzac's search for the sublime was a search for beauty in all its spaciousness, as distinguished from that of his later counterpart, whose sense of musical space, if any, derived primarily from his greater suppleness in working with the art, in blending its rolling movement broadly into the same rhythms of his *temps retrouvé*. Both saw music as ennobling, but while one stressed spiritual elevation, the other embraced its moral quality;[7] here Vinteuil himself becomes a role model.

Consistently, Balzac and Proust appear as the reverse sides of the Euterpean medal. My point is that it is the same medal. Even with more confidence in the intellect, Gambara might easily have uttered the Narrator's "Swann held that musical motifs were real ideas belonging to another world, another order—ideas veiled with shadows, unknown, impenetrable by the mind, but which for all that are perfectly distinguishable one from the other, unequal among themselves as to value and meaning": hence the art's ability to uncover our intimate, usually unsuspected, private world. In the words of one critic, "Those illuminations, making the Narrator see (as Vinteuil's *petite phrase* did to Swann) the unhoped for possibility of a new existence, and making those invisible realities sensible to his soul, free as it was from hesitation—those illuminations inspired, together with that desire for inner renewal, an impulse to dedicate his life to them."[8] And just as Wagner's music brought Baudelaire around to himself,[9] "the [Vinteuil] music helped me to descend into myself, to find something new there," as we read in *La Prisonnière*, and Modeste, Ursule, Pons, Massimilla on hearing Rossini; Montriveau on hearing "Fleuve du Tage"; or Balzac himself on hearing Bellini's *La sonnambula*—all find themselves subject to the identical psychic force. But what distinguishes Proust's analysis in the long run is the subtle, refined, and remarkably accurate psychological probing in the face of the dual factors of memory and repetition:

Swann, then, was not wrong in believing that the Sonata's phrase really existed. Human as far as this perspective went, it certainly still belonged to a supernatural order of creatures that we have never seen, but which we nonetheless recognize with delight when some explorer of the invisible manages to capture one, to drag it down from the divine world to which it has access, and to shine for a few moments above ours. This is what Vinteuil did for the *petite phrase.* . . . There were admirable ideas there that Swann had not distinguished at first hearing and that he perceived now, as if, in the vestiary of his memory, they had got rid of their uniform disguise of novelty. . . . Perhaps what is lacking the first time is not understanding but memory.

These pasages from *Du côté de chez Swann* and *A l'ombre des jeunes filles en fleur* identify Proust himself as that "explorer of the invisible."

No technical knowledge of music, as Balzac attempted to acquire, is necessary for such an exploration. Proust proceeds by sensations. Indeed, no technical comments inform his novelistic text, just as no allusions to instruments are to be found in the fragments of his *carnets*, though one critic claims he became early interested in woodwinds.[10] In self-defense, he tells us through Swann's narrator: "Perhaps it was because he did not know music that he was able to experience such a confused impression, one of those impressions which yet may be the only purely musical ones, unextended, entirely original, and irreducible to any order of impressions." Sensation was fundamental, and even the technically educated, Proust thought, approached the art on this level, whether they realized it or not. A sentence in *Les Plaisirs et les jours* underscores this: "The musician, who yet claims that he only enjoys a technical pleasure in music, still experiences significant emotions, but wrapped up in his own way of conceiving musical beauty which hides them from his own eyes."

These and other reasons have always led me to suspect that Proust reacted to sound more than to "music," formally speaking, as an art. Sound, after all, constitutes the root element of the psychological stimulus, insofar as feelings relate to the sound factor. As has been suggested, "the description of music is less important than the feelings that entice it."[11] Seen this way, it is not surprising to come across many bewildering appreciations of his that would equate noise with music—in the manner of John Cage today—except that Cage evolves an aesthetic around the concept of noise, whereas

Proust plays with the random and often unlikely associations of which the mind is capable. Sounding frequently contrived because of the highly subjective nature of the narrator's expression, they are not always convincing, but they do highlight Proust's irony vis-à-vis the unsophisticated social climbers and help give a tonality to his universe and that society to which he applies his psychological scalpel. I am referring to the "music" of the train in *A l'ombre des jeunes filles en fleur:* "First four equal semiquavers, then a furiously precipitious semiquaver against a *noir*"; of the automobile in *Pastiches et mélanges* ("En mémoire des églises assassinées"): "From time to time—St. Cecilia would improvise on an even more immaterial instrument—[the chauffeur] touched his keyboard and got from it one of the scherzos *[jeux]* from those organs concealed inside the automobile whose music we hardly recognize, which is nonetheless continuous and changes its registers with the shifting of gears; the music is, so to speak, abstract, made up entirely of symbol and number, making us think of that harmony which, they say, the spheres produce when they turn in the ether"—a notion complemented in *Pastiches et mélanges* when young Proust imagines the anxious emotions of his awaiting parents at the sound of the klaxon as he is being driven home:

I thought that in *Tristan und Isolde* (first in the second act when Isolde waves her scarf as a signal, then in the third act with the arrival of the ship) the first time it is to two notes, repeatedly strident, undefined, and more and more rapid, whose succession is sometimes produced by chance in the disorganized world of noises; and the second time it is to the reed-pipe of a young shepherd, to its growing intensity, to the insatiable monotony of its slender song, that Wagner, through an apparent and genial abdication of his creative powers, entrusted the expression of the most stupendous anticipation of happiness that ever filled the human soul.

With reference to Wagner, I am referring also to the music of the door on the landing that closes with a draft in *A l'ombre des jeunes filles en fleur,* which performs "the hatching of voluptous and sighing phrases that lie above the Pilgrims's Chorus toward the end of the overture to *Tannhäuser*." Beethoven can also be called into play, in the same work, with reference to the music of the valve by the fireplace: "like the famous bow-stops with which the Symphony in C Minor begins." And so can Bach and Debussy, in *Le côté de Guermantes,* where the shrill laughter of Charlus resembles the "little trumpets that are necessary to perform certain works by Bach," and where the snail vendor raises the price of his gastropod mollusks like modulations

in *Pelléas et Mélisande*. And in *Sodome et Gomorrhe*, it is the telephone
that provides the musical frame, when Marcel listens for the call that will
let him know if Albertine will spend the evening with him: "I was tortured
by the constant return of my desire, ever more anxious . . . , clamoring to
appeal; . . . suddenly, mechanical and sublime, like the scarf waved in
Tristan or the shepherd's reed-pipe, I heard the noise of the telephone."
Given this musical sensitivity to noise, the snoring of Marcel's aunt and the
throat rattling of his grandmother, which become "more melodious" as they
"change register," do not come as a surprise. When it comes to Wagner
especially, one commentator can easily lament the fact that Proust did not
consult the score of *Tristan und Isolde* more closely.[12]

These—for me—basically ludic free associations, make André Coeuroy
think of, among others, Balzac,[13] but in my opinion nothing could be more
distorted. Balzac never subjectified and interiorized music to such a free-
associational extent; he shared with us its sublimity without feeling he had
to invite us into "the vestiary of our memory" and introduce us to his private
convolutions. Outside his own world, Proust's analogies are surely forced.
In matters of portrait, he met Balzac only on the level of the physiological,
of Massimilla's and Genovese's traumas, though Proust's descriptions are
necessarily ironical: the neural reaction detectable in Mme Verdurin's facial
twists as she listens to the Sonata, Mme de Cambremer's salivary glands that
"enter a phase of hypersecretion" the moment she talks of music, and the
Narrator's association of the scent of roses with *Pelléas et Mélisande*: "It is
so strong in the score that, since I have hay-fever and rose-fever, it made
me sneeze each time I heard that scene."

Balzac always referred to "good music"—*la bonne musique*. Not so Proust
who, some commentators find, is refreshing in that he can unabashedly,
from the individual intimacy of his private world, write about "bad music."
In his *Les Plaisirs et les jours*, we read an "Eloge de la mauvaise musique,"
a piece betraying less a sensitivity to the formal art than a responsiveness to
the ready pleasure of sound, in this case to what has an immediate appeal
to the masses, however cheap, through an "annoying refrain" or a "bad
romance." "Hate bad music, don't despite it. . . . It became slowly filled
with the dreams and tears of man. . . . Its place, it has none in the history
of art, is immense in the sentimental history of societies." Balzac has been
chided for loving "Le Songe de Rousseau" or the "Fleuve du Tage" by those
very persons who would find keen wisdom in Proust's "What does it matter

that houses have no style, that tombs disappear under inscriptions or ornaments of bad taste? Before an imagination sympathetic and respectful enough
to silence for a moment all aesthetic disdain, there can swarm from that
dust a flock of souls gripping in their bill a still green dream that makes
them sense the next world or that makes them cry in this one."

Balzac's Euterpean heroes were Beethoven, Rossini, Mozart, Bellini, Ci-
marosa, Paganini, Weber, Liszt, Chopin, Palestrina, Berlioz, Gluck—and I
might add Meyerbeer except for the fact that the composer of *Robert le
Diable* ultimately paled in the presence of the composer of the Fifth Symphony.[14] (I am reminded here of the *gaminerie* of Proust's Morel in *Le côté
de Guermantes*, who played a Meyerbeer march which the whole unsophisticated audience found admirable, thinking it had listened to a piece by
Debussy.) Proust's heroes included some of Balzac's (Chopin and Beethoven
primarily,[15] through the latter's quartets like nos. 8, 11, and 14), but focused
significantly and more resrictedly on his contemporaries, notably Wagner,
Debussy, Saint-Saëns, Franck. . . . This means to me that Proust's range
of sympathies was much more confined and parochial than Balzac's, which
was more historical. Admittedly, during the first half of the nineteenth century the musical stage belonged to Beethoven and Rossini, and during the
first part of the twentieth it belonged to Wagner and Debussy—and to this
extent each writer's breathing the cultural ecology of his day is understand-
able. But omitting Ravel and Verdi from the private pantheon of one's early-
twentieth-century universe is quite strange. If the traditional Verdi made
him shudder in his basically Northern boots, what could possibly have made
Proust insensitive to *Falstaff*? More puzzling: If any composer fit the Proustian mold—structurally, melodically, and rhythmically—it was Ravel. Even
Vinteuil's Septet has a way of reminding the reader of the *Introduction et
allégro pour harpe, quatuor à cordes, flûte et clarinette*. Yet, *A la recherche
du temps perdu* contains only one insignificant reference to the composer,
and in associating him with Palestrina, in *Le côté de Guermantes*, he shows
that he is as impervious to the French impressionist as he is ignorant of the
Italian contrapuntalist. Indeed, in contexts of this kind it does appear that
as a "musician" Proust has been overrated and Balzac underrated.

But on balance the connection between the novelists remains steady and
strong. Does not Proust elaborate on Gambara's Panharmonicon when he
writes in *Du côté de chez Swann:* "He knew . . . that the field open to a
musician is not a meager seven note keyboard but an immeasurable key-

board, still almost all unknown, with millions of keys, here and there, separated by thick and unexplored shadows"? The madman's instrument, which
for him produced "celestial harmonies" that bore him upward to the door-
step of angels, is converted subliminally into a metaphorical keyboard with
"keys of tenderness, passion, courage, serenity . . . , a universe inside another universe." Wagner seemed to Proust to be this universe inside a universe, which was Gambara's dream, and it is natural, therefore, that a fundamental affinity exist between an author who adumbrated Wagner and an
author who admired him. Gambara's vision exploded with theories to which
post-Wagnerian twentieth-century schools of composition have confessed—
something that has labeled Balzac "the commentator of Wagner before
Wagner." Both Gambara, through is opera *Mahomet*, and Wagner were
concerned with treating a divine drama while representing human nature,
with the reconcilability of their means to the symbolism of ideas. Both molded
expression as closely as possible on idea, avoiding fancy manner for its own
sake, developing a symphonic style into the fabric of the drama, applying
bold modulations to accompany movement through a lively transposition of
orchestral colors. Gambara pursued the history of humanity, "the depiction
of the life of peoples," in the form of a trilogy that foreshadows the *Ring*
tetralogy. (The idea of treating the story of Siegfried did not come to Wagner
until eleven years after the publication of *Gambara*.) Balzac's harmonic description of major thirds, fourths without sixths in the bass, fifth, seventh,
octave, and ninth chords is clearly Wagnerian, and when we add to it his
suggestion of the whole-tone scale, we introduce Proust's other great deity,
Debussy (and Moussorgsky). Gambara also broached the vibratory theory of
sound when it was nearly unknown and made persistent parallels between
music and light (so did Frenhofer for painting in his anticipation of Paul
Cézanne and Juan Gris), to which he accorded an importance equal to that
of sounds in the production of ideas. Scriabine is around the corner. I like
to say that post-Wagnerian composers like Schönberg and Berg, the masters
of atonality, inherited Gambara's "deafening cacophony," and that *Mahomet* in theory and *Die Walküre* in practice are links in the chain that
stretches across the last century into our own.

   Not the least important connection is Balzac's interest in the idea of a
continuous melody, which was to characterize *Mahomet*, and particularly
in the leitmotif—Berlioz's *idée fixe* and Weber's innovations notwithstanding—that melody or phrase "which doubles back onto itself" (*qui revient*

sur elle-même), as he aptly says. As usual, Proust internalizes and expands the principle. He rejects the Beethovenian aesthetic of not stuffing into one sonata ideas sufficient to nourish ten of them, but he is careful to exploit the one principle that alone gives coherence to his entire work, the leitmotif, diffusing it in all possible directions. His only rivals in this context are Mann and D'Annunzio. "In all the work of Wagner," writes one critic of Proust, "there is no leitmotif employed more significantly and capably than that *petite phrase* of Vinteuil, from the moment it presides over the birth of Swann's love, accompanies the phases of that same love, reanimates remembrance, then passes into the service of the narrator himself, leaving the image of Odette and attaching itself to that of Albertine."[16] Says Proust in the first book as the phrase "doubles back onto itself":

Even when he was not thinking of the *petite phrase*, it existed latently in his mind in the same manner as certain other notions without equivalence, like notions of light, sound, relief, physical passion, that are our rich possessions with which our inner life is diversified and graced. . . . Because of that, the Vinteuil phrase, like a theme in *Tristan*, for example, which also represents for us a certain sentimental possession, had wedded our mortal condition, acquired something human—which was quite touching.

It has also been claimed that Marcel's musical reflections correspond to the dynamism of the creation of Albertine and that the lyrical dimension of Wagner's music gives an illusion of life created by the repetition of leitmotifs.[17]

Under the category of musical expressiveness, Proust brings to mind his contemporary, Gabriele D'Annunzio, about whom I shall permit myself a perhaps gratuitous, yet for me congruent, digression in order to place the Frenchman's accomplishment into a more definable perspective. More often than not, here we come face to face, not with the *idea* of music, but with its applicability to style. With D'Annunzio, in time his Nietzscheanism and Symbolism yield to musical Decadence in the best and most airy sense through his desire to melt words into music. While his visual and lyrical Impressionism is sensory like Proust's, it is also more fragile, and not infrequently fragmented (especially in his poetry). As a Wagnerian, he is well known; his *Il Fuoco* and *Vergini delle roccie* are cases in point, as is his often noted interpretation of *Tristan und Isolde* in *Trionfo della morte*—an interpretation, I might add, not more penetrating than Proust's, though stylistically equally sensitive. An adept employer of the leitmotif, D'Annunzio gives verbal undulations and sinuosity to his language in a manner mastered by Proust and never even attempted by Balzac. In his nocturnal diary *Notturno*, for example, all his themes—love of the sensory life, self-celebration, self-lamentation, lyrical cries and sighs, dream, remembrance—come together, after having wandered throughout the text, into a final, "musical" resolution. One critic refers to a gathered, internal music, to images dense with recollections, especially to images of the night in variation, "like a leitmotif, in fact, like a reprise of the note that would like to remain the dominant tone."[18] In a sense, the Italian poet takes Proust a step further in verbal subtleties and the sentiment that fades into rhythmic mellifluousness (because often he does not care to match his syntax with what he is describing), given as he is to a desire to transfigure reality rather than to penetrate it like Proust. But he frequently sounds like Proust. *Il Fuoco* describes the arrival of the queen in Venice:

A new clamor, louder and longer, arose between the two tutelary granite columns while the eight-oared boat moored by the congested Piazzetta. As the black and dense crowd undulated during the pause, the empty spaces in the ducal loggias were filling with a confused noise similar to that illusory roar that animates the whorls of marine spiral shells. Then, suddenly, the clamor climbed up again into the clear air, broke up through the slender forest of marble, surpassed the fonts of the tall statues, reaching the pinnacles and the crosses, and dissipated in the crepuscular distance. Unperturbed, above the agitation below, during a new pause, continued the multiple harmony of the sacred and profane architecture over which the ionic modulations of the Biblioteca drifted like an agile melody, while the summit of the naked tower rose like a mystic cry. And that silent music of the immobile lines was so powerful that it created the almost visible phantom of a more beautiful and richer life, superimposing it onto the spectacle of the restless multitude. It felt the divinity of the hour.

Moreover, he is not sensitive to the virtues of continuous melody. Any one of his texts illustrates this, including his *Il libro segreto:* "Oh that smell of tranquil honey and of still moist bread under the crust that a guilder, idle because of lack of golden foil, tempered in the oven's mouth to the maximum richness and delicacy of his home-made guilding." It took *Le Martyre de Saint Sébastien* to bring out the full power of his verbal music, unbounded by strictures of structure and like the dissolution of musical phrases in its fragmentariness, and to take a definitive step beyond Proust. He wrote it in (archaic) French and—appropriately—in collaboration with Debussy, that "airy inventor" (his words), whose slow and wandering music had affected his *Canto novo*, and whose suggestive, languid, tender, fragmented, and fragile craft fit the tenor of his drama perfectly (see the Prélude, Canticus Geminorum, Chorus Seraphycus, and Sébastien's ecstatic dance). "Debussy . . . , I believe, taught Gabriele D'Annunzio something of his secret, of his weightless art."[19] With his lofty vision, Balzac might have hailed this stylistically musical feat, though not emulated it. Proust does, but with the signal advantage of treating music not just metaphorically, like D'Annunzio most of the time (since for him it was ultimately a matter of style) but, rather, like the veritable art of sounds it represents.

Proust's greatness, then, comes in his structural elaboration of the musical presence and in the intimate relationship he establishes between style and subject. Balzac talks musical theory; D'Annunzio transforms music into words; Proust employs music. Albertine and the use of leitmotifs is hardly the only example to be adduced. Marcel Butor likes to stress Proust's metaphor of the prism—"the spectrum exteriorizes for us . . . the harmony of a Wagner," we read in *La Prisonnière*—and the Septet indeed acts that way, broadcasting color tones throughout.[20] I would not relate the prisms' seven colors to the seven instruments of the chamber work, but I would stress, with Souza,[21] its "architectural" function: by having it performed during that evening at the Verdurins, the revelation in *Le temps retrouvé* is prepared. In fact, the very expansion achieved by the *petite phrase*, modulating and expanding from sonata to quartet to quintet to a planned sextet to a finished septet to even a symphony, as was anticipated, becomes like an engulfing evolution that has caused Vinteuil's phrase to be considered the key to Proust's art and soul. In its own way, and because of the moving and shifting associations of its leitmotif quality, it floats inside the text as a form of continuous melody, exercising its prolonged action in ways that Balzac could not have envisioned but creating what Balzac, an admirer of the organ and the function of the pedal-point, would have called an "intimate humming" *(bourdonnement intime)*. Not unlike D'Annunzio's, Proust's writing process is that "humming" like a Ravel quartet realizing itself as it moves along, discovering itself through execution, writing like Balzac under the stimulus of a musical inspiration (perhaps little more than a comment by Strunz or Hahn) but using, instead of Balzac's *passé simple*, the imperfect, the *éternel imparfait*. This allows for musical overlaps, thematic intertwining, the ambiguities of fragmentary melody, ultimately brought together in recaptured time. If we need to reread Balzac, it is to grasp the nuance that slipped by the first time; if we need to reread Proust, it is because we have to, in order that memory clear new paths for us, in the same spirit that we listen again to a symphony we have heard, or dip again into the night of D'Annunzio's *Notturno*.

For both Balzac and Proust, the ubiquitous reality of love was subjective, a disposition of the individual soul that music blends with and fully stimulates, fostering a desire, with all its anxieties and presentiments, for the absolute, which Balzac seeks in the sublime and Proust in the subliminal. Music is often the heartbeat of *La Comédie humaine* and usually the mindset of *A la recherche du temps perdu*, Ganymede's intoxicating cup and Ariadne's discovering thread, because it furbishes dream and substantiates memory.

[11]

MOTIF AND LEITMOTIF:
MANN IN SEARCH OF WAGNER[1]

A terminological confusion usually characterizes the transference of nomen-clature from one art to another. Literary critics in particular, who, more zealously than their counterparts in the other arts, seem keenly bent upon coining new terms to describe new approaches, seize upon musical termi-nology and twist it to do their bidding. Thus "counterpoint," instead of signifying several independent ideas sounded simultaneously yet in comple-mentary posture, comes to mean simply a juxtaposition of two thoughts or characters or actions, whatever their timing or relationship. The same hap-pens to the term "polyphony" or "fugue" which, like counterpoint, is fre-quently violated by being thought of merely as a multifaceted presentation, with no concern for the fact that the facets, like layers, must sound together, vertically, working into and affecting each other's patterns.

Leitmotif has suffered from similar misuse. It has become an imposing Germanism, like *Weltanschauung* or *Doppelbegabung* (world view or mul-tiple talent would do just as well if not better), to mean motif, or nonmus-ically speaking, theme. So employed, it has become a mere snobbism. Thus, we read about the leitmotifs of death, disease, art, sexuality, the forbidden married woman, the father-son syndrome, the bourgeoisie, and the like, that cross the entire opus of Thomas Mann, when in reality each provides nothing more than a theme or motif, a characteristic ingredient of all good extended fiction. Any number of critics has confused leitmotif with symbol[2] or broadened the meaning of motif into leitmotif from a single work to the author's entire opus[3] (example: the "leitmotif" of death from *Buddenbrooks* to *Doktor Faustus*), thus depleting the musical term of its significance and value. The recurrence of a sense of death, for example, without intertextual links of a recalling or associative order, does not make it a leitmotif. Nor does the reappearance, in a single work like *Der Zauberberg,* of a hat (characteristically worn by middle-class newcomers to Davos who still thought in Flatland terms of proper attire). Nor does the repetition of the word *unheimlich* (uncanny), with which Hans Castorp describes so many of his experiences in the sanatorium. And when another scholar writes, "two *leitmotifs* are sounded to confuse each major appearance of the 'loved one' [Clawdia Chauchat]—the *Pribislav Hippe* pattern [Hans Castorp's association of Clawdia with a strong adoration he had felt in school for a classmate] and the *theme of death* [his feelings of love for Clawdia always accompanied by injury, dread, or disease],"[4] he is only talking of the traditional themes of love and death that flow in and out of each other in Hans Castorp's *Liebestod* experience at the Berghof. One might also include among such motifs examples of Mann's oppositional bias in *Der Zauberberg,* a juxtaposition of two elements in dialectical relation resulting in the fusion of a double state or a double activity. The sensation of a hot forehead coupled with cold feet repeatedly grips Hans Castorp; the elements merge on the physical level of his body the way any number of emotional or intellectual antipathies will meld to inform his integrated experience on the mountain. In like fashion, "das Unheimlische" creates a confrontation over and over again between the known and the strange. Again, the protagonist's notion that "accustoming" (*Gewöhnung*) lies in "getting used to not getting used" (*dass man sich nicht gewöhnte*) promotes the motif of the oppositional.

   To convert any of these motifs into leitmotifs is to misuse the Wagnerian model that Mann had placed before himself. From the literary perspective, the best definition of leitmotif has been articulated by Calvin Brown: a formula which is deliberately repeated, in music or in literature; which is easily recognized at each recurrence; and which serves, by means of this recognition, to link the context in which the repetition occurs with earlier contexts in which the motif has appeared.[5] Richard Wagner, who associated it with the fixed Homeric epithet—not dissimilarly from Hector Berlioz's notion of the *idée fixe* or from Carl Maria von Weber's or Giuseppe Verdi's fashioning of repeated phrases—and who further infused it with distinct, psychological associations, would not have quibbled with this definition. In searching for a way to transpose the musical into the literary, Mann experimented in *Tonio Kröger* with a common, mechanical, indeed crude incorporation of the device based on sheer repetitions known stylistically to other writers from Goethe to Dickens to Zola. He realized the artificiality of the results; the searching effort was too evident and the effect too unliterary. Music thrives on overt as well as on covert repetition that in a novel can become an irritating stylistic fallacy. *Tonio Kröger's* recurrent phrases, sometimes with insignificant changes, do nothing for the narration (e.g., "a tall, carefully dressed man [the hero's father] with thoughtful blue eyes, who always wore a wild flower in his buttonhole"; "shoving back his cuffs with his little fingers"; "over the Millwall and over the Holstenwall"; "we are not gypsies living in a green wagon"; "[Ingeborg's] narrow blue eyes"; "the man who was perched upon the last"). In his 1936 Preface to *Stories of Three Decades*, the author wrote that in *Tonio Kröger* he first saw music as a shaping influence in his writing through "a weaving of themes, as a musical complex of associations" which he employed later in *Der Zauberberg* with a "less mechanical, more musical character," not in the context of form alone, but in that of "emotion and idea" as well. Even so, there are carry-overs of the mechanical, purely formal (though less crude) use of the device in *Der Zauberberg:* Hans Castorp's repeated self-reference adopting Settembrini's epithet, "delicate child of life" *(Sorgenkind des Lebens)*; the many allusions to the vulgarity and stupidity of Frau Stöhr; or Madame Chauchat's slamming of the dining room door each time she passes through it, thus providing, among other things, a percussive component for the novel's symphonic texture.

But *Der Zauberberg* is also structured along more subtle lines involving the leitmotif. One consequence of the greater subtlety—meaning the more intricate employment—is the less frequent appearance of individual motifs. Writes Ronald Peacock comparing the earlier novella with the later novel: "While [in *Tonio Kröger*] the fabric of the leitmotif is extremely dense, [in *Der Zauberberg*] it is relatively thin."[6] The reader can make his way through several hundred pages of narration without reencountering a motif. For this reason, Mann himself suggests that the novel be read more than once to feel the leitmotif structure: for a leitmotif pushes a memory button and need not be recalled immediately to remain itself, just as it can be changed and modified according to varying situations and still retain its identity.

Selectively, four veritable leitmotifs can be identified to indicate Mann's Wagnerian touch—by which we mean that, while enjoying their own development, they are all interrelated in a finely woven tapestry of images, ideas, and symbols. Their importance is underscored by the fact that each claims a chapter or two in which it is stressed, like an emphatic statement of the motif, and thereby brought to a heightened awareness in the consciousness of Hans Castorp. They are the *Devil*, the *Middle Ages*, the color *White*, and the phenomenon of *Music*. There are more, to be sure, but the intent of this selection is purely illustrative.

1.   *The Devil*. Several chapters are devoted to him: "Satana" and "Vom Gottesstaat und von übler Erlösung." The theme, most closely connected with Settembrini, the Mephistophelian character or Tempter, first appears in "Satana" connected with the Italian humanist in a sanatorium equated with Hell where the doctor is the devil. Two kinds of devils are immediately established: the rebellious, critical spirit of the Italian poet Giosuè Carducci's fiend, admired by Settembrini (the critical mind), and the medieval spirit of darkness and disease, equated with the Settembrinian rhetoric concerning the forces at work in the Berghof sanatorium. The Devil leitmotif combines the material and the spiritual. The first corresponds with the Mephistophelian element in the worldly humanist as he tries to beguile and influence Hans Castorp. The second belongs to the religious sphere represented by Naphta, where God and Devil merge to oppose *Lebensbürgerlichkeit*. A complex leitmotif, the *Devil* combines these two forces. In contrast with these juxtapositional devils, the novel peppers the diabolical image with innocuous everyday allusions, such as Hofrat's warning to Hans Castorp: "If you continue along that vein down there, my dear sir, the devil will have your lung before you can blink an eye." Later in the novel, the English patients play a parlor game called "Did you ever see the devil with a nightcap on?"—an innocent use of the word that prolongs a tonality in the novel, revealing, to the attentive reader, how the motif expands into a multi-leveled mechanism creating associations and recognitions.

2.   Not surprisingly, the theme of the Devil connects evocatively through the *Middle Ages*; the bridging chapter is "Vom Gottesstaat und von übler Erlösung." The fixing chapter is "Operationes spirituales." The embodiment of medieval doctrine, combining the spiritual and material worlds with a spirit of terrorism, is Settembrini's opposite, Naphta. Asceticism and solemnity reach Hans Castorp through the solemn bearing of the medievally portrayed grandfather portrait. Settembrini associates the medieval with illness and the praise of suffering, remarking about the sanatorium: "Here is much that strikes one as medieval." And indeed, there is an aristocracy of illness among the patients—a grotesqueness mirrored in Naphta's "Pietà," a Gothic painting that strikes Hans Castorp as both ugly and beautiful (the oxymoronic syndrome of opposites) at the same time. A certain praise of disease and suffering prevails, making these "medievally" associated conditions more attractive to the protagonist than the wordly, unmystic rationalisms of Settembrini. The Middle Ages program Hans Castorp's mood in the frame of timelessness, or time-remoteness, an awareness of which reaches him only through symbols; a dialectical fusion of good and evil, of the spiritual and the material, without even a yin-yang distinctiveness, strikes an outsider like Settembrini as "a disgusting hodgepodge" (*ein ekelhafter Mischmasch*).

This *Mischmasch* shapes the mood of Hans Castorp's experience as it recurs with expanding significance.

3. In the novel, *White* operates referentially on many levels. To begin with, the sanatorium is essentially white: "The walls shimmered white and bright" *(hart)*, and within them one talks of the dining room shimmering with milk or sees antisceptic white furniture. In chapter one, the mountains lie under "everlasting snow," and it is not surprising to see Clawdia Chauchat's skin and clothes portrayed in the same color, or to read of Dr. Krokowski's phosphorous complexion. Neither is it to be told of Hofrat's white coat or of Myneer Peeperkorn's crownlike halo of white hair. But the color finds its most complete and rewarding expression on the eternal snow of the mountain, in the appropriately entitled chapter "Schnee," where it becomes the nothingness that dissolves calendric time and, interconnectedly with music, serves to produce a dreamlike state that prepares the protagonist's epiphany. A mere purveyor of mood at the outset, "white" expands into an idea.

4. All this culminates in the structural leitmotif by which the sanatorium seems to breathe: *Music* itself, present at Hans Castorp's arrival and sounding its refrains throughout the novel, thereby interconnecting his experiences. The patients walk to the beat of a march; the amorous couple next to room 34 moves to the tempo of a waltz. Hymns, polkas, dances are constantly heard, infiltrating most of the novel's concerns, just as music itself, in Mann's view, connects with the phenomenon of narrating or writing, given their common denominator in time. "Narrative is like music in that it fills time." Thus Hans Castorp cannot be disassociated from the art of sounds, not only because of his veneration of it, as illustrated in the chapter "Fölle des Wohllauts," but also because of its capacity to induce a certain passive emotional state—one which the rationalist Settembrini finds "politically suspicious," as if echoing a distant Platonic diffidence. Before the vision of Hippe, Hans Castorp is singing, and as he sees his heart in the X-ray room and realizes his mortality, he makes a "musical" face: "To this he made a face as he was used to doing when he listened to music: somewhat dull, sleepy, and pious." Yet the art accompanies each of the protagonist's epiphanies; indeed, in the snow epiphany, the entire scene is filled with music. It might even be argued that a hidden reason for Hans Castorp's finally leaving the sanatorium was the shallowness of its inhabitants, who looked at music brainlessly and without his own passionate involvement. Music becomes a mindscape in which Hans Castorp plants his successive learning experiences.

These leitmotifs interconnect with fine sartorial skill. One of the novel's major concerns being Time, Mann states in his Preface that Hans Castorp's story stems "out of the depth of the past," that it is "covered with historic mold." Therefore, the leitmotif of the Middle Ages offers us the needed remoteness from the present, the time of the "Flatland" and the linear, progressive concept of chronology in the twentieth century. For the Middle

Ages, time was circular, just as the notion of history was figurative, not linear. *Der Zauberberg*, states Mann, possesses the quality of a legend, which is a timeless story.

In the medieval legends, the Devil received full, mythological expression, representing worldliness and the dark forces that tempt man away from Eternal Salvation. Drawing from medieval remoteness, the leitmotif of the Devil underscores the novel's legendary quality while emphasizing the demonic forces that underlie civilized man and that reach a heightened sensibility on that mountain, so removed from the everyday world. In this, the presence of the Devil throughout the novel parallels the vision of the blood sacrifice in Hans Castorp's epiphany: the evil upon which or out of which, like a Freudian sublimation, stems the good. Moreover, the notion of the Devil as tempter also suits those who see the novel as a *Bildungsroman*. The protagonist feels himself pulled both ways between Naphta and Settembrini, who fight over his soul "like God and the Devil in medieval legends." In an epilogue, Mann notes that the lesson Hans Castorp learns is "that one must have a knowledge of sin in order to find redemption."

The color White, which is present throughout the novel much as it is in Anton Chekhov's *The Cherry Orchard*, achieves its highest symbolic function as a void in which time has stood still. It is out of this nothingness that Hans Castorp creates his dream poem of humanity in the chapter "Snow." Prevailing everywhere in the sanatorium, White establishes it as a place suspended above ordinary concerns, like a white void, a gap between the moments of linear time where Hans Castorp's subjective time receives full expression. The sense of what was is sublimated as it passes through the filter of white snow to become a sense of the human. Thus, the tone of "pastness," fixed by the leitmotif of the Middle Ages, contributes significantly to this suspension.

The unity of form and content that characterizes *Der Zauberberg* is established by the leitmotif of Music itself, present like White throughout the novel. By gathering all themes unto itself, it induces for Hans Castorp that magical, receptive state which permits him to undergo his epiphanies, his insight into things. If we view the content of the novel as his inner experience—his inner time—then the musical form, involving the use of leitmotifs, also constitutes the content by developing it as well as by shaping it. In the words of one critic, "The inner life of man is actually a complex of motifs which surface, disappear, and resurface—thus of leitmotifs."[7] Structuring the novel with leitmotifs thereby exposes the character's consciousness.

The motifs intratwine through intratextual correspondences, recurring to signal associations with their own earlier contexts as well as among themselves. In other words, they grow into leitmotifs. For Hans Castorp and also for the reader, this subtle art of recall through associative nuances evolved into a veritable "process."[8] Mann's search for Wagner indeed took the capabilities of literature beyond *Der Ring des Niebelungen* and *Tristan und Isolde* in the sense of working out an even broader network of interpenetrating contexts than was customary for the master of Bayreuth. Mann's leitmotif, then, is a short literary "subject" that inflates and acquires extended and expanding resonances of meaning. Each leitmotif acquires increased psychological associations as the *Bildungsroman* advances a structural condition which would seem to take the work a step beyond what we hear so impressively in that operatic scene between Tristan and King Mark (who has discovered his subject's and his queen's disloyalty), when the English horn and the oboe over the bassoons bring together the hero's history (the Tristan leitmotif), the potion theme which doubles as the Isolde leitmotif, and their relationship. In Mann, even more themes infiltrate one another. Thus, in reading—and rereading—*Der Zauberberg*, a work that portrays by symbols and uses characters less as people than as representative figures or vehicles for ideas (e.g., Joachim = devotion to duty, Settembrini = the rational, Naphta = the emotional),[9] we come to realize that its conceptual impact is forged by its aesthetic structure and that to know the novel means to experience it musically.

12

BEETHOVENIAN OVERLAYS BY CARPENTIER AND BURGESS: THE NINTH IN GROTESQUE JUXTAPOSITIONS

If an overlay is an overspreading flap superimposed on the thing itself—call it the truth and not, then, the thing itself, the outwardly imposed and arbitrary use of Ludwig van Beethoven's Ninth Symphony in such novels as Alejo Carpentier's *Los pasos perdidos* and Anthony Burgess's *A Clockwork Orange* becomes highly suspect as to its purpose and also appropriateness. This comment must have a strange ring to it, since both authors are musicians and musicologists who can monitor the technical pulse of musical reality even more closely than a writer like Thomas Mann, and yet both choose to overlay with negative associations one of the supreme compositions in the musical repertory. I am aware of the modern tendency to take bulwarks of our culture and through them, as modernists would have it, revise our view of our culture under a private heading of disillusion, dejection, and disgust. To do so, they will *use* a Ninth Symphony directly to point up Western moral bankruptcy or indirectly to question Western achievement. The technique is simple: grotesque juxtaposition. We need only look at that striking chapter, "Faith, Hope, and Love," in Günther Grass's *The Tin Drum*, part of which, after wading through the dense imagery, reads:

It is the same butchers who fill dictionaries and sausage casings with language and sausage, there is no Paul, the man's name was Saul and a Saul he was, and it was Saul who told the people of Corinth something about some priceless sausages that he called faith, hope, and love, which he advertised as easily digestible and which to this very day, still Saul though forever changing in form, he palms off on mankind.

Saint Paul's Epistle to the Corinthians (I), juxtaposed with concentration camps in Nazi Germany—the grotesque treatment fits a modern pattern. But its salubriousness for society's constant struggle to better itself, or simply its appropriateness within a broader philosophical context in so overlaying the West's supreme achievements, cannot but be questioned.

Carpentier's intellectually flamboyant work tells of a disaffected composer in New York in the throes of typically existential nausea—anxiety, isolation, futility, automatism, sexual dissatisfaction, recourse to drink, desire to escape—who undertakes on behalf of a museum a journey deep into the South American jungle in search of the earliest instruments known to man; who at first thinks of swindling his employer with forgeries but who eventually feels re-created by the dark and distant primeval regions to the point of beginning a magnum musical opus; but who must return to civilization to procure writing materials, after which he can no longer retrace his steps and find his inspiring origin of worlds. With sometimes overpoweringly rich conceptual allusions and images matched by great stylistic sophistication, the novel—recounted by an anonymous narrator but admittedly autobiographical—represents a journey backward on the Amazon river of time from the twentieth century to the earth's year zero, where all is "authentic," and suddenly forward again to today's metropolis, where all is "synthetic."

Carpentier wastes few words before introducing the symbol of his disillusionment in Chapter 1, then again in Chapter 2, and still again in Chapter 3, by which time a pervasive tonality has been set: Beethoven's Ninth Symphony. Seeking shelter from a storm (itself symbolic in context), the narrator enters a concert hall, only to leave "in disgust" when he recognizes the Ninth and thinks of its nauseating, "sublime" Schillerian *Freude, schöner Götterfunken, Tochter aus Elysium*. Later, in a distant corner of South America and in the company of acquaintances—self-exiled artists from the United States, none of whom could praise Western culture or "the Europe of that 9th Symphony"—the Beethoven theme returns in the gloomy setting of "this Dionysus, the officer Nietzsche, . . . in *Reichswehr* uniform," a "prophetic prefiguration of the god of horror." And finally, in a remote inn, he recognizes the symphony dimly over the radio by its initial crescendo, but instead of turning it off this time, he listens to it, sustained by "echoes that I found in myself," referring to recollections of childhood—of his father, who played the horn and ghost-conducted the Ninth at home using his own cracking voice as the orchestra and chorus (movement I); of his mother, who played the third movement from a piano transcription; of her death (movement II: scherzo); and of his yearning for lost happiness in the maternal abode and his youthful affection for a girl named María del Carmen (movement III: adagio/andante moderato). The narrator's father had spoken to him so enthusiastically about European human primacy that, after his death, he had made a pilgrimage to the revered continent to experience the cultural sublimity of the German land whose workers took their families to hear the Ninth Symphony on their days off. But at this time, just weeks before the outbreak of World War II, he had found Beethoven's homeland more interested in military parades and Nazi book burnings than in the spiritual values of universal brotherhood. The "Turkish march" motif in the final movement encourages this particular flashback. Germany was insensitive to the Mansion of Shudders (concentration camp ovens and torture chambers). Hence, in the novel we read of a painter's "maimed and flayed figures . . . which should symbolize the spirit of the times." The key sentence in the context of the Ninth reads: "I could never have conceived such total bankruptcy of Western man as that to which that residue of horror [crematories, ordure, heaps of bones] bore witness." Such a tonality in the "key" of the coldest historical barbarism cannot bring the narrator to an understanding of the nobility of Schiller's "Ode to Joy" (movement IV), coming after a clash of symbolically dissonant notes, an attempted amalgamation of the themes of the previous three movements, "broken, maimed, twisted, merged into a chaos that was the gestation of the future." The supposedly culminating intoning of the ode by soloists and a chorus of human, jubilant voices, can only sound ironic. The narrator turns off the radio before dignifying Beethoven with his conclusion. In his world view, the Dionysian cult has prevailed; in the purity of the aboriginal jungle, Beethoven's appears as "a symphony in ruins."

This philosophical dénouement, an admixture of Spenglerianism and existentialism, is legitimate as far as it goes. But the grotesque light in which the master of Bonn's creation is cast still confounds the reader and amounts to a misuse, in my opinion. It is never clear in the novel whether the author or the narrator likes the symphony, which the West has not lived up to, or dislikes it because it is made up of the West's fatuous and hypocritical pretensions. Critics have tacitly assumed that a musician like Carpentier who has been so attracted to Beethoven in other writings (*El acoso* is structured

around the Third Symphony *[Eroica])* naturally admires the Ninth as a
work of art, but that in *Los pasos perdidos* he uses it to symbolize (by juxtaposition) Western bankruptcy. However, whatever the case, the Ninth
Symphony is defamed—by implication or association or innuendo. Stressing
not the composer's vision but the narrator's experience of the world, in an
autobiographical piece of writing on top of it, degrades the symphony. It
can be argued that "Carpentier maintains his distance from his narrator,"
but if "no simple identification of author with narrator can be made,"[1] conversely no simple separation of author from narrator can be made either.

If the Ninth qua Ninth is merely incidental to the pessimistic thesis, then
any noted composition would have done, from Mozart's Symphony no. 40
to Mahler's *Das Lied von der Erde.* But as a landmark of Western culture—
like the *Divina Commedia,* the *David,* or the cathedral of Chartres—the
Ninth Symphony is naturally a convenient target, since for all its sublimity
it has not come down to us without its detractors. The final, choral movement especially has drawn unenthusiastic comments. Mann himself, uneasy
over Beethoven's "half-wild inarticulateness," said after a concert: "Never
had I more deeply admired the scherzo and the adagio—but once again I
could summon up no affection for the variations of the disjointed last
movement"[2]—incidentally, the model for Adrian Leverkühn's final work,
Doctor Fausti Weheklag, a negation of Beethoven's work, in the novel *Doktor Faustus,* in which we read something that might have been penned by
Carpentier's narrator: "It ought not be . . . , the good and the noble, what
one calls human, though it is good and noble—what men have fought over,
stormed Bastilles for, and compliers have jubilantly proclaimed—that ought
not be, that will be retracted, I will retract it . . . . : the Ninth Symphony."
In fact, instead of writing an "Ode an die Freude," Leverkühn writes a
"Lied an die Trauer." Like Mann, Giuseppe Verdi admired Beethoven, but
the master of bel canto had to qualify his praise with some justified (listen
to the awkward use of the human voice in *Fidelio)* sarcasm: "No one will
ever approach the sublimity of the first movement, but it will be an easy
task to write as badly for voices as is done in the last movement."[3] Nietzsche,
we know, liked the music but condemned Schiller's verses. And I could go
on—but the point is made, perhaps ending with this choice bit of screaming
by an anonymous reviewer:

The whole orchestral part of Beethoven's Ninth Symphony I found very wearying
indeed. . . . It was a great relief when the choral part was arrived at, of which I

had great expectations. It opened with eight bars of a commonplace theme, very much like Yankee Doodle. . . . As for this part of the famous Symphony, I regret to say that it appeared to be made up of the strange, the ludicrous, the abrupt, the ferocious, and the screechy, with the slightest possible admixture, here and there, of an intelligible melody. As for following the words printed in the program, it was quite out of the question, and what all the noise was all about, it was hard to form any idea. The general impression it left on me is that of a concert made up of Indian warhoops and angry wildcats.[4]

Romain Rolland's Jean-Christophe (in *Jean-Christophe*) learned after a lifetime that critics misunderstand and condemn and that works like Beethoven's Ninth are not spared.

If we take *Los pasos perdidos* alone, we must ask if Carpentier is among such critics. His protoganist's disillusion dooms him, beyond frustration, to failure, and the Beethoven-impregnated novel tells us that his Sunday New Year never comes. But neither does a clear sense of Beethoven or of the Ninth as music. The narrator, who runs from the concert hall or turns off his radio, also says, in a passage that reminds him of what the author does himself: "But nothing had made such an impression on me as this putting on trial, this resurrection for punishment and profanation of the tomb of him who had concluded a symphony with the chorale of the Augsburg Confession." We are faced here with enormous ambiguity. Carpentier's methodology relies on intellectually ensconced oversimplifications and on unending contrasts, so black and white in nature that, as Priestley remarks in another context, we cannot approach *Los pasos perdidos* from the standpoint of "sociological polemics but [as] a poetic symbolic novel."[5] I agree fully with the critic who queries: "How do we know that the influences [Carpentier] describes as responsible for his rootlessness, his alienation—the oppression of society, his wartime experiences, the debased culture he has absorbed—are not part of an elaborate mechanism of self-excuse? [I might add his comments about the Ninth.] If they are, this helps to explain the naive oversimplifications, the black and white contrasts, that seem to flaw the novel. Perhaps, at the level of the narrator as an individual, we are reading an account of a prolonged delusion." This same critic then quotes another scholar who emphasizes the presence of "an orthodox unreliable narrator, with the ironic subversion of his account."[6] In other words, we are dealing with a case of Sartrian "bad faith." The narrator, after all, always embraced notions of brotherhood, as in the Schillerian ode, from the first page of the novel when he referred to the enthusiasm of tree planting—"when we had lent our hands to the common enterprise," to the powers which joined dog and man—a "relation of brotherhood."

Part of the problem lies in an elliptical process of thought and language employed (deliberately?) by the author/narrator. In the "mental gymnastics" he adopts to keep up with the "acrobacy of culture," he can find justification for any number of "moral aberrations," and the acrobatics lead to shifting expressions of values—the jungle is "duplicity" and "artifice" but is also "beautiful" and "friendly"—perhaps all dictated by a desire on the part of both author and narrator to become visible: "this subconscious confession that I wanted to 'hear myself performed.' " Nothing, after all, stands out more visibly than contrast and contradiction. This is hardly an appeal to authenticity. The novel is written with such elaborate sophistication by an author who debases the culture that was capable of producing such sophistication that indeed any examining jury would suggest "bad faith." Were this not the case, the novel's style would have had to be more in line with Chinua Achebe's *Things Fall Apart*. But then Carpentier could not have revealed the conflict involving a creative consciousness[7] and a consciousness predicated on nature.[8] Such an ambiguity cannot be more fully exploited than by the infinite contrasts expressed in *Los pasos perdidos* between the jungle and the metropolis, the "authenticity" (the narrator's word) of primitive consciousness and the inauthenticity represented by the Ninth Symphony.

This question of authenticity lies at the root of the whole of the narrator's experience and, I must believe, of the whole of the author's ideology. It accounts for the attempted filling of the void between the subjective creativity of the author and the objectivity of nature by means of the literary technique of reflexivity. Yet the author does not advance toward establishing a dialogue with his culture, so that, in order to achieve some form of authenticity, he must objectify himself, view himself from a dispassionate perspective, as if "interrogating his own mask."[9] But this, too, is merely a device of convenience; the objectification does not obtain, for some reason, when the Ninth surfaces in the text. For reasons of his own, though insufficiently clear for the reader, Carpentier renders indistinguishable the nonrepresentative, authorial "I" and the representative, narrative "I." Within and without the Beethovenian allusions, the reader cannot pry the two consciences apart, ascertain what we are to accept at face value and what we are to ascribe to the personae involved, whether author or narrator. The overlay gets too thick. And if for the protagonist authenticity is the *summum bonum*, applicable to the spirit of the jungle, why deny the same applicability to the spirit of the Ninth Symphony?

Carpentier may well play with ambiguity intentionally, but what does the game achieve? On the one hand, like a Classicist, his narrator seeks order, Europe's "Apollonian soul" as well as the coherence of the virginal forests "where not one gesture was made without cognizance of its meaning"; he breathes "a sigh of relief at an affirmed tonality" after various stormy measures of the Ninth Symphony, and is ill at ease when a young musician plays a twelve-tone atonal theme, a Schönbergian indication of supposed musical progress. On the other hand, like a Romantic, he yearns for the disheveled, tangled vegetation of the deep Amazon and its untampred beauty, for free mores and natural integrity; he rejects what he had hailed as a "return to order, a necessity of purity" and sets himself to composing a piece in which he would avoid such "spiritual subjection." Not surprisingly, this ambivalence leads the narrator to heaping blame, not upon himself, but upon the outside civilized world, sniffing out the negative over the positive and locking out the possibility (until the very end when he feebly admits to his "weakness") of his possessing no creative capacity. He confuses Beethoven's authenticity with his own inauthenticity. Perhaps this is why, on the very first page, his steps under the portico have a "hollow ring"; and this hollowness, reminiscent of T. S. Eliot's "Hollow Men," fixes the tonality of his final defeat. In such a debilitating setting, Beethoven's Ninth suffers from considerable incongruence.

But there is more. In Carpentier's *El reino de este mundo*, abstract figures of a puppet theater travel through jungles and over seas. I feel that the characters in *Los pasos perdidos*, too, are puppets whose strings the author manipulates to give his intellectual overlay more meaning than his human underlay, denying them an inner life in favor of his conceptual construct. Beethoven's Ninth also is manipulated, pulled by strings. The characters' lack of psychological depth has been alluded to by various critics; the search for an ultimate integrative synthesis—city/jungle, nature/history, learning/creation, even author/narrator—tends toward abstraction. Only puppets, after all, would have such one-sided backdrops as a "caricature" of New York and an impossibly "idealized" Santa Mónica de los Venados.[10] Therefore, while admiring the author's learnedness, we cannot feel profoundly moved by this

Spenglerian novel about the decline of the West. In fact, I am tempted to go further and conjure up the word "allegory" in Balzacian fashion, since the narrator is alienated *Western Man* and estranged artist in society (like the finally frustrated seeker Raphael in Balzac's *La Peau de chagrin)*; Ruth, his actress wife, is "make-believe," "artificial," "automated" *society* (like Balzac's Fedora); Mouche, his mistress, is fleshy and flashy *vulgarity*; Rosario, his Gauguinian forest lover, is primitive *wholesomeness*; the guide, the Adelantado, is *governance*; the Curator is *history* (like Balzac's antiquarian); and so on, including the river as *time*, the city as *falseness*, the jungle as *purity*, the fifteen street lamps in Los Altos as all kinds of things, dutifully interpreted for us by the author. And Beethoven's Ninth. . . .

Beethoven's Ninth is treated inflexibly from the disaffected narrator's viewpoint, as if petrified, a disillusioning marble monument, like the frozen expeditionaries by the mouth of a volcano, "their faces crystal-covered [overlayed] like a transparent mask of death." But, contrary to the tenet of Carpentier's mentor, Jean-Paul Sartre, whereby essence is attained only with the end of existence, namely death, art invites no such formulation. The Ninth can never be crystallized into an essence: it is forever becoming, self-renewing. It is man who must live up to it. In the novel, the Kappellmeister uses Beethoven, "resigning himself to deafness," as a symbol of perseverance amid the adversities of a typical Latin American revolution that had erupted; the narrator might do the same to overcome his spiritual depression, though the author has the conductor accidentally killed.

But the depression runs too deep. In the history of his own vocation, music, the narrator sees only a development of insincerities, especially in the modern games of Schönberg and those who imitate primitive rhythms without knowing their meaning. The Impressionists indulged in exaggerated stylization. The Neoclassicists, too, in applying their formal rhetorics, wrote music that forgot about the soul. Beethoven, we know. Apart from Heitor Villa-Lobos, whose quartet he admires because of its "assimilation of landscape, songs, nature, and popular tunes," he accepts only the old medieval church composers, those who predate polyphony, harmony, and counterpoint, whose "masterly manipulation of the ancient modes and ecclesiastical tones [achieved], by way of authentic primitivism, the most valid objectives of certain contemporary composers."

It was in this mode that he conceived his magnum opus—again an example of ambiguity. In his heart of darkness, his creative feelings are aroused and he dreams of a "threnody." "I hoped to arrive at a combination of polyphonic and harmonic writing, concerted, mortised, in keeping with the most valid laws of music, within the framework of a vocal, symphonic ode, gradually rising in intensity of expression." The title, of course means dirge, but its would-be composer does not envision a "Lied an die Trauer"; instead, he gives it an altered definition, more in keeping with archetypal ritual: "a magic song intended to bring a dead person back to life." This sense of resurrection, analogous to his escape from the city, recalls in him one of his "misbegotten" enthusiasms of adolescence, a cantata based on Percy Bysshe Shelley's *Prometheus Unbound*. If Beethoven's Ninth is the novel's tonality, Prometheus as liberation and Sisyphus as subjugation are its dominant images. Therefore, even if the cantata pertains to the city as opposed to the threnody, which pertains to the jungle, the idea of the Prometheus composition keeps returning. Indeed, with his ideal of assimilating cultures, he thinks of incorporating Shelley's work into his new opus as "an emergence from darkness, most appropriate to the original conception of the threnody." He cannot do so, however, because he does not have the text. Then, with characteristic black-and-white contrast, the author has the narrator leave his outline of the threnody with a piqued Rosario as he is about to abandon her and fly back to civilization, anticipating an "irresistible [desire] to go to work on *Prometheus Unbound*" and, in the very last pages of the novel, waiting for Rosario to show up (she will never return), he works "with Shelley's text, cutting certain passages, to give it a more authentic cantata quality."

The continued attraction of *Prometheus Unbound* for the author may be explained by the dethroning of Zeus, the symbol of evil, by Demogorgon, the primitive power of the world; by the Oceanid Asia, the symbol of nature, who rebecomes beautiful when united with Prometheus, the symbol of humanity; or by William Godwin's philosophy, embraced by Shelley, that evil is not inherent in human nature, that man must keep perfecting himself, and that love will prevail over suffering. But for someone who rejected as nauseous the fourth movement of the Ninth Symphony with its "Ode to Joy," an attachment to a dramatic poem whose fourth and final act is a hymn to joy over Prometheus's victory, singing of peace and fraternity, strikes me as ambiguous, not to say contradictory. Owen Jack, the protagonist-composer in George Bernard Shaw's *Love Among the Artists*, who does complete a "Prometheus Unbound" cantata, is firmer as to what he means, and his fellow character Charlie Sutherland, perhaps aware of Beethoven's own attraction to the legend (*Die Geschöpfe des Prometheus*, some of whose themes went into his *Contretänze*, into his Piano Variations opus 35, and into his Third Symphony), praises Beethoven more clearly, within the fictional context: "We heard the Prometheus. By Jove, Mr. Jack, that *is* something to listen to! The St. Matthew Passion, the Ninth Symphony, and the Nibelung's Ring are the only works that are fit to be put behind it."[11] Emil Ludwig, too, we may recall, was even clearer, hearing in the Ninth the "defiant challenge . . . of the new Prometheus."[12]

Still, the Ninth Symphony, with its lofty reputation, is not *ipso facto* always an object of celebration, and it continues to appear in grotesque contexts. With the author of *A Clockwork Orange*, Anthony Burgess, it is once more demythicized and overlayed with negative associations. Here again, the Ninth is treated, not as a work of art, but as a device in the novel whose dystopian vision centers around politics (the authoritarian socialism of future society), the media (thought control through technology), and morality (actually the immorality of the curtailment of freedom of choice). Carpentier's narrator thought he had found goodness in the jungle; Burgess, who replaces contrast with irony and seeming allegory with whimsical reality, sticks to the urban setting. At the end of *The Wanting Seed*, the question is asked: "Do you think people are fundamentally good?" The reply is grim: "Well . . . they now have a chance to ge good"—grim in light of *A Clockwork Orange*, where a conditioning process assures stability by eliminating freedom, and where the impossibility of distinguishing good from evil anymore in a totally mechanical environment results in "good" human zombies assembled like a clockwork. Like Carpentier, Burgess critiques the West, though less for its spiritual bankruptcy than for its idealistic faith in natural goodness. Free choice provokes anarchy, conditioning establishes control.

Carpentier's intellectually sophisticated language gives way to what has been called a Technico-Russo-Anglo "slanguage"[13] called Nadsat, replete with neologisms to fit the society portrayed but also pleasantly rhythmical, indeed musical. The narrator Alex, after all, is a hoodlum who loves classical music, especially Beethoven, and his jargoned idiom, where neologisms act as dissonances, betrays a musical affinity. In the words of one critic, "It is hardly coincidental that Alex's favorite piece of music is Beethoven's Ninth, rich in dissonances that only the professional ear can detect, but filled also with as many untapped, infinite (so it seems) harmonies."[14] As an example, I might single out one passage; after a successful "drasting" with his buddies, Alex writes:

when we got into the street I viddied that thinking is for the gloopy ones and that the oomny ones use like inspiration and what Bog sends. For now it was lovely music that came to my aid. There was an auto ittying by and it had its radio on, and I could just slooshy a bar or so of Ludwig van (it was the Violin Concerto, last movement), and I viddied at once what to do.

Alex, a lad of fifteen, is "ultra-violent," and the music he loves primarily is German, a preference that combines artistic greatness with the naked horrors of two world wars. Carpentier would agree. His motto is antiestablishmentarian: *Non serviam*, or "Kiss-my-sharries." He and his gang of three masked "droogs" commit all kinds of atrocities, "drasting" and "tolchocking": more than robbery and theft, they beat up an old professor and a drunkard to a pulp, attack another gang with razors and chains, savagely kick a pair of lovers, invade a writer's "HOME" and rape his wife. After breaking into an elderly, cat-loving woman's house and knocking her unconscious, Alex is arrested; sent to jail, where he is number 6655321 and accidentally kills a homosexual inmate; and is turned over to Dr. Brodsky for a reclamation treatment called Ludovico's Technique: brainwashing through films and drug injections that cause Alex to become violently ill the moment he starts experiencing pleasure at violent thoughts. The chaplain has reservations about the treatment: "The question is whether such a technique can really make a man good. Goodness comes from within, 6655321. Goodness is something chosen. When a man cannot choose he ceases to be a man. . . . It may be horrible to be good." But Alex sees this as the only way out of prison. He undergoes the cure and is declared cured, "ready to be crucified rather than crucify," by the doctors and state officials. Released, he is rejected by his parents; attacked by the old professor; rescued by his former "droogs" (now policemen), who beat him mercilessly for having previously beat up one of them during an argument; revisits "HOME", where the writer, a liberal out to "dislodge this overbearing government," at first recognizes him as a victim of that freedom-choking Ludovico Technique, later as the rapist who violated his wife—at which point he metes such excruciating punishment on the narrator through music that Alex attempts suicide by jumping out of a window. In the hospital he is restored to his former "ultra-violent" sex-maniacal self (the state is under pressure over its methods) and the Minister of the Interior makes a deal for his support in order to discredit the writer's political party. In one version of the novel, a final chapter (Chapter 21)[15] has him mature to realize that "ultraviolence is a bit of a bore, and it's time he had a wife and a malensky googoogooing malchickiwick to call him dadada."[16]

In this gruesome fantasy, Beethoven plays a telling role, with a helping hand from Johann Sebastian Bach and George Frideric Handel. For Alex, music is a salvation, "gorgeousness and gorgeosity made flesh," producing "a cage of silk around my bed," resembling "silvery wine flowing in a spaceship, gravity all nonsense now": "Great Music . . . and Great Poetry would like quieten Modern Youth down to make Modern Youth more Civilized. Civilized my syphilised yarbles. Music always sort of sharpened me up, O my brothers, and made me feel like old Bog himself." Therefore Alex, who strikes his friend for simply ridiculing a woman singing opera at the Korova Milkbar, retires to his room afterward and masturbates while listening to Beethoven. After beating and bloodying the writer's wife, and with feelings of violence racing through him in bed, he again experiences an orgasm listening to classical music:

I wanted something starry and strong and very firm, so it was J. S. Bach I had, the Brandenburg Concerto. . . . Listening to the Bach, I began to pony better what that meant now, and I thought, slooshying away to the brown gorgeousness of the starry German master, that I would like to have tolchoked them both harder and ripped them to ribbons on their own floor.

And in prison he is allowed to listen to the "holy music by J. S. Bach and G. F. Handel," even while reading the Bible: "While the stereo played bits of lovely Bach I closed my glazzies and viddied myself helping in and even taking charge of the tolchocking and the nailing in."[17] But his favorite composition is Beethoven's Ninth. He picks up two ten-year-old girls at the bar and rapes them, incited by the symphony:

Then I pulled the lovely Ninth out of its sleeve, so that Ludwig van was not nagoy too, and I set the needle hissing on to the last movement, which was all bliss. There it was then, the bass strings like govoreeting away from under my bed at the rest of the orchestra, and then the male human goloss coming in and telling them all to be joyful, and the lovely blissful tune all about Joy being a glorious spark like of heaven, and then I felt the old tigers leap in me and then I leapt on these two young ptitsas.

Alone later he falls asleep "with the old Joy Joy Joy crashing and howling away." Indeed, there is black humor as well as grotesque irony attached to this type of Beethovenian overlay, like that of the cat-loving woman who

tries to protect herself against the invader wielding a bust of the master from
Bonn, or like that of the dream he has of Beethoven, during which he hears
a violence-ridden parody of the ode:

> Boy, thou uproarious shark of heaven,
>   Slaughter of Elysium,
> Hearts on fire, aroused, enraptured,
>   We will tolchock you on the rot and
> kick
>   your grahzny vonny bum.

It dawns upon us at one point that in the name "Ludovico's Technique"
Ludovico is really Ludwig, "Ludwig van" in Alex's parlance. When the
narrator is subjected to the horrid state-sponsored rehabilitation process,
complete with wires, drug, and film ("a very good like professional piece of
sinny"), the background music turns out to be Beethoven's Fifth Symphony,
which then produces such an abhorrence for this music which up to now
has aroused his sexual violence (the old "in-out in-out"), that the revengeful
writer conceives of locking him up in a room and having symphonic music
piped in, a diabolical punishment of hypercruelty.[18] Even Alex, now sixteen, begins to realize the degrading nature of what is taking place:

I don't mind about the ultra-violence and all that cal. I can put up with that. But
it's not fair on the music. It's not fair I should feel ill when I'm slooshying lovely
Ludwig van and G. F. Handel and others. All that shows you're an evil lot of
bastards and I shall never forgive you, sods.

At the end, as part of the deal with the Minister of the "Inferior" and to
make sure he has been returned to his original self with his "bloshy" musical
ways, he asks to hear the Ninth Symphony (end of Chapter 20), and he is
convinced in a manner Beethoven might not have appreciated:

Oh, it was gorgeosity and yumyumyum. When it came to the Scherzo I could viddy
myself very clear running and running on like very light and mysterious nogas,
carving the whole litso of the creeching world with my cutthroat britva. And there
was the slow movement and the lovely last singing movement still to come. I was
cured all right.

As in Carpentier, this network of musical references may well provide a
unifying factor in the novel, identifying the protagonist's individuality
throughout, an individuality that in A *Clockwork Orange* threatens and in
Los pasos perdidos opposes the status quo.[19] But here, too, one must wonder

about the suggestion, in the former work, that the mathematical music of
Bach or, more pervasively, the lyrical and jubilant music of Beethoven,
sparks even more violence than the hoodlum had in him originally. Similarly, one must wonder about the appropriateness, in the latter work, of
associating the Ninth Symphony with violence after a token tribute to childhood memories. It is not enough to say that we are merely dealing with a
whimsical selection, a convenient image, or an interesting device. For some
reason, something about Beethoven—his titanic stature or what he represents in the cultural patrimony of the West—activates a devil's advocate's
adrenalin in the authors of *Los pasos perdidos* and *A Clockwork Orange*.
Grass reacted similarly toward St. Paul. To be sure, other works by Carpentier and Burgess, like *El acoso* and *Napoleon Symphony*, pay homage to the
master, at least to the extent of their structural transpositions of the Third
Symphony. But then again, look in passing at Richard Ennis in Burgess's *A
Vision of Battlements*, who incites an antiaircraft unit to combative violence
with words about this same master: "Beethoven was a musician. . . . He
had absolutely no respect for authority. . . . He was independent, fearless,
alone, no base crawler." We cannot overlook Dr. Brodsky's remark, either:
the "sweetness and most heavenly of activities partake in some measure of
violence—. . . music, for instance." Hence Alex's unwittingly profound
observation: "It was like as though to get better I had to get worse." Is it that
in a clockwork, mechanical world good derives from bad like peace from
violence—a restatement of Charles Baudelaire's *Les Fleurs du mal* or Giovanni Papini's *Un uomo finito*? Or that man has reached a hopeless impasse
in his savage quest for improvement? But the existential messages of Kier-
kegaard, Nietzsche, Dostoievsky, Pirandello, and Kafka have already been
recorded. Carpentier's narrator hurts spiritually under authority; Burgess's
challenges it physically. One feels like a Prometheus for a moment in the
jungle but knows he is too weak to be one and that he will get worse before
getting better; the other feels like a "fruit" who ultimatley *is* that clockwork
orange and that, if he has been made better for society, it is actually worse
for society. Thus, we are left with paradoxes in the throes of a Manichaean
dialectic: the Apollonian or the Dionysian, freedom of choice or submissive
choicelessness, the authentic or the synthetic? More troublesome still, is
either side of the equation possible today? If the culture of the Western city
has not found fulfillment, is the alternative the primitive jungle? And if the
promise of social governance has not matured, is lawless instinct the only

avenue left? Answers to these questions are never clearly suggested. The ends of both novels are open-ended—indeed, unhealthy in light of their inconclusiveness. And it is the Ninth Symphony, incongruously, that shapes the contexts.

Yet the language of Beethoven's composition rings too lucidly with vitality and conviction to provide backdrops for such ambiguities and paradoxical modes. The overlays obfuscate the truth. As one critic has commented, "if the mode of a novel should say something about its meaning, or at least carry us forward so we may debate it, then we might have wished for a less open-ended conclusion, one that defined as well as disturbed."[20] Without the definition, Beethoven is merely "used." In "Beethoven's Ninth Symphony and the King Cobra," the poet Edgar Lee Masters sounds more convincing:

> Beethoven's soul stepped from darkness to brilliant light,
> From despair to the rapture of strength
> Overcoming the world.

13

ROMANTIC IRONY
IN MUSIC

A device developed in one art form usually transposes with difficulty into another, and when to begin with the device finds uneasy definition in the original art, one must exercise extreme caution when assessing it in terms of the other. Though there are those scholars who would justifiably insist that Romantic irony is a world view, it could also be argued that it is such a device, a special effect in literature cultivated by writers around the end of the eighteenth century and associated with Friedrich Schlegel's ideas describing a poet's attitude toward his own subject matter. In this sense, as has been suggested, "artistic irony" would seem a better term, also because, particularly in the case of music, it allows a necessary extension of application to the years immediately preceding and following the period we normally identify as the Romantic era.

The critics' incessant reversion to Schlegel to seek a definition of Romantic irony has confused more than it has helped. Whereas we may assemble a few guiding principles from his *Fragmente*,[1] he ends by giving Romantic irony, without ever referring to it as such, a metaphysical overlay, elevating it to a general, shaping force, much the way the Romantics lifted aesthetics onto a primary level of thinking, imagining, and feeling. Hence, the variously identifiable ingredients of such irony, some of marginal and others of central value to music—for example, distance, aloofness or detachment, ambiguity, conflation, contradiction and juxtaposition, incongruity or anachronism, destruction (of an illusion)/re-creation, buffoonery, caprice (*Willkür*) or sudden change, conflict, absolute freedom, chaos and agility, finite versus infinite (or the ideal), double meaning, dynamism, elusiveness, license, mirroring or parody, naïveté, objectivity versus subjectivity, paradox ("Irony is the form of paradox"),[2] exaggeration, play within a play, wit, playfulness, serious jest ("all jest and all seriousness"[3]), and confusion—become, in his thinking, profound, universal forces of transcendental significance, forces which bind and dissolve and re-create through the artist who thereby relates God to Nature to Man. Playfulness, for example, is not simple jocularity. Its overstated form, buffoonery, is not enough by itself; to fit the context of Romantic irony it must be "transcendental buffoonery."[4] Life is so fearful that the mind, to maintain sovereignty, can only make a plaything of it, present chaos and transcend it, then transcend it again (like a play within a play) and, by "hovering" between poles or between the "opposition of the undetermined and the (pre)determined", render a creative response to the unresolvability. It must turn things around and embrace the hovering positively: "Romantic poetry [can] hover in the middle on wings of poetic reflection, free from all real or ideal interest, between that which is represented and that which represents, and potentiate this reflection again and again while multiplying it in an infinite series of mirrors."[5]

Trying to identify these principles and ingredients of Romantic irony in music without qualifiers could prove meaningless. Schlegel's thrust was literary, and he makes no mention of music. Furthermore, the metaphysical cast is too conceptual to find translation into the musical idiom. This does not mean that Romantic irony cannot exist in music; though less profusely than in literature, it exists as easily as it does in *Der gestiefelte Kater* of Tieck, who did not write with Schlegel's superior, integrating concept of wholeness in mind, and to whom the author of the *Fragmente* hardly pays tribute as a Romantic ironist. In other words, Romantic irony may be more wisely deduced from the practices than assembled from the theories. And in this light, we must at all times be sensitive to the context of a work and, especially in the case of music, take into account the necessary qualifiers: the composer's ironic *intent* and his composition's *direction*—how it may point to itself. The modern word is "self-reflexiveness." This suggests that more than ever there exists a special relation of the creator and/or his creation to the audience (which Schlegel barely considers).

Without the factor of ironic intentionality clearly directed on the self—whether on the author or the work—Romantic irony would not differ appreciably from Classical irony. The latter tends to be objective; the former, subjective. Classical irony exists through its function in a work, with the author's intent taken for granted and with the work objectively never turning against itself, as it were. Hence, along Aristotelian lines (pursued by Cicero and Quintilian), we may discern intended or unintended irony emerging through a character or an event (involving tension, paradox, coincidence—of marginal value when it comes to music), which ranges from Socratic self-deprecation or Sophoclean ignorance (Oedipus) to Juvenal's or Swift's or Parini's or Ionesco's manipulation of derogatory or pointedly contrived circumstances. On the other hand, where the formula is reversed and the work subjectively (or self-reflexively) points to itself as a result of the author's pronounced ironic intent, we face a more involved question. Then the focus is on the author, and the tension, paradox, and coincidence yield to ambiguity, parody, and playfulness—of central value when it comes to music. By manipulation, the author calls attention to his work, to how he has written or composed it, less to what it says than to how he says it (or to how the work presents itself). To do this, he needs to handle adroitly the factor of subjective distancing—self-abstraction—that paradoxical, involved withdrawal which has been looked upon as a mixture of simultaneous immanence and transcendence.[6] We then contemplate a formal irony relating to structure—one which, through the exercise of freedom or license, agility, caprice, incongruity, or wit—disrupts easy illusions, preassumptions, or anticipations, and by calling attention more than usually to the author endows the work (or that portion of it) with a distinctive "twist" of its own. While not necessarily Romantic in origin (e.g., Boccaccio, Cervantes, Beaumont, Holberg, Sterne), it was the Romantics, as we know, who gave this kind of irony currency (Tieck, Byron, Pushkin) and made us feel the contradiction between the seeming meaningfulness of the work and the reminder that it is just a work, an artifact, and therefore meaningless in itself.

On the basis of this hovering between opposites, one would expect that Romantic irony would find a welcome vehicle of expression in music, since it was with Romantic composers that distinctions between private and public music began to be made. Hoffmann's Kreisler exemplifies the composer caught between music as a way of escaping reality *(Sehnsucht)* and as an applied art in the theater filled with philistines who would destroy his true vision. Music written for those knowledgeable of the art differed from that written for greater popularity (and therefore for a composer's wider "success"). The difference that separates Schubert's D Minor String Quartet from the popular *Forellen* Quintet, or Schumann's Fantasy in C Major from his well-known *Kinderszenen*, indicates less a composer's simple desire to write in different veins than a recognition that "intimate" music—Beethoven's last quartets—would no longer win masses over to music as an expression of a serious, artristic conscience. In fact, as Einstein remarked about Berlioz's awareness of the cleavage separating artist from public, "he could have written string quartets or piano pieces only if he had wished to make fun of himself."[7] Who is to say, then, that the composer's adoption of colossal means of expression does not contain at least a tinge of irony? Is the *Symphonie fantastique* only the heady product of a new, serious aesthetic of 1830, or is it partly an ironic comment, as the title itself would encourage us to believe? Its program and its astonishing (for its day) melodies, harmonies, form, and tone color invite public response, and of this concession the Romantic composer was not unaware. In this sense, all the great composers' Romantic music which thrives on virtuosity may be considered somewhere under the heading of "Romantic Irony" (at least during that period when virtuosity flashed with brilliance for its own sake—à la Liszt and Paganini— and before it settled down into an integrated aesthetic). Indeed, we might wish to take matters even further and argue that, since we can only hear any piece of music—Romantic or otherwise—as performed and interpreted by others, perhaps the subtlest aspect of irony lies in the very nature of music, in the contradiction between the seeming concreteness of the instrumental or vocal sounds and our own awareness that they represent a mere reproduction of what the creator heard in his mind and thought he transcribed on paper. We must constantly transcend the paradox while preserving it.

Apart from these speculations, however, the fact remains that Romantic composers did not engage heavily in "ironic" compositions. Most felt their art so intensely that artistic distancing became difficult. Romantic philosophers never talk of music in terms of irony, sarcasm, or parody. Herder sees it as a new language of feeling, without ulterior intentions. For Wackenroder, who well summarizes the attitude, music appeals to certain areas within us by associating tones (sounds in the strictest mathematical sense) with human emotions, the fibers of the heart, and by affecting them in a direct and unreflecting way. With no space between two elements in the affective process, he leaves no possibility for distancing, for irony to infiltrate. In his own way, Hanslick, like Herbart, does the same thing when he describes music as a self-contained art with no reference to anything outside itself. Since music has no "meaning" because it is only developed thematically in tonal patterns, it cannot express a state of mind, which is what irony is: a mental attitude become construct.

Only one critic, as far as I know, has substantively considered the question of Romantic irony in music: Rey Longyear, who limits his discussion to Beethoven.[8] But Longyear does not always apply the qualifiers of intent and direction strictly and at times is too prone to identify Romantic irony with simple humor, or to label it the instant he spots one of the ingredients. Beethoven may have been "attuned temperamentally to the idea of romantic irony,"[9] but ironic, biographical data really have no bearing on a discussion of Romantic irony in music.[10] Where is the Romantic irony in the fact that the composer's friend, Bernhard Romberg, trampled the cello part of the second movement of String Quartet, opus 59, no. 1, under foot because he did not like it? As for the musical application of Romantic irony, Longyear makes a number of interesting disclosures as well as a number of questionable identifications. Among the latter, we might allude to the supposedly surprising Scherzo of Violin Sonata, opus 96, which follows an adagio and is written in minor for a work in major, or the "ironic" Bagatelle, opus 126, no. 4, "which destroys the sublime mood created by the preceding bagatelle." Is the intent ironical here—that is, is there here a capricious destruction of illusion occasioned by "the juxtaposition of the prosaic and the poetic"—or is this simply the aesthetic principle of contrast at work, which is as necessary formally as it is psychologically in any work of art, and which Beethoven did so much to cultivate? Unless ironically intended, changes of mood constitute normal aesthetic procedure, like the would-be confounding Coda of Chopin's Nocturne in B Major, opus 32, no. 1. Again, are the unexpected juxtapositions in the second movement of the same Beethoven quartet Romberg would not appreciate, or the cellist's drumbeat in the first movement, examples of arbitrary caprice or ironic wit? Are the "rhythmic complications" of the syncopated Scherzo of String Quartet, opus 18, no. 6, or the "unexpected sforzandos" in the second movement of Piano Sonata, opus 31, no. 3, paradoxical parodies or ironic contradictions?[11] Are the distorted recapitulation of that same opus 59, no. 1, and the "wrong key" restatement (first movement), along with a "sudden tonal shift" (to the submediant which introduces the second theme in the Finale of the Eighth Symphony), an "irregular resolution" of a diminished seventh chord or the "surprisingly unexpected irregular modulations emphasized by silences" (in the quartet's Coda), "exaggerated pathos," and a "muddy and apparently purposeless [according to Longyear] mock fugato"[12] conveyors of serious jocularity, self-mocking ironic surprises and incongruities, *Willkür?* And does Beethoven really "create the effect of musicians who have gotten lost" (Scherzo of String Quartet, opus 131), presumably to mock what may have happened during rehearsals or performances of his works, or does he really inject a "rude sawing" effect (principal motive, second movement of String Quartet, opus 18, no. 4) to raise the listeners' consciousness of his devices, comparable to Tieck's making his audience "aware of the machinery of stage effects" in *Die verkehrte Welt?*[13] In my opinion, Beethoven, in his later and deafness-afflicted years especially, Beethoven the artist, so passionately committed to music, did not necessarily engage in so many ironies and practical jokes. He never indicated that he shared Schlegel's literary notions of ironic transcendency. This is not to say that there is no humor in many pages of his music; this is merely to say that in most instances he did demand more and more expressiveness, more and more of music itself—and of the players. Mozart and Haydn wrote, by comparison, "pat" quartets whose performers, for Beethoven, were amateurs. His inner ear and musical vision needed to encompass ever changing amalgams of sounds and possibilities which eluded conventions and shocked, which forged his own language, but which had nothing to do, usually, with ironic idiom. It might be sentimental, or "romantic," but untrue, to say that Beethoven's unconventionality represents a metaphysical insufficiency, that is, the artist's inability to capture and hold the ideal in music, except perhaps—and significantly—in his last quartet and last sonata. Aldous Huxley alludes to the composer's impulsive idiom, without reference to Romantic irony:

Meditate on Beethoven. The changes of moods, the abrupt transitions. (Majesty alternating with a joke, for example, in the first movement of the B flat major Quartet. Comedy suddenly hinting at prodigious and tragic solemnities in the scherzo of the C sharp minor Quartet.) More interesting still, the modulations, not merely from one key to another, but from mood to mood. A theme is stated, then developed, pushed out of shape, imperceptively deformed, until, though still recognizably the same, it has become quite different. In sets of variations, the process is carried a step further. Those incredible Diabelli variations, for example. The whole range of thought and feeling, yet all in organic relation to a ridiculous little tune.[14]

This passage might suggest ingredients of Romantic irony but not Romantic irony itself. Here again, Beethoven's posture resembles that of Hoffmann's

Kreisler, who wanted to open new realms of music and did not care about its communicability to an audience.

Sometimes circumstances seem to endow the musical expression with special jocularity, and Beethoven's Violin Sonata, opus 96, written after scenes of Goethe's sarcastic, dramatic joke, *Der Triumph der Empfindsamkeit*, surely is an example of irony. As Schering says, we detect "caricature" in the music, "resonances of the heart and overexaggerated emotional pathos next to each other."[15] Such "frivolities" *(Lächerlichkeiten)*[16] as displayed also by enormous tonal leaps differs from those leaps in the first movement of String Quartet, opus 59, no. 3, where the composer explores a different mode of expression or, better put, "a new order."[17] In any event, the jocularity is induced by the text, and to what extent this might reflect a self-deprecatory quality of Romantic irony may be debatable. Longyear is correct to caution that in Beethoven's humorous works we are dealing, not with Romantic irony, but with simple playfulness.[18] We should do well to add that where *Spiel* is its own structuring force, without calling attention to something other than itself, we are outside the periphery of Romantic irony. However, when Mozart uses *opera buffa* melodies in the Finale of String Quartet in G Major, K. 387, thereby playfully underscoring the learned quality of a serious fugue, or when he cites one of his own themes from a previous work ("Non più andrai" from *Le nozze di Figaro*) in the ominous "Commandant" scene in *Don Giovanni*, thus breaking the heavy moralistic illusion and reminding us that we are merely witnessing an opera—a musical artifact— then we are in the throes of Romantic irony, shaped by both intent and direction, by parody, destruction and re-creation, and wit.

It would appear that the Rondo a Capriccio, opus 129—with its apparently deliberate dissonances and strange improvisations that do not bespeak a search for a "new order" as much as sheer playfulness mocking itself or, through its transparent caprice, seeming to mock the very notion of humor in music—would qualify for Romantic irony. So would sections of Beethoven's last work, String Quartet, opus 135, an interpretation colored by the inscription in the finale "Must it be? It must be!" *(Muss es sein? Es muss sein!)* and about which Einstein queries whether it was composed "in jest or in earnest?"[19] If anything comes close to Schlegel's transcendental "serious jest," this Finale does, primarily through the inversion of the "Muss es sein?" motif which comes through as the "Es muss sein!" phrase. *Muss* being more resigned in German than *soll* (despite the exclamation point), the inversion

in the musical structure points to the disparity between the implication of
the question and the reply. The reply is resigned, and the resolution is the
inversion, a musical trick. Life, the deaf composer is known to have said,
transposes all our expectations, and he uses form, the symbolic significance
of the musical device of inversion, to suggest this. In this sense, where
music reaches beyond itself to point to an ironic resignation, Romantic irony
may be detected. Does Thomas Mann maintain anything different in *Doktor Faustus* where music teacher Kretzschmar comments on Beethoven's
last piano sonata (opus 111), on the passage ending the arietta where the
music dissolves into trills, making of itself something else and enabling
Kretzschmar to remark that ultimately "art always throws off the appearance
of art"?[20] To the "Muss es sein?" theme we might apply Ernst Behler's
words: "ironic counterpointing of illusionary fiction and empirical reality
. . . in an inverted procedure"[21]

Mozart, as we know, could be a master of the "inverted procedure," but
this was largely because, apart from his witty, rococo temperament, in his
day performance was to be clever, among other things; the orchestra, which
often enjoyed no conductor except the harpsichordist or the concert master,
played more freely, not bound by today's rigid rules and practices of execution. We must, then, be aware of what represents objective wit and what
represents subjective irony in his writings. If, without ulterior motive, he
quotes a phrase by another composer, he is merely being witty, like Schumann, who quotes a theme from Beethoven's Piano Sonata, opus 31, no. 3
(the minuet's trio) in the allegro of his *Faschingsschwank aus Wien*, opus
26. Beethoven *seems* ironic when he bases the scherzo of the A Minor String
Quartet, opus 132, on phrases of Mozart's Quartet in A Major, but he is
not, and neither is Chopin, who bases his Etude in G♭ Major, opus 25,
no. 9, on Beethoven's Vivace from Piano Sonata, opus 79. Beethoven who
quotes Leporello's "Notte e giorno faticar" humorously in one of his Diabelli Variations is not being any more ironic than Mendelssohn who quotes
his own song, "Ist es wahr?," in his String Quartet in A Minor, opus 13,
no 2. This represents straight (not ironical) parody, in the musicological
sense of the word, like Luther's use of plainsong in his hymns, or the Renaissance use of consecrated melodies for secular purposes. Negro spirituals
are parodies of Protestant gospel-hymn tunes, and their intent is not ironic.
Charles Ives's use of "My Old Kentucky Home" in *March III* is really not
ironic, and the modern jazzing of the classics has as little to do with Ro-

mantic irony as Mozart's or Chopin's (but not [Gilbert's and] Sullivan's) use of the Italian *bel canto* aria in their (piano) music. Parody as stylistic criticism, however, displays an incongruity typical of Romantic irony. This might be said of Debussy's spoof on the Prelude to *Tristan und Isolde* in "Golliwog's Cake Walk," or of Wagner's use of a Romantic love theme heard between the lines of the Lutheran chorale in the opening scene of *Die Meistersinger*, though we might question the purpose of the composer's incongruity. This might surely be said, too, of Mozart's *Ein musikalischer Spass*, with its ludicrous parody of the serenade tradition through an incompetently composed and executed serenade, or of Debussy's "La Sérénade interrompue" where the romantic serenader is ridiculed as he is subjected to endless interruptions. This might not be said of (Giovanni Bertati's and) Giuseppe Gazzaniga's simple mimicking of orchestral instruments at the end of (their) *Don Giovanni* (possibly Da Ponte's source for Mozart), but when Mozart, at the end of his *Don Giovanni*, creates a witty sextet with a bouncy fugue that destroys the pre-assumptions of the recent tragic encounter, or when Verdi ends his *Falstaff* with a mighty fugue whose joviality points to its satirizing self, mocking life as a jest and therefore sardonically, in purely musical terms, chastising all happy endings and leaving the last laugh to irony, then something beyond straight wit is involved.

Something beyond wit is involved in Schumann's insertion of strands from the "Marseillaise" in the *Faschingsschwank aus Wien* which was performed in Vienna—and the title underscores the irony—where the French anthem was forbidden. His use of the anthem thereby differs basically from Tchaikowsky's (in the *1812 Overture*) or even Debussy's (in *Feux d'artifice*—like the suggestion of "God Save the King" in his *Hommage à S. Pickwick, Esq.*). Schumann's ability to mock suited his decision to set Heine's ironies to music in his *Dichterliebe* cycle and the poet's *Stimmungsbruch*. According to one listener, he makes the piano laugh.[22] Mendelssohn, too, enjoys the same "ironic" success in his settings of Heine's *Neue Liebe*, and the second movement of his Cello Sonata in D, opus 58,[23] is so wandering, so freely recitativelike, that one could argue that the composer is making a comment on the idle and slack lyricism of some of his contemporaries. To these examples I might append the descriptively (literarily inspired) ironic musical scenes of *A Midsummer Night's Dream*, especially where the clowns discuss their respective roles (III, 1 and V, 1). One of the masterful examples of Romantic irony—again literarily inspired but this time developed through purely musical means—may be found in Liszt's *Dante Symphony*, in the first movement or "Inferno" section, where in the recapitulation he reintroduces in variational form appoggiature originally heard in the exposition. The original appoggiature translate the sighs and groans of the damned, and the later ones the comically yet pungently ironical utterances of the devils sneeringly mocking the sinners with their own sounds. Such parodistic means he also used in the *Faust Symphony*, in which Mephistopheles' evil spirit finds expression through a distortion of the previous themes associated with Faust.

Romantic irony in literature opened up a new manner of expression, and its practice was not abandoned in music after the height of the Romantic period. Two legacies in particular, caprice *(Willkür)* and destruction *(Vernichtung)*, spark a number of compositions which, by anachronism, conflation, license, and ambiguity, mark much of twentieth-century music. Parodying chaos and buffoonery obtain. To quote Jean-Paul's foresighted criticism: "abandoned caprice" gives rise to a poetic nihilism that "egomaniacally destroys the world and the All, only in order to vacate for itself room for play within Nothingness."[24] In Romanticism are sunk the roots of that aestheticism which has led modern art to an impasse in an aesthetic Nothingness, particularly through the self-destructiveness of irony.[25]

The parodistic techniques of Mahler, as in the Scherzo of the Ninth Symphony, have been disclosed.[26] Musical caprices and exaggerations and abrupt contrasts à la Richard Strauss which go nowhere, or the ambiguous tension of being caught between the program idiom of Berlioz and Liszt and the absolute, pure idiom of Brahms—these are ideas which emerge when least expected in his music. Suddenly, negative vibrations amplify. The famous "Totenmarsch" from the First Symphony, ironic,[27] brooding, and sultry, inserted before the final movement (ambivalently labeled "Dall'inferno al paradiso"), suggests itself as a case in point. Seemingly tragic but actually a mock funeral march using "Frère Jacques" (Bruder Martin) as a theme, its self-deprecation communicates through understatement, and its ironic dialogue in the sonata form, with the B section based on "Die zwei blauen Augen von meinem Schatz," indicates a withdrawal from the world through dream and reminiscence before returning to the "Frère Jacques" of A. Put all this together and the whole piece says something negative or destructive to the listener as his mind reverts to the unsettling and distorted realities of life. And irony is its language, connotative irony scoring a condition of negation that makes the ambiguity of hovering between program and pure music a meaningless, academic concern, since, however perceived, the music will always convey the same message, or, more abstractly, create the same mood. The pop tune that becomes solemn designates itself unmistakably by contrast and reminds us of the *Scherz* and *Ernst* dialectic.

Richard Strauss sometimes also engaged in conveying ironically a sense of negation in the context of his compositions.[28] The stage audience which insists on the impossibility of performing an opera within an opera in *Ariadne auf Naxos*—Commedia dell'Arte within *opera seria*—is somewhat obvious, but Strauss can be more subtle. The fugue, for instance, in *Also sprach Zarathustra* turns out to make, for one critic, a destructive comment on science: "We find the fugue used . . . to describe almost sarcastically the dark, complicated frigidity of science."[29] Here again, the composer's method intentionally produces something that goes beyond purely musical significance. Schumann would have commented that such jests have dark veils. And at times the wilder the jest, the darker the veil, that is, the destructive comment. Is this not the case with Erik Satie, whose daring harmonies outdo Wagner, and whose deliberate buffoonery pokes devastating, ironic fun at Wagnerism and Romanticism as a whole? Dissonance as dissonance, stylistic gaucheries of all kinds, burlesque advice to performers, notational clowning (see his bizarre enharmonic writing: the A-Minor triad, for example, as Gx, B♯, E), and similar deliberate license characterize such works as *Parade*, "Airs à faire fuir," and "Morceaux en forme de poire." The single cannon of Tchaikowsky becomes a plethora of mechanical, percussive noises promoting a sense of chaos: typewriters, sirens, engines, pistols . . . ; a *dépouillé* style à la *caffé-concert* destroys with its banality as much as it self-destructs.

More temperately, Ravel's *Tombeau de Couperin* calls veiled attention to itself by contrasting the measured cadences of the seventeenth-century composer with varied stances and virtuosities. But the intention here may have been only marginally ironical. More pointedly, however, we note in *La Valse* an ironic parody in the form of a gradually unraveling paraphrase of the waltz, a conflation outdistancing the comical exaggerations of the serenade in Mozart and Debussy. Ravel's *Valse* ends by combining all waltzes, one would say, into a final explosion of madness. If we remember that Romantic irony cannot be confused with the mere exuberance and healthy spontaneity of wit—which is positive—and that it is negatively inspired, then we may observe the destructive valence that has carried over into the twentieth century.

Yet there is a constructive side, too. Anachronism, which generally represents a parodistic device, can re-create when used to paraphrase a style or a composition. In the former instance, Prokofiev's *Classical Symphony* comes to mind, whose parody reshapes the classicism of Mozart or Haydn or Vivaldi, paraphrasing classical form and structure in such a way as to restructure them for the new *Zeitgeist*. In the latter instance, we might single out Stravinsky's *Pulcinella Suite* (supposedly derived from Pergolesi), where "artful nuances of melodic-rhythmic emphasis, harmonic idiom, instrumentation . . . transform [as does Prokofiev] the past into the present. And, what is more, the piquant paraphrase is more vital and vibrant than the original."[30] By the time of Prokofiev and Stravinsky, however, Romantic irony, which inspired the method, remains peripheral in intention, for these composers' meticulous use of the past is exceptionally serious and re-creative, and to the extent that this is true the margin of irony dwindles.

The above examples of Romantic irony in music do not pretend in any way to cover the whole range of possibilities. They illustrate, if anything, the elusive fabric out of which the literary device is woven when transferred onto a musical loom; in carrying the seemingly ironic thread the shuttle often slips. Only attention to intentionality and direction can keep it from falling altogether, and if so contemplated we may even be surprised at how broad an influence in the art of music Romantic irony exercised, despite the relatively sparing use composers in general have made of it. This manner, which may well have originated in music when the banal pretentiousness of *opera seria* was countered and shredded by the lively mockeries of *opera buffa*, relates primarily in spirit to proto-Romanticism or to that transitional period when Mozart leads to Beethoven, and from some of its valences—especially *Willkür* and *Vernichtung*—the twentieth century has derived a number of expressive benefits. After Wagner, as the saying went, no more music was possible, at least diatonically. Hence the predicament, hence atonality. Dissonance understood as dissonance is probably the final expression of Romantic irony in music. It spoofs the human ear. What now? We must still explore further the metallic sounds of Satie (the fur-lined teacup must always be invented), and—who knows?—in a dehumanized, science fictionalized, brave new world, through the inherited posture of Romantic irony, we shall be giving an appropriately appreciated parametric music to a civilization of cold technology in which the works of Mozart, Beethoven, Berlioz, Schumann, Chopin, Mendelssohn, Liszt, Verdi, Wagner, Debussy, Mahler, R. Strauss, Ravel, Stravinsky, and Prokofiev, among others, will appear as interesting artefacts of a primitive, emotional culture.

(1977)

14

MUSIC AS FANTASY

[La fantasia] . . . è l'officio del poeta . . . e . . . del Musico.

Music is in the mind of God.

Fantasy in literature constitutes a form of musical thinking.

BACKGROUND

It is best to begin by averring that no one knows what music really is: not the psychologist, though the art represents a pure form of psychic emotion; nor the anthropologist, though the primitive cultures he studies are usually grounded in musical rites; nor the physical scientist, who does not go beyond measuring vibrations and acoustical ratios; nor the sociologist, whose quantitative statistics stop the thought process at percentages; nor the philosopher, who stands uneasy before anything that defies the formulation of conceptual constructs. Among the latter, even those who have confronted the phenomenology of musical aesthetics have experienced difficulty in making themselves understood, including to themselves. In the modern period, only Arthur Schopenhauer, whom Richard Wagner credited with having been the first to recognize the primal position of the art among its sisters,[1] stressed music's essentialness as a real, metaphysical, and cosmic essence underlying the instinctive drive of the entire organic world, and his compatriot one century later, Oswald Spengler, also privileged the art with a noble primacy above all else. Wrote Spengler:

The beyond lies where the boundaries of the light-world [the self-contained world of the visible] are, and salvation means deliverance from the spell of the light-world and its facts. The ineffable magic and the very real power of salvation that music possesses for us resides precisely in this. For music is the only art whose means lie outside the light-world that has for so long become coextensive with our total world, and music alone, therefore, can lift us right out of this world, break through the steely spell of light, and allow us the sweet illusion that we are reaching the soul's final secret . . . , a world of the ear.[2]

But even so, the notions remain intangibly metamorphical.

Perhaps the best proof that nobody knows what music is reveals itself when we ask the musician himself—the composer, performer, or teacher—whose best answer, if one is forthcoming, dates back to 1798 when Johann Wolfgang von Goethe's composer friend, Friedrich Zelter, wrote to Friedrich Schiller:

You can well ask me what I understand by musical, and so I shall tell you immediately that I myself do not really know; that I know from other musicians that they also do not know; and that the majority among them is so unaware that they do not know that they do not know. . . . We musicians [have] no concept of what we call musical.[3]

It pleases me that the question shall never receive an adequate answer, that the reader and critic will never penetrate the haunting core of attraction in Thomas Mann's *Doktor Faustus*, or that the listener and scholar will never decipher the cosmic ecstasy of spirit in Ludwig van Beethoven's String Quartet no. 14 in C♯ Minor, opus 131. Music is the only art that enjoys ubiquitous ties: it has been variously considered a promoter of thought and provoker of feeling, a therapeutic drug and an exciter to action, a fascinator of primitives[4] and an enchanter of the civilized, a social coagulator and a psychological activator, an educational tool and a commercial requirement, an inducer of dark satanic powers and an emanation of luminous divine blessedness. More scientifically, it has been argued that the basic metaphors for cosmos, history, and human society used in the *Rig Veda*, for instance, or by Plato in his dialogues, not to speak of much ancient literature reflecting arcane sources, are drawn from a construction of musical scales from a monochord by successive divisions of numerical powers, allowing for mathematical tuning systems and for the resolution of problems of consonance and dissonance by setting limits to the number of intervals generated in each scale. "The structure of these scales . . . constitutes for such ancient literature the basic metaphor for all complex systems such as the cosmos, human and exemplary history, the social order and city planning."[5] It is not by chance, then, that the universally significant and archetypal descent and ascent of Orpheus was powered by his lyre and his song. To arrive at a *definition* of what is *musikalisch* would be as counterproductive as to assess what makes fantasy *fantastisch*, or, in literature, to delineate the exact boundary between fantasy and reality for the benefit of a few academic committees.

THE NATURE OF MUSIC

In point of fact, *all* music is fantasy. It is its most fundamental, pristine, and purest form, unequaled by the other arts. Think of the magnificent, inimitable fantasies of Giuseppe Verdi's *Falstaff.* Music's vital force stems from the fluidity of tonal events constructed around sequences or unions of note sounds that are never fixed *precisely* once and for all as to rhythm, tempo, dynamics, and the like, and as a result we enjoy as many different performances of the same work as there are performers. I have enjoyed at least a dozen *different* performances of *Falstaff*, whose imaginativeness is inexhaustible. A score is not defining; its verbal indications are not notational, which means that its "language," semiotically speaking, exists like fantasy in a fluid state, modifying by deviational degrees its communication from performance to performance, thus compounding the composer's original fantasy with the fantasy of the artist, to say nothing of the private fantasy of the listener. The notational system of a score "furnishes no means of identifying a work from performance to performance."[6]

What we have, then, in music as in fantasy, is an emotional construct of imaginative vitality that communicates essentially—some would say fantastically. The Mazzinian saying, "Music begins at the point where poetry ends,"[7] has poetic merit, but, apart from being overused, it falsifies the nature of the phenomenon. Marcel Proust voiced it in a glimpsing flash, though he misunderstood his own insight when he considered the following a possibility that has ended "in nothing":

And just as certain beings are the last witnesses of a form of life that nature has abandoned, I asked myself if music was not a unique example of what could have become a communication among souls, if the invention of language, the formation of words, and the analysis of ideas had not interfered.[8]

This is what one critic means by calling certain music "psychological hieroglyphs not yet decoded."[9] We are here in the true realm of the *Fantastisch* because at this point, science fictional in temper, we meditate beyond the context of what we are used to on a quotidian basis: ordinary reality as experienced naturally. We are in Tzvetan Todorov's definition of the fantastic as "that hesitation experienced by a person who knows only the laws of nature, confronting an apparently supernatural event."[10]

Music literally swirls with many shapes because it moves fluidly through linear space, despite the synchronic connections some analysts like to look for.[11] Unlike verbal language, its fantasy depends entirely on rhythmic speed, duration, intonation, and intensity, fashioning an aggregate system of interrelationships, and incorporating, in the words of Robert Morgan (discussing tonal space) "all elements of compositional structure . . . [in such a manner that] the ways in which [these relationships] occur are open to infinite variation."[12]

As a self-referring art in the first instance, the note signs point to each other, each being a member of the whole and assigned a different function—reminding us by analogy of what Bruce Morrissette says about Alain Robbe-Grillet's scenes in *La Jalousie*, that without commentary they exist "in the pure domain of phenomenological semantics."[13] But to leave music in its self-referential state the way John Cage does when he emphasizes that sounds should simply "be themselves rather than vehicles for man-made theories or expressions of human sentiments"[14] leads to a needless dehumanization that forgets the elementary fact that nothing exists independent of the human sphere, not even the noise made by the proverbial tree falling in the remote forest. The human, teleological dimension cannot be brushed aside. Aleksandr Scriabin's well-known mystical chord—$C–F\sharp–B\flat–E^1–A^1–D^1$—communicates its fantastic, eerie vibrations only to the human ears, beyond whose reception only unrelated silence exists. So, while the musical idea depends for its compositional—and therefore expressive—structure on the rhythmic and durational relationship between tonal event 1 and tonal event 2 and on how the relationship's complexities are developed and concluded—what makes music also a self-evolving organism—this self-referring, centripetal as it were, quality is constantly countermanded by the fluid, expressive, centrifugal nature of music itself. Musical time, Cage should consider, is not identical with the duration subjectively experienced by the human ear, which makes its own expansions and contractions in receiving sound. However objectively constructed, there can be no art without subjectivism. What else does Henri Bergson mean when he suggests to us that we listen to a melody and allow ourselves to be lulled by it?[15]

THE PLATONIC MISGUIDANCE

Self-contradictorily or not, the poetic Plato distrusted fantasy, and with characteristically logical and associative consistency he harbored a similar attitude toward music (the word for which in Greek designated both poetry and melody). Because rhythm and melody affect man's emotional life most deeply, he regarded music as superior to the other arts, but by the same token—and because of its uncontrollable abstractness, ultimate inscrutability, and dubious stimulations—he also saw its dangers if mismanipulated or misapplied. Well applied, it fosters citizenship and strengthens the State. But all around him, he sensed misapplications. Hearing dissonance, the virtuous mind, as he would have it, can only eschew it, even metaphorically.

Plato was greatly conscious of the human ear, whose tolerance for dissonant relationships is limited. This consciousness had much to do with the fixing of harmonic ratios according to generated intervals. Different scales, for the Greeks, produced different modes to the ear, and in turn each harbored a different psychoaesthetic association. Dorian, Phrygian, Lydian, and Ionian scales, together with Pythagorean, Just, Archytas, and Ptolemaic tuning systems, created peculiarities that the Athenian philosopher was not ready to accept by simply suspending diffidence or disbelief. Truth, and by extension the Good, could not be served by an unstable, therefore manipulatable, art unless severely controlled. And the implementation of this control, together with the way the musical phenomenon was rationalized, came as close to denuding music of its inherent fantasy as anything has ever come. It has been pointed out by Ernest McClain that the root meaning of the *Timaeus* numbers is musical and underlies the structure of the heavens metaphorically. The ratios (frequencies) derived from the tuning of a monochord, when precise, produces defined pitches, but since the ear is not that precise and can conceive the same total interval through different ratios, both the instability of the art and its potential for degenerating into dissonance became worrysome harbingers of a faltering moral structure belying the eternal model. Comments one critic:

Music, with its mathematical and sensible components, is the fundamental analogue of the relation between the eternal and the sensible [and] the temporal flow of the sensible world is like a song sung now in one, now in another musical scale . . . ; it is inevitable that degeneracy and disharmony creep into the transpositions of all musical scales, [leading] to the decay of regularity and virtue and to social or cosmic chaos.

Hence, Plato's construct of ideal, utopian cities; in the technical words of the same critic, which demonstrate for my purpose the extent to which the Athenian philosopher defantasized the phenomenon, albeit with "scientific" fantasies of his own[16] that attached moralistic principles to musical modes:

> Plato . . . , in projecting his ideal or celestial city of Callipolis [the "beautiful city," *Republic* 423–25], limited it to 1000 inhabitants, because in its musical analogue, the Dorian and Phrygian scales generated by the numbers 2^p, 3^q (Phrygian tuning: p, q integers), certain basic disharmonies are removed by limiting the notes of the scale to those and those only for which the notes are represented by integers less than 1000. The worst city . . . , Atlantis [the "most corrupt and luxurious city," *Critias* 113–21c], has 12,960,000 inhabitants: its musical analogue is a scale generated by the numbers $2^p . 3^q . 5^r$ (just tuning: p, q, r integers) and it includes all intervals represented by integers not greater than 12,960,000 which are grouped so closely together that they generate a cacophony. Likewise, Ancient Athens [the "best city," *Critias*, 109b–12c] as the model for the best city, and Magnesia [the "second-best or practical city," *Laws*, books IV–IX] . . . of the second-best, both have structures derivable by analogy from their characteristic musical scales and are limited in size by a number chosen to exclude a chosen level of dissonance.[17]

So is music reduced by Plato to a set of integers and ratios, intervals and vibrations. Thus conceived, it can be stabilized, and the morality of the State controlled.[18]

Now, fantasy in literature constitutes a form of musical thinking. Plato sensed the connection. Hence, for him, the importance of a binding, indeed exclusive and "stabilizing," relationship between literature and reality—not fantasy—whereupon, along with his pupil Aristotle, he proceeded to lay the ubiquitous though misguiding foundations of a Western critical theory that "assumed mimetic representation to be the essential relationship between text and the real world."[19] Fantasy lies; music, as he saw it developing, is therefore dangerous.

The imaginative vitality of music is tantamount to that of fantasy, and both subsist on the energy of *innovation*. But in his quest for stability, Plato did not welcome novelty—the kind that unsung (wordless) music would represent. He would have decried Beethoven's opus 131, for only the traditional practice of a musical accompaniment (music being abstract and a nontransmitter of reason) to lyric poetry (the word being a direct expression of reason) could be tolerated. A Greek text had always been set to music syllable/note by syllable/note, and the new practice of superimposing a text onto an existing melody, or worse, of outright melismatic expression, or of engaging in ornamentation—the ultimate heresy—sent chills up his spine. On the grounds that sound actualizes perception, meaning that it engenders new perceptions, he denounced musical innovation. In the *Republic*, we read:

The evolution of our rulers should be directed—[so] that music and gymnastic be preserved in their original form, and no innovation made. They must do their utmost to maintain them intact. And when anyone says that mankind must regard "the newest song that the singers have," they will be afraid that he may be praising, not new songs, but a new kind of song; and this ought not to be praised, or conceived to be the meaning of the poet; for any musical innovation is full of danger to the whole State, and ought to be prohibited. [Book IV, 424]

Plato conveniently argued musical simplicity (what could come closer to what sounds traditional?), lest novelty inveigle the listener and, like fantasy, function as sorcery. He admired the Spartans because they allowed no imaginative deviations in music. Timotheus, who dared expand the seven strings of the lyre to a dozen, uttering "I do not sing of the past; in novelty is power . . . [and] to Hades with the old Muse,"[20] tarnished Plato's Hellenic ideal. So did the Ionian and Lydian modes, whose relaxing effeminateness undermined the State and needed to be banished, in contrast with the more vigorous Dorian and Phrygian, though even from these he would retain like the Spartans only those aspects that were military in effect. And Aristotle echoed his teacher's bias: "The right measure will be attained if students of music . . . do not seek to acquire those fantastic marvels of execution which are now the fashion" *(Politics, 1341a).*

With its imaginative juxtaposition, and in quality not unlike virtuosity, polyphony, then in its embryonic stages, represented political betrayal and aesthetic confusion. And so it went. Music, which is fantasy, could not be permitted any freedom of development according to its inherent forces and innovational imperatives. In society, it had to have what in literature was extolled as mimetic value, namely, a functional or representative rather than a fantastic or imaginative aesthetics. Plato was but the fountainhead of a repressive musical conservatism in whose lineage we meet, among others, the Christian Fathers, St. Augustine, Charlemagne, Martin Luther, John

Calvin, Immanuel Kant, Lev Tolstoy, and the theorists of the Soviet Union, to whom, as Sergei Prokofiev and Dimitri Shostakovich and so many others found out, innovative imaginativeness constitutes rebellion.

In researching my argument, I was attracted to the words of all those literary critics who have contributed to a definition of fantasy. I found particularly useful Kathryn Hume's essay,[21] which surveys the field very coherently with good historical sense. In so many cases, the musical concept may substitute for the literary concept of fantasy, remembering her fundamental statement that "theories of fantasy can be characterized by the portion of the contextual system they emphasize, and by the amount of the system they encompass."[22] Various definitions alluded to may be adopted to encompass the musical system. If we work with W. R. Irwin's rule of "overt violation of what is generally accepted as possibility," we can see that, in music, any violation of what is *expected*—given music's forever recurring reliance, unlike literature, on repetition—would fall under the same psychologically based heading. Hume continues with Eric Rabkin, for whom fantasy appears where "the perspectives enforced by the ground rules of the narrative world must be diametrically contradicted." By the simple contrivance of contradicting the perspectives enforced by the basics of musical expression, we link music with fantasy unequivocally through the medium of innovation, here meaning surprise and relating to Irwin's opinion, as I shall attempt to show later when I consider the *poiesis* of musical fantasy as a superimposition on the basic level of its *praxis*.

Certainly, the definition proffered by Todorov and adopted by Christine Brooks-Rose, and which comes down to defining literary fantasy by the relationship between reader and work—the final logos of Irwin's and Rabkin's utterances—can be transferred only too easily to the context of music, and Harold Bloom's focus on an unusual selection of literary elements, despite his mythicized English, can still be transferred to the musical dimension, to what Plato would have abhorred ("Fantasy, as a belated version of romance, promises an absolute freedom from belatedness, from the anxieties of literary influence and origination") because if for the Greek "imagination" was dangerous enough, "innovation" was worse. What would have disturbed Plato about the above notions is the creation, development, and establishment of a logical impossibility. He detested the possibility of fantasy's—and music's—subversiveness through the simple gimmick underlying all art (of course, not philosophy!), that is, the game, the ludic exercise. He could not have abided the "exercises" of Dante Alighieri, Ludovico Ariosto, E. T. A. Hoffmann, Edgar Allan Poe, Franz Kafka, and Samuel Beckett, or anyone else, according to Darko Suvin's definition of science fiction as "the presence and interaction of estrangement and cognition," not to mention Bertolt Brecht's notion of *Verfremdung* or Victor Shklovsky's notion of *ostraneniye*, or defamiliarization.

In contrast with fairy-tale author J. R. R. Tolkien's joyous and consoling assessment of creative fantasy, I could not help associating Rosemary Jackson's sulking, Marxist view of fantasy and the fantastic—a "negative rationality" with subversive qualities that "may lead to social transformation"—with Plato's apprehensions and prescriptive desire to control the art of music. For the Athenian feared the inevitable addition of intensity, the emotional factor, to quantity, the functional factor, or the poetic irrational to the mimetic rational, producing a "negative rationality."

PRAXIS AND POIESIS

In his *Manifeste du surréalisme*, André Breton criticized the West because of its excessive rationalism and materialism which bans fantasy (*chimère*):

We live under the rule of logic. . . . Absolute rationalism, which remains in vogue, permits us to consider only facts that are closely tied to our experience. . . . Under the banner of civilization, with the pretext of progress, we have managed to ban from the mind everything that, correctly or incorrectly, can come under the heading of superstition, of fantasy.[23]

I call music in its original state—the one that sprouts from its own "rule of logic [and] absolute rationalism"—fantasy to the first power, or F^1. On this level, I would use Leonard Meyer's articulation with reference to "evident meanings," namely, "those which are attributed to the antecedent stimulus in retrospect, after the consequent has become a tonal-psychic event and when the actual relationship between the antecedent and consequent is apprehended."[24] In the long run, it evolves into what the human ear in time becomes accustomed to and therefore demands because it is comfortable with it—something like how the West embraced mimesis after the Platonic and Aristotelian decrees. I refer to the allowable musical relationships that come into existence with the composition as it reflects an innate, deep structure, "a system of structural conventions not unlike those of the grammar of a language,"[25] say the I–IV–V–I harmonic progression. On this level, we have *musica practica,* not in Roland Barthes's ingenuous sense,[26] but in the sense of *praxis* operating functionally. Praxis equates with F^1; F^1 expresses itself through a codified system of relationships perpetuated by a mimetic tradition (its literary analogue). Whereas it is imaginative to the extent that all music is fantasy, it cannot be called innovative because it takes for granted an implied and emotional condition that very often in its most obvious consequence—as, on the elementary level, "Happy Birthday to You," "Fra Martino companaro," "Ach, du lieber Augustin," and "Sur le pont d'Avignon" indicate—finds the end presupposed in the beginning. These are just examples, but they happen whenever each sound, without imaginary departures, is assigned a different yet structurally identifiable function.

F^1, of course, need not be demonstrated with simplicities. Any number of Johann Sebastian Bach's sarabandes fit the praxis dimension, or the slow movements from some of Wolfgang Amadeus Mozart's piano sonatas (like the C Major), or the Trio in the third movement of his Symphony no. 41 in C Major (the *Jupiter*), K. 551, even most of Frédéric Chopin's Prelude in D♭, opus 25, no. 15, not to speak of some of Francis Poulenc's piano Improvisations—the C Major, for example. These compositions are not simplistic; they are "mimetically" conceived on the ground level of fantasy, with preordained rules of musical logic that suggest evident meanings.

There exists a superior level, however, and this level I call *poiesis,* fantasy to the second power, or F^2, which is as inherent in F^1 as fantasy is in literature. Robert Scholes goes rather far when he claims that all writing is construction (not mimesis), a view that would even deny praxis in favor of poiesis.[27] But ultimately, in principle, given the overriding necessity of F^2 in the creative process, it is acceptable, in the sense that a novel or a symphony is great to the extent that it is constructed or furbished by F^2. I am reminded of Honoré de Balzac, whose visionary powers, whether in creating Gambara, Goriot, Frenhofer, Claës, or Vautrin, flow out of and finally leave behind the deep inner structure of reality, and what would otherwise be mimesis in fact reflects a world created fantastically inside his own head. Poiesis derives from praxis; Vautrin the spirit of evil emerges from Vautrin the escaped convict. Shifting to music, the dominant seventh chord may be related functionally to the subsequent chord, according to the "rule of logic" and the condition of "obvious meaning," since the ear expects the resolving relationship, but the introduction of something more visionary or transcendental—if only a 9th or an 11th, and so on to Scriabin's mystic chord—creates a unique, uninstitutionalized response of incomparable freshness, thanks to its innovative character. Just experience the use of secondary 7ths in much of Claude Debussy's piano music—I am thinking particularly of the *Jeux*. In painting, Odilon Redon would call it *logique imaginative*. On the first level (F^1) reigns the practical triad, and on the upper level, it yields to harmonic and melodic departures of poetic breadth. The genius of any composer reveals itself when his departures invigorate the composition. Indeed, the degree of F^2 is a test for evaluating the music, just as in literature the existence of fantasy sets up the true quality of a novel, if as examples we compare Balzac with Joris Karl Huysmans, Alessandro Manzoni with Luigi Capuana, or Charles Dickens with Thomas Hardy.

The composer engages in a dialectic between the established and the spontaneous,[28] superimposing F^2 onto F^1, the artificial (in the good sense) onto the natural, leaving the final judgment to the ear and combining "a procedure which relies on tradition . . . [with] a procedure which . . . still wants to subject the system of musical sound" to elaboration.[29] This happens to be quite consistent with that part of the Romantic theory of art that believes that there exists not only "a mimetic artistry" but also a "pure . . . artistry which springs spontaneously from within the soul."[30] What else is Hume formulating when she points to the two impulses of literature, *mimesis* and *fantasy* (for me, F^2), or "the desire to change givens and alter reality: out of boredom, play, vision, longing for something lacking, or need for metaphoric images that will bypass the audience's verbal defenses,"—to which I add: or that will raise the listener's auditory perception and consciousness? Above all, F^2, to adapt her words, "helps activate whatever it is in our minds that gives us the sense that something is meaningful."[31]

Innovation is the catalyst. My use of words like "irrational" and "spontaneous" notwithstanding (which refer to the *spirit* communicated rather than to the process undergone), composing or constructing the enigmatic fantasy of music remains a self-conscious act, even if the composer adopts random procedures, or if he utilizes for themes naive musical phrases whose brevity makes them sound almost thoughtless. To create much from little is to engage in F^2. What can appear more random or naive or brief than the opening phrase (nothing more than a rhythmic schema become melodic) of Beethoven's Symphony no. 5 in C Minor, opus 67? Or the three-note theme of César Franck's cyclical Symphony in D Minor? Or the typical three- to five-note leitmotif in Wagner? Or the short, incantatory and ritualistic patterns of Carlos Chavez? All innovation represents an act of artistic self-awareness, the superimposition of fantasy upon fantasy denounced by Plato, the departures, the "overt violation" and "diametrical contradiction" of the ground rules that surely produce "hesitation" before the *Fantastisch*. Greatness and innovation go together because the latter has, historically and psychologically, expanded our consciousness and sensibility—which is not at all to say that greatness can come at the expense of nuance, elegance, subtlety, stylistics, refinements, and humanity. The importance of F^2 in the creative process, however, cannot be overstressed.

The composer uses many devices to express his inspiration and arrive at poiesis, and an exhaustive enumeration here would tax our tolerance. Apart from those already alluded to, a selective sampling of F^2 devices should suffice to make my point. Bach was kind enough to provide the fundamental example of how poiesis is to be distinguished from praxis by writing the same sarabande twice (*English Suite* no. 3 in B Minor), first in the basic, plain, and direct style I associate with F^1, and then with "agréments," in the more elaborate, imaginative, and embellished style I associate with F^2. The "agréments" he relies upon most frequently are ornamentations or filigree notes known as mordants and inverted mordants—enough to give the two versions, while recognizable, entirely different personalities.

Bach's example (another is the sarabande of the *English Suite* no. 2 in A Minor) allows us to appreciate what is with reference to what can be; the latter gives fantasy its full range, revealing temporal sequences as they shape synchronic conventions. Similarly do Debussy's arabesques add to the straight lines of his melodic inventions. They are equally obvious as in Bach, but they need not be. Chopin weaves ornamentation into the texture of his melody so as to become inseparable from it (in principle, the same as the *grace-gamaka*, or curves of sound, of Indian music—not simple ornaments but essential parts of the melodic structure), and the ultimate of this type of workmanship might very well be Franz Liszt's piano transcription of Niccolò Paganini's "La campanella." Closely related to all this is the well-known form that proceeds directly from praxis into poiesis, often compounding the latter beyond belief, called "Theme and Variations," and for which a single example should suffice: Beethoven's thirty-three "Veränderungen über ein Walzer von A[ntonio] Diabelli," opus 120, for piano, as close to a prolonged F^2 tour de force on a single instrument as we can find.

A simpler and effective deviation, sometimes confused with musical humor, comes at the very end of Mozart's Symphony no. 35 in D Major, K. 385, the *Haffner*, the first theme of whose last movement behaves like a rondo by being repeated intermittently and identically, until the final return when the last note, A, is surprisingly stepped up to a B. Against all expectation, Mozart extends the space for his fantasy to take place, and keep the listener from thinking with anticipated boredom: "What, again?" Too much evident meaning can invite boredom, and at this point another device comes into play. Through the heightened fantasy of poiesis, the tendency toward the tedium of maximum certainty, regardless of whether the ear is comfortable with what it has become accustomed to (the systemic certainty, among other anticipations, of knowing how the piece will end), is obviated because of

the *designated uncertainty* introduced by the composer. . . . We should expect designed deviations, delays, and ambiguities to be introduced as systemic probability increases. . . . C. P. E. Bach, for example, writes that "embellishments are best applied to those places where the melody is taking shape, as it were, or where its partial, if not complete, meaning or sense has been revealed."[32]

Related to the device of ornamentation are the cadenza, whether in the first movement of Felix Mendelssohn's Violin Concerto in E Minor, opus 64, or in Vincenzo Bellini's "Casta diva" from *Norma*, and the technique of virtuosity—Aristotle's denounced "fantastic marvels of execution"—what Barthes says belonged to the "new Romantic deity, the interpreter."[33] Indeed, the more the poiesis deviates from the praxis and elaborate techniques prevail, the more the interpreter becomes the dazzling technician. Hence, too, the development of an aesthetic along the lines of purposeful complication, to combat tedium. The Renaissance courtly madrigal or the popular *frottola* exemplifies one of the most significant devices of purposeful complication in the history of music: polyphony, that counterpoint by which each part unfolds its own voice and which can go so far as to create artificial rhythm unrelated to melody—in other words, polyrhythm inside polyphony. Béla Bartók emphasized polyrhythm by the use of polymetrics, the separation of the accents of each rhythm. Repetition identifies the theme of Igor Stravinsky's *Le Sacre du printemps,* but its development proceeds rhythmically either by elimination or by metrical amplification. Giacomo Puccini's sparklingly ingenious juxtaposition of a whimsical lovers' argument with passionately serious lovers' declarations in the same quartet (*La Bohème,* Act III) is still unmatched in the operatic repertoire. A madrigal is overt polyphony; this quartet's is, as it were, covert. Polyphony, the most natural outgrowth from F^1, since it combines in its simplest form two or three F^1s, has become too fundamental a type of musical expression to be debunked. Not even the Central Committee of the Supreme Soviet, in accord with Tolstoy's reactionary synthesis in *What Is Art?* of the musical aesthetics of Plato, St. Augustine, Luther, and Calvin, has been able to ostracize its fantasy in the name of public corruption, incomprehensibility to the people, aesthetic realism, and decadent formalism.[34] When the committee leveled its charges against Shostakovich and Prokofiev, it failed to realize that music is less concerned with shaping systems of elementary objective relationships (F^1) than with constructing systems of tendencies, fantasy characteristics (F^2) that arouse the imagination, the aesthetic consciousness, be they unexpected structures, new melodic entities, tonal departures, clashing rhythms, or novel acoustics.

More examples of what I call poiesis might include retrograde structures in Anton von Webern and Alban Berg (the device's early practitioners), through which the music, having reached a certain point, reverses itself, to arrive at its point of origin (this has been called an image of negation); the seemingly directionless, chaotic prodigality of Heitor Villa-Lobos, whose density of detail in the *Choros* must be rendered with immediacy of improvisation and no more than a scheme of rhythmic relationships between each section; the opulence of Enrique Granados in *Goyescas* which strikes the listener with its chromatic sequential writing; the inward, evolutionary nature of Liszt's thematic metamorphoses in the *Dante Symphony* and the *Faust Symphony*, or the "Fantasia quasi una sonata" composed after reading Dante, to mention but a few examples in which the composer sometimes suspends structural motion and moves, as in the Inferno section of the *Dante Symphony*, through harmonic oppositions without modulations, thereby replacing modulation with juxtaposition[35] (as good an example as can be found of the relationship between literature and music where the nature of musical fantasy is dictated by the form of the work and its plot). I might mention finally Luigi Dallapiccola's *Canti di prigionia*, whose music abets dramatic expression by virtue of double and triple canons; distrait polyphony; and the final two flutes (symbolizing eternity), one of which plays the other's part backward (a comment on the nature of inescapable suffering).[36]

Similarly, we should not forget that Arnold Schönberg's innovative fantasy of the *Tonreihe*, or twelve-tone scale, came about as a deviation from basic musical syntax's reliance on the melodic-harmonic relationships derived from the major-minor tonal system. It represented a departure from what had been established on a praxis basis for centuries as a rule of musical logic. All these examples illustrate how poiesis takes shape, not to mention the obvious device of syncopation, which also violates intrinsically the rule of logic by contrasting musical accent with strictly rhythmic accent, and which cuts across all types of musical idioms, from Indian tablas to George Gershwin's "Fascinatin' Rhythm" from *Porgy and Bess* to Stravinsky's *L'Histoire du soldat* and *Petrouchka*.

Music, unlike literature, depends also on *technical* innovation, which in turn promotes automatically the development of an F^2 dimension. All we need to recall is Beethoven, whose inventive mind had already ventured through all the devices of modulation, who used a valved horn in his Symphony no. 9 and prefigured the revolution in the orchestra. We can guess with accuracy at what Plato would have said, even before the use of artillery by Pyotr Tchaikowsky! And since the range of music, by function of its self-evolving fantasy, keeps expanding, we do not have to wait long, historically, before eight—as distinguished from the traditional two and four—muted (in addition!) horns mimic the bleating of sheep in Richard Strauss's *Don Quixote*, and by absorbing the world of solid objects into music, give us, ironically in my context, what Anthony Burgess calls the Platonic ideal of bleating sheep.[37] The addition of the bass clarinet and contrabassoon have worked their own guile, and today the introduction of electronic, synthesized, and computerized instruments—from the experiments of Maurice Martenot (his *Ondes*) to frequency oscillators and the current modifications in the very concept of musical sound—augurs a further expansion of what the ear, in its automatic, namely conventional acceptance of F^1, will hear in coming elaborations stemming from technological innovation.

The radical shift involved in psychoaural aesthetics became pronounced one and a half centuries ago when Hector Berlioz conceived his more than symbolic and keenly symptomatic *Symphonie fantastique*, opus 14 (we must place special emphasis on the adjective). Indeed, the symphony encloses a literary fantasy (emphasized by the presence of opium) inside a musical fantasy. Berlioz created original auditory facts, new revelations in sensuous sounds achieved by the constant transformation of these sounds through the continual imposition of new forms. His imagination was originally described as "Babylonian and Ninevehan" (enough, one would say, for any F^2 designation) by none other than Liszt, and he was imaginative enough to use spacial direction as a compositional resource. This means that he placed his performing sources in an unusual, "illogical," innovative way to produce unusual, unfathomed, innovative effects: the *Requiem's* four subsidiary orchestras in the four corners of the performing space, producing fantastic configurations of sound that adumbrate Luciano Berio. Berlioz, indeed, harbored such arrogant confidence in the effect of the *élan vital* of poiesis, or the *Fantastisch*, that, like Richard Strauss, he arrived at the belief that words represent an inferior mode of expression, and that musical language can replace verbal language, suggesting that in time, given human evolution, the art of music will take over the art of language.

In fact, one of the most significant deviations in the elaboration of musical poiesis has involved the phenomenon of the human voice, supposedly on its way to being taken over by Berlioz's vision of the future, in the production of what Barthes calls "musical chimaera (the voice rising out of the symphony)—. . . all . . . deployed under the musical code of the West, tonality."[38] I am referring to a phenomenon that goes beyond the compendious effect of the solo and choral score of the last movement of Beethoven's Symphony no. 9, or of Gustav Mahler's Symphony no. 2 in C Minor (the *Resurrection* symphony) and Symphony no. 8 in E♭ Major (the *Symphony of a Thousand*), and reaches something akin to the mystic alliance, reflecting the origin of worlds, sought by the protagonist deep in the "heart of darkness" of the South American interior in Alejo Carpentier's *Los pasos perdidos*. The father of modern linguistics, Ferdinand de Saussure, has impressed upon us the arbitrary nature of words, where the quality of vowels has more to do with what is signified than we might have presumed. Berlioz aside, words and music constitute a formal, primal unity. The qualitative sound of vowels particularly is not remote from musical expression, as we have known for a long time, and something African tribes like the Bantus (e.g., their Duala language) do not even begin to question. Spoken sounds also transform constantly; ultimately, they may be considered articulated noises, not unlike the articulated notes of an instrument, and those who would follow Cage would then justify his denial of any distinction between the structured sounds of music and the noises, human included, of the external world. But though we may conjecture theoretically that even cacophonous rackets and clamorous hubbubs, in the name of F^2 departures, will eventually shape their own tradition, we must recognize the sensibilities of the human ear which are nothing more than easily offended extensions of bodily rhythms placed in us by nature, and Cage might have to wait a long time before our acceptance of noise under the heading of music is unchallenged. Rock 'n' roll (I refer primarily to acid rock) is bad enough, with its neurophysiological attacks on the cochlea: harmonic insignificance coupled with melodic aridity on unrelentingly mechanical rhythms and unrelieved high-decibel intensities, codified to stimulate animalistically rather than to inspire spiritually.

Music as an *art* still reaches us as graspable and pleasurable fantasy; noise startles us but cannot hold our attention. The spoken word, however, thanks largely to its vocalic structure and without becoming the *eidos* of the work as in a cantata or opera, can take its place acoustically and artistically alongside all registral placements of pitches, timbres, and rhythms. Words, we have been acculturated to believe, have conceptual meaning the way tones have emotional meaning, but nothing is to prevent us from doing as Berio did, that is, veil both and bring the two together in a kind of fantastic, generic newness. This opens a door to a future orientation in music and offers a way out of what Scholes sees as our linguistic limitation when it comes to imagining a world free of connection to our experiential world (reality). I submit that music, through the *Fantastisch* of poiesis, *can* "conduct the human imagination to a point beyond this reality"[39] (writers of science fiction take note) without unmooring our sensibility from the human coastline. In a sense, we return to the geometric ontology of Plato's *Timaeus* that reduces nature to a mystical pattern of numerical relationships, humanly perceived but without the moralistic implication and goal of the judicious life.

Berio's generic newness engenders heightened consciousness and a shift in aesthetic outlook. Like his *Momenti* and *Omaggio a Joyce*, his *Sinfonia of 1968* and, a significantly, *Voci* (1984) almost sound like ultimate deviations and are cases in point. *Voci* builds on human realities from the lives of Sicilians: songs of work, play, and love, lullabys, even street cries—folkloric transcriptions whose material is scrambled into experimental tone-color variations, what he calls his "philological abuse." Downstage, he arranges a heterogeneous orchestral group centrally around the conductor, and another, with a wide gap in between, peripherally upstage in a semicircle curling around the sides with total disregard for instrumental families, so that a violin plays next to a trumpet next to a bass next to a clarinet next to a drum—and so on. Unimaginable dimensionalities of sound emerge, reminding us indeed of numerical relationships. *Sinfonia*, whose title refers not to Classical form but etymologically to the "sounding together" of instruments (including the human voice) as well as ideas and references, goes even further. Human voices speaking human words in various languages do not convey a text but "instrumental" sounds. Yet a human mooring is retained. The first movement begins with a text from Claude Lévi-Strauss's *Le Cru et le cuit* dealing with the structure and symbology of Brazilian myths, a theoretical premise then exemplified in the second movement via a tribute to Martin Luther King, Jr., the words of his name suddenly surfacing intelligibly. The central third movement combines excerpts from Beckett's *The Unnamable* with a fantasized homage to Mahler, whose Second Symphony's Scherzo sounds pervasively—and, like a receptacle, gathers into itself, thereby transforming their "language" according to the new context, phrases from Bach, Schönberg, Beethoven, Richard Strauss, Johannes Brahms, Stravinsky, Berg, Pierre Boulez, and others. Berio calls them "characters" to fit the constantly changing fantastic landscape with a sense of anthropological evolution. The "texts" of the three preceding parts unite in the fourth movement, and in the final fifth the various fantasies are recapitulated and concluded (the original snippets from *Le Cru et le cuit* being fleshed out into narratives), uniting the whole through what the composer calls "the 'Language' [sic] of the composition itself." We are leagues away from Claudio Monteverdi's then forward-looking aesthetic whereby harmony must achieve an expressive relationship between tone and word, because Monteverdi, himself not free of Platonic biases, still thought in terms of moral categories. Berio rejects them : "Categorical statements, such as right and wrong, beautiful or ugly, typical of the rationalistic thinking of tonal aesthetics, are no longer useful in understanding why and how a composer today works on audible forms and musical action."[40]

When words communicate as melodic sounds, the latter become signs and adumbrate the realm of semiotics. But this inquiry I leave to others. I stop with Berio's mind-expanding poiesis where their affective power functions superbly. Jonathan Cullar states that any sphere of human activity, "from music to cooking to politics," can be approached semiotically,[41] thus substantiating Charles Peirce's "We think only in signs,"[42] and no doubt any analysis of the music of the future will deal with the signs and symbols and the enlarged fantasies that will shape and structure our perception of new worlds through art. The listener will fit together the pieces of music he receives, restructure things for himself—for *himself*, because the subjective reception will not disappear. Cage's criticism of that mentor of experimental music, Edgar Varèse, for teleologically injecting his personality into music ("Varèse is an artist of the past; rather than dealing with sounds as sounds, he deals with them as Varèse."[43]) just cannot obtain, even in science fiction.

Fantasy, communicated through verbal signs or musical visions, still relates to the *human* mind, though it may involve nonhuman entities of nature. Olivier Messiaen comes to mind, from the sensory, nondeveloping harmonies of his early works yielding to melismatic arabesques, to the *Ile de feu's* Indian-based *(ragas* and *talas)* magic fantasies leading later to emulations of the cries of birds: in his view, humanity reborn through the language of the birds (a noteworthy expansion of the F^2 already evidenced by the recorded nightingale in Ottorino Respighi's *I pini di Roma*). Therefore, Messiaen "has created a language . . . , and that language has made considerable impact upon twentieth-century music."[44] Thus, the composer furnishes space for poiesis, emerging from praxis, to take place. And as even the guarded Kant would have said, it is essential that everything spatial be experienced in the depths of the imagination—where fantasy works its in-novations.

POSTSCRIPT

So long as the ear and the human moorage are not abandoned, audiences will in time assimilate the heightened and novel principles of musical fan-tasy; when the shock and hesitation before the overt violations pass, what may have disquieted will be prized and viable critical criteria will be devel-oped. Aesthetic constructs will shape themselves around the artistry of the advanced innovations with which fantasy will flow, for only poiesis invigo-rates and ennobles music. In music's interrelation with literature, science fiction might well lead the way, becoming a new humanism through which our tried, recalcitrant—however well intentioned—modes of thinking and feeling can find invigoration. "I have now the conviction that pure science is pure art."[45]

Unfortunately, writers of science fiction have not paid sufficient attention to the undefinable, heiroglyphic phenomenon of music,[46] whose semantics like its semiology eludes us but whose fantasy, as Giuseppe Mazzini ob-served, is "the algebra of the soul whence lives humanity."[47] Perhaps some-day they will *utilize* (not merely allude to, as Isaac Azimov does) music in their futuristic explorations of new worlds, simply because music will always remain at the Schopenhauerian core of all that is organic as well as, now, inorganic. Perhaps they will find in Franz Joseph Haydn's *Il mondo sulla luna* and Leos Janaček's *The Adventures of Mr. Bronček* and *The Makropou-los Case* implications of which the composers themselves were unaware. I should like to see these writers give music more substance by going beyond Yevgeni Zamyatin's *We*, where it becomes a process of psychic control in the Single State—material music (analogous to the single existence in that State of iambic pentameter in poetry), however, that reminds us of Plato and the Spartans again, but from which the character I 330 tries to break away by heightening her listener's consciences by playing, yes, Scriabin. A substantive musical dimension to science fiction might corroborate Ferruc-cio Busoni's[48] opposition to Spengler's historical, musical cynicism concern-ing our civilization's current and final phase before it collapses into anarchy and dissolution (Plato again?):

What is practiced as art today—[like] music after Wagner—is impotence and false-hood. . . . What do we possess today as "art"? A faked music, filled with artificial noises of massed instruments.[49]

At one time, John Stuart Mill could be seriously tormented by the thought of the inexhaustibility of musical combinations—let alone the superimposed effect of massed instruments!—by which he meant, on the one hand, the seeming paucity of the five-tone/two-semitone octave that, on the other hand, can produce so awesomely much. These fears are mere philosophers' constructs that make no allowances for the grandeur of the phenomenon of fantasy, of poiesis, because, as Giacomo Leopardi observed, if the philosopher is not a poet his is not philosophy. Burgess once said that music, after all, is the mind of God. Leopardi was both poet and philosopher, someone whose imcomparably rich notebook, I have found, provides us with profound views on just about any issue. Music is no exception. He first saw (in 1823) Plato's system of ideas as the Greek himself did, as "a fable," and then proffered what could be the final word (italics added):

The principle, indeed the true art of the *inventors* of music, and the true, proper music and the great effect of their *inventions*, can only be seen . . . when their melodies are such that the people, and generally all the *listeners*, are *struck* and *amazed* by them, as if they were listening to a *new* melody. . . . Which proper effect, indeed the *only* effect *proper* to *true* music, the only *great, vibrant,* and *universal* effect, can only be obtained through *adornment* and *embellishment,* through judicious *variation,* in order to *ennoble,* so to speak, to bring together and arrange in a *new* way, to *present with a new aspect* [F²] melodies that have become absolutely and *formally* popular [F¹] . . . , that is, melodies that the *ear* knows more or less, and has become *used to.* The poet is no different; his art . . . consists . . . in choosing *lesser known* things, in clothing them newly through *adornment* and *embellishment* with *novelty* and the harmony of his verse, with *metaphors* and every other bright stylistic device, . . . almost as if by *magic* incantation. . . . He takes, for example, the *creatures of nature* and makes them speak naturally . . . so that the reader, recognizing . . . that *language* . . . , still finds it *new* and more *beautiful* at the same time . . . , because of the poetic *adornments* and the *new style,* in short, the *new form* and the *new body* that drape it. Such is the task of the poet, and such, no more and no less, of the Musician.[50]

LITERATURE IN MUSIC

PERCEPT AND CONCEPT:
ON HUGO'S *HERNANI*
AND VERDI'S *ERNANI*

When the acerbic but astute music critic George Bernard Shaw turned his attention to Victor Hugo's *Hernani* and Giuseppe Verdi's *Ernani*, he commented with reference to the character of Don Carlos: "In the play, Charles is sublime in feeling, but somewhat tedious in expression. In the opera, he is equally sublime in feeling, but concise, grand, and touching in expression, thereby proving that the chief glory of Victor Hugo as a stage poet was to have provided libretti for Verdi."[1] Musical drama, he implied, provides a natural stimulant to sublimity, thus elevating it above spoken drama in its ability to communicate deep emotions. Shaw followed up his comment when, on the subject of Pietro Mascagni's transposition of Giovanni Verga's *Cavalleria rusticana* to music, he wrote about the "superior intensity of musical expression [which makes] the opera far more real than the play."[2]

We must exercise care with Shaw's use of the term "real" if the implication is that Hugo's drama does not do something it should do, namely, adhere to principles of verisimilitude. By "real" Shaw means that the emotional realities of the play are much better served and communicated, in his words, by "the grandiose Italian opera in which the executive art consists in a splendid display of personal heroics, and the drama arises out of the simplest and most universal stimulants to them."[3] The critic appears to subscribe to the general opinion that Hugo's play is too laden with gestural modes and artificial stylizations, not to mention psychological absurdities, to handle the suspension of disbelief that musical drama instills as a matter of course, divorced as it is from artistic naturalism through its reliance on accepted conventions. As far as "reality" is concerned, we know that usually the reverse of Shaw's opinion obtains, and spoken drama will normally claim far greater verisimilitude than musical drama. Suspension of disbelief results in spectator permissiveness. Peter Conrad has said that "Music pardons all faults,"[4] while W. H. Auden, when asked why he wrote librettos, replied more openly that for him opera was the last refuge of something he appreciated: high style.[5] Both comments implicitly deny the need to emphasize reality altogether. Yet Shaw would praise Verdi's opera above Hugo's play for being more "real."

The question is why, and the reason, I believe, is twofold: first, a misjudgement of the play; second, inattention to an important focal point of the opera. If by percept we mean a mental impression of something imagined (as well as perceived by the senses), a basic component in the formation of concept—which is a concrete idea or human understanding of something—then Hugo's motivation was an aesthetic percept, Verdi's an ethical concept.

Certainly Hugo did not try to pursue the path of verisimilitude; his aesthetic perception encompassed different and more striking horizons. We know, as he also did, that his dramas stemmed from the melodramatic tradition, à la Guilbert de Pixérécourt, who evolved a form of popular tragedy that cultivated the sensationalism of astonishment, farce, suspense, and horror. It is as unfair to judge Hugo by what he never intended to do as it is not to recognize that a man of his high intellectual stature knew perfectly well that *Hernani*, say, was unrealistic, what Balzac dismissed as not commonsensical, "an enormous idiocy," since it contained no illusion of truth.[6] Even that admirer of Hugo, André Breton, chastized the poet's unverisimilitude in a "monotonous and artificial" theater,[7] and a modern critic minces no words in declaring the plays "ridiculous and very dreadful."[8] We have heard all too often that Hugo did not care to control his imagination, that his dramatic encounters rested on coincidences and disguises, that his thought process was provoked visually and stoked by antitheses, that he stressed sonority, spectacle, and eloquence at the expense of characterization, psychological justification, and human consistency.

What we have not heard often enough is that the point of *Hernani* is not the contrast in Don Ruy Gómez between honor and baseness or senile jealousy and patriotic faithfulness, or the incongruity of Don Carlos the royal lover and the political moralist, or the improbable single-mindedness of Doña Sol, or even the Castilian self-sacrifice to principle of Hernani himself. The play *Hernani* demands our own suspension of disbelief. In so doing, to use

the unfavorable words of one critic paradoxically, we can reverse the traditional relationship between poetry and drama: "It is not the purpose of the
poetry to develop or illuminate the dramatic issue; it is the purpose of the
drama to contrive situations in which the characters can launch themselves
into poetic speeches."[9] Constructing credible developments and plausible
ties between character and situation does not coincide with Hugo's aesthetic
percept, which is to orbit the imagination, using love, jealousy, hate, honor,
and politics as mere ingredients for a lyrical fantasy, indeed a historical
fantasy, given the political setting and the local color, but a fantasy nonetheless, with all the magical and moving qualities of an epic—meaning a
romance epic à la Ariosto. Despite the fated horn or Don Carlos's lengthy
monologue in Act IV, there is no adult sense of Sophoclean fate; there is
fantasy, which suits the youthful reader—and the two protagonists, like the
King, are adolescents, in their teens or barely out of them[10]—moving in a
world where only chance can be detected, not fate for which they are too
young, too full of explosive energy and passion. Fate renders everything too
"real." *Hernani* cannot be weighted down with tragic emotions under these
circumstances, only with pathetic feelings, in the sense of *pathétique*. If the
protagonist declares that "I am a force that moves," I interpret the statement
not in the context of a chilling destiny, but in that of nature, of the impassioned youth seeking the free life, the elegy of love, through magnanimous
actions and under lunar nights. His sense of restlessness does not derive
from the human condition, as has been pompously suggested, but simply
from eager anticipations. And his gloomy tones, when we hear them, especially during his oaths, emerge less from a philosophically tragic sentiment
of life than from overyouthful language that outdoes its own context.

As I believe this to be the case, I also believe that subjecting this aesthetic
percept to rational analysis opens the door to ridicule only too easily. It
falsifies Hugo's art, which invents situations that acquire magic and suggestive powers *because* they are unreal, because we are dealing with a poetry of
transcendence, indeed high-style drama (as Auden liked) making us witness
illusion, not reality. Hugo is picturesque in the finest sense: his language
contains tonalities, and these tonalities make us conjure up mental images,
impressions, perceptions that in turn become musical. We go to see *Hernani*, not to think about the events, but to listen to its sounds. It is no
surprise, then, that the noted musicologist of the last century, Eduard Hanslick, thought mainly about Hugo when he described French plays of the

time "less [as] tragedies against which music would do violence, than librettos which have not yet been composed."[11] Did not Hugo himself say, in the famous "Préface à Cromwell," that the dramatist employs "the fascinations of opera"? We have almost come back to Shaw.

Justly, then, it has been said that *Hernani* has an operatic quality, and unlike Classical drama in which soliloquies fulfill dialectical functions, in this Romantic play the plot provides the framework for what could be solos, duets, arias, and recitatives.[12] Hugo can claim all he wants that drama has an imitative function; this is not how he writes, for he is too rhetorical for mimesis. Verdi's librettist Francesco Maria Piave, on the other hand, did not have to preserve the rhetoric. The music would do that automatically, for it possesses inherently the ability to communicate and arouse passions. Verdi had one of the keenest theatrical instincts in history and knew well that, especially in the case of *Hernani*, music would allow verse to fill the dramatic, emotional frame and handle the otherwise questionable *coups de théâtre* with acceptable nonchalance. Years later, Ferruccio Busoni was to say: "What I desire from an opera text is not only that it conjures up music, but that it allows room for it to expand."[13]

It was Verdi who outlined the libretto for Piave, shortening Hugo (125 pages reduced to 40, for example, and 5 acts to 4), changing a few names (Doña Sol becomes Elvira; Don Ruy Gómez de Silva becomes known simply as Silva); altering a few events (only Ernani dies at the end, instead of Hernani, Doña Sol, and Don Ruy Gómez, and the instrument of death is a dagger instead of poison); and, as if to appease Shaw's sense of the "real," giving the characters psychological motivations. But he respected Hugo, not wishing to tamper with the play's substance and retaining the abstract themes (mystery, crime, love, plots, surprises, disguises) which would resound expressively through his music. He insisted that music remain properly deferential to dramatic values,[14] and he recognized Hugo's "operatic quality": "In *Hernani* [signor Piave] would only need to condense and tighten up; the action is all ready-made; and it is immensely gripping."[15] Again: "Urge Piave to take particular care with the verses and not to omit any of those powerful phrases in the original which always have such a fine effect in the theatre."[16] Still again: "in the last two [acts] the closer we keep to Hugo, the greater will be the effect. I think those two acts are divine."[17] In other words, as his biographer Carlo Gatti says, "Verdi sowed in the furrow plowed by Hugo."[18] And Piave maintained some of the youthful quality of the play when he has Don Carlo, about to become Emperor Charles V, sing nostalgically of his "green years" ("verd'anni miei") and invoke the disappearing "Beauty . . . youth!" (Bellezza! . . . gioventù!") among the tombs in Act III. But the characters impress us as being older. In addition, he leaned, like Verdi too, toward the rapidity and violence and lurid hues of Hugoan Romanticism, certainly if one looks back to the previous operas *Il Nabucco* and *I Lombardi* (composed with a different librettist).

But the new quality of *Ernani*, and what makes Verdi's motivation an ethical concept, that which humanizes the characters and makes them—in addition to the musical sculpting—more "real," is the sociopolitical dimension. In Hugo it is a mere motif; in Verdi it becomes a dramatic core. A true product of Italian Romanticism, which, similar to Norwegian Romanticism, was more political than metaphysical like the German, nature-oriented like the English, or sensational like the French, Verdi "needed the inspiration of appropriate political and social subjects to inspire his lyrical muse."[19] The Risorgimento's struggle for national unity and liberty—with all its problems of power and authority and its mitigation between public order and private freedom—focused Verdi's muse on immediate, human concerns, rather than on sweeping political philosophizing, which was more Richard Wagner's style. The composer worked best in the arena of immediate actuality; as Auden put it, "The quality common to all great operatic roles . . . is that each is a passionate and willful state of being."[20] This quality offended Hugo's aesthetic percept; immediate actuality is far from what he had in mind for his historical fantasy. Massimo Mila has noted that when the Hugoan *Hernani* was transplanted across the Alps to become the Verdian *Ernani*, the subject acquired an explosive force that Hugo could never have suspected:

this Elvira who invokes the bandit Ernani to come to steal her away from the abhorred embrace of that old man Silva, what else was she if not the young Italy extending her arms to someone who would come to free her from her old masters? . . . [See] the conspiracy scene with that captivating male chorus, full of incendiary phrases, where it was so easy for the spectators to substitute mentally the word Italy for the word Iberia.[21]

The reference is to Act III, Scene 4, "Si ridesti il Leon di Castiglia," which the censors at first did not allow, though the persuasive Verdi prevailed by modifying a few verses. "Out of context," writes one observer, "the Lion of Castile chorus sounds banal, but in the opera it not only serves its immediate purpose admirably but also is capable of awakening feelings of group solidarity and togetherness, as is proved by the meaning the Venetians [the opera's premiere took place in Venice's Teatro La Fenice] imposed upon it, and the use they made of it in substituting 'Venezia' for 'Castiglia.'"[22] To this may be added the use the Romans made of it to praise the newly elected Pope Pius IX, or, more significantly, the political demonstrations the opera aroused in Paris, to Hugo's instant anger,[23] where a new title for the opera had to be found—*Il proscritto*—and where the characters's Hugoan-Iberian names had to be changed to Italian.[24]

Judging from the immense popularity of the opera all over Europe,[25] it is clear, whether Hugo liked it or not, that Verdi had used the French poet to express the spirit of the generation of 1848. The chorus has little to do with the actual story of *Hernani*, but it functions as a disguised Risorgimento ode,[26] as indeed do the other scenes with political stresses. It is interesting that, where Hugo happens to be more political in the play, there Verdi and Piave changed less for the libretto. Still, all in all, the composer was careful to conceal the sociopolitical meaning under the protagonists' love duets and solos. And the blend of the love story, about which Hugo fantasized, with the immediate historical reality, of which patriot Verdi was aware, created characters more three dimensional than Hugo's, and therefore, for Shaw, more "real." They are more adult, and the music makes them more prone to recognizable sorrow; and "sorrow is the climactic moment in [the] process of a character's humanization, from which flows, with a sense of commiseration, the typical Verdian melody."[27] This is the direct result of Verdi's personalization of history, where "every allegiance implies an emotional commitment and every situation becomes a repository of emotional trust."[28] Thus did the ethical concept supersede the aesthetic percept.

Moreover, through the music the action gains a certain cogency that the fantasy-driven spoken drama could not have. A single example suffices: that of the horn motif. Hernani has vowed to kill himself at his rival's, Don Ruy Gómez's, command after both have avenged themselves of King Don Carlos's willful intrusion in the life of Doña Sol. The command: a blast of the horn. Verdi's Preludio begins adagio with this pledge motif, which overshadows the ensuing romantic love theme by returning. In the opera, in other words, as distinguished from Hugo's play—with the ethical overshadowing the aesthetic, with sociopolitical considerations alive, and with more adult protagonists—there *is* a sense of fate, an inexorable nemesis. Unlike Wagner, Verdi was a pessimist. The motif recurs in Act II and again in the end, activating but still suspending suppressed emotions between recitative and song, each restatement acquiring a more intense, expressive symbolism. In Hugo, the horn can come into play only in Act III, and when the pledge is alluded to in Act IV, it is, says one critic, a "non-effect."[29] In the history of music, we are here in the presence of an early form of the leitmotif, "which [Verdi] has been often accused of appropriating from Wagner."[30] Here again we can see how Hugo's ideas were more adaptable to the musical medium.

Verdi wrote for the contemplating listener; Hugo, for the listening reader. Verdi is sometimes uneven and magniloquent; Hugo, startling and full of speeches. Both, however, are vigorous and compelling. Among other things, Hugo offered Verdi excellent opportunities for characterization that were not the French poet's intention to exploit on the human, social scale: the outlaw-lover Hernani; the opportunistic, self-gratifying monarch (before imperial responsibility ennobles him) Don Carlos—that is, the lover and man of destiny; the paternally erotic Don Ruy Gómez de Silva; the exquisite, anxious, and hapless Doña Sol. Hugo aroused the fascination of other composers as well: Vincenzo Bellini wrote sections of an *Ernani* in 1832, but with censorship astir, he prudently shifted his music to *La sonnambula;* later in the century, Alberto Mazzucato wrote an *Ernani,* and Victor Duvernoy composed an overture. But it was Verdi who produced the significant work. Hugo's percept of a fantasy epic necessarily heroized the real, while Verdi's political concept deheroized the epic to make it real. And if epic and novel now exist in some kind of symbiotic relationship, I am tempted to say that *Hernani* is a *roman manqué,* while *Ernani* is a *drame réalisé.* Yet, for all that, it was Hugo who provided the libretto, without which the operatic composer cannot work. As Busoni commented, "To me, the all-important condition is the choice of a libretto. While for the drama there are almost boundless possibilities of material, it seems that for the opera the only suitable subjects are such as could not exist or reach complete expression without music—which demand music and only become complete through it."[31] With uncanny, heightened perception, Hugo seemed to invite the notion of music, including of chorus, when in Act V, Scene 3, just before the dooming horn is sounded, he wrote:

>   . . . Car la musique est douce,
> Fait l'âme harmonieuse, et, comme un divin choeur
> Eveille mille voix qui chantent dans le coeur!
> Ah, ce serait charmant!

>   (. . . For the music is sweet,
> Makes the soul harmonious, and, like a chorus divine
> Awakens voices by the thousands singing in the heart!
> Oh, would that be charming!)

[16]

A MATTER OF INCOMPATIBILITY:
PUSHKIN AND TCHAIKOWSKY

The Russians, we read, turn to their beloved poet, Aleksandr Pushkin, for consolation and positive thoughts, for springtime and optimism, for mirth and the pleasant joys of yesteryear. Their dark lot of hardship and endurance—unmodified, one might say, since they began recording their history—induces forced convictions of happiness and laughter (translated politically, this means a sense of primacy) that block out, in sporadic outbursts, what Miguel de Unamuno calls the tragic sentiment of life. See, by way of just one example, how many Soviet critics insist that Anton Chekhov's melancholy—some would say tragic—*Vishnevyy sad* is a riotous, side-splitting comedy.[1] That they are not necessarily alone in this is not the point. The fact that it fits a pattern, however, is. But the reverse side of the coin also obtains; for during the silences between the outbursts, a dim moroseness of resignation can quickly spread to tint the world view. A gloomy side to Pushkin surely exists, strongly underscored by the pervasiveness of his irony, however gently it flows from his pen, and his masterpiece *Yevgeniy Onegin* is not the only case in point. It becomes, nonetheless, a telling piece, especially when Pyotr Tchaikowsky gets hold of it and—disregarding the poem's irony, detachment, and mordant wit—converts it into an opera of heavy, impassioned, dim, and tragic love. As the Russian saying goes, nothing succeeds like excess.

Fyodor Dostoievsky called the poem, through Tatiana's last words to Onegin (whose late advances cannot replace his earlier rejection: "But I am given in wedlock to another, and I will be faithful to him forever"), an apotheosis of resignation. This is what Tchaikowsky did with his music, write an oratorio of resignation and not, as one reviewer of Pushkin's work claimed, a capriccio in which "the poet is constantly playing, now with a thought, now with an emotion, now with imagination; he is alternately gay and pensive, frivolous and profound, derisive and sentimental, spiteful and good-natured; he doesn't let a single one of our mental faculties slumber, but he doesn't hold on to any one and he doesn't satisfy any one."[2] Indeed, the composer stresses only the pensive, the emotionally profound, the sentimental, and in the long run, thinking his opera contains too many bland, unincisive, and notationally wordy pages, it does not even satisfy his own mental faculties. His inclusion of country airs and mazurkas and courtly airs and waltzes does nothing to restore the cynical, derisive vivacity of the original. In fact, he drains every ounce of Byronic irony, sharp humor, and titillating ambivalence out of the text and leaves only a pathetic story to furbish the drama and sustain the listener's interest. Biographers are quick to tell us that in reading the novelistic poem Tchaikowsky saw in Tatiana the anguish he must have caused his future wife Antonina Milyukova when he so indecorously rejected her and that, when he created his musical portrait, he poured himself totally into her emotions. A glance at his correspondence makes this hard to deny: "I am under the spell of Pushkin's verse, and I am drawn to compose the music as it were by some irresistible attraction." But a glance at his overall musical production makes it equally hard to deny that Tchaikowsky was incapable of ironizing musically and that his ability to use the musical scale for wit was very limited. Whether or not his autobiographical thrust made him disregard the poet's oscillating meanings and polysemantic utterances and focus exclusively on dark truths, and whether or not his high specific gravity made him disregard Pushkin's ability to transform experience without running away from its sadnesses so as to leave space for affirmative energies to rise,[3] Tchaikowsky ended by composing an opera not based on *Yevgeniy Onegin* as Pushkin wrote it but on *Yevgeniy Onegin* as he, Tchaikowsky, thought it could be. In so emasculating the original and slighting the springtime and the optimism, as it were, he probably never asked himself why he did not give the characters different names and the opera a different title.

Tchaikowsky's incompatibility with the work of his predecessor has been very well described by Gary Schmidgall, who wrote: "Between the intentions of Pushkin and Tchaikowsky lies a strange aesthetic warp that seems to divide—and make mutually exclusive—the essential qualities of poem and opera."[4] He has shown how the heart with its "stress of love" (Tatiana's letter, Lensky's final aria, the last Tatiana-Onegin dialogue) and not the intellect dictates the composer's expression; how sympathy replaces deflation;

how the composer identifies more with love-smitten Lensky, including his inertia and naïveté as well as his sentimental yearning, than with cool, volatile, witty, and ingratiating Onegin; and how he avoids Tatiana's dream and the foreshadowing of Lensky's death (too ironical?).[5] The same Tchaikowsky of the Overture to *Romeo and Juliet* who took the fresh and clean love of two teen-agers and amplified it into the troubled, full-bosomed passion of adulthood also took the genuine, simple, and pure feelings of a country maid and injected them with lyrical plenitudes of parodic proportions. When Pushkin's Tatiana rummages through Onegin's abandoned library and, in trying to better understand the man's character, is surprised at what she discovers: "Might he not be, in fact, a parody?" (Tchaikowsky naturally did not touch this passage), the operagoer might in fact ask the same of the composer's work. The famous letter scene, with its eight anxious changes in feeling in the music corresponding to the shifting moods in the letter Tatiana is composing, is hardly an innocent celebration of pure love. Its specific gravity keeps pulling our emotional resistance lower through the heaviness of the downward moving orchestral phrase, abetted, as in the Overture to *Romeo and Juliet,* by the sighing and lamenting horns:

It is important to make this observation, because Tchaikowsky began the composition of *Yevgeniy Onegin* with this letter, which then cast its agitated spell onto the rest of the opera. Indeed, the four-note core idea that occupies the Prelude:

also a "descending" motif, weaves its way throughout the musical drama, like a motto theme. The Russian romantic flattened sixth scores highly, as do dropping fourths and fifths by the flute, clarinet, and horn which do not, as someone has suggested, convey the naïve character of the writer and the act of writing itself.[6] The music makes everything thicker.

I can certainly accept Schmidgall's conciliatory conclusion that "as a faithful translation of literature, [Tchaikowsky's *Yevgeniy Onegin*] is a catastrophe, but it is nevertheless an *operatic* success."[7] And there is something to another scholar's claim, that when a great work of literature gets "translated" into a musical work, critics tend to measure the result against its source[8]— which perhaps they ought not do. Still, if the composer does not change the title of his opera, the impatience of the knowledgeable reader/listener is unavoidable; in no way can he react as if he did not know the original, and to say that the opera would be fine if he could obliterate Pushkin from his mind is to say to nothing. Verdi and Boïto knew this when they worked out *Otello* and *Falstaff*, and even if Shakespeare was the source, they came through magnificently—let alone Puccini, who did wonders with Murger's *Scènes de la vie de bohème* in *La Bohème*, or Mozart and Lorenzo Da Ponte who did the same in *Don Giovanni* with Tirso de Molina's *El burlador de Sevilla*.

I am not in agreement with Schmidgall, however, who is ready to put part of the blame over Tchaikowsky's failure to convince us that he was "under the spell of Pushkin's verse" on music's inability to establish the needed ironic distance that Pushkin's narrator, who is nowhere in the opera, establishes in the poem.

For the impact and communicative power of music are direct; music cannot alone say other than what it 'means'—cannot itself create ironic distance. . . . Not only because Tchaikowsky was preoccupied with the direct impact of strong emotions but also because opera finds uncomfortable the complexities of an ironic perspective, it was perhaps inevitable that the composer should banish Pushkin's narrator from his opera.[9]

Otherwise put, there can be no Romantic irony in music. This opinion, to me, is erroneous. Humor is one thing, and we all recognize it in Rossini's *Il barbiere di Siviglia* or Donizetti's *Don Pasquale*. But parody is quite another, and it does acquire a musical language in Mozart's *Così fan tutte* or R. Strauss's *Ariadne auf Naxos*; and irony, too, creeps into many an operatic product, like Busoni's *Doktor Faust*, and I should say especially in Verdi's *Otello* (through Iago) and his *Falstaff*.[10] As for ironic distance, Romantic irony is *almost* as much a possibility in music[11] as it is in Byron's *Don Juan* or Tieck's *Der gestiefelte Kater*. There is no reason that Pushkin's phraseology cannot find correspondence in the art of sounds: "Now my Onegin is at large: hair cut after the latest fashion . . . , and finally he saw the world"; "How he was able to seem new . . . , conquer by means of wit and passion . . . , pursue a love . . . , and afterwards, alone with her, amid the stillness give her lessons!"; "He sang parting and sadness, and something, and the misty distances, remoteness, and the romantic roses. . . . He sang life's faded bloom at not quite eighteen years of age"; "Why is Tatiana, then, more guilty? is it because . . . she . . . in her dreams believes? Is it because she loves without art?"; "Tragiconervous scenes, the fainting fits of maidens, tears, long since Eugene could not abide . . . "; and so on. Pushkin's dandy can be shown through musical methods to be quite self-controlled in a society that accepts any sign of learnedness shallowly and delights in the superficiality of anecdotal conversation: think of Mozart's ability to treat such a circumstance, and think of how Verdi would have treated the final crushing irony of Onegin's capitulation to passion. Irony, including ironic distancing, like parody and humor generally, is not outside the purview of musical expression. In fact, ironic humor has contributed to the aesthetic psyche of the musical experience from Mozart to Mahler, and if we wish to extend our point of view historically, to Erik Satie, Gian Carlo Menotti, and John Cage. There is no justification, therefore, in rationalizing Tchaikowsky's treatment of Pushkin's work and continuing to call it by its original name.

With his setting of Pushkin's prose story *Pikovaya Dama*, on the other hand, we need not rationalize too much or develop the impatience we feel before a false musico-literary correspondence. Yet, strangely enough, critics have paid less attention to this Pushkin-based opera of Tchaikowsky's than to the popular *Yevgeniy Onegin*. Not that Pushkin's parodic temper receives due recognition and translation. The writer's offhand manner, as Viktor Shklovsky pointed out in a comparison with Laurence Sterne's *Tristram Shandy*,[12] remains the hallmark of his style, which is antipathetic to the composer's irrepressible need for involvement, and, as another critic put it, "the question and quality of parody is never far away in Pushkin."[13] Tchaikowsky could not handle the implied thrusts at the Romantic predilection for ghost themes, madness, unrequited love, demonic power, and secret meetings; if they are there, he plays them straight, as he does with the insidious theme of sexuality—covert with Liza, more overt with the Countess[14]—by converting the former into love (the invitation to her room) and the latter into melancholy (the Grétry air reminiscence of yesteryear), and by avoiding entirely the irony of the bishop's funeral oration. And this, not to mention the Countess' wily "wink" in her coffin and Hermann's copying his love letters from a German Romantic novel. Furthermore, the ending is altered to fit Tchaikowsky's weighty Romanticism: instead of marrying prosperously someone else after rejecting Hermann because of his duplicity, the opera finds Liza jumping to her death into St. Petersburg's cold river (Tosca's leap from Rome's Castel Sant'Angelo is far more convincing), and instead of going mad after losing his entire fortune of 47,000 roubles at the gambling table when the queen of spades shows up instead of the desired ace, Hermann dies of a stroke on the spot and the opera ends with a liturgical motif.

Still, these omissions and alterations do not interfere radically with even our "literary" appreciation of the opera because in the Pushkin story the parodies and ironies are considerably underplayed in comparison with *Yevgeniy Onegin*, where they are essential. The composer, more operatically at ease in 1890 than in 1879 when he had put together *Yevgeniy Onegin*, had developed more artistic control of the operatic medium and—apart from the simple fact that the plot of Hermann's and Liza's story is easier to shape into an opera than Onegin's and Tatiana's—he was, to his credit, able to sustain a lyrical impetus (à la Puccini) without stopping the action more successfully than he had in his previous musical drama. And the chromatic extensions of his harmonies contain what might easily have become explosions of furious lyricism. If some feeling of incompatibility with his literary source still lingers, it is again due to the problem of the exclusion of ironic possibilities. But these do not loom as serious; the opera is a better balanced, hence a finer achievement. His symphonies, I would argue, are even finer works because he was primarily a symphonist and thought in instrumental terms (his most successful arias, like the Prince's love song to Liza [Act II, Scene 1] might sound better if given to a clarinet or horn), and his most engaging melodies belong to them. I might argue, too, that the dramatic requirements of characterization lured Tchaikowsky to "enter" his characters (Hermann "can become Tchaikowsky"[15]), especially in his first opera (Tatiana through his Antonina and Lensky through himself), whereas the mere process of scoring a moving line for an instrument allowed him greater emotional distancing.

It is difficult, however, to refrain from thinking that the combination of Mozartian levity and depth would have better served the Pushkin tales. Alluding to Aldous Huxley, one Russian critic has seen the point: the British author "has rightly observed that although Mozart's music seems gay, it is in fact sad. The same can be said about . . . Pushkin. . . . The artistic expression of sorrow . . . is so filled with light . . . that the content appears joyful."[16] Tchaikowsky's waters are too troubled and run too deep for the purpose of translating Pushkin. The large Russian audiences that flock to hear their favorite *Yevgeniy Onegin* as well as *Pikovaya Dama* obviously leave the literary texts at home and do not expect Tchaikowsky to hand them springtime and optimism. The darker valence obtains. But they may well go to the literary text for the brighter valence. A. D. P. Briggs properly quotes Lev Shestov to capture this spirit:

Dangers, disasters and misfortunes, far from undermining the Russian writer's creative spirit, strengthen it. He emerges from each new trial with renewed faith. . . . Pushkin . . . was the first to stand his ground when confronted by the terrible sphinx. . . . The sphinx asked him: How is it possible to look at life and still believe in truth and goodness? Pushkin replied: Yes, it is indeed possible, and the mocking and terrible monster disappeared.[17]

17

FROM *OTHELLO* TO *OTELLO*: IRA OVER *GELOSIA*[1]

The interrelation of *Othello*, sometimes considered one of William Shakespeare's weaker plays, and *Otello*, usually considered one of Giuseppe Verdi's better operas, has received broad coverage. And not a few are those who contend that the opera represents an improvement over the play. Such comparisons put us on slippery slopes, for the requirements of verbal drama differ too widely from those of musical drama to provide a functional common denominator over which to link valid comparisons. Be this as it may, there are still aspects of the interrelation—structural rearrangements and shifts of emphases—that remain to be analyzed in order to appreciate better Arrigo Boïto's work as the librettist and Verdi's genius as a "Shakespearean" composer whose affective power is at least equal to that of his literary model.

As Joseph Kerman points out, opera as drama must not be measured exclusively in terms of plot or according to some notion of naturalism relating to character, locale, or detail.[2] Rather, the criterion must be the physical and psychological response of the characters to the action; the heavier the response, the heavier the drama. Music must function less as a mood setter than as an interpreter—an imaginative catalyst that stokes, not the surface of action and emotion, but their *quality*. Words address this quality specifically, but the unspecificity of sounds allows them to say more. Yet "each art has the final responsibility for the success of the drama."[3] Herbert Lindenberger distinguishes between the mimetic and the rhetorical[4]—between the play, with its emphasis on imitation over effect, and the opera, with its effect and intense immediacy of communication. Quality amounts to a wedding of mimesis and rhetoric that permits various levels of stage action to dovetail into the production of a unified impact.

This impact must be accomplished, not despite the compressions, distortions, and omissions required to transpose verbal into musical drama, but because of them. Gary Schmidgall says of these compromises: "The subject of literature as opera is largely one of compromise between the excellences of the written or acted word and the unique and separate splendor of musical expression."[5] Creative compromise would be a better phrase, to allow each art its prerogative and identity. And creative compromise ultimately means an aesthetic congruence respectful both of the original drama and of the artistic prerogatives of the musical medium. The librettist excises and shrinks; his fundamental art is terseness, in Gaetano Donizetti's words, "Brevity, for heaven's sake, brevity," while the composer restores and expands—in Verdi's words, "music will do the rest."

Musical drama can "do the rest" especially well when the original verbal drama has operatic qualities, like Friedrich Schiller's *Wilhelm Tell* or Maurice Maeterlinck's *Pelléas et Mélisande* or Shakespeare's *A Midsummer Night's Dream*. Or when it can gain by expansion into the orchestral dimension. Ferruccio Busoni commented that the only suitable operatic subjects are those that need music for full expression—something that is equally applicable to a great work like *Faust* and to a modest work like *Hernani*. Like good wine, good opera deriving from verbal drama results from a fermentation, a breakdown of the organic compounds of the play into a concentrated blend. *Otello* represents such a blend, since, as has been recognized, music is inherent in the poetry.[6] "*Othello* is a play by Shakespeare written in the style of an Italian opera," mused G. B. Shaw.[7] We should exercise caution, however, in how we perceive the orchestra. Using Jago's "Credo" as an example, some would say that through orchestration opera merely exteriorizes that impressive soliloquy with which Boïto wisely presented Verdi, giving it a public quality that Shakespeare's intimate and self-conscious soliloquy does not have.[8] But the composer and the educated listener know that the orchestra works both ways. It does not perform only a ceremonial, externalizing role, for its true role is to further internalize the thoughts and emotions—in this case, Jago's—in order to express what words by themselves cannot. What seems outwardness to the eye and ear is inwardness to the mind and heart.

Now, what Boïto/Verdi do so remarkably is to effectuate that concentrated blend of the inward and the outward in *Othello*. A telling example of this relates to the felicitous shift of emphasis from a private to a public emotion, from the play's punctuating motif of jealously to the opera's pervasive tonality of wrath *(ira)*. If Dante is any guide, the lion—Othello is, after all, the "Lion of Venice"—stands for violence, beginning with anger. To be sure, jealously is only commonly *perceived* to be the principal motivator in *Othello*, and not many scholars go along with this perception. Nonetheless, the "green monster," as Iago calls it, compels our attention, and, judging from the direct allusions in the drama, clearly supersedes its derivative, anger. Both ideas surface in Act III, Scene 4 as if in resumé, the first mitigated by question and conditional, the second underscored by proverbial wisdom:

IAGO

Can he be angry? I have seen the cannon
When it hath blown its ranks into the air,
And, like the Devil, from his very arm
Puffed his own brother, and can he be angry?
Something of moment then. I will go meet him.
There's matter in 't indeed if he be angry.

EMILIA

But jealous souls will not be
   answered so.
They are not ever jealous for the
   cause,
But jealous for they are jealous.
   'Tis a monster
Begot upon itself, born of it-
   self.

Verdi's succinct description of the Moor to Boïto—"he loves, he is jealous, he kills and is killed"[9]—reflects a common reading of Shakespeare; but after a hearing of the opera, it is difficult to agree with the critic who asserts: "Otello is Jealousy and Iago Envy."[10] In fact, if it comes to an apportionment of the two emotions, it is Jago who turns out to have more *gelosia* in him and Otello more *ira*. While retaining the inward self-consciousness of *gelosia*, Boïto's libretto compresses the action and stresses the *ira*, whose outward displays enhance the dramatic effect. For Verdi's purposes, the blend was perfect. In doing "the rest," the music could now integrate the instrument of jealousy, the handkerchief, and its abstract image, the ensnaring web (Shakespeare's "There's magic in the web of it" [Act III, Scene 4]), with the movements and symbols of anger (the shift of the storm from the play's Act II, Scene 1 to the opera's opening scene, thereby setting the tone of wrath, was a brilliant stroke). And the whole, amplified as it is by irrational human elements, is swept along by the fury of Nature acting under the canopy of destiny *(Fato)*. The following outline suggests the process.

| | ACT I | |
Shakespeare's *Othello*	Boïto's *Otello*	Comments
Act I, 1:9–33; 55–57 and I,3:303–308; 362–366[11]	Act I, from "Roderigo, ebben, che pensi?" to end of "È una cagion dell'ira"	Boïto establishes motivation for Jago's villainy, and introduces motif of *ira*
I,3:130–168 Othello tells Doge of his courtship of Desdemona	Courtship related by the couple to each other	Showing and telling are joined in Boïto, for the famous love duet; motif of 'bacio'
Act II,1:1–30; 53 "A sail!" mention of storm, Turkish fleet, and Othello's triumph	Opera opens with the actual storm, and "Una vela! Una vela!"	Boïto shows the *ira* of nature, the storm; *ira* bound to "Veneta fortuna . . . e il Fato"—link with Otello
II,1:169–170 Iago: "With as little a web as this will I ensnare . . Cassio"	Appears in handkerchief duet of Act III	Fusion of means with end in Boïto: device of concretization
II,1:186–199 Othello: "If after every tempest come such calms . . ."	"Tuoni la guerra . . . dopo l'ira immensa viene quest'immenso amor!", then love duet	Shakespeare places after the physical storm, Boïto after emotional storm of Cassio's disgrace
II,2 Herald announces celebration, bonfires	"Fuoco di gioia" chorus	Themes of storm and love joined by Boïto; adumbrate more *ira* than *gelosia*; two interpretations of "fulgido incendio che invade il cor": joy can become its opposite
II,3:17–258 Othello breaks up fight between Cassio and Montano: mentions their rage, his own: "Now, by heaven, my blood begins my safer guide to rule; and passion, having my best judgment collied, assays to lead the way. . ."	Otello alludes three times to *ira*: "O la turchesca *rabbia*," "Ah! l'ira volge l'angelo nostro tutelare in fuga!" and "dopo l'ira immensa," "l'ira immensa"	Both authors foreshadow Iago's artificial production of *ira* in Othello with that of *ira* via wine in Cassio; externalization of *ira* motif in the duel, emphasis of its impact on individual and society

Shakespeare's *Othello*	Boïto's *Otello*	Comments
	ACT II	
	Act II opens with this scene, with the two 'innocents' coming together more naturally	Shakespeare emphasizes concern with loss of reputation; Boïto, Jago's manipulations
II,3;319–333 Iago convinces Cassio to go to Desdemona for intercession with Othello		
II,3;356–367 Iago's soliloquy, "Divinity of Hell!"	Jago's 'Credo'	Boïto again introduces motif of *ira*, now as man's basic nature: "Credo in un Dio crudel che m'ha creato simile a sè e che nell'*ira* io nomo"
Act III,1 Cassio sends musicians to serenade the newlyweds	Modified to serenade of Desdemona by Cypriots; a 'positive proof' which only momentarily sways Otello in Desdemona's behalf	Reinforcement in Boïto of innocent and virtuous image of Desdemona: correlation to the Madonna
III,3;34–40; 92–163 Iago and Othello enter, seeing Cassio with Desdemona: "Ha! I like not that": the temptation scene	"Ciò m'accora." Faster, more powerful treatment of Jago's poisoning of Otello's mind: Otello is rather easily convinced of her guilt	Desdemona does not interrupt in Boïto as she does in Shakespeare; thus, intensification of tempo
III,3;164–170 "O, beware, my lord, of jealousy . . . the green-eyed monster," says Iago	"Temete, signor, la *gelosia!* È un'*idra* fosca, livida, cieca, col suo veleno sè stessa attosca, vivida piaga le squarcia il seno"	Boïto specifies the form of *gelosia*, because it forms so much a part of Jago himself
III,3;190–192 Othello gives logical sequence of doubt-proof-resolution: "Away at once with love or jealousy!"	"Pria del dubbio l'indagine, dopo il dubbio la prova . . . amore *e* gelosia vadan dispersi insieme!"	"or" becomes "and"—Boïto's Otello is already decided about his wife's guilt
III,3;258–268 Otehllo's soliloquy as to *why* Desdemona may be unfaithful	In Boïto, but Otello is wrapped up in himself: he ruminates in Desdemona's presence, ignoring the tender expressions of her love and respect	Boïto places this *after* the hanky's loss; Shakespeare before: his Othello is trying to see clearly

III,3;278 Othello: "If she be false, O, then heaven mocks itself! I'll not believe it!" inspired by the mere *sight* of Desdemona	Othello conquered by the serenade, not by sight of wife: "S'ella m'inganna, il ciel sè stesso irride!"	Shakespeare places this even *after* her first petition for Cassio, but Boïto only before; greater emphasis on guilt
III,3;283–320 Appearance of hanky: it is accidentally dropped; Emilia willingly gives it to Iago. Little tension involved	Otello ill-humoredly throws away the hanky; Emilia takes it up but does not want to give it up to Jago: tension and threats, fear	*Ira* appears directly and indirectly in this scene between Emilia and Jago: "il tuo nefando *livor*" and "l'*irosa* mia man"
III,3;321–329 Iago's plans for the hanky: "Trifles light as air are to the jealous confirmations strong as proofs of holy writ"	"Con questi fili tramerò la prova del peccato d'amor." Extension also to proof of sin *against* love, which is jealousy itself	Hanky = veil = web = trap; motif begins, now that *ira* motif is established; hanky as metaphor for love and woman
III,3;333–451 Othello's "False to me!"; his farewell speech; and his demand for "ocular proof" from Iago; if empty suspicion, Iago must answer to his "waked wrath." 'Proofs' of Cassio's dream, possession of hanky: Othello now believes her infidelity—"One [life] is too poor, too weak for my revenge. . . . O, blood, blood blood!"	Same sequence, but strengthening of *ira*: "Vò una secura, una visibil prova! O sulla tua testa s'accenda e precipiti il *fulmine* del mio spaventoso *furor*. . . . Una [vita] è povera preda al *furor mio*"	Joining of storm and *ira*: nature and man united for a spectacle akin to the wrath of God. Return of destiny motif: "Il rio destino impreco." Otello's *ira* intensified and joined with *gelosia*: "Nelle sue spire d'angue l'*idra* m'avvince! Ah! sangue! sangue! sangue!" With this second allusion, *idra* becomes a central image
III,3;460–476 Othello's and Iago's oath of vengeance: "Now, by yond marble heaven, in the due reverence of a sacred vow I here engage my words"	"Sì, pel ciel marmoreo giuro! Per le attorte folgori! Per la Morte e per l'oscuro mar sterminator! D'*ira* e d'impeto tremendo presto fia che sfolgori questa man ch'io levo e stendo!"	Intensification, emphasis on Otello's passions, for vindication and rage: end of scene with "Dio vendicator!" Otello *is* this, in a transference in Boïto from Act I. Shakespeare emphasized objective claims of justice, Boïto the subjective

Shakespeare's Othello	Boïto's Otello	Comments
	ACT III	
III, 3:77 Othello makes Iago his lieutenant after the oath	Boïto moves this to Act III, *after* Otello has seen the hanky in Cassio's possession	Note placement: only after "ocular proof" has been provided does Boïto change Iago's rank
III,4:37–100 Desdemona and Othello play out their mutual obsessions, Cassio and the hanky; Othello rushes out and Emilia and Desdemona discuss jealousy; Iago joins them and in seven lines four times says "Is my lord angry? . . . Can he be angry?" Only joining . . . in Shakespeare of *gelosia* and *ira*	Act III, placed after Iago promises to have Cassio incriminate himself before Otello; play of obsessions here reveals Desdemona's perception of Otello's *ira:* "nella tua voce v'è un grido di minaccia! . . . in te parla una *Furia*"	Introduction of this act in Boïto is built on motive of *gelosia:* this is a private emotion, in which knowledge of truth causes suffering. *Ira* is a public emotion: ignorance of truth, thus suffering. (NB: the Furies stood for *wrath*, not jealousy, in the Middle Ages and in antiquity)
Act IV,1 Othello with Iago, whose poison is working; Othello works himself into an epileptic fit with "Handkerchief—confessions—handkerchief"	This closes Boïto's Act III, but only *after* Otello has made a public display of both *gelosia* and *ira* before the Venetian ambassadors: his private life destroys his public one	Union of the two emotions is maintained throughout Boïto's Act III, with crescendo at end in Otello's 'fall' and Iago's triumph, to prepare for the worse events of Act IV
IV,1:81–179 Othello overhears Cassio's 'confession' and sees hanky as proof: Iago: "As [Cassio] shall smile, Othello shall go mad; and his unbookish jealousy must construe Cassio's smiles, gestures and light behavior quite in the wrong." Bianca brings the hanky to Cassio, thus indicating the double betrayal of Othello (Desdemona with Cassio, Cassio with Bianca): Othello's utter and complete humiliation due to this	As Otello watches, he repeats "Dio frena l'ansia che in core mi stai" When hanky is shown by Cassio: "Ruina e morte! Tutto è spento! amore e duol." Hanky duet between Cassio and Iago, which stands as a metaphor for two views of love and woman. Iago: "Questa è una ragna dove il tuo cuor casca, si lagna, s'impiglia e muor." Cassio: "Miracolo vago . . . più bianco, più lieve che fiocco di neve, che nube tessuta dall'aure del ciel." End with trio of: "Miracolo vago!" "Tradimento!" "Troppo l'ammiri—Bada!"	One of Boïto's rare uses of dramatic irony: Iago is speaking clearly to Otello in his duet with Cassio. Concentration of symbolic motifs in Boïto: hanky = web = trap; imagery of hanky intimately related to that of woman/love in general, Desdemona in particular: cf. the words and images of the Cypriots' serenade, as well as the Classical allusions in Cassio's greeting to Desdemona in Shakespeare. Note similarity of Iago's description of the hanky to the action of the *idra* felt by Otello: "Nelle sue spire d'angue l'idra m'avvince!"

IV, 1:180 "How shall I murder *him*, Iago?" which Iago channels toward Desdemona: "Strangle *her* in her bed, even the bed she hath contaminated." "Good, good: the justice of it pleases"

IV, 1:226–292 Public scene between Othello, Desdemona, Venetian ambassadors: she asks, "What, is he angry?" when Othello speaks under his breath to her; but no one knows his true state. He treats his wife like an automaton after he strikes her (260–270) and calls her devil. Ludovico reflects on how much Othello has changed from his noble Venetian self: "Is this the noble Moor whom our full Senate call in all sufficient? Is this the nature whom passion could not shake? Whose solid virtue the shot of accident nor dart of chance, could neither graze nor pierce?"

"Come *la* ucciderò?"—transference immediate, for brevity. Otello after Jago's suggestion: "Questa giustizia tua mi piace." After Jago says he will slay Cassio, Otello only now makes him his lieutenant

Otello has Cassio summoned for torment/proof when he learns of his recall to Venice. Emphasis on *ira*: Otello seizes Desdemona 'furiously'; Ludovico says "Egli la man funerea scuote anelando d'*ira*." Return of the motifs of storm and destiny in the choral soliloquies—Cassio: "L'ora è fatal, un fulmine sul mio cammin l'addita . . . un'onda d'uragan"; Roderigo: "S'oscura il mondo, s'annuvola il ciel coll'atre pugna." Scene ends with Jago's hypocritical "È l'*ira* inutil ciancia" and his incitation to revenge. Otello unleashes his fury on all present: "Chi non si scosta è contro me rubello," and, 'convulsively, deliriously' works himself into a paroxysm of *ira*, due to which he faints

Shakespeare's Othello is still in love: "The pity of it, Iago!" Note the objective tone toward justice his Othello maintains, whereas Boito's is thoroughly subjective, focused on both Otello *and* Jago

Boito has made it clear throughout that Otello is *not* the steadfast hero who has finally fallen, but rather a man who has been slowly consumed by his native Moorish nature—*ira*. Otello's past and present states are juxtaposed by both authors, with Boito showing rather than telling; he exteriorizes the workings of the soul, emphasizing Otello's literal and metaphorical fall via its counterpointing with the Cypriots' hailing of the Lion of Venice from outside. This apex is countermanded by the nadir, as Jago exults over Otello's inert form: "Ecco il Leone!" effectively echoes "Vittoria! Sterminio!" of Act I. Before his fainting occurs, however, another allusion to the *idra* image: Jago explains to the crowd that "Lo assale una malìa che d'ogni senso il priva," after which Otello babbles "Vederli insieme avvinti . . . il fazzoletto! Ah! . . ." and faints

Shakespeare's *Othello*	Boïto's *Otello*	Comments
IV,2:1–94 The 'bordello scene,' and Desdemona's innocent reaction: "I understand a fury in your words, but not the *words*." In 49–64 his ambivalence toward her is still evident: "Had it pleased heaven to try me with affliction. . . ." Discussion of Othello among her, Emilia, Iago [not present in Boïto, though perhaps his choral soliloquies create a parallel]	Placed after the play of obsessions, and before the "ocular proof" of the hanky, from Otello's "Alza quegli occhi!" to "quella vil cortigiana." It is here that Desdemona is aware of the "Furia" in him: "*la sento e non l'intendo*." Otello's "Dio! mi potevi scagliar . . ." as a soliloquy of profound dejection after he has forced her out of the room	In Boïto, Desdemona is not innocent of the world: she understands the import of Otello's *words* but is puzzled by his manner: he changes 'suddenly from anger to the most terrible, ironic calm'; he is very much alien to her understanding and her experience
IV,3:11–59 Desdemona has been sent to bed by Othello, and Emilia asks her "How goes it now? He looks gentler than he did." The 'Willow Song' follows: "Let nobody blame him; his scorn I approve—Nay, that's not next"	ACT IV Emilia's words open this act. The wedding sheets in Shakespeare become "la mia candida veste nuziale . . . se pria di te morir dovessi mi seppellisci con un di quei *veli*." Variation of 'Willow Song': "Egli era nato per la sua gloria, . . . Io per amarlo e per morir"	Reprise of 'velo' motif: now it becomes her literal shroud, just as it was the symbolic cause of her death. Shift in song's content illustrates author's conception of singer's personality: Shakespeare's heroine is very submissive, a sacrificial lamb; Boïto's is more aware of husband's basic nature, and the incompatability of her love with it
IV,3 This scene ends with Desdemona and Emilia's discussion of adultery: Emilia endures retaliation: "The ills we do, their ills instruct us so." Desdemona responds: "Heaven me such uses send, not to pick bad from bad, but by bad mend"	Boïto alters this into a prayer by Desdemona to the Virgin Mary: "prega nel peccator, per l'innocente, e pel debole oppresso e pel possente, misero anch'esso. . . . Prega per chi sotto l'oltraggio piega la fronte e sotto la malvagia sorte. . ."	As above, these provide different modes of insight into her character; Boïto balances out his more wordly wise and stronger willed heroine with extensive religious imagery and attitudes

V, 2 Othello secretly enters Desdemona's room to slay her; his soliloquy includes "Put out the light [the candle], and then put out the light [Desdemona's life]"	Stage directions for Otello's entrance are a literal translation of the verbal into the visual: 'He stands before the candle, undecided whether to extinguish it or not. He looks at Desdemona, then puts out the light'	Boïto's Otello is more decisive in his actions than his Shakespearean counterpart: he is also not given to self-analysis
He kisses her and she awakes; he tells why he must kill her: "By heaven, I saw my handkerchief in [Cassio's] hand. O perjured woman! Thou dost stone my heart, and makest me call what I intend to do a murder, which I thought a sacrifice"	No self-inquiry or objectified justification of why he must kill her; his *ira* predominates, especially in the almost hysterical exchange between them over her crime and her attempt to postpone his revenge	Boïto's Desdemona puts up a more emotionally energetic struggle for her life than her Shakespearean counterpart: comment has been made about the 'shift' this causes in the libretto—it is no more Otello's tragedy, but Desdemona's
Othello strangles her, then uses a pillow: "I that am cruel am yet merciful; I would not have thee linger in thy pain"	Desdemona shrieks as she is strangled, while Otello is apparently very cool: "Calma come la tomba" in his comment	Remnants of Othello's great love are still present in Shakespeare, as well as his inherent nobility and sensitivity
Revelation of Iago's villainy, though Emilia questions Othello's affirmation three times. Emilia: "Villainy hath made mocks with love!" Iago is brought in: "I told him what I thought, and told no more than what he found himself was apt and true"	More concentrated. Otello: "A Jago il chiedi." Emilia: "A Jago?" "A Jago." "Stolto!! e tu il credesti?" "Negarlo ardisci?" When Jago is brought in and Emilia asks him "Hai tu creduto Desdemona infida? Parla!" he answers only "Tal la credea"	Shakespeare emphasizes throughout his play the perceptual element, and self-illusioning: thus the prevalence of dramatic irony. Boïto defines his Otello and Jago in terms of *ira* and the satanic, thus simpler, more concentrated lines and treatment
Othello mentions the handkerchief as proof positive of Desdemona's guilt: Emilia reveals Iago's part in this, and she is slain by Iago	Same, except for Emilia's death; however, there's an extensive variation on the 'velo' motif via related words—Emilia: "Tutto *rivelo!* . . . costui dalla mia man quel fazzoletto *svelse* a viva forza." Montano: "Rodrigo morente mi *svelo* di questi'uom l'arti nefande"	Boïto echoes words and imagery to concentrate and unify primary motifs and themes of the opera—Otello to Jago in Act II: "Dunque senza *velami* t'esprimi, e senza ambagi"; Desdemona to Otello in Act III, after she sees the "Furia" in him: "Mi guarda! Il volto e l'anima ti *svelo.*" We also recall the first words of the opera: "Una vela! Una vela!"

Shakespeare's *Othello*	Boïto's *Otello*	Comments
Iago flees, and Othello recognizes his own cowardice: "I am not valiant neither, but every puny whipster gets my sword. . . ." His reflection on his fate and his view of Desdemona [similar language is in Boïto], with his own self-weighing and concern for his fame in both the personal ("then must you speak of one that loved not wisely but too well") and the public ("I have done the state some service, and they know 't") realms. His words at his suicide: "I kissed thee ere I killed thee: no way but this: killing myself, to die upon a kiss"	Same action, but Otello's reaction presented in different terms: "E il ciel non ha più fulmini?"—his storm of rage recalls the real storm of Act I, just as the calm of Act I's ending is recalled with his suicide and the reprise of the love duet: "Un bacio . . . un bacio ancora . . ah! . . . un altro bacio. . . ." This haunting motif closes the opera	Shakespeare is primarily concerned with the tragedy of the hero Othello, a great man brought low through a fatal flaw: thus, there are noble speeches and references to the great general of Acts I and II (Boïto has no corresponding act for Act I, in which the hero's qualities are firmly established). Boïto also, however, recalls *his* Act I, but emphasizes not the great *man* now fallen, but rather his *flaw itself* (storm, *ira*), and what he lost because of this flaw; thus, there is a return of the 'bacio' motif of the love duet, the one moment in the opera when Otello and Desdemona were in complete and blissful accord. And symbolically, the word may end, but the musical phrase on "-cio" does not
The play ends not here, but rather with the reestablishment of justice and order: Ludovico consigns Othello's goods to his next of kin, his office to Cassio, as well as the proper trial for Iago for the murder/suicide. As in Boïto's opera, this too is a kind of circularity, for the word ends with a completion and return to the tenor and status of its first act		

After thus dissecting Boïto's *Otello,* we become aware of the overriding motif of elemental *ira* and of how it moves through the text. The raging storm with which the opera opens foreshadows what will happen to Otello himself: he is the commander of the vessel ("della veneta fortuna") being tossed about ("or s'affonda, or s'inciela") by a storm that is associated with the wrath of God ("Iddio scuote il ciel bieco, come un tetro vel" [the "hand-kerchief of jealousy," too, will become a "tetro vel"]). This storm ends well, however, for the Turks are defeated and Otello "s'inciela," ascends to the peak of his glory: "Evviva Otello! Vittoria, vittoria!" But soon the Cypriots' song of victory is ominously juxtaposed to death: "Vittoria! Sterminio! Dispersi, distrutti, sepolti nell'orrido tumulto piombar." This will prove the key to the whole opera, even though Act I itself strikes the victorious tone—not that of "s'affonda"—closing as it does in utter calm and unity with the tender love duet between Otello and Desdemona.

The opening of Act II prolongs this peacefulness, as Jago holds out to Cassio the promise of reconciliation with their lord through the intervention of Desdemona. But this apparent resolution grows, through Jago's machin-ations, into Otello's raging emotional storm, stirred by his oath of "vittoria, sterminio" over Cassio and Desdemona. Thus the end of the second act returns to the opening of the first, with Otello's *ira* replacing that of God and the elements, and his victory becoming one that will destroy, not con-serve, nature and human relations. Appropriately, Act III begins with a brief but false lull, when Jago tells Otello how they will obtain the "proof" the latter so desperately seeks. Yet soon it too develops, from the suppressed storm between Otello and his wife as each plays out his own obsession, into a grand public spectacle in the scene with the Venetian ambassadors. The "Evviva! Evviva Otello!" of the Cypriots is juxtaposed to the lord's decision to slay his wife that night (his moral fall) and his fainting after his paroxysm of rage (his literal, physical fall). Jago's comment, "L'eco della vittoria porge sua laude estrema," is apt, for it applies not only to Otello's situation but also to his own; his victory over his superior is complete, in that he has achieved the "sterminio" of the very soul and conscience of the Moor. The "lion" has been caught in the "web" of the handkerchief, and a tragic Fate is about to be fulfilled.

Like the previous act, Act IV opens with an ominous calm: Emilia and Desdemona find themselves in the eye of the hurricane as they await Otel-lo's entrance. His turbulent rage increases until it reaches its fateful denouement in the murder and suicide. The physical storm of the first act is re-called in his words "E il ciel non ha più fulmini?" when he realizes the horrendous magnitude of his actions. The tempest of nature and wrath of God have been rejoined, just as the emotional tempest of rage in Otello has spent itself; only now can there be a return to the absolute calm which ended Act I, the calm symbolized by "Un bacio . . . un bacio ancora . . . ah! . . . un altro bacio." The temporal union of two loving souls has been replaced by the eternal state of a dual death.

With either "inspiring simplicity"[12] or variegated texture, the orchestra carries the structural burden of translating *ira* (and *gelosia*) into music. Verdi uses common compositional devices with an artistry which tends to defy analysis due to its deceptively unassuming sophistication that is dramati-cally—mimetically *and* rhetorically—suited to the quality of the action pro-posed by Boïto's, let alone Shakespeare's, evocative vocabulary. Sometimes the techniques are so subtle as to slip by unnoticed, yet they remain unfail-ingly effective. As an example, we might point to the first act's bonfire, scored to make the chorus' and other participants' snippets of melody dis-appear in the ensemble the way tongues of fire disappear into the atmos-phere. A fragment of melody is as common a musical fact as its use in Verdi's bonfire becomes subtly symbolic. Chromatic runs, echoed by se-quences in the minor second, used with specific reference; diminished chords held in ominous suspension; trills and quavers used less in humor or orna-ment than for purposes of thematic portrayal; shifts from major to minor, however imperceptible, exteriorizing what the libretto wants to signify—these devices and others color and distinguish the scoring with reference to the substance of the action.

Take, for example, the shift from major to minor in the "Vittoria! Ster-minio!" passage of Act I; it follows a "Vittoria, vittoria!," rendered in B, and continues the tonality but falsely, for soon we realize that the positive B Major is merely the dominant of the negative E Minor, into which key the music slips when the word "sterminio" is used. Similarly, "Fuoco di gioia" sounds in E Major, but with the ambiguous "Fulgido incendio che invade il cor" we have been lowered into E Minor. We are thus made aware that different types of fire may exist—all a matter of interpretation. Making full use of the minor mode's tenebrous psychological connotations, Verdi fre-quently introduces the minor third cross-referentially. After Jago has re-minded Otello of the handkerchief in Act III, the same interval sounds when the Moor warns his wife angrily of "il fazzoletto." Such a simple device gives tonal unity to the fundamental direction of the opera's action.

If Verdi has an interval bias for the minor third in this opera, he also has a harmonic bias for the diminished chord, which he establishes with the orchestral introduction (allegro agitato) to Act I, purposely not resolving it (only murder and suicide at the end "resolve" things), and which he employs to underpin the text's first use of the word *ira* (Act I: "E la cagion dell'ira, eccola" [Jago to Roderigo about Cassio]). The *ira* in the opening statement of Jago's "Credo" is similarly underscored. A dominant bias accompanies that triple rhetoric of wrath at the end of the act ("O turchesca rabbia" and "Ah! l'ira volge l'angelo nostro tutelare in fuga"), but, significantly, the third allusion ("dopo l'ira immensa") is rendered in the positive context of G♭ Major, since the subject has turned to sweet reminiscences, dulcified by a muted cello, soon joined by three more. The sense of a dominant ninth resolving elliptically provides an exquisite lead-in to the famous love duet. And when, on the issue of the handkerchief (Act II) now appearing like a web for entrapment, the dominant G seventh resolves in C, we hear a major of (foul) determination, surrounding music with "stabbing accacciature figures always on the off-beat, like a thought that emotionally gnaws at the brain."[13]

The chromatic scale is a standard rhetorical device for agitation; Verdi supplements this commonplace by making it also a device—indeed, a near leitmotif—for evil and jealousy and therefore for association with Jago and with the handkerchief. The instances abound, the phrase usually proceeding in a descending direction: Jago hinting at his evil (Act I, immediately following the first use of *ira*); the diffident exchange between Jago and his wife Emilia (Act II: "Su te l'irosa mia man s'aggrava" [Jago], and "Il tuo nefando livor m'è noto" [Emilia]); Otello raging in a manner recalling the storm motif (Act II: "fulmine del mio spaventoso furor"); the heavy chromatic accompaniment supporting Desdemona's feeling of entrapment (Act III: "l'angoscia in viso e l'agonia nel cor"); Otello's paroxysm of *ira*, shouting "convulsively, deliriously" at the thought of the handkerchief (Act III); and the loud chromatic runs in the orchestra as he queries despairingly: "E il ciel non ha più fulmini?" (Act IV). Most intriguing is the use of downward chromatics in the first act's jovial drinking song, where one would not expect to encounter this device so commonly associated with injurious moods; but Verdi subtly gives the runs, not to the chorus or to Roderigo or Cassio, but, of course, and appropriately, to Jago, who plots evil inside the general merriment. Even more striking is the slithering chromatic scale in his hypocritical advice to his lord (Act II): "Temete, signor, la gelosia," with full orchestra on pianissimo, not unlike—in effect more than in structure—the curling line with voice and accompaniment in unison on the image of the hydra, Shakespeare's "green monster" (Act II). The jealousy-provoking account of Cassio's dream (Act II: Jago to Otello) on a monotone pianissimo actually harbors a chromatic intensification in the orchestra, as happens in the stirring oath taken by Jago and Otello at the end of this act. Here, another clever subtlety occurs: when sung by the Moor, the oath, "Questa man ch'io levo e stendo," enjoys a clear, open tonality (A Major), without chromatics, but his part acts tellingly as a countermelody to Jago's, the leader in the whole affair, who sings over chromatic lines in the orchestra.

Minor seconds constitute the basic unit of a chromatic phrase, like a phoneme to a syllable or word; similarly, to the more extended chromatic scale, they may be handled cheaply as fill-ins, and penned by a less genial composer they would sound exactly so. But Verdi's fashioning of them is always significant and is usually associated with the presence of the handkerchief as an ensnaring web. Minor second sequences are highly suggestive of the weaving process, to begin with. But more than that. In the 6/8 allegro brillante description of the handkerchief, "Quest'è una ragna dove il tuo cuor casca," where, more to the point, "il tuo cor . . . s'impiglia e muor" (Act III), we hear an "embroidered" staccato that moves in and out of itself—a true "nube tessuta." The hydra motif is intoned by the cellos, but quavers on the flute, piccolo, and violins seem to shimmer like a web in the light; they reflect by contrast Jago's heavy, low-brassed envy in Act II, and imprint in our ears the correlation between what we heard as viola semiquavers and the idea itself of jealousy. These quavers complement the trill, effectively used by Verdi to underscore wrath (as through the violas and clarinets at the moment of *ira* in the "Credo" [Act II], or the flurries of semiquavers supporting Otello's enraged, triple insistence on the "fazzoletto" over Desdemona's unrelated utterances [Act III]), to suggest that diabolical combination in Jago of good humor and evil intent (the music becomes insidiously innocent), and to intensify jealousy. The handkerchief trio (Act III), for example—with Otello's furious "È quello!"—is full of negative devices, "cross-rhythms, unisons on diminished sevenths, savage trills."[14]

Shakespeare has far from suffered in Verdi's musical translation. The shift

of emphasis from jealousy to wrath for Otello and the transference of jealousy to Jago encourage a heavier response to the events by the characters
and—consistent with the rhetorical requirements of musical drama—make
possible a unique quality in the interrelation of text and music. Like any
great play, *Othello* contains too many complexities to be covered by an
opera; yet Verdi, in compressing and intensifying his mimetic material, could
not reduce his Otello to sheer blind jealousy and his Jago to sheer villainous
evil. Boïto served him an artfully blended concentrate, and the composer
welcomed it, sculpting (as literally as this term can be used for music) an
orchestration that bridged all potential gaps between action and accompaniment, and filling in untold internalizing nuances of which the reduced text
was incapable by itself. Indeed, the music did "the rest."

18

THE *KALEVALA*, SIBELIUS, AND THE MEANING OF INWARDNESS

Then old Väinämöinen sings up a hazy blue wilderness,
into the wilderness he sings a sturdy oak and a strong rowan. . . .
Steadfast old Väinämöinen got his harp,
sat down to play, began to play beautifully.
Everybody starts to listen to that, to marvel at the joyous music,
the men in a good mood, the women with laughing mouths,
men with tears in their eyes, boys on their knees on the ground.
The people grew weary, the country folk get worn out;
all the listeners fell asleep and the onlookers sank down;
the young slept, the old slept to Väinämöinen's music. . . .
Steadfast old Väinämöinen played the harp a long time,
both played and sang, so that it was joyful, indeed.
The music was heard as far as the moon's dwellings, the joyous sound heard up to
    the sun's windows.
The moon comes from its house, steps onto a bend in a birch branch;
the sun came out of its fine house, took its place on the crown of a pine
to listen to the harp, to marvel at the joyous music. . . .
There he began to sing. He sang magically for his last time,
sang up a copper boat, a copper-decked vessel.
He sits down in the stern, set out for the clear expanse of sea. . . .
"Let time pass, one day go, another come;
they will need me again, be looking, waiting for me
to fetch a new Sampo, to prepare a new instrument,
fetch a new moon, free a new sun
when there is no moon, no sun nor any worldly joy."
Then old Väinämöinen sets out quickly
in the copper boat, in the flat-bottomed copper craft
toward the upper reaches of the world, to the lower reaches of the heavens.
There he stopped with his vessel, out of weariness stopped with his boat.
He left the harp behind, the fine instrument for Finland,
the eternal source of joyous music for the people, the great songs for his chil-
    dren. . . .

. . . "I blazed a trail for singers,
blazed a trail, broke off tree tops, broke branches, showed the way.
Thence the way goes now, a new course stretches out
for more versatile singers, for ampler songs
in the rising younger generation, among the people growing up."

Thus, from beginning to end, the epos of Finland, the *Kalevala*, reveals its secret, always taken for granted and so never stressed—and therefore near forgotten: music, its central impulse and generator of a cultural, artistic vitality that has come down to us in the compositions of Oskar Merikanto, Erkki Merlartin, Armas Launis, Kerl-Muller Berhaus, Robert Kajanus, Leevi Madetoja, Johan Filip van Schantz, and, among others, especially Johan Julius (Jean) Sibelius. It is not enough to say that the *Kalevala* takes its place alongside all the other popular epics—from the *Iliad* and *Odyssey* to *Beowulf* and the *Niebelungenlied* (with stress on the *Lied*)—which, as characteristic of the oral tradition, were transmitted through their *jongleurs* by song, for the Finnish epos, as the above passages suggest, is far more steeply rooted in the concept of music.

The songs of the *Kalevala* are popular runes—natural poetry with only a dawning tendency toward art, springing spontaneously from the viscera of a classless society, and bound by the classless phenomenon of the musical principle. The *Kalevala* we read has been called on a conflagration and concatenation of traditional songs, lyric, magic and narrative, sung by unlettered balladeers—a main singer *(laulaja)* and a supporting singer *(puoltaja)*—from North Karelia near Archangel,[1] using a small, usually five-stringed harp called a *kantele*. We now have many of the runes in some kind of loose, narrative order through the massive, creative effort of Elias Lönnrot (and some of his students, like David E. D. Europaeus) in 1835 and 1849, aimed at picturing—what formerly would have been designated singing—the life, thoughts, and customs of the ancestral Finns, and centering, for the sake of homogeneity if not unity, around the magical "mill," the Sampo, and the struggle between the Kaleva District *(Kalevala)* and the North Farm *(Pohjola)*. "Lönnrot is hence the Homer of Finland, not the Homer-poet of old literary tradition, but the Homer-collector . . . , [yet] much more than a simple stringer of songs,"[2] since he broke up the runes, distributed the passages, considered the variants, and established the fundamental text of each song. It has been pointed out repeatedly that one does not look for organic unity or artistic coherence in this kind of creative compilation, which depends on external connections; a guiding moral or sentimental motive, not to mention the factor of style itself, is understandably not there. But, while Finnic scholars have been reluctant to state that the *Kalevala* represents a coherently unified structure, they have also not been ready to declare that it is totally lacking in unity.

I suggest, then, that due to the constant focus by critics on the work's social and anthropological dimension, insufficient attention has been paid to the one element of continuity of *Kalevala* does present, what amounts to its internal connection: music. For the idea of the poem, as it came to Lönnrot, was latent in the mass of songs, in particular the magic song "which originates the myth [and] serves as a root to the epos: it formulates also the idea of the hero."[3] We need only look at the triad of heroes: Väinämöinen, Lemminkäinen, and Ilmarinen. In this natural epos, it is music that reaches inside Nature itself, producing all kinds of spells or feats of magic through their singing:

VÄINÄMÖINEN:
. . . I was created a singer, became a singer of magic songs. . . . [rune 21]
Then old Väinämöinen quietly sings.
First he sang one side [of the "firm-ribbed boat"] full of sleek-haired youths,
sleek-haired, with powerful hands, with finely shod feet.
He sang the other side full of maidens with tin head ornaments,
tin head ornaments, copper belts, with lovely gold rings on their fingers.
Väinämöinen further sang the rowers' benches full of people. . . . [rune 39]
Then old Väinämöinen sings softly
on the doors of the copper mountain, on the sides of the stone stronghold.
Now indeed the gates of the stronghold were moving. . . . [rune 42]

LEMMINKÄINEN:
Then reckless Lemminkäinen now began to sing.
He sang up rowans in farmyards, oaks in the middle of farmyards,
sturdy boughs on the oaks, an acorn on a branch,
on the acorn of golden ball, on the golden ball of cukoo. . . .
Lemminkäinen kept on singing, kept on singing and speaking magically,
sang the sand into fresh-water pearls, all the rocks till they were glistening,
all the tress till they were reddish, the flowers the color of gold.
Then Lemminkäinen sang, sang up a well on the farmstead. . . .
He sang up a pond onto the meadow, onto the pond green mallards
with brows of gold, heads of silver, all their toes of copper. . . . [rune 29]

ILMARINEN:
Shall I now begin to sing . . . ?
. . . Craftsman Ilmarinen now indeed began to sing,

got angry to the point of singing magically. He sang his wife into a seagull
to scream on a little island, to echo out on reefs in the water,
to whimper on the tips of headlands, to rock on headwinds. . . . [rune 38]

Similar musical enchantments also belong to others, to be sure, like the
master of North Farm (rune 27); Vipunen "skilled in magic songs" *(virsikäs)*
(rune 17); and the powerful and tragic Kullervo, "son of Kalervo" *(Kalervon
poika)* (runes 34 and 36). But essentially the musical idea formulates the
three protagonists, and especially the most important among them, Väinämöinen, who is the "eternal sage" *(tietä iäikuinen)* but who is, more significantly for me, also the "eternal singer" *(laulaja iäikuinen)*, and who as
such appears in the greatest number of runes (31 out of 50).[4]

Commonly, the three heroes have been associated with the qualities of
wisdom (Väinämöinen), craft (Ilmarinen), and recklessness (Lemminkäinen). And, while the qualifications are acceptable, I prefer to shift the emphasis slightly according to their actual roles in the epos whereby sportive
recklessness converges with Love (Lemminkäinen is, after all, most hand-
some and a lady-killer [see rune 12]), workaday craft with Industry (Ilmarinen forges the all-important Sampo [see rune 7]), and above all charmed
wisdom with Art (more often than not, Väinämöinen's true wisdom is expressed through his music). Love, industry, and art shape the essence of
life. And, by extension, I should argue that that strange and enigmatic
Sampo—perhaps simply an ideal of prosperity, which as a three-sided mill
grinds out grain, salt, and money—has some trilateral connection with the
three heroes's essential qualities. More significant, however, is the fact that,
while the craftsman forges the Sampo, it is Väinämöinen who arranges—
one could say inspires—it.

Through Väinämöinen, the divine merges with the human by virtue of
an identity of names; the Väinämöinen who takes part in creation may not
be the same as the Väinämöinen who appears in the poem as the son of a
mortal, but the appellation establishes a spiritual kinship nonetheless. The
eternal singer, whose birth begins the poem, acts as the mentor of the divine
art; all of rune 41 portrays him as a Nordic Orpheus who with his harp
gathers and delights all living creatures, even denizens of the air, the earth,
and the sea.

He took the instrument in his fingers, on his knees tuned the instrument with a
       tempering frame,
the harp under his hand. He uttered a word, spoke thus:

"Let him come to hear who previously may not have heard
the joyous music of eternal lays, the resonance of the harp. . . .
Now joyous music resulted in joyous music, rapture after rapture burst forth,
the music seemed like music, the song was like a proper song. . . .
The very geniuses of the air, lovely virgins of the air,
marveled at the joyous music, listened to the harp. . . .
There was not that creature, not indeed a single-finned creature
moving in the water, not the finest school of fish
that did not come to listen, to marvel at the joyous music. . . .
Then old Väinämöinen played one day, played a second.
There was not that person or brave man,
not man or woman or girl with luxuriant hair
who did not start to weep, whose heart did not melt. . . .

As the mentor, who in the manner of a patriarch wants only happiness for his people, he stresses the joy of music: "Singing he steered over the water, over the billows striking up joyous music" [rune 40]. . . . 'Stay now, torch holder, slight so that I may see to sing. My turn to sing is coming, my mouth desires to ring out.' Then he sang so that it resounded, sang joyfully throughout the evening," and in so doing he wishes the Kaleva District a happy life in times to come (rune 46). Finland would seem to be grounded in the musical principle. Tapio, the presiding woodland deity in the forested land, knows the force. In Väinämöinen's words,

In any event allow, God, another time, true Creator,
Tapio's horn to sound, the woodland pipe to sound out shrilly
in this little farmyard, in this confined farmstead.
By day I would it might be sung, by night that joyous music be made
in these parts, in these districts, in these great farms of Finland,
among the rising generation, among the people growing up. [rune 46]

The mentor is also the theorist and the shaper. He advises that no chanting is to be performed on the waters or singing on the billows, for "songs hold up rowing," and that music must be controlled, appropriate, as he warns Lemminkäinen, for there are times when it can be "[too] early for singing, too soon to make joyous music" (rune 42). Hence his wisdom; and hence, too, his art, if great poetry needs the virtues of timing and talent. Väinämöinen does not shape his harp until rune 40, from a pike's jawbone which, like Ulysses' bow, many attempt to use without success. In the attack against North Farm, during which the eternal singer's playing brings the adversary company to sleep (rune 42), the instrument disappears in a storm at sea, after which Väinämöinen constructs a lovely new birchwood harp and again "made the music resound beautifully":

> Then old Väinämöinen fashioned the birch into an instrument. . . .
> "There is the body of the harp, the frame of the eternal source of joy. . . .
> I got the pegs for the harp, screws for the curly birch frame.
> It is still lacking a little something, the harp lacking five strings. . . .
> Give me, virgin, some of your hair, some of your tresses, charming maiden,
> to be strings for a harp, to be the voice of immortal music." . . .
> The instrument is got ready. . . .
> Väinämöinen played with his fingers, the harp resounded with its strings.
> Mountains echoed, boulders crashed, all the crags shook,
> rocks splashed into the billows, gravel boiled in the water;
> pine trees rejoiced, tree stumps jumped about on the heath. . . .
> There was not indeed a wild animal that did not come to listen
> to the lovely instrument, to the resonance of the harp. . . .
> Then old Väinämöinen indeed played prettily,
> made the music resound beautifully. . . . [rune 44]

At the end, in rune 50, Väinämöinen's song must tire: "Why, therefore, should not a song get tired, delicate songs not slow down from a long evening of joyous music . . . ?" Then he adds: "a good singer [does not] sing everything he knows. It is a better idea for one to stop than to be cut off in the middle." This final rhapsody ends with Väinämöinen's bequeathing his harp and his great songs as a heritage for his Finnish people.

It is impossible, then, to conceive the heartbeat of the *Kalevala* as other than musical. Its sociological and anthropological interest lies in the history books, but its spiritual interest centers around the cultural meaning of music in that Nordic civilization. Music, suggests Väinämöinen in rune 21, is a necessary and integral part of life; its lack is felt deeply in rune 25, for it acts as the vocal chord of Nature, and man communes with it by correspondence: "The moon comes up from its house, steps onto a bend in a birch branch; the sun came up from its fine house, took its place on the crown of a pine to listen to the harp, to marvel at the joyous music" (rune 47). It fosters human activity, so that at the beginning of the epos the "*Competition in Song* is of the highest importance in the definition of the nature and essence of the Finnic epos; for in it is concentrated the feeling which vibrates in the magic songs, and accompanies, like a symphony, all the heroic action of the epos."[5] Such is the spirit that impregnants the *Kalevala*.

Ceremonial singing by the peasants underscored the musical substance;

hands and knees touching and bodies moving gently to the flow of sounds—
this is what Lönnrot saw in his day, and Sibelius some years later, in the
early 1890s when he visited Karelia and heard the runic singing of Larin
Paraske. Nearly unvaried, the melody of the *laulaja* was always the same,
just as the rhapsodies were never of great length. Moreover, parallelisms and
substantial repetitions of idea and objects, with only slightly different words
in successive verses by the *puoltaja*, abetted by formulas and stock epithets
(often made possible by the isochronous verse), further enhanced the musical experience. Sibelius was drawn to the *Kalevala* less because, as a patriot,
he saw the possibility of spawning a prideful national consciousness at a time
during the 1890s when the Finnish autonomy within the Russian Empire
was being eroded,[6] than because the legendary subject matter contained fe-
cund and inestimable elements to which his musical temperament was au-
thentically suited. Indeed, the *Kalevala*, whose hero for once in the world
of the epic is not a warrior but a wizard, is indifferent to history, and this
explains why the composer's fascination lasted far beyond the final decade
of the last century and well into the twentieth, by way of either new compositions or of the reworking of older ones.[7] Related directly or indirectly to
Lönnrot's epos, Sibelius's works span his creative life, from *Kullervo*, a long
orchestral work, sometimes as morose as its hero, for orchestra, male chorus, soprano, and bass of 1892 based on runes 31—36 (its centerpiece being
the dramatic exchange "Kullervo and his sister") and the tone poem, *The
Swan of Tuonela* of 1893, inspired by runes 16 and 17 (reworked in 1897
and 1900), to the *Song of Väinöö*, from rune 23, for mixed voices and
chorus of 1926 and his culminating and summing up *Tapiola* for orchestra
of 1925–26. In between appeared the orchestral *En Saga* (1892; reworked
1900–1); the other three *Legends* to complete the tetralogy with the *Swan*:
Lemminkäinen and the Maidens of Saari (1895; reworked 1897 and 1939);
Lemminkäinen in Tuonela (1895; reworked in 1897 and 1939); and *Lemminkäinen's Homeward Journey*, based on runes 11–15 (1895; reworked 1897
and 1900); and more works: the choral *Song for Lemminkäinen* (1894); the
Scènes historiques I, which originally included "Väinämöinen's Song" (1899);
the *Origin of Fire* cantata (1902; reworked 1910), known as "Ukko the
Firemaker," describing from rune 47 how the god of heaven kindles fire for
a new moon and sun to replace the vacuum created by Väinämöinen's seduc-
tive playing; the tone poem *Pohjola's Daughter*, complete with quotations
from the appropriate rune (8) and depicting Väinämöinen's journey north

to Pohjola, the beautiful girl's sitting on a rainbow, her conversation with Väinämöinen, the impossible tasks she asks of him, and his sad return journey (1906); the tone poem *Luonntar* for soprano and orchestra, based on rune 1 and the creation of the heavens from a union of winds and waves with the virgin of the air (1910; reworked 1913); the orchestral tone poem *The Bard* (1913, 1914); the Kylliki Suite for Piano (about this time); the six a capella part *Songs* for male voices; *Tiera* (Lemminkäinen's companion) for wind band (also around this time); and other compositions unrelated to the *Kalevala*, including seven symphonies. It is not quite true, then, that it was his nationalistic fervor of the 1890s alone that brought him to the Finnic epos and that he later evolved into a pure symphonist. The *Kalevala* colored his entire musical career, most of which could fit spiritually under his geographic title, *Karelia Suite*.

Like the repeated opening chord sequence of the tone-poem *Finlandia*, Sibelius's music strives for something inner and deep, resulting in an inwardness matched in music history only by Beethoven's last quartets. This inwardness has usually been described superficially with the words "gloom" and "brooding," but in fact the limitations of verbal language are such that the words disserve the composer. I prefer to say that his tonalities simply enter the concealed recesses of the soul—his own in correspondence with that of his thickly forested native land. I agree fully with Veikko Helasvuo's statement: "The white summer nights, snowbound winters, vast forests, dismal swamps and blue lakes of Finland have been read into works that would offer incomparably richer material for analysis on psychological, philosophical and, above all, purely abstract musical grounds."[8] To be sure, Sibelius himself provided a quatrain for *Tapiola* which encourages a literal understanding of the dusky expressions:

> Wide they stretch, the dark forests of the North,
> Primeval, mysterious, brooding wild dreams;
> Within them dwells the mighty god of the Forest,
> And in the gloom woodland spirits weave magic ways. . . .[9]

But the slow orchestral sonorities, enhanced by many tonic resolutions in the major key, betray an inner heroic search, not depression. The final *Tapiola*, with its magical and imaginative, strange-sounding visions of an unpeopled world presided over by the god Tapio—where the forces of nature and the myth of man blend and where the human and the arboreal, as it

were, dissolve into infinity and eternity—ends not untypically with an assertion of the tonic triad. Consider the affirmative endings of *Kullervo* or of
Lemminkäinen's Homeward Journey. Even *The Bard,* whose predominant
harp points directly to the poetic patriarch Väinämöinen, ends in a major
statement. Gloominess, then, is not the word; introspection is, and the realm
of the dead, *Tuonela,* yields to affirmation.[10]

Many devices serve the composer to reach inside himself and Lönnrot's
national epos, but none is as telling as the single continuous tone in the
bass held against changing upper figures known as the pedal point, or what
has been referred to as "the pedal-notes of nature." One visitor to Sibelius
in 1910, with whom she visited the great rapids of Imatra, wrote: "Sibelius
had at that time a passion for trying to catch the pedal notes of natural
forces. The pedal note of Imatra no man has gauged, but Sibelius often
seemed satisfied with the results of his rapt listening, when he caught the
basic sounds of forests, or of the wind whistling over lakes and moorlands."
Another visitor described to the composer his impression of Finland approaching it by ship as low, reddish granite rocks emerging from a pale blue
sea, "solitary island of hard, archaic beauty, inhabited by hundreds of white
seagulls"—to which Sibelius commented: "Yes, and when we see those granite
rocks we know why we are able to treat the orchestra as we do."[11] Hence
when he overhauled *En Saga* in 1902, he elongated rather than contracted
the pedal points, just as he reduced key changes from forty-eight to thirty-
four, thereby allowing the music to have a more sustained quality, all of
which forced an internalization, as opposed to an externalization, of his
idom. The process climaxed in *Tapiola,* with its long, internal, spacious,
and meditative pedal points.

In searching the depths of Tapio's woodland, Sibelius penetrates, like Alejo
Carpentier's protagonist in the jungle of *Los pasos perdidos,* to the source of
the Finnish spirit. However, runic expression influenced him less immediately than spiritually; rhythmic structures and modal habits of mind turn his
melodic and orchestrational thinking inward. What makes *The Bard* a masterpiece of introspection is the way in which the nineteen-page score is built
on the slenderest materials: Part I has no theme but a three-note cell that
moves up and down, and the brassy Part II uses two trumpets and three
trombones with only six notes between them. Elsewhere, in *The Swan of
Tuonela,* the introspection is achieved by the absence of bright instrumental
colors (no flutes, clarinets, or trumpets, and an oboe merely reinforces one

note and one phrase of the English horn, representing the bird) and by a complex use of *divisi* strings (divided into eight parts, then at the end into fourteen, nine of which with double stops and ten groups *col legno*). Devices such as these fully invite meditation by pointing inward and suggesting, in the words of one critic, the internal cycle of nature: "He introduces thematic fragments and proceeds to unite them in the development, then dissolves and disperses the material back into its primary constituents. . . . The peculiar strength and attraction of this method of construction consists in the fact that it is the method of nature itself; Sibelius's most characteristic [compositions] are born, develop and die, like all living things."[12] Moreover, the meditative quality remains uninterrupted, thanks to his mastery of transition and to the concomitant organic integration of all parts, the inner connection that exists among all the motifs, as Mahler said of Symphony no. 7. Steady increases in dynamics up to stirring summits draw from the music's inner reaches; their drama surfaces from the musical concept without being something imposed from without, and the typical, sustained brass chords beginning sforzato, then dropping subito pianissimo and moving into a slow crescendo, suggest quest and the effort of penetration as convincingly as any device at the composer's disposal.

Many insist on Sibelius's pictorial or descriptive features, but I would argue that, granite rocks and forests notwithstanding, it is the meditative feature that domintes and corroborates the Kalevalan background. This holds true whether the work enjoys a programmatic base like *Kullervo,* the *Four Legends, Luonntar,* and *Pohjola's Daughter,* or suppresses any story in poetic landscapes without figures reflecting, not nature's outward symbols like mountains and rivers, but its inner forces—which supposedly makes the composition more "symphonic," like *En Saga, The Bard,* and *Tapiola.* More precisely, it is the very merging of the symphonic with the programmatic, the story line (when there is one) seeming hardly identifiable, that shapes Sibelius's personal language of inwardness and that profound sense of inner self-discovery. *Pohjola's Daughter,* for example, is programmatic because of Väinämöinen's story and is symphonic because each musical idea urges the music forward by establishing its own internal logic.

Perhaps the notion of pictorialism has come about because of Sibelius's use of folkloric material. But this, too, is a misrepresentation. He insisted that he never used folk music, and whatever images the mind evokes have at best only inferential interest. Surely, he did not transcribe folk melodies with the ethnic zeal of a Smetana or a Granados. True to his aesthetic of inwardness, he did not attempt to harmonize folk strains inside a composition, which would have given that composition an immediate flavor of outwardness. The most that can be said is that he used the falling fifth with accented upper note (sometimes becoming a falling octave with its accompanying tinge of sadness) and the rising third with accented lower note— both frequent in Finnish folk music—but these archetypal intervals that we hear in *Lemminkäinen and the Maidens of Saari* and in *The Swan of Tuonela* in no way justify Aaron Copland's ingenuous remark, "Sibelius is, by nature, a folk composer"![13] More appropriate is the remark by popular composer Oskar Merikanto: "We feel these melodies to be our own, even though as such we have never heard them before."[14] The inward movement could not be better expressed.

To put this aesthetic of inwardness into perspective, one need only look contrastively at the tone poems of Richard Strauss. Leaving aside *Ein Heldenleben*, *Also sprach Zarathustra*, and that lofty achievement *Tod und Verklärung*, the obvious examples are *Don Juan*, *Till Eulenspiegel*, and *Don Quixote*. Here, Sibelius's stress on substance over sonority is inverted into a stress of sonority over substance. The themes, while progressing through evolution, cannot be spoken of as readily in terms of evolutionary thematicism as Sibelius's because they rely more on manipulation than on evocation. This affects formal construction, for the Finn tends to be essentially symphonic while the German delights in dramatic, psychological, and picturesque movements. In the long run, Strauss's musical grammar or rhetoric—his language—crops up in all his works, outspoken, not private. To a greater or lesser degree, the same rules and formulas apply to all, and one does not sense a profound discovery of the self, an inner conviction and identification. Despite *Tod und Verklärung*, there is no *Tapiola* in his repertoire.

The music is thoroughly—and beautifully—descriptive, every inch a pictorial feat. Devilish and impudent, the music of *Till Eulenspiegel* (1895) rings with appropriate extravagance, with no attempt made to turn us from the issues of rascality, sacrilege, and impenitent prankishness, or from concrete details like soldiers returning from war or lovers quarreling over a woman, let alone the sickening struggle of Till's hanging, and even so the composer penciled onto the score annotations which translate the events and emotions of the medieval practical joker. Strauss manipulates his two themes to reveal the scapegrace's transformations; the realism achieved is palpable even to the untrained ear. If *Tapiola* is intrinsic, *Till Eulenspiegel* is extrinsic. The same may be said for his earlier *Don Juan* (1889). The swashbuckling and amatory conquests are "visible," and if for his tone-poem Strauss liked Nicholas Lenau's version that stressed the hero's *Weltschmerz*, his idealistic disillusion and satiety with unfulfilling carnal possession, one cannot say that he penetrated the lover's insensate desires. We hear the conquests and his increasing desire with each repetition, but all is rendered outwardly through the woodwind chromatic scale that easily suggests resignation, even disgust. When, then, we engage the "fantastic variations on a knightly theme" (*Don Quixote* [1897]), the aesthetic of outwardness climaxes. The variations link to particular episodes in Cervantes's novel: there is no mistaking them descriptively. Our attention is guided reliably by the solo cello (Quixote) and solo viola (Sancho Panza). Don Juan's outward mood, which has become Eulenspiegel's outward actions, is now Quixote's outward fantasy, complete with externalizing wind machines for the windmills and an array of eight bleating horns for the sheep: brilliant, forthright, energizing, but hardly intimate, probing, meditative. The closest Sibelius comes to Strauss's outwardness is in *Lemminkäinen and the Maidens of Saari*, where the second subject—gaily twirling maidens' figures—with a fitting horn call, roguish accents, and a purposeful drone exact a near sense of Straussian verisimilitude (Sibelius had heard Strauss's *Don Juan* in Berlin in 1890).[15] Sibelius's tone poem shares with Strauss's a certain ludic quality, but the Finn was never literal, even in the vivacissimo portrayal of the abduction, and if Lemminkäinen has the last word, like Till, his reappearance is fleeting and, expectedly, much more subdued, almost apologetic.

Sibelius's chamber work, a string quartet, he called "Voces intimae." The adjective reflects the intimacy of inwardness. Various zones of musical influence creep intertwiningly through his music, not as ambiguities or uncertainties, but as directionalities. Sibelius was a Classical craftsman who could not isolate the elements of his musical themes; rather, he forced them to find their inner unity and thereby to integrate, direct themselves into the coherent aesthetic tonality I call inwardness. We cannot scalpel out their private design, whether by way of tonal contrasts or correspondences, harmonically or melodically. An echo, internalized by the listener, tells us much, a medieval descant in his twentieth-century diaphone. Sibelius's true, intimate, and perhaps inexplicable personality remains as a function of his compositions, especially those based on the *Kalevala*. His music is inwardly responsive to the wild, shadowed beauty of Suomi—the awe and the mystery of the dark forests, promoting the presence of Tapio, not as a monster, but as the embodiment of all that is primitive and unspoiled. And his music grows with symphonic inevitability, deepening after each section, as the natural mood intensifies, beckoning a poetic vision, in the manner of Väinämöinen, who casts aside all surface peripeteia and thinks only of penetrating the vast expanses of nature he has been divinely called upon to animate with his harp. We must think of him as of Sibelius himself, the spirit who combines spanned melodies with concise motifs, or epic expansiveness and aphoristic brevity whose insights, like the tone-poem's germ cells, germinate in many ways. Sibelius always makes the structure of his music the product of inward processes. And inwardness must finally terminate in silence. Väinämöinen ends the epos inwardly: "I . . . did not get words from outside, phrases from farther off" (rune 50). Similarly, Sibelius, who did not care for the Russian Six or Schönberg or Stravinsky (but who liked Bartók), preferred not exploratory music, which by inspiration is outwardly oriented, but traditionally symphonic ways; he sank into a silence lasting a third of a century after *Tapiola*, leaving the unexplored to the explorers, he who had concentrated on penetrating deep into the cultural forests of his land, and giving us biographical reason to ponder with Väinämöinen: "a good singer [does not] sing everything he knows. It is a better idea for one to stop than to be cut off in the middle."

19

THE AMBIGUOUS FAUNS
OF MALLARMÉ AND DEBUSSY

Sylvain d'haleine première
Si ta flûte a réussi
Ouïs toute la lumière
Qu'y soufflera Debussy.[1]

Gabriele D'Annunzio described Claude Debussy as a moment in French sensibility. This moment happened to fit the Impressionistic contours of that literary aesthetic we have come to know as Symbolism, distinguished by Stéphane Mallarmé among others, in particular by his famous eclogue "L'Après-midi d'un faune." Given this poem's stress on musicality, frequent comparisons have been made with the other arts. The analogy with music especially invites consideration on purely formal grounds, since in the general area of Impressionism, tonal sequences and a poet's language, like the brush strokes of Claude Monet, seek to manipulate less the content of a vision, idea, or sensation than the material used to express it. Semantics becomes syntax; and this syntax in each art is loosened, whether it is that of language for poetry, outline for painting, or tonality for music. It moves about more freely; some would say it breaks down, yielding to phonology, as it were, challenging subservience to conventional rules or accepted usages. Grammar is discarded—or, shall I say, a metagrammar is formulated—stressing effects and divorcing form from meaning as we normally conceive it.[2]

The result is ambiguity, a key concept; and fragility, a key sensation. By definition, ambiguity cannot be resolute; it cannot function as an imperative. So in painting we get light washes of color in Renoir; the glimmering *pointillé* frailty of Seurat; or, more genuinely Impressionistic, the blurred edges and outlines of Monet, whose cathedral of Rouen, we have heard repeatedly, is observed through a wet window pane, just as the sounds of

Debussy's "La Cathédrale engloutie" emanate from under the water. Nothing represents anymore; all suggests. All is a matter of evocation, allusion, suggestion, not description. "Monuments, the sea, the human face, in their fullness, indigenous, retaining an otherwise attractive virtue that a description will not veil—say an evocation, what I consider an allusion, a suggestion."[3] Lyrical verse, said Mallarmé, "must ravish the ear"; to be poetic, thought must pass through "the study of sounds and of the color of words, of music, and of painting."[4] Thomas Munro calls this "vacillations of light and shadow."[5] In music, with Debussy, we go a long way toward losing the sense of tonality, or the feeling of being confined to an identified key. Chromaticism militates against key restrictions. Already accorded a certain importance by Beethoven and raised to prominence by Liszt and Chopin, it figures centrally after Wagner in the expression of Impressionism's musical tableaux. And devices such as pauses to invite suspense (Mallarmé designates them typographically), avoidance of distinct closure to forgo assertiveness, successive chords to suggest vague melodic lines, diminished sevenths in chord or arpeggio sequences to abandon the comfort of tonality, and movement by whole tones to enhance the sensation of keylessness—all become the focus of Debussy's new aesthetic.

Music from Bach to Debussy illustrates clearly an evolution from clarity to ambiguity. We have but to be reminded of the mathematical rigor of Bach's grammar, much loosened in the elegant coherence of Mozart's graceful syntax; then of how the grammar begins to be wrenched out of place as a result of Beethoven's impatient disregard for regulated rhetoric; and after that of the flowing freedoms taken by Chopin and Liszt with what we might call (to keep up the linguistic metaphors) their lyrical sentence structures. As Leonard Bernstein (who takes a clue from Mallarmé and uses these metaphors) has shown in his *The Unanswered Question*, when we get to Debussy we observe the final stages of disintegration of musical rhetoric in favor of a more diffused expression, all the more intoxicating in this moment of special sensibility because it is less logical, less Cartesian. A formerly consistent aesthetics has become a "delicious aestheticism." And while, as in Mallarmé, we may still somehow speak in terms of "tonal and syntactic containment,"[6] after Debussy and Mallarmé we remain wary of how fragile the containment is, of how quickly it crumbles just a few years later as we cross into the twentieth century.

In poetry the breakdown in rhetoric translates into a stanza like the following one by Gerard Manley Hopkins, in "The Candle Indoors," written in 1879:

> Some candle clear burns somewhere I come by.
> I muse at how its being puts blissful back
> With yellowy moisture mild night's blear-all black,
> Or to-fro tender trambeams truckle at the eye. . . .

Hopkins was influenced by Mallarmé, who three years earlier had written "L'Après-midi d'un faune," an elegiac verse monologue uttered by Pan, if we wish to identify the faun, during a hot, sleepy afternoon perhaps in mythical Sicily. In light of the coming musical analogy, a brief summary of this well known but always esoteric poem may be in order:

Pan half wakes; he has been dreaming of the rape of nymphs and with eyes still shut tries to prolong the voluptuous vision ("Those nymphs, I want to perpetuate them"). The illusion of his dream is so strong that he still sees the luminous forms of the goddesses, though with a doubt: "Did I love a dream?" But he sees that he was alone, alas! and had merely dreamed. Yet his subtle spirit meditates a hypothesis: were there two nymphs in his dream, one suggested by a spring, the other by the breeze? No, the only sound in this wood is that of the flute which the faun has been playing. So, following his own inspiration, he sings of his own dream. "I was cutting here the hollow reeds," he muses, and saw these vague forms which took flight and dispersed at the first sound of the pipes, the moment the musician sounded "the A" on his "malicious Syrinx." Too bad; as he rises the faun feels on his breast what might be the memory of a "mysterious bite"—so perhaps it was not a dream after all? But alas again: his breast is "virginally clean of proof." Pan looks to music as the only conscious means of evocation. Only his flute has the key to the enigma, the syrinx which now dreams only of amusing the youthful beauties by a musical imitation of their forms, transforming softly the curves and sinuosities of thighs and backs into the undulations of "a sonorous, vain and monotonous line." There is no expectation of turning the line into reality. The faun will content himself with memories and imaginary pleasures, akin to fashioning a syrinx out of a hollow reed, just as when he sucks grapes he blows up the empty skins and contemplates till evening the light shining through them, enjoying the illusion. Here the story is taken up again, with Pan suddenly finding at his feet two nymphs asleep; he seizes the couple, carries them off, covers their bodies with kisses. But the anger of the gods is aroused at that "disheveled forelock of kisses," and a sudden feebleness, a "vague sense of death," makes him loose his grasp of them. They escape. The end approaches as the satyr begins his musing again, in a relaxed strain. He consoles himself at the thought of future delights, even flattering himself with the thought of a sensational rape, that of ravishing Venus herself. But . . . "O certain punishment . . ." The faun is falling asleep again, succumbing to the heat. He takes his leave of the nymphs, about to plunge into sleep to find again that night wherein dreams float and dissolve. "Goodbye, you two, I go to see the shadow that you became."[7]

To this extent the eclogue *may* be verbalized in summary, but over and beyond all this its effectiveness lies not in what it expresses but in its expressiveness. Among other things, the poem asks: Is the beginning the beginning? What nymphs? Am I dreaming, or am I awake? Or was I? Were there two nymphs? Was the flight of swans or of naiads? Since there was no water or breeze, were they real? Were they part of me? Were they but a creation of my desire? Is this Sicily? Did a licentious act occur? Am I a poet, or am I deluding myself? How could *une morsure* be *vierge de preuve?* Was that love real? Was the kiss real, or was it a dream? Did the trees confuse me? Should I sleep? Is it better to renounce effort? Will memory or musing adduce an answer? Will I actually possess Venus? Is sleep better than striving for an unattainable poetic ideal? Posed this way, the questions create arabesques of rises and falls, convolutions and involutions of language gliding from one query to another, from sensual abandon to perceptive self-inquiry, highlighting only essentials—catching, as Charles Mauron comments, only the "spontaneous impression" and using "what at first seem the wrong words so as to allow of metaphorical obliquities, and subtlety and fluidity of thought." All of this draws ambiguous, "long arabesques."[8] There is a literary alchemy at work which transforms—sublimates—the very words of the poet (or the faun) into evaporating dreams partly sustained by memory, dreams of art and erotic love, dreams of poetry and creation, given life by the intervention of music.

Perhaps, as Henri Peyre believes, Mallarmé's musical culture was limited, since intellectually he had to reject the supremacy of music over poetry—to which we might add that, after reading such writings as "La Musique et les lettres" and "Richard Wagner: Rêverie d'un poète français," we come to feel that Mallarmé placed more emphasis on music as a metaphorical concept than as an artistic projection. In a letter to René Ghil, he speaks of musical rhythm and color, relating them more to reason and passion than to pure movement and shading.[9] Ironically for this "pure" poet, "pure" composers like Bach and Mozart offer little corresponding inspiration; and to this Symbolist, who always pursued analogy, the burning ecstasy of a Wagner—his "splendid bravura" or "scintillating will"[10]—could not be compatible with the desired ambiguity and fragility of literary Impressionism. As we know,

Mallarmé's "demon" is analogy ("Le Démon de l'analogie"), which includes metaphor and arabesque; he is haunted by the grouping of words, like an assemblage of nymphs, and the spacial sounds and sensations or associations they generate. Music, for him, remains associative; a passage like this variously quoted one[11] from *Divagations* rings with associations which by their very nature can be termed "musical," voiced by a "musician of words," but music itself cannot advance beyond analogical communication:

Note that instruments separate, by a magic not too difficult to ascertain, what we might call the summit of natural landscapes; they evaporate them and bring them together again, floating in a superior state of being. Look at how, to express a forest bathed in its green crepuscular horizon, one needs only a chord unrelated to a memory of the hunt, or a lea, with the pastoral vision of a fluidly passed afternoon, that reflects itself and flees from the river's reminders. Just a line, some vibration— briefly, and all becomes discernible.[12]

The suggestion is complete. Music is entrancement, which is a main part of poetry; obscurity and ambiguity fashion their spell; in other words, abstraction is the only zone in which pure ideas (ideas not related to an easy, immanent meaning) can float. Only a metagrammar can handle abstract reality in any pure way. Local grammar shapes the idiom of a botanist, who sees the flower as the reproductive organ of certain vegetables. But when Mallarmé speaks of a flower, or indeed when his faun speaks of a nymph, he evokes the ideal thing that does not appear in a bouquet: "the flower one will never see, that one will never pick, in brief, a new kind of flower that our senses do not let us know but that our minds see arise by virtue of the simple fact that it gives it a name." In this twilit, green horizon, abstraction or ambiguity is only a means of suggesting reality without stating it. "Abstraction is music thought out."[13] Hence Mallarmé's assertion: "I speak and say: a flower, and . . . musically, the one absent from all bouquets arises."[14]

Musically, he says, for a set of musical scales is the vehicle for movement, for modulating from one landscape to the next, or from one object to its ideal form. As one idea recalls another, so does one tone call another. The faun gives his dream life through his syrinx, or panpipe. "From now on, all modulations are possible: a work of art is an arabesque freely traced by the mind between what exists—our inner or outer experience of the world— and what does not exist, going through the various gradations of dream."[15] So we modulate between and among the four summits of that landscape, as suggested by A. R. Chisholm[16] in terms of motifs: Sensuality (the faun's erotic obsession), Art (his literary obsession), Dream and Memory (the shape and motor of these obsessions). The faun needs sensuality to sense life, dream to counter the crudities of reality, art to perpetuate the experience, and memory to give it a dimension, a fullness. Not that the faun attains satisfaction, physical or otherwise: He is only dreaming, after all, blowing into the empty grapeskins, and even so, when his music evokes too earnestly, when the tuning A is struck, the nymphs slip from his would-be arms and disappear. Only that state of "untuned" fragility can hope to safeguard their presence. The syrinx can be an "instrument of flights," but, Giacomo Leopardi might have said, "in this sea is foundering sweet to me" ("L'infinito"). And Mallarmé drowns us in the sounds of his verses, crawling over each other in waves of evocative alliterations and assonances. As Debussy submerged his melodic line in a rustle of notes, Mallarmé "immerses" his narrative line in a rustle of words. If the verse is alexandrine, the feeling of the Classical twelve syllables is drowned in silences and enjambments, which give the alexandrines the kind of suppleness Debussy accomplishes through repeated changes in tempo. This allows for a sense of fragmentation, in the poet's own analysis, for "an infinity of broken-up melodies that enrich the texture without one's sensing an equally stressed cadence."[17] Many, therefore, beginning with Mallarmé himself, have referred to the music or musicality of the eclogue. The poet gave his poetic line "a musical accompaniment"; indeed, he "orchestrated" the poem.[18] After him, among others, Paul Valéry spoke of a "literary fugue"[19] and Albert Thibaudet of a "transposition of the symphony into a poem."[20]

It is easy to see how and why Debussy would have found Mallarmé's verses, indeed his whole poem, coincident with his own musical idiom. Ultimately what counts is not audience gratification through understanding but rather gratification through what we might call involuntary (because of its dreamlike quality) sensory perception. Hence the ambiguity, hence the fragility. And hence, too, other typical qualities in both music and poetry: a kind of winning softness which permits us to savor, in melancholy moods common to us all (for such music and poetry are usually quite melancholy), attenuated sensations, hidden compenetrations of emotions. Or the quality of vagueness, of incompleteness, which, as in Monet's painting, serves both to obfuscate the artist's deep lyricism, denying it all sharpness—let alone blatancy (remember the nymphs that vanished when the syrinx got too sharp)—and to invite in the reader or listener or viewer at all times the pleasurable intercalation of private feelings. In "L'Après-midi d'un faune," these are pleasant feelings because the mild agitation which accompanies this aesthetic as still another of its qualities aims at something beautiful, pleasing like the summits in Pan's landscape. Dissonances enrich, not corrode, the minor modes, when indeed they may be detected in words, colors, or sounds. The halo of Mallarmé's "L'Azur" is made up of pure sound.

This is what Debussy's musical interpretation of the poem creates.[21] Mallarmé had to admit that "this music prolongs the emotion of my poem."[22] Speaking clearly, the composer enjoins us to seek the emotion and not the kind of one-to-one relationship between words and notes which we might discover, say, in Liszt's rendering of Dante's *Inferno*.[23] "The music . . . is a very free rendering of Mallarmé's beautiful poem. It makes absolutely no pretension to synthesize the latter. Rather, it creates successive settings whereby the faun's desires and dreams move about filling the heat of that afternoon."[24] In fact, we notice that Debussy does not call his work by the same title as the poet: instead of "L'Après-midi d'un faune" we are told it is "Prélude à 'L'Après-midi d'un faune.' " The idea of prelude (that allusion in verse 30?) is important—something used to set a mood rather than to articulate. It is, in Calvin Brown's words, "a preliminary establishment of the languorously idle and sensuous mood of that hautingly vague work,"[25] and as an early edition of the score described it ("a sensuous pastoral rhapsody following no fixed form"[26]), it becomes a counterpart of that poetry which has been called "hypnotic poetry."

Yet, Debussy's disclaimers notwithstanding, a number of links between the eclogue and the prelude do come to our attention, and the composer himself invites us to recognize them, if, as Mauron reports, Debussy declared that he wrote the piece following the poem "verse by verse."[27] Indeed, one critic surmises that "it seems more than coincidental that the number of lines of the poem is identical to the number of lines of music."[28] Debussy cannot possibly have meant "verse by verse" literally (the flute opening, for instance, does not translate "I want to perpetuate them," and when he reaches the "long solo" section Debussy, though the opportunity for literalism is golden, makes no salient use of the flute), but figuratively he did imply a *close* reading of the poem. The "successive settings" he alludes to do structurally translate the poem's succession of sensations.[29] The four harmonic variations of the opening theme stem from key changes corresponding to shifts in the faun's thinking. Without reading accuracies into

the score as if the notes translated individual words, but with a continuous
sense of the movements and transitions of the text without arriving at an
actual synthesis of it, we may surely infer a progression of "settings."[30] We
know the composer wanted to render "the general impression of the poem,
for, to follow it more closely would stifle the music."[31] Hence his friend,
the poet Pierre Louÿs, referred to the "Prélude" as "a delicious paraphrase."[32] Like the poem, whose opening verse causes the faun's story to
evolve digressively from query to imagination to resignation, the music's
opening phrase spawns into a series of versions. The sole motif generates all
subsequent material—Debussy's desired method: "with a single continuous
motif."[33] Like the poem, the music moves without interruptions or divisions; all is flow, even through the silences. Like the poem, the music must
suggest without stating. Arbitrary as inferences are, we still hear the "sonorous, vain and monotonous line" of the panpipe at the outset sounded by
the unaccompanied flute, as if the faun were playing without any distinct
purpose in mind other than to whittle the time away. Furthermore, the flute
motif reappears periodically in both poem and music. It is the binding agent
which spawns further motifs—the "perpetuation." The sleepy hesitations and
imprecise recollections, too, are there, in the third horn, along with the
very significant blank measure of suspenseful query (measure 6: and the
dominant seventh chord) and the drowsiness of the glissando passages in the
harp.

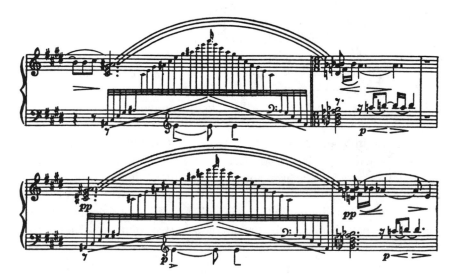

We are reminded of Verlaine's

> la nuance seule fiance
> le rêve au rêve et la flûte au cor.[34]

> (only nuance weds
> dream to dream and flute to horn.)

Silences characterize the beginning and end of the composition as they characterize the beginning and end of the poem. We can, if we wish, detect the questioning of measures 19 and 20 ("Did I love a dream?"), lapsing into the faun's resolve to follow his own inspiration and continuing with the dispersal and flight of the naiads (measure 21 onward, with the suggestive arpeggios of the harp and the rapid thirty-seconds of the flutes, later the clarinet). In measure 31, "Mysterious bite" comes in poignantly,

followed by the flute's imitation of the nymphs' forms or the transformation of the sinuosities, rendered seductively by the oboe (beginning measure 37):

In Matisse-like fashion, the "arabesque"—the sinuous melody—lines made in the poem by the eye tracing the nymphs' "back" and "side" become in the music the sonorous flute lines akin to the melodic lines of the verses themselves.[35] Indeed, Debussy admitted that the arabesques were "dictated" by Pan's instrument.[36]

Then the "malicious Syrinx" may be heard (flute and oboe) as the tempo accelerates at measure 44, and the expressive passage which begins on measure 55 with the whole woodwind section suggests the faun's contentment with his memories and imaginary pleasures:

The ardor of the central scene, with the "disheveled forelock of kisses," between the faun and the virgin nymphs is hard to miss around the fortissimo in measure 70, as is the subsequent "vague sense of death" presented tenderly by the horns, the clarinet, and the oboe (measure 74 on). When we hear the return of the panpipe theme by the flute, we must be reminded of the passage in the poem where the poet begins the recital again in a relaxed and somnolent strain (measure 79), and the impishness of measures 83 to 85 suggests the faun's thought of future delights:

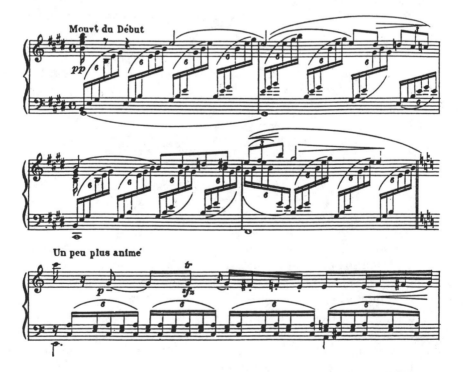

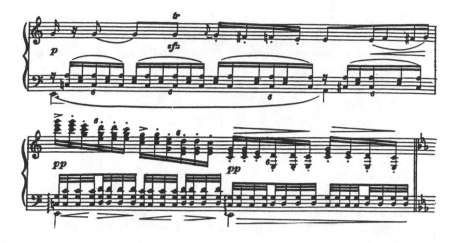

While sleep sets in around measure 86, the thought of Venus herself, in very animated tempo, agitates the woodwinds and the harp (measure 90 onward), just before the faun begins to doze off again (the return of the panpipe theme in measure 94), succumbing to the heat (measure 102), and delivering his "Adieu" to the two nymphs with the same theme, now heavily and drowsily harmonized (measure 106 to the end):

Thus, Pan's final resignation to the "shadow" of the nymphs he had originally wanted to "perpetuate" finds an echo in the coda which repeats resignedly (since two notes of anticipation—E and G♯—are omitted) the opening statement.[37]

Throughout these fugitive impressions and intertwining of sensations, it is equally possible on a broader level to detect the four motifs of the poem—art (measure 1), memory (measure 31), dream (measure 37), and sensuality (measure 83)—entering and exiting elusively throughout as the music unfolds one hypnotic effect after another. What we might call musical equivocation blurs the boundaries between reality, recollection, and fantasy. All this takes place inside an A–B–A[1] structure roughly corresponding to the poem's confused questioning, sense of vicarious fulfillment, and attempt at sublimation.[38] Twenty-three time changes, sixteen major tempo changes, and ten key changes produce a mesmerizing effect, paralleling the plethora of assonances and alliterations in the poem. Tonic-dominant relationships drift unresolved, mounting a fragile structure of hanging seventh chords. Scales range beyond the common major and minor audibility. Mallarmé's nuance that replaces clarity becomes in Debussy the tonal subtlety that replaces direct statement. Nuance is especially effective in breaking down "grammatical" relationships, in allowing chords not to resolve, indeed, in not overusing basic chords lest they start sounding bland, even banal.[39]

The grammar is truly geared to the ambiguity of indistinct sounds and moods, of those involuntary sensory perceptions. Woodwinds properly dominate the sylvan pastoral, conducted, one might say, by the flute, whose opening chromatics and dozing rhythm (reminiscent of the "long solo" of verse 45) set the tone of vagueness. Melodic fragments and fragile harmonies set the pastoral during the whole first third of the "Prélude," what has been called "the aesthetic of the short breath."[40] The rising and falling arabesque becomes the breathing pattern of the whole piece: moderato, ritenuto, *tempo primo*, animato, più animato, *tempo primo*, sostenuto, *tempo primo*, animato, *tempo primo*, molto animato, *tempo primo*, ritenuto, lento.[41] In this sense, too, we modulate from one landscape to the next, and between them that flower "absent from all bouquets" rises before our mind's eye. Like the faun, we breathe in a state of *perhaps*, never sure of what might be or might not be. The irregular length of Debussy's measures fits the movement of Mallarmé's verses. Then there is the matter of key. As Bernstein asks,[42] What key are we in when we hear the first two panpipe measures? Only the third suggests the key of E♮; but then ambiguity sets in two measures later when we find ourselves in the most unlikely dominant seventh not of E♮ but of E♭! Debussy's language speaks in such allusory harmonies that are not traditionally logical or closely tied to functional references.[43] The opening theme, moving downward from C♯ to G, then E to A♯, shapes itself around the tritone (three whole tone steps producing an augmented fourth), the most unstable of intervals and Debussy's "basic structural principle; . . . the interval is our leading clue to penetrating the vagueness and ambiguity of the piece as a whole, which carries out, to the very end, all the harmonic implications of the initial tritone."[44] And when the melodic line eliminates it, the eliminated note may be heard in the bass (see measure 31). Similarly, the repeated chordal progression from E to B♭ is tritonic and deliberately provokes an unclarity which a normal progression to the mediant G or subdominant A or dominant B would not create. So, while the composition ends unmistakably in E♮, all the way along the composer has teased us with questions, like the faun's, about exactly where we were. The only *tutti* in the score occurs in a D Major, in the middle. "That follows the ascending movement of the poem," wrote Debussy.[45] Otherwise, he keeps hinting at E but always slips away from it, the way the naiads elude Pan. The queries: Were they nymphs? Was I dreaming? Am I a poet? Was that love real? translate into: Are we in E♮? E♭? No, is it D Major? Here's a B♭ seventh— but is it actually A♯? Is the E Major triad tritonic, since the line ends on an A♯, that is, B♭?

If one extends the diatonic orbit far enough, tonalities can no longer be recognized and ambiguity is intensified. Then if one introduces whole-tone scales, entrancement prevails and "all becomes discernible" in its own veiled way, "with a single continuous motif." Consistent with the tritone, Debussy plays with the whole-tone scale (the tritone falls naturally in the whole-tone scale), which, softly struck, has a fragile, soporific quality largely because, without a perfect fourth and fifth (E/F♯/G♯/A♯/C/D/E), it cannot relate to a tonic or a dominant statement. Without this relation, which provides anchorage for the musical line, all kinds of phrases can be set adrift, much the way all kinds of abstract associations can be made with a phrase in poetry which has become unmoored and has abandoned the firmness and security of rhetoric. Yet, as we know, we are ultimately not adrift. Like the poem and despite the comment in the early edition that it has no form, the "Prélude" is carefully structured on the tritone and whole-tone scale; furthermore, we *are* in the key of E, just as the poem *is* classically conceived in traditional alexandrine, twelve-syllable rhymed couplets and straight hexameters: "the alexandrine in full dress."[46]

And, let me add: just as we know that Pan had *really dreamed* and is now about to sleep once more. Abstraction or impression is only half of Mallarmé's and Debussy's art, which in its intimate form is as concrete as any complex of sensitive calculations can make it. Those ambiguous fauns of theirs are willed to the last syllable and to the last note.

(1985)

20

FAUST AND
THE MUSIC OF EVIL

Music has always taken its place alongside the Faust legend to become a traditional part of it. From the medieval puppet plays to the present, the art of sounds has given the tradition an especially rich added dimension that other thematic legends—like Oedipus, Prometheus, even Don Juan—do not possess to the same degree. Remarks Ferruccio Busoni's poet to the spectators before his *Doktor Faust* begins: "In dieser Form allein ruft sie nach Tönen, Musik steht dem Gemeinen abgewandt; ihr Körper ist die Luft, ihr Klingen Sehnen, sie schwebt. . . . Das Wunder ist ihr Heimatland" ("It calls for tones only in this form: music wards off the ordinary; its body is the air, its sounds are desire, they soar . . . Wonder is its homeland"). And the tale, of course, has evoked its own *Wunder*, since it has to do with mankind's perennial fascination and concern with the problem of evil, to which music as an art has not been conceptually and mythically unrelated. Thomas Mann was among the most recent to remind us of this.

Indeed, the attraction composers have found for the Faust story assumes itself legendary qualities, if only by virtue of the long line of artists who have sought to give it musical shape. The formal lineage—in which we come across such early works as J. E. Gaillard's musical pantomime in London, *Harlequin Faustus* in 1715, and Ignaz Walter's Singspiel *Doktor Faust* under a century later—was seeded by Wolfgang Goethe, whose famous drama *Faust* presented musicians with their most formidable challenge. Before it, even the gradiosity of Giacomo Meyerbeer, who could set nuns of damnation to music in *Robert le Diable*, had to retreat when he refused the project of writing an opera on the great drama, calling it an "Ark of the Covenant" which must not be profaned with music.[1]

Yet, many composers recognized that, far from defying music, the drama demanded it. Goethe himself had consulted his Berlin friend and advisor on musical matters, composer Karl Friedrich Zelter, who recommended that Prince Anton Heinrich Radziwill do settings for *Faust,* and these were eventually performed in Berlin in 1819. Ten years later, a friend of the poet's family, Karl Eberwein, wrote music for it for a performance in Weimar. At first, Goethe had favored a melodramatic approach to the long monologues, with words spoken over music, an idea he discarded in 1821. At that time he began to see his drama in more complex aesthetic terms, beginning as a tragedy which would require a great tragic actress and ending as an opera in which Helena would have to be both actress and singer. And at the end the voices of a chorus would ascend musically toward heaven. In his opinion, the end of Part II *needed* music, that "Medium for the inexpressible." Though Busoni reverted to the early legend of the "Puppespiel" (puppet play) and, like Meyerbeer, did not care to wrestle musically with Goethe's thought ("Doch was vermöcht', gen Zauberer, ein Meister?" ["Yet, what power has a master against a magician?"], queries his poet), he finished very close to it and understood the "magician's" fundamental theatrical vision when he insisted that "Goethe thought of his second *Faust* as partly 'operatic,' " and he confirmed that the author wanted choruses to be sung throughout, Helena to be both tragédienne and prima donna, and that in general, especially in Part II, the presence of music was imperative and indispensable.[2]

With such interest demonstrated by the master himself, those who wrote musical versions of the legend, or parts of it, became legion.[3] Among those who set their sights on longer works, nine, in my opinion, have contributed significantly to the musical lineage, though for different reasons and with varying degrees of success: Louis Spohr, Hector Berlioz, Robert Schumann, Franz Liszt, Charles Gounod, Richard Wagner, Arrigo Boïto, Gustav Mahler, and Ferruccio Busoni. While turning primarily to Goethe's work, most of them recognized the impossibility of transcribing totally such an "Ark of the Covenant," which the author himself had assessed as unmeasurable, or "incommensurable" *(inkommensurabel).* With this in mind, others limited themselves to transcribing impressions: tableaux, scenes, songs, incidental pieces, episodes, or portraits, with or without words. These nine, however, attempted numbers of discernible comprehensiveness and magnitude.

But to get to the essence of the Faust story and to be able to say that *Faust* was "put to music"—that is, that the work was given not just a mu-

sical accompaniment or a setting through impressions but a musical interpretation, as it were a philosophical presentation through the art of sounds—
means to come to grips with the question of evil. For the story is principally
moral, and the emphasis that many composers have necessarily put on the
final outcome, redemption, like Schumann and Mahler, acquires significance only in the context of its opposite. The conquest or triumph it represents must be juxtaposed to evil. If the Faust idea culminates in the attainment of spiritual freedom through service to mankind, it is preceded by
the struggle against the limitations of the finite and the imperfect and, in
the process, against the temptation of worldly pleasures. Therefore, if music
is to "interpret" *Faust*, it must normally encompass both Part I and Part II,
and it is up to the composer to penetrate all the phases of ethical emotion,
damnation as well as redemption.

Because the sinister aspect of *Faust* has related so closely to prevailing
world views, musicians of both the nineteenth and twentieth centuries have
sought a protagonist other than Faust and have found him in Mephistopheles, whose name, Boïto reminds us in his Introduction, means "enemy of
light." Not that damnation attracted the Romantics and their followers more
than redemption; it simply received in their cosmos greater focus than in
previous eras and was made to blend with the heroic features of human
volition and purpose. "This power of the heroic will is the magic medium
that has guided our thinkers, scholars, and artists."[4] This notion Boïto thoroughly understood, as the title of his opera indicates, but it is not quite true,
as has been suggested, that musical interest in the problem of evil in *Faust*
originates with him. His view coincided with Romantic vision. In point of
fact, Mephistopheles is merely the Mephistophelian in Faust; in addition,
he is no less God's servant than Faust and is condemned to work good
through willing evil. As Boïto, his own librettist like Busoni, has his sinister
protagonist identify himself (following Goethe's "Teil von jener Kraft, die
stets das Böse will, und stets das Gute schafft"), he is

> Una parte vivente
> di quella forza che perpetuamente
> pensa il Mal e fa il Bene.
>
> (A living part
> of that force that perpetually
> thinks Evil and works Good.)

A successful musical approach to the question of evil must take into account this peculiar moral vagary which has made the question itself problematic to Goethe scholars for a long time. It has certainly focused attention on Mephistopheles. Though the German review that Busoni, along with Gerhard Hauptmann and Ludwig Justi, founded in Berlin received the title of *Faust. Eine Rundschau (Kunst und Mythos)* because it sought to muster toward reconstruction civilization's "inner composure, the concentration of all ideal powers and the foundation of a unified world view," the fact remains that its thrust was to thwart Mephistopheles's gaming hand which had shaped, according to the first issue's prefatory statement of 1921, "the fragmentation and confusion of the modern spiritual life," particularly in a country that was just emerging from the depths of an experience of evil in all its horror, "a consequence of the cultural catastrophe of the war." Mephistopheles reaches the life of the spirit through subtle evil, the temptation of lucid, unbound minds. Therefore, says Paul Valéry, he is "the devil with light eyes," an "observer . . . , a spectator of the destinies of our species who, placed a bit above us humans, [considers] our condition."[5]

Of the composers mentioned, the only ones to give the problem of evil due prominence—otherwise put, the only ones whose music strikes me as an artistic response to the moral issue—are Berlioz, Liszt, Boïto, and Busoni. If the sensuous, frolicsome, and diabolical abandonment by Mephistopheles of the sacred for the secular is not addressed by the music, then, however musically worthy the composition, the philosophical lesson disappears, leaving in its place, if only salvation is addressed, a theological sermon. Hence, the sense of oratorio that emerges from the works by Schumann, Mahler, even Gounod, whatever their technical, musicological designation. In this context, I make no distinctions between instrumental and vocal music; I am not interested in what a text might force the music to "say," but in what the music "says" by itself,[6] in the way an idea conceived in the mind shapes itself into musical utterance.

To Louis Spohr goes the credit—hence the historical significance of his work—for having written the first opera based on the Faust tale (he went not to Goethe but to old sources),[7] but his Mephistopheles does not possess the qualities referred to above. In fact, all the opera's music may be sung to the librettos of other operas of his day; the musical distinctiveness that would lend itself to ethico-musical analysis is not there. Carl Maria von Weber complimented the composer for a score with some carefully and felicitously devised melodies which weave through the whole work like delicate threads, holding it intellectually together. Indeed the role of Mephistopheles, among others, is made coherent through an associative system of leitmotifs which anticipate Wagner, but the musical phrases themselves are not sufficiently romantically free to be descriptive of evil. If anything, they are eclectic and do not develop their inner potential. Spohr's straddling the line between Mozartian Classicism and Romantic inspiration was not the case with Wagner, whose *Eine Faust-Ouvertüre* in D Minor continues the interest already expressed in his *Sieben Kompositionen zu Goethes Faust*, opus 5, of 1832 in making structural use, well before the *Rienzi* Overture, of the leitmotif.[8] The D Minor suggests the depressed state of mind the composer was in during the early 1840s, and as such the highly Romantic composition inspires the ominous—brooding or agitated—moods of the story, yet with contrasting measures in a confident major adumbrating salvation. The low-pitched beginning, its terse, somber, broken phrases, yields to a motif in the major, then returns to a restless minor with a savage outburst in the strings through rising and falling musical lines, before a rapid rush to an upward climax of redemption. Night yields to dawn. The problem is that the sense of evil—here rendered by low-register scoring, agitation, confusion, and ominousness—tries hard to make a statement but needs more communicative power. The first subject by the violins is vague, though the second, reminiscent of Elsa in *Lohengrin*, is attractive as it increases in anxiety before losing itself in a full orchestral despair. Diabolical evil needs more conviction—something Wagner must have sensed, since he remained forever unsatisfied with this composition and kept revising it for years. As if reminiscent of Mephistopheles's contractual demand, Liszt is supposed to have said, in promoting the piece: "Every note is written with a poet's blood!"

By far the most popular setting of Goethe's work has been Gounod's opera *Faust*,[9] but the composer, who among other things did not feel he could write well in the minor key, put together a work of sublimated moods—indeed inspiring in their own right—without a metaphysical sense of the drama and without endowing evil musically with its necessary lurid, netherworldly challenge. Méphistophélès's first appearance ("Me voici!") is sounded on a descending octave, in $C^\flat$, appropriately the same as his very last word in Act V, "Jugé." But Gounod's dulcet manner makes him more amiable than fearsome; the composer relies almost exclusively on agitated rhythms and heightened dynamic levels, occasionally on cries of horror by the chorus, to give evil credible expression (see the end of Act III, from "Tête folle" to the laughter—an allegro with simple harmonies and a few injected fortissimos, or the "Duel Scene" in Act IV, ending with "Voici notre héros, étendu sur le sable"—something handled more convincingly by Richard Wagner with a varied, additional use of augmented and diminished harmonies). If Méphistophélès gets Faust to sign the pact and indicates "Làbas, allons, signe!", the musical phrase is at best only pleasantly ominous and is followed by a duet in a comforting major. The same applies to his "Le veau d'or est toujours debout" of Act II, though in C Minor and underscoring "Et Satan conduit le bal." Yet the roseate music does little to stress it. Again, agitation (this one in an allegro maestoso) produces a lurid effect, but without more substance than that, the effect is lost. Gounod's Satan mocks reasonably well when he interrupts Wagner's trying to sing the "Song of the Rat," but in the sublimated context he sounds incongruously lyrical, especially over the harp's arpeggios, in "O nuit, étends sur eux ton ombre," despite his ulterior motive. And, finally, his sneering serenade, "Vous qui faites l'endormie," merely attempts to be minor; the evil is gentle; the horrible laughter engaging. As Berlioz remarked, the most convincing music in the opera underlies the emotion of love, like Marguerite's "Il m'aime! quel trouble en mon coeur!"—this was Gounod's "passionate inclination," and he may not be unhappy today that the bacchic *Walpurgisnacht* of Act V is generally omitted in performance. For someone who believed that love is the only condition for human happiness, it is proper that Goethe's drama be limited to Part I and to the Christian setting of error, atonement, and transfiguration, and that it reflect less the combat in the penitent soul than the heavenly transformation. The irresistibly onward movement of the organ prelude to the "Cathedral Scene" speaks eloquently for Gounod's vision in that it obviates any fatefully sinister sense the music might wish to convey. In this way, Gounod ably circumscribed his limits and remained faithful to Goethe's episode.

Both Schumann and Mahler view Goethe's drama from the vantage point of its outcome: the former emphasizes it, the latter concentrates on it exclusively—both advancing their music steadily to the poem's culminating verses, "das Ewig-Weibliche zieht uns hinan" ("the Eternal Feminine draws us upward"). There is no question that evil represents a power rebuked and defeated: *Garettet ist* ("Deliverance"). Gounod's work particularizes in human love a more universal spirit embraced by Schumann and Mahler. Part I of *Szenen aus Goethes Faust*[10] focuses on Gretchen, her love, remorse, and despair with fear of retribution. Part II, derived directly from the drama's Part II, highlights Faust, his growing and self-seeking awareness of grace leading to a desire to serve others, and his final self-sacrifice and death. Part III is the suavely mellifluous conclusion in the form of a transfiguration and apotheosis. Schumann's Faust exudes a spirituality that precludes any real concern with evil. He sights the reward. Hence, the part of Mephistopheles appears minor; he has no role at all in Part III, for example. This being the case, the composer could not underscore with dramatic intensity his presence in the preceding parts without detracting from the unifying, redemptional tone of the oratorio. Even so, he uses strategies and devices to suggest unmistakably Mephistopheles's insidious influence, and to the limited extent he does he makes a more pungent suggestion of evil than Spohr and Gounod managed to do. At times, he is too restrained: in the opening (I, 1), Mephistopheles's "Es ist wohl Zeit zu scheiden!" ("It is high time to part!") has no stygian character. But he uses this surly theme effectively as a recall. Though the orchestration suffers from too many tremolos—not the most illuminating way to describe the nefarious dangers of temptation—the abbreviated sonata form of the Overture (in D Minor) successfully produces a sense of conflict, and its somewhat Baroque figurations in Romantic garb and uncomfortable appoggiaturas and clashing notes convey well their reprobate meaning. Above all, the Overture introduces the theme (as a second subject) which, while not fiendish or foreboding, establishes its presence in such an insinuating way as to suggest the felonious spirit: in the accompaniment to Pater Ecstaticus's solo (III, 2), briefly in the "Chorus Mysticus" (III, 7), in introducing the accursed one in the "Garden Scene" (I, 1), and especially in the "Cathedral Scene" (I, 3), where Gretchen is taunted with damnation. Faust's encouragement—"O schudre nicht!"—is therefore not misplaced. Effective, too, are the downward phrases in the lower orchestra before Mephistopheles joins in, and the open, downward fourths of his "Weh dir" (I, 3); the bold musical lines and chromatic motif (in the strings) in quick, staccato rhythm of the Four Grey Women (II, 2); and the hard way Schumann pushes the texture, orchestration, harmonies, and dynamics— all to convey tension and evoke a strange hollowness—in the awe-struck aftermath of Faust's death (II, 3). Above all, Mephistopheles's "Hier gilt kein künsterisch Bemühn!"; the deep, trombone tones of mischief that appear in the mocking, four-square ditty of the lemures;[11] the vocal drops in fourths in the profligate's "von keinen Graben, doch vom Grab" (contrasting with the upward movement of Faust's "Verweile doch, du bist so schön!"); and the eerie scoring of his "Die Uhr steht still," followed by the midnight sounds of "Er fällt! es ist vollbracht"—these passages draw our attention to the presence of evil. But the overall atmosphere of ecstasy and of serenity, happiness, and reverence betrays the composer's strong attachment to Christian ethics and his avoidance of subjects that come face to face with damnation in favor of those ennobled and spiritualized by repentance and self-sacrifice, by the lofty reaches of redemption. His music breathes sermonically emotions that stem rather from the ethical than from the sensual.

The same last scene of *Faust* that Schumann set in a conservative oratorio style became the second half of Mahler's Symphony no. 8 *(Symphonie der Tausend)*,[12] written in a continuous, ever shifting, innovative series of tableaux embracing a Classical symphony's second (slow), third (scherzo), and fourth (finale) movements. From the "Accende lumen sensibus" of the first movement—built around the ninth-century hymn "Veni, creator spiritus"—to the "Gerettet" of the second, the symphony demonstrates longing for deliverance through the spirit and the consciousness of salvation bestowed upon ever struggling man. Redemption is its name and inspiration, and as such Mephistopheles again has no active role. In fact, there is no role for him at all, and his spirit is alluded to only once, albeit with stirring orchestral colors in the hour of heavenly triumph, throughout the long work:

> Böse wichen, als wir streuten,
> Teufel flohen, als wir trafen
> Statt gewohnter Höllenstrafen
> Fühlten Liebesqual die Geister;
> Selbst der alte Satans-Meister
> War von spitzer Pein durchdrungen.
>
> (Evil yielded, as we spread,
> The Devil fled, as we struck,
> Instead of the usual shrieks of Hell
> The souls were filled with pangs of love;
> Even old Master Satan
> Was pierced with sharp pain.)

Since Mahler sought to link the second with the first movement through complementary musical ideas and similar motivistic, thematic treatment (e.g., the "Veni, creator" theme is quoted in the "Chorus Mysticus" at the end of the work), the presence of even a reappearing surly theme like Mephistophe-les's "Est ist wohl Zeit zu scheiden" in Schumann's work becomes incongruous, structurally as well as conceptually. The music's ruminative, brooding tones, slowly working their way toward light and the brass of victory, reveal a sense of earthly suffering that Mahler possessed more deeply than Schumann, but in no way do they invite an ethico-musical analysis focusing on the workings of evil. Though his symphony points back to the idioms of Berlioz, Liszt, and Wagner, Mahler is not a descriptive composer; his musical, Romantic *Weltschmerz* opened up onto spiritual states, and in this number, damnation was not one of them. The intense, polyphonic design, however, backing a gigantic vocal and instrumental ensemble, lends credence to the composer's satisfied claim that in this symphony "the whole universe bursts into music"—something Goethe, in search of music for his noble ending, might well have considered a dream fulfilled.

Keen as it may have been, the intellectual insight of the above composers falls short—intentionally, in most cases—of realizing the great, successive motives of the shifting moral situation which pivots around Mephistopheles's manipulations and Faust's responses to them. For this reason, Berlioz, Liszt, Boïto and Busoni stand out. Through more than a fitting play of musical sounds, however skillfully scored (as in Wagner, Gounod, and Schumann), these musicians have portrayed musically the sensuousness, frolicsomeness, and devilishness of the protagonist of evil, bringing out with varying degrees of emphasis the enticement, irony, and destructiveness that these three qualities possess. What was said to Schumann after the Dresden premiere of his oratorio may be said with greater stress for the three composers in question who set their music to words—namely, that the music clarifies the text, and for the fourth, it may be said that he illustrated it. Their music casts a spell of the infernal and the iniquitous. Berlioz is more gripping than Schumann in sensing the degradation rather than the elevation of the human soul, Busoni more intense than Spohr in fashioning decay out of musical sounds, Liszt more plausible than Wagner in his mockery of peace and happiness, and Boïto more persuading than Gounod in stripping evil down to its heinous glow. They possess the tools for a music of pessimism.

Like Boïto, Berlioz, through the title of his work, leaves no doubt as to where he places the tale's emphasis. Though *La Damnation de Faust*[13] drew the criticism of having mutilated a monument (since Goethe saves

Faust), the feisty composer retorted quickly, as we read in his *Avant-propos:*
"The legend of Doctor Faust can be treated in all sorts of ways: it is in the
public domain." As a refinement of the previous *Huit scènes de Faust,* which
he deemed badly written and sought to destroy, the four tableaux of the
"dramatic legend" *(légende dramatique)* or the "concert opera" *(opéra de
concert)* that the *Damnation* represents impressed Liszt to the point of his
writing one of his best piano transcriptions on it (as he did also for Gounod's
popular waltz, to which Busoni later wrote a cadenza). What Mahler did
for the redemption, Berlioz did for the damnation, and Méphistophélès is
treated, especially toward the end, with proper musical reprehension. His
lines are in flexible musical prose, with harmonic surprises and chromatic
inflections, usually not based on even four- or eight-bar phrases but on
phrases of irregular lengths. His style permeates and informs the composition. The work's opening melody, with its flattened sixth and the modal
flavor it creates, is typical. Méphistophélès's entrance occurs on a descending line ("O pure émotion!"), perhaps not the most telling words to begin
his part of the drama, but the orchestra is heavy, with strings scratching a
tremolo *sul ponticello.* The same downward musical motion self-de-
scribes Méphistophélès: "Je suis l'Esprit de Vie," adumbrating Boïto's "pensa
il Mal e fa il Bene." So do Faust's "Eh bien! pauvre démon, fais-moi voir
tes merveilles!" and his "J'y consens," the fiend's "suis-moi!" and "change
d'air!", and the scene's last mockery, "Et laisse le fratras de la philosophie!".
All of these fix a pattern of physical gravity which continues in "Auerbach's
Cellar" in Leipzig and in Méphistophélès's "Flea Song," judging from the
conspicuous triadic cadences.

It might still be argued, however, that much of the music up to this point
lacks a villainous flair. It is harmonically clean, at times conventional in
the wake of Gluck and Beethoven, as Méphistophélès's beautiful "Voici les
roses" (Scene 7) proves, a questionable mood which he protracts when he
joins the chorus of gnomes and sylphs following Faust's dream. Granted,
his plan is to seduce Faust alluringly into sleep, but where are the hints of
wickedness? As in much of Schumann and Gounod, not to speak of Spohr,
there is little up to here of the characterization of malevolence we find in
Liszt and Boïto. Occasional chordal blasts, as with the quick opening notes
of Scene 10, do not suffice. Yet Berlioz's chordal writing manages to be
expressive if not functional. Often one chord does not lead into another
progressively. As with Busoni, it just exists individually, and the notes change

enharmonically (even if Berlioz did not care for enharmonic movement) according to need. Like Wagner, Berlioz makes good use of diminished intervals, and the resulting tension-bound sonority with much spacial distribution of sound—again like Busoni—heightens our sense of the warped and unseemly.

Berlioz prefers cumulative codas to thematic development, the principle of *idée fixe* notwithstanding.[14] Furthermore, his use of a second theme is minimal, so that, without its developmental resources (so coherent in Mahler), he achieves a Lisztian mood of discontinuity that fits the jagged outlines of evil. This is what happens in the evocation (Scene 12, "Esprits des flammes inconstantes"), whose awkward intervals now begin to portray Méphistophélès as the vicious spirit who joins the wills-o'-the-wisp in a serenading "chanson morale . . . pour perdre [Marguerite] plus sûrement." Berlioz engages rarely in the tension of contrasting characterizations. (As an example, we might recall the trio ending Scene 14, when Faust and Marguerite must escape Marthe's approach and the music quickens its pace; but the double mood combining and contrasting Méphistophélès's boast "Je puis donc te traîner dans la vie, fier esprit!" with Marguerite's rapturous "O mon Faust bien aimé, je te donne ma vie!" over Faust's ecstatic "Je connais donc enfin tout le prix de la vie" is lost, and Méphistophélès's black taste of triumph simply melts into the pleasant harmonies.) Yet his music portrays a scampish Méphistophélès, seemingly reduced to singing the ditties of the "Song of the Rat" and the "Song of the Flea," though in effect recording the victory of matter and the flesh. And his demonism erupts fifty-two measures into Scene 18, in Faust's and his "Ride to the Abyss" on two black horses, amid the cries of terrorized people and the cacophonous blasts in nine measures of trombones and bassoons, joined immediately by the bass clarinet and tuba and followed by the screeching of piccolo and flutes. "Quels cris affreux!" exclaims Faust.

Méphistophélès abets the orchestral anxiety with his satanic punctuations on the word "Hop!" Eventually, Faust falls into the abyss under Méphistophélès's high E♭ cry, "Je suis vainqueur!"—musically a dissolute prologue to Scene 19's apocalyptic Pandemonium. A feeling of evil stuns the listener with rapid, harmonic changes and tainted open fifths: "Je suis maître à jamais. . . . Il signa librement" (Méphistophélès's last words and the final accomplishment of degradation). The inexpiable gibberish of the victorious devils say more, in this concert opera, than the chorus beckoning Margue-

rite to heaven in the concluding Scene 20. The musical lines exist throughout, not as melodies with accompaniments, but in coloristic, contrapuntal
relation; not as traditional fugues (which Berlioz viewed as inexpressive and
mocked in the "Amen" joke in Scene 2), but as fugatos. And the fugal
openings of Scenes 1 and 2 establish an atmosphere—like the fugato after
Brander's Song—of conniving complexity. They also inject an element of
sensuousness in the piece. Thus, the portraying strategies of evil in Berlioz's
work vary, from nonhomogeneity remedied by brilliant orchestration to
disorienting harmonies and impulsive contrasts. The music promotes the
text. Berlioz paved the way musically for the ethical concern with damnation evident in those composers who took to penning music for *Faust* after
him.

Liszt does not use timbre in as free combinations as Berlioz, but he has
a broader grasp of the fullness of orchestral resources and becomes thereby
the richer illustrator. These resources he uses as effectively, in expanding or
contracting volumes, as Busoni. It was imperative for him to give his interpretation of *Faust* as broad a set of dimensions as possible within the reduced context of portraiture, particularly Mephistopheles's portrait, since he
was always haunted by the legend and by its sinister prince. Faust himself
he regarded as a bourgeois character, but Mephistopheles was different; he
was, in Goethe's words, "the spirit who always denies." It is said that Liszt's
walking stick was engraved with images of St. Francis (the life of the spirit),
Gretchen (reverence for women), and Mephistopheles (cynical diabolism),
three components of the composer's personality admired by Berlioz, who in
1846 thought it fitting to dedicate his *Damnation de Faust* to him. Liszt's
fascination with the tale took him to Nicolas Lenau's *Faust* as well, on
which he wrote *Two Episodes from Lenau's Faust*, a double symphonic
poem consisting of the dazzling *Mephisto Waltz* (on an episode called "The
Dance in the Village Inn") and the subtler *Procession by Night*.[15] In fact,
he kept writing Mephisto music: there is a subsequently expanded *Second
Mephisto Waltz*, an outstanding *Third Mephisto Waltz* (which Busoni transcribed for piano), a *Mephisto Polka*, and an unfinished *Fourth Mephisto
Waltz*.

Lenau's Mephistopheles may be more truly evil than Goethe's, but he is
also less intellectual and witty,[16] and the Mephistophelian in Liszt admired
wit or, better still, its discrediting face, irony. Though he admitted that
anything having to do with Goethe was dangerous for him to handle, he

was more given to musical sarcasm than to blatantly scurvy expression. The way he has the devils parody the plight of the sinners in the first movement of his *Dante Symphony* illustrates this point. Therefore, he went to Goethe in his *Eine Faust-Symphonie*,[17] which he promptly dedicated to Berlioz. Since he felt more comfortable with Lenau's succession of episodes or tableaux, he adopted the scheme of musical characterization—a convenient way of avoiding the "dangers" of the master's total drama. Besides, the scheme fits his propensity for program music, about which he had evolved a personal theory. Despite the near one-to-one program relationship with literary events one finds in the "Inferno" movement of the *Dante Symphony*, this theory departed from the specific manner of Berlioz, who saw music and literature as one and the same art. Liszt wishes to be less precise, using the text as a mere springboard, as in the "Purgatorio" and "Paradiso" sections of the symphony on Dante, to open up musical ideas that then follow their own laws of development. In his words, his theory relates more to Beethoven's *Egmont Overture*, where the music is not simply descriptive or decorative. For this reason, to follow *Eine Faust-Symphonie* with text in hand warps the composer's intention, which was to provide the listener with a dramatic synthesis of Goethe's work based on three characters—Faust, Gretchen, Mephistopheles—each one individually occupying by himself the three movements of the symphony.[18]

The first movement gives a complex sense of Faust with its gradual introduction and the first, meditative theme sounded in a *lento assai* by cellos and violas *con sordino*. Marked by diminished fourths, the theme moves slowly downward until it rises in augmented intervals to reach a *dolente* G♯ on the oboe. The character's *Sturm und Drang* appears in an allegro agitato section followed by an expressive statement by the clarinet and oboe in E♭ and then by a loving affettuoso in E Major by horn and clarinet over bassoon, cello, and tympani. In terms of the meditative and emotional side of Faust's character, all has been said. What follows is the intellectual side of decisive ambition and energy in the second theme, a grandioso for *tutti* in E Major based on five chords in tonic-subdominant-tonic sequence. Both are developed by juxtaposition (the ending on a dying version of the second suggests Faust's insecurity). The second movement is characterized by Gretchen's sweet simplicity, introduced by an oboe andante soave in A♭ Major and continued in a dolce amoroso in the strings. The orchestral feeling approximates to that of chamber music. A horn's patetico recalls Faust, and with the intertwining of themes the lovers's union is intimated before the movement ends on a modified return of the first part.

The masterstrokes come in the third movement, where Mephistopheles engages our attention, for here we hear a parody of Faust's themes. Since creation lies outside Satan's purview but deformation does not, Liszt allows Mephistopheles no motives of his own: he cunningly twists and breaks, through melodic and rhythmic changes, the two themes of the first movement. The archfiend's only "external" phrase, a short one, is itself derived from one of the composer's early pieces with the telling title of *Malédiction*. The movement is labeled not just an allegro vivace but an allegro vivace ironico, at the beginning of which the oboe, *dolente* for Faust and *soave* for Gretchen, penetrates the texture sardonically. The spirit of negation could never sound more clearly; in Boïto it whistles, in Liszt it contorts and gnarls. Indeed, the chromatic rise in allegro tempo on the mutilated first theme, from $A\flat$/G to $E\flat$ by the violas over clarinets and cellos, then bassoons, complete with *pizzicatos* and a scherzando, sounds as frolicsome as it sounds vicious, not to mention the allegro vivace play on the diminished fourth by the strings. The mood progresses to another contortion, that of Faust's second theme, like a mockery of decisiveness and great expectation, given in sixteenth triplets by the whole orchestra in an allegro animato, marked additionally for its sarcastic gait, giocoso. It picks up the E Major of Faust's phrase. With symbolic mockery, at the end of the cadence when the high E is reached, the line plunges downward in open fourths and fifths, ending in the tympani, whereas in Faust's statement it had ascended with the strings in a major tonic arpeggio. Then when the two motifs are heard in fugue by the strings, the irony is complete, a fine example of what Liszt meant by "transformation of themes." Gretchen, untainted by negation, is heard (a sudden pianissimo) through her theme stated without modifications, but only briefly. The orchestra returns fully with its whipping sonority, and the whole then yields to a choral finale in praise of the Eternal Feminine and the virtue of redemption. This represents a necessary coda for those who know the drama, but the Devil, though defeated in the end with the sinking of the music, has obviously done his evil. The scoring, then, is highly expressive, full of the tension of harmonic and melodic counterstatement, and also highly conceptual. For, apart from the destructive irony, Liszt's using the same motifs and transforming them from the first movement to the third signals to the listener that Mephistopheles is the Mephistophelian in Faust himself, perhaps the soul of the portrait.

Portraiture distinguishes Boïto's writing as well; like Busoni's, his Mefistofele may gain ascendancy in the end, but more than any other composer he makes his depravity alluring; it is simultaneously enticing, ironic, and destructive. The music revels in characterization, all the more remarkable a feat since, of all the musical Fausts derived from Goethe, his is the most encompassing and arguably the most moving. But the broad scope does not discard the particularization. His Mefistofele commands attention, not just for the text (Boïto was a poet as well, with a fine dramatic sense that made his libretti for Giuseppe Verdi's *Otello* and *Falstaff* among the best in operatic literature), but also for the music which communicates an ominous sense of a whole cosmos from seemingly wide orchestral sentences that turn out to be melodically constrained, at times smashed with harsh harmonies and spastic vocal effects (the baritone who sings the role must be a superb actor). The text, of course, helps; his self-identification is stunning:

> Son lo Spirito che nega
> sempre tutto; l'astro, il fior,
> il mio ghigno e la mia bega
> turban gli ozi al Creator.
> Voglio il Nulla e del Creato
> la ruina universal.
> È atmosfera mia vital
> ciò che chiamasti peccato,
> morte e Mal!
> Rido e avvento questa sillaba:
> "No."
> Struggo, tento, ruggo, sibilo:
> "No."
> Mordo, invischio,
> struggo . . .
> fischio, fischio, fischio, fischio, fischio, eh!
> . . . Parte son d'una latebra
> del gran Tutto: Oscurità.
> Son figliuol della Tenebra
> che Tenebra tornerà.
> S'or la luce usurpa e afferra
> il mio scettro a ribellion
> poco andrà la sua tenzon,

v'è sul Sol e sulla Terra
Distruzion!
Rido e avvento questa sillaba:
"No" . . .

(I am the spirit who denies
everything, always: the star, the flower;
my sneer and my wrangle
disturb the Creator's leisure.
I want Nothingness, and the universal
ruin of Creation.
My vital atmosphere is
what you called sin,
death and Evil!
I laugh and I hurl this syllable:
"No."
I waste, tempt, roar, and whistle:
"No."
I bite, snare,
destroy . . .
I hiss, hiss, hiss, hiss, hiss, ha!
. . . I am part of a recess
of the great All: Darkness.
I am the son of Shadow
that will revert to Shadow.
If light now usurps and grabs
my sceptre of rebellion
the contest will be short,
on the Sun and on the Earth
is Destruction!
I laugh and I hurl this syllable:
"No" . . .)

But it is the fever of the music that puts the character across. Far different from Gounod's almost gentlemanly spirit and Berlioz's near "galant, bon vivant,"[19] Boïto's sensuous and frolicsome emanation is also caustically diabolical. Even during the most beautiful arias ("Dai campi, dai prati," "Lontano lontano lontano," "Spunta l'aurora pallida," "Giunto sul passo estremo"), his presence is felt.

Influenced by Baudelaire, Boïto considered the problem of evil a centrally disrupting factor in the human condition, in the form of the contradictions between the positive and the negative, or the irreconcilable struggle between angel and demon. This dualism is evident in his ode, "Dualismo," of 1863, with its conflicting contrasts between light and shade, butterfly and grub, or in his other opera, *Nerone*, for which he chose a title symbolizing the evil of decadent Roman paganism rather than the good of dawning Christianity. In fact, Boïto came close to writing for Verdi not *Otello* but *Iago*. Hence, his opera is not *Faust* but *Mefistofele*; like the only true Romantic in Italian letters, as Benedetto Croce saw him, he had a sense of the autonomy of evil. Little surprise, then, that of all the composers considered, his constitutes the really "Faustian" effort to embrace an impossibly vast subject through a heroic condensation, and he knew—self-critical that he was—that more existed in his mind than he could write. Far from being disjointed or thin or uncertain, as has been claimed, *Mefistofele* impresses us with its erudition, its fullness, and the perversely rich quality of the music swirling around its protagonist.[20] It does not try to cram too much into a small space, though necessarily it cannot have the sweep of the original drama. But, like it, it is episodic; more than that, as a philosophical narrative in music, it says more covertly than overtly. That is, barring the few arias (themselves quite restrained by comparison with the effusiveness permitted to traditional bel canto numbers), the music does not come totally forward, does not round out its every emotion, so that the resulting art is one of reflection that invites the listener to provide his own interepisodic material, which cannot fail to relate to the central issue, evil. Sometimes the intellectualism falls short of its desired goal and reminds us of an academic exercise (for example, the love quartet in Act II, Scene 1); the flow of Gounod simply does not inform the Garden Scene (II, 1), despite its "Amor mistero" and the great climax. Normally, however, the music remains vibrant and alluring.

Boïto's ethical purpose directed him more to Goethe's Part II than Part I. In his Introduction, he says that, without such a continuation, the drama would remain imperfect in its highly moral scope and development, and to end the opera with Margherita's death and not Faust's would mean never to fulfill the bargain between God and the Devil. Pursuing this perspective of inclusiveness, the music provides its commentary; like the first and last words of Faust, the theme of the Prologue is repeated in the Epilogue (just as the poem ends as it began), and in the latter it is the orchestra that translates Goethe's four obscure figures around the dying Faust as he is troubled by hallucinations, for sounds are more incorporeal than words. All Faust needs to say toward the end is "Il real fu dolor, e l'ideal sogno" to set the tone for the remainder of the opera, whose grandiose, powerful conclusion remains tainted by this statement. For if Mefistofele sinks into the ground under the weight of flowers—and here the music, mixed with the redeeming assurance of Faust's "Arrestati, sei bello!" eliciting the Celestial Chorus and the arch-fiend's defiant "Trionfa il Signor, ma il reprobo fischia," could not evolve a more ironic contrast—he has made his dismal presence known.

Boïto respected the supremacy of the voice. He has Mefistofele twist it in all ways, including shouts and chilling whistles, the opera's trademark of chaos and destruction. Without prolonged melody (symbolically, Mefisto-fele has no aria) but with clipped phrases, as in Act II, Scene 2, when witches and warlocks of the Witches' Sabbath recognize "nostro Re" and he sings "nel pugno mio serrar," the voice becomes a purveyor of psychological insight. One cannot listen to something as simple as the arrangement of notes in Mefistofele's lines without sensing something more: the moral qual-ity of the character. If the melodic lines of the arias rely on tonality, Mefis-tofele's rely on timbre; the psychological strategy leads to tonal devices. This is consistent with part of the composer's aesthetic practice: to allow the great-est possible tonal and rhythmic development and to obliterate formulas, or the mechanical sequence of arias without dramatic reason. Thus, Mefisto-fele's spirit can punctuate the whole drama, even when not present. The folly of the Easter celebration (I, 1), the cadences underlined with tympani of the "Mantle Song," the fugato of the internal powers feasting the Sab-bath, the interruption of the Heavenly Chorus at Margherita's death, the uneasy undertones as the heathen contemplates the maiden's "Greek Dance" during the "Night of the Classical Sabbath," the wild orgiastic "Fuga Infer-nale" ending the Brocken scene—the wily spirit pervades. Antiphonal fan-fares in the "Prologue," along with augmented and diminished intervals, majors shifting to minors and vice versa, the chromatic writing in the de-scending "Sono lo Spirito che nega" (I, 2); the chromaticism in Margherita's mad prison scene (III) and in Elena's "Notte cupa" as she recalls the horri-ble carnage of Troy (IV); the selected use of low tones and low-range or-chestration throughout all these season the overall concept with an appur-tenant flavor of gloom. The orchestral voices stimulate the human.

But the main technique at Boïto's disposal is contrast, again an aspect of *dualismo,* a metaphorical reflection of the struggle between Good and Evil in the legend. The Prologue introduces contrasts immediately, like the shifts form major to minor. Sometimes they exist inside the same musical moment, sometimes in the juxtaposition of tableaux. "Odi la pia pace serena" counterpoises the screeching piccolos at the Prologue's end. The relaxed "Dai campi, dai prati" is shaken by the turbulence of Faust's "Olà! Chi orla?" (Mefistofele's entrance). The impurity of Mefistofele's phrases in low register counterstates the purity of Elena's lines in high register in Act IV. The Witches' Sabbath and the Classical Sabbath find themselves in automatic juxtaposition. Evil being buried under flowers, even a statement like "Le membra ho corrose dai raggi e dai fior," with appropriate musical ambiguity, creates an ambience of irony which originates in Mefistofele himself. For this reason his music is heard centripetally, for it drags all unto itself. The salubrious effects of the Celestial Host (in the Prologue), whose harmonies resolve in a strong major, cannot last the moment we hear the wrangling clamor of the "Fuga Infernale." In this context, redemption cannot appear as pure as it does in Schumann and Mahler, despite the peripeteia in the oratorio and symphony before it is reached. "L'opera del male distrugge Iddio col suo stolto perdon," boasts the protagonist, to the accompaniment of pungent harmonies. The work, it has been said, reveals more a pagan than a Christian hue; perhaps this is why. Mefistofele quickens the questioning, striving impulses in man and, therefore, comes forth more sensuously than, say, Schumann's villain. The music shapes this sensuousness and, in the process, delivers its most ironic messages, whether intended by Mefistofele for God ("Di tratto in tratto m'è piacevol cosa vedere il Vecchio . . . ; è bello udir l'Eterno col diavolo parlar si umanamente") or for mankind ("Eccoti . . . il mondo inter"). The orchestration mocks. It derides humanity as easily as the globe shatters in Act II. George Bernard Shaw understood the music well: "Gounod has set music to Faust, Boïto has set Faust to music." He speaks of the "great rolling crashes and echoes of brazen sound [in the Prologue] that transport us into illimitable space at once," of the "tremendous sonority of the instrumentation at the end with the defiant devil mocking each climax of grandeur [which] literally makes us all sit up."[21] And, between, all belongs to evil.

If Liszt's and Boïto's psychological strategies and tonal devices achieve aesthetically a chilling effect, Busoni achieves a veritable necromantic effect. *Doktor Faust*[22] rings with shrill clarinets, vehement brass, daring wide intervals, and bizarre modes of orchestral expression in a personal, atonal manner which, through its leanness and muscularity, exposes the text's nerves and sinews. Not abiding by the old tonalities, Busoni's style possesses inherently a cynical quality of exclusiveness; indeed the passages in the opera that demand irony become ironic almost spontaneously, aloofly, as if through the very nature of atonality and without the structural calculations of Liszt. Both as a composer, then, and as a philosopher observing the ugly realities of his pre- and postwar world, Busoni felt the spell of the Faust idea. His *Musikalische Fauststudien* of 1912 as well as his "Entwurf eines Vorwortes zur Partitur des 'Doktor Faust' [which he was composing, based on his own libretto of 1920], enthaltend einige Betrachtungen über die Möglichkeiten der Oper,"[23] published in 1926 after the opera, show how Goethe's drama, primarily Part II with its choruses, lends itself to music. His is a score of magic and sarcasm, in hectic colors and an expressionistic, nearly athematic and "futuristic" idiom; as he said, "solo chi guarda verso l'avvenire ha lo sguardo lieto,"[24] and not only Mahler but also Pfitzner, Hindemith, and Schönberg ride in his wake. In his opera, we find no traces of formulaic, thematic developments as in Spohr and Gounod, no abandon to sentimental impulse as in Berlioz or Liszt, no dictation of melody by harmony as in Wagner, and no reliance of the melodic line on timbre or tonality as in Boïto or Schumann. These anti-Wagnerian and anti-Impressionistic attitudes constituted his aesthetic credo, to which, for the opera, like Boïto he added a belief in the supremacy of the human voice, that conveyor of melody, limited only by speech and text. This makes for a concise, expressive music that abets the words as they are sung in clear lines, lyrically expansive in spirit but restricted by their expansiveness in utterance. Constantly refined by its own imperatives, the music arrives at a highly concentrated expression of evil by means of the same devices used by the other composers but endowing them with more audibility or sharper immediacy.

As we have come to realize, one of the common devices employed by composers to make us infer evil is a downward movement in the melodic line or in the harmonic progression. We hear it immediately in the descending thirds of Busoni's Overture and the opening "Pax" chorus of Vorspiel I where, as previously, they combine with minor seconds to produce unusual sonorities. The orchestral interlude before Vorspiel II contains upward melodic attempts constantly pulled downward, and in the agitated section of "Luzifer! . . . Hierher zu mir!" the music resists elevation. The same occurs in the "Hauptspiel," Scene 2, during the philosophical discussion on Plato, in the Theologian's effective "[Alles] zerfällt in Nichts!" and in the Protestant-Catholic students' argument where each party wishes the devil on the other in a jagged allegro rhythm in which the melodic line has no direction, except that a gravitational pull is felt. And in the Letztes Bild, the flute lines move rapidly downward commenting on Faust's "Meine bösen Geister sie trieben ihr Spiel." The contrast in meaning with upward moving lines, such as in Faust's devoted beseeching before the crucifix in the same scene, "Ich will wie ehemals aufschauen zu dir"—or later, following his last, inspiring words when the clarinet rises symbolically—is only too clear. In the same vein we note another common device, the use of low notes, generally sustained to create an atmosphere of reprobation and made poignant when juxtaposed to higher sounds, often hard and agitated, hammered by the brasses and winds. In Vorspiel I, for example, the juxtaposition comes with a shrill trumpet accompanying the overboiling of the crucible on the hearth "with loud clatter" (*mit lautem Geprassel*), and in Vorspiel II with Faust's "movement of disgust" (*Regung des Widerwillens*) after a movement of repulsion when Mephistopheles has given his name. In the Letztes Bild, the opposition finds a loud orchestra headed by heavy brasses (followed by unearthly low tones after "So sei das Werk vollendet"). This type of musical description falls under the category of orchestration and orchestral color, again noticeable following the organ intermezzo where a high oboe punctuates the low notes of the scene between the soldier, Faust, and Mephistopheles. Since it is not a simple matter of effect (Busoni was too intellectual a composer for that), much of this would not be possible without the composer's predilection for tenuous polyphonies, or polyphonically derived harmony and orchestration that produces a properly disturbing experience in the context of evil. The polyphony is also linear, befitting his emphasis on melody, with chordal formations and notes aligned more horizontally than vertically. This makes for continuous, false tonal relations, the perfect language for a broken world view.

Needless to say, ambiguity becomes a trademark of the scoring, something Busoni adapts skillfully to give appropriate passages in his opera a portentous cast. Again, the effect operates by contrasts, not sweeping like Boïto's, but contained. When, for instance, in the Hauptspiel, Scene 1, in the Ducal Park in Parma, the music announces and accompanies Faust's magic tricks, the writing (in which the woodwinds play a large role) is quite clear for all its atonality, full of comfortable allegros, as it is (though more gently paced) in the Duchess's subsequent dreamy, "high" mood emphasized by her acquiescent "Ja, ich komm." But the powerful line of Mephistopheles that follows—"Die Macht des Bösen ist nicht unterschätzbar"— almost comments sarcastically on the preceding music's clarity as the high mood descends with implausibly wide intervals. And the scene ends in shattering orchestral chords, stressing seconds, when Mephistopheles's (as the court's chaplain) blessing hand "spreigt sich zur Kralle." Gounod, Schumann, Berlioz, Liszt, Boïto—all make successful use of intervals in weird and fantastic situations, but in Busoni's dissonant context the gaps become foreboding. They permeate the opera, beginning in the Overture and continuing through Wagner's eerie announcement of the "Clavis Astartis Magica" in Vorspiel I, the orchestral interlude, Mephistopheles's self-identification, his scornful "drei Ratten in einer Falle" ending Vorspiel II, the haunting musical phrases of the magnificent Sarabande, and the arrogantly hollow horns ending the students' simultaneous emptying of their glasses in the Hauptspiel, Scene 2. The separation of lines on different planes of tonality produces a pertinently ambiguous effect of disembodiment.

Another device, used especially well though less frequently by Boïto, who passed it on to the composer, acquires a peculiar audibility in Busoni's atonal idiom: the rapid shift from the minor or the dissonant to the major, one would say mainly to suggest the concept of Mephistopheles's willing "das Böse" and working "das Gute" (something masterfully worked out in the beginning when Faust signs the pact in blood while the chorus sings an "Easter Credo" and "Hallelujah"). An example occurs in the intimation of redemption in the "Sarabande," following suspenseful appoggiaturas—the major chord and serene melodic line given by the strings, quickly suppressed, as it were, by a final, atonal five-note phrase ending on descending minor thirds. Another example occurs in Faust's exciting valedictory, "Ich, Faust, ein ewiger Wille!" when the trumpets inject themselves in the major. Such shifts do not go without their element of irony, of course, since they rely on an abrupt distortion of tonal perspective. The role of Mephistopheles is naturally full of distortions, including his own vocal range which, seemingly paradoxically, is that of tenor (stemming from Lucifer's servants in Vorspiel II, who appear as six tongues of flame in ever shriller notes). Chosen by Faust because he is as swift "als wie des Menschen Gedanke," he operates with alert impatience, and hardly ever with the support of major chords. The historical period in which he wrote made Busoni view him with austerity; in fact, though he reverted to the original Puppenspiel, he eliminated the humorous popular figure of Kasperle and converted all potential humor into irony. (The Parma episode and the drunken student scene merely contain traces of humor.) Humor is discarded because the music must deal seriously with man's future and high aspirations in the throes of vicissitude. As an illustration, in Vorspiel II, when Mephistopheles induces the peccant to agree to his pact—"Höre, Faust"—by reminding him of being pursued by creditors, the brother of the violated girl, and the clergy ("der Scheiterhaufen wartet deiner!"), the music, which might have provoked smiles, acquires a threatening, ironic bounce, breaking into a false baroque cadenza that almost sneers, and ringing with crisp punctuations by brass and tympani alongside the "no more" of Mephistopheles's enticement: "Ein Wort von dir, und sie sind nicht mehr!" In such instances, Busoni's musical sarcasm is far more to the point than Berlioz's and Gounod's, and in sheer intimacy of text and music it outdoes even Boïto. Another high point of scornful hypocrisy takes place with the playful, childlike line given by the woodwinds under the passage: "Ich hoffe, diese Geschichte klingt gänzlich ohne Harm; ich berichte die Geschichte noch eben brühewarm . . . Nehmt's nicht zu tragisch," and the mock pathos when burning the straw (-child), which leads to an evocation of Helena; through the legato melodic phrase of wonder, Mephistopheles jabs his allegro ("He he he he he he!"—so much nastier than Gounod's, though not as horrible as Boïto's whistle), whose cynicism clearly contrasts with the following straightforward allegro of the students' congratulating Wagner as Faust's successor to the position of Rector Magnificus. If the "He he he" represents humor, its color is black.

Doktor Faust is a landmark in the musical history of the Faust legend and more specifically in the history of the musical depiction of evil. It was Busoni's "grandiose theme" *(ungeheuere Stoff)*, in the words of the poet of the Epilogue, a genially contained expression that for all its severity bursts emotionally in a deafening portrayal of damnation. Mephistopheles carries off Faust, who has bequeathed his energy to the youth bearing the Ideal's blossoming branch as he rises from the corpse of a child—a form of redemption. But the last words are those of Mephistopheles, disguised as a night watchman, and the words are suddenly not sung but spoken, stark and unaccompanied: "Sollte dieser Mann etwa verunglückt sein?" The orchestra then explodes in loud, dissonant chords, which die away, suggesting that the story of "das Böse" is not over. Boïto had intimated as much. Says the Epilogue's poet: "Noch unerschöpft beharren die Symbole, die dieser reichste Keim in sich begreift" ("Still unexplored remain the symbols which this richest of all buds contains in itself"). Indeed the symbols are not exhausted. Berlioz may have come to grips with the problems of evil and perdition, Liszt painted their ironic portraits; Boïto synthesized the totality of the Mephistophelian presence; and Busoni placed a metaphysical overlay over the whole world view, but, in music at least, the legend will always lure those composers for whom the art of sounds is not just a pleasurable aesthetic pastime but a profoundly human activity of the ethical spirit in man—*[che] guarda verso l'avvenire* ([that] looks toward the future).

(1983)

[21]

LISZT'S JOURNEY
THROUGH DANTE'S HEREAFTER

With the Romantic rediscovery of Dante's *Commedia* came several attempts to render in music the poem's awesome majesty, the best remembered of which remain Liszt's programmatic *Dante Symphony* and Tchaikowsky's fantasia, *Francesca da Rimini*. However, apart from the enormous difference in scope between the two pieces (the former encompassing the three canticles and the latter only one episode from the first), they cannot be discussed in the same manner. Tchaikowsky's work—with its suggestion of passion, the whirlwind storm of the lustful, and the soloistically instrumented voice of Francesca—may easily lure the critic into a false musico-literary commentary, one based purely on inference and not, as it should be, on strict analysis.[1] For in this case analysis finds it has nothing to say about Dante; remove the title and the composition might apply just as conveniently, say, to the stories of Romeo and Juliet or Dido and Aeneas. If anything, Tchaikowsky's music stresses Francesca's romantic experience rather than her personality and her reality. The piece does not lend itself to a musico-literary study, except in the vaguest of terms. Nor was it intended to.

If Tchaikowsky had a genuine appreciation of the great Florentine, Liszt had a deep understanding of him. This understanding is less in evidence in his "Après une lecture de Dante: Fantasia quasi Sonata" for piano (inspired by Victor Hugo's poem, "Après une lecture de Dante"), a long and tempestuous composition, full of the fiery passion and ebullient dazzle that marked the Romantic movement,[2] than in the *Dante Symphony*. The symphony represents the best example of a true musico-literary interrelationship, the kind that lends itself to analysis because the music is not generally but specifically descriptive of the poem,[3] at least in the opening movement.

In typically Romantic fashion, Liszt preferred to work with large designs, in the spirit of his century's cult of Totality. Besides, as an intellectual and man of letters, which he also was, he looked to many writers around whom he could shape his large designs: Shakespeare, Byron, Longfellow, Hugo, Goethe, Lenau, Schiller, Heine, Petrarch. As for Dante, we know that Countess Marie d'Agoult and Liszt often read parts of the *Commedia* together in the 1830s. Sometimes during the heat of day they sat in the shade of plantains in the Villa Melzi by Lake Como reading the poem at the feet of Cornelli's statue, *Dante led by Beatrice*.[4] And his companion, the countess, was a Dantean in her own right, having published her dialogues on Dante under her usual pseudonym, "Daniel Stern." It did not take Liszt long, under these favorable circumstances, to conceive the idea of more than a symphonic poem, indeed of a programmatic symphony with the three canticles of the *Commedia* appropriately translated into three separate movements. By 1847 the principal themes had been sketched, and Liszt's enthusiasm burst beyond the original idea. Now he hoped that the painter Buonaventura Genelli would design lantern slides to be projected simultaneously with the performance of the music—a *Gesamtkunstwerk* of sorts that might have elicited wonder even from the Florentine bard. But he did not reach the point of composition until 1855, and by then the visual project was forgotten. Not so, however, a spectacularly grandiose third movement, or finale, complete with climaxing fanfare and powerful percussion, supposedly depicting the *Paradiso*—until Wagner, to whom the symphony is dedicated, suggested that fire and brimstone did not fit the spirit of Dante's Heaven. Liszt then replaced the movement with a Magnificat for boys' choir, and the symphony has come down to us in this final version: an agitated "Inferno", a meditative "Purgatorio", and an ethereal "Paradiso" in brief choral form.

When Liszt spoke of a "transposition of art" (i.e., through a "transformation of themes," using one art to do what another had done), he implied a strong measure of interpretation by one art of the other, accessible to analysis and not merely suggesting a "reaction to" the original subject. Even if he tended to think of a program as "any foreword in intelligible language added to a piece of pure instrumental music by which the composer intends to guard against an arbitrary interpretation, and direct the hearer's attention in advance to the poetical idea of the whole, to a particular point of it," and added that "the programme has no other object than to indicate the spiritual moments which impelled the composer to create his work, the thought which he endeavored to incorporate in it"[5]—something that would fit Tchaikowsky's *Francesca* Fantasy and his own "Après une lecture de Dante" well—he still insisted on subordinating purely musical concerns to the original subject, that is, to the program, thus fostering closer literary awareness.

In the so-called classical music the return and thematic developments of the themes are determined by express rules, which are considered inviolable, although the composers who originated them had no other precept for them than their own imagination, and themselves made the formal dispositions which people wish now to set up as law. In program music, on the other hand, the return, change, modification, and modulation of the motives are conditioned by their relation to a poetic idea. Here one theme does not, according to the law, call forth a second theme; here the motives are not the consequence of stereotyped approximations and contrasts of tone-colours, and the colouring as such does not condition the groupings of the ideas. *All exclusively musical considerations, though they should not be neglected, have to be subordinated to the action of the given subject.* Consequently action and subject of this kind of symphony demand a higher interest than the technical treatment of the music material; and the indefinite impressions of the soul are raised into definite impressions by an expounded plan which is here taken in by the ear, similarly as a cycle of pictures is taken in by the eye. The artist who proffers this kind of art work enjoys the advantage of connecting with a poetic idea all the affections which the orchestra expresses with so much power.[6] [emphasis added]

Liszt's achievement in the *Dante Symphony* consists in avoiding subordinations, in the successful blending, particularly in the first movement (the "Inferno"), of program considerations with concerns of musical form, indeed of the traditional sonata form, in such a way as to permit not a translation of one art into another (for literature and music necessarily remain two very different forms of expression), but a transposition (or transformation) by which the musical art interprets in its own idiom what the literary art has inspired.

I

In the first, or "Inferno", movement, Liszt concentrates on five passages from the poem in a general but clearly identifiable A–B–A, sonata-form disposition of material: the entrance through the ominous portals of Hell and the awesome inscription above them (Canto 3), the agonized cries and groans of the wretched souls (also Canto 3), the defiant pride of some of these souls (like Farinata, Capaneus, Vanni Fucci, Nimrod, Antaeus): these episodes constitute Section A. The pathetic encounter with Paolo and Francesca (Canto 5) constitutes Section B, and Section A—the recapitulation—brings back the cries and groans, this time mockingly heard through the sneering devils (Cantos 21–22), the sight of Lucifer (Canto 34), and the inscription again.

Verses 1–3 of the inscription are written into the score at the trombone level, as well as the famous concluding verse, "Lasciate ogni speranza . . ." ("Abandon all hope . . ."), given to the trumpets and horns:

Most appropriately, this theme of "abandoning all hope" becomes the leit-motif that unifies the whole movement, as indeed it consolidates the whole canticle of the Inferno. We are, not surprisingly, in the minor mode. Liszt's initial problem had to do with writing infernally horrible music, particularly at a time in the history of the art when the notion still prevailed—Grétry's utterances about realism notwithstanding—that music should be only sweet and beautiful and not concern itself with the characteristic, let alone the ugly. Mozart's and Gluck's renderings of Hell were striking but not ugly, and if something fearsome emerged it was more the operatic context than the notes themselves that caused it.[7] Along with Liszt, his fellow composers Berlioz, Wagner, and Boïto turned the aesthetic table around enough to show that, if by nature music cannot avoid beauty, it can also at least be beautifully ugly. Understandably, much depends on the orchestration, and Liszt emphasizes the low register throughout the first movement, producing dismal effects with instruments like the bass clarinet, the contrabassoon, two sets of tympani, a bass drum, a gong, cymbals, two harps, a harmonium, and an organ. Thus, we have an acoustic sense of the torments and despair that Dante witnesses, and of the abyss after abyss that opens before his eyes. The opening measures of the inscription and the motto theme—the proclamation of hopelessness—set the infernal tone.

The inscriptional motif, which begins in D Minor, relies for its effect on the interval of the tritone, since its two characteristic phrases before the cadence end on a G♯. In most musical traditions, the tritone, or augmented fourth, is an unpleasant interval, difficult to frame in singing, for example; theoretically it was forbidden in fourth- to sixteenth-century Western ecclesiastical music because it was considered injurious to the ear. Accordingly, it was referred to (conveniently for Liszt's purposes!) as the "diabolus in musica." Liszt makes frequent use of the agumented interval progression, though this or any other device he uses in the symphony (in the *Faust Symphony*, we observe, he focuses on the augmented triad) is not necessarily untypical of his general musical manner. The point is that here, quite apart from whatever he does in other musical works, the devices fit the literary context snugly and so abundantly that there can be no question about his aim to parallel the poem closely in the first movement. Such closeness of analogy does not characterize the *Dante Symphony*'s spiritual sister, the *Faust Symphony*, or, for that matter, the former's "Purgatorio" and "Paradiso" sections.

After stepping through the gateway, the awful tumult begins: Dante hears the groans of grief and reviling and the cries of anger and despair:

> Quivi sospiri, pianti e alti guai
>   risonavan per l'aere sanza stelle,
>   per ch'io al cominciar ne lagrimai.
> Diverse lingue, orribili favelle,
>   parole di dolore, accenti d'ira,
>   voci alte fioche, e suon di man con elle
> facevano un tumulto, il qual s'aggira
>   sempre in quell'aura sanza tempo tinta,
>   come la rena quando turbo spira.
>
> (Here sighs and cries and loud laments
>   echoed across the starless air,
>   which at the outset made me weep.
> Strange tongues and horrid utterances,

words of pain and sounds of anger,
voices shrill and faint, and beating hands
together made a tumult that always whirls
in that timless turbid air,
like sand when whirlwinds blow.)

[*Inferno* 3.22–30]

A turmoil of this sort can best be rendered in music by an established rhythmical combination associated with movement: the triplet. While the use of three notes in lieu of two gives a slow tempo greater flow, it gives an agitated tempo greater restlessness. Dante's Hell combines movement with purposelessness. It is important to note, then, that Liszt not only uses triplets but uses them chromatically and in a descending scale:

One of his finest devices is the symbolic use of musical line to produce the desired atmosphere in accordance with Dante's patterns. This chromatic scale, with its concomitant rhythm, not only produces an eerily jagged effect through its *pizzicato* but also, by nature, has no identifiable tonality, no central tone, therefore no centralized, purposeful motion. And if to this sense of disorder we add the quality and downward direction—a device that pervades the first movement—then we begin to absorb phonically the true mood of the poem.

A passage for the lower strings set against tympani rolls is followed by an *allegro frenetico* in 2/2 time, sounded by bassoons and violins; the groans and cries of anguish are rendered—again most appropriately—by Liszt's next device: appoggiaturas, downward and upward pulsations that describe the pained restiveness of those souls:

The appoggiatura, the leaning note that cannot stand by itself, creates a momentary suspension, and thereby a feeling of restless insecurity, the kind that characterizes most of Hell's damned.

Most, but not all. Alongside them Dante occasionally meets those who adopt postures (however vacuous) of defiance, especially Capaneus and Vanni Fucci, to recall whom Liszt switches from minor to major and sets down a motif for trumpets, horns, and trombones in the shrill key of B:

From the musical point of view, as well as from that of Dante's narrative, the change provides both psychological and aesthetic contrast. Any shift from minor to major does this, of course, but this instance possesses the double virtue of being dramatic and yet not so dramatic as to overdraw our attention. This is as it should be; in fact, defiance being to no avail, the motto theme or leitmotif of hopelessness slices through it eventually without resistance, punctuated by the tympani.

In listening to the first movement, we note that the composer, in order better to render Hell's disorder and disjointedness, extends the scope of the musical phrases from one formation to another without modulations. Because any melodic or chordal progression pivoting on a common note or chord unavoidably makes for coherence in the form of a graceful or serene transition, Liszt underscores the jaggedness by moving forward without modulations. A common note would imply concordance. We can appreciate the meaning of this when in Heaven we hear the celestial harmonies of the Magnificat moving upward from one sphere to the next in an exquisite modulatory process—ascending modes, like "Palestrina" scales, suggestive of Dante's continuous, harmonious rising toward the Empyrean. The harshness created by a total lack of modulation strains our traditional perception of beauty and, by reversing the aesthetic table, as Dante did in the *Inferno*, invites the oxymoronic designation of beautiful ugliness.

The middle section of the first movement is a slow andante amoroso, featuring harps, flutes, and violins, describing the Paolo and Francesca episode in the circle of the lustful. The storm subsides to allow Dante to address the adulterous lovers, but it is Francesca who does most of the talking. In a recitativelike solo passage, the bass clarinet intones her theme, the words of which Liszt again writes into the score:

Nes - sun mag-gior do - lo - re   che ri - cor - dar - si del tem - po fe -

sf ━━━ *p*   *fp*

li   -   ce   nel - la mi - se - ri - a.

After the swirling orchestral storm, Tchaikowsky too uses the solo instrument to signify Francesca's presence, but Liszt makes us aware of the accompanying presence of Paolo as well, through the most obvious harmony of two persons, namely thirds, played by two clarinets. For while Francesca tells her doleful story, her companion only sobs; yet the sobs are of love and complicity, of that sinful togetherness which spelled their downfall, as the sighing motif of the appoggiaturas reminds us:

There are, too, in Francesca's musical story, canonic devices, which also denote the presence of Paolo, the silent echo of the heroine. If given the opportunity to speak, he would say the same thing as she; hence the transpositional value of the canon. At times, as in Dante, the melody achieves a certain serenity. Francesca is a fine lady who clings to her dignity even in disgrace, giving herself the illusion of hope where none exists. It might even be argued that for a fleeting moment she seems to forget her misery. But Liszt (in contrast with Tchaikowsky) makes sure that the melodic line moves inevitably downward; in fact, all lines move downward: the melody and of course its canon, the appoggiaturas, the arpeggios, and the bass. A gravitational pull exercises its force to keep the voice from rising to reach where it is not permitted to reach:

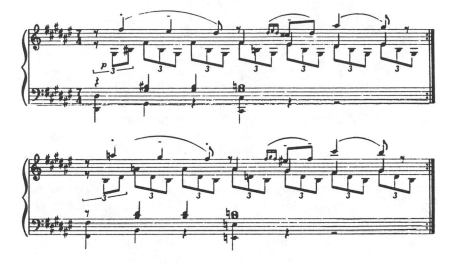

The chromatic involutions seem to reflect the manner in which Francesca keeps bringing her account back to herself, to her personality and reality, as an analogue of Guinevere in the tale of Lancelot that she and Paolo had been reading the day her husband discovered and killed them. The queenly fabric she has woven for herself, however, is soon marred by the thread of hopelessness, a subdued reminder by the motto theme, which Liszt inserts at the end of Section B.

The tympani reset the mood for the recapitulation, a new fantasy on the previous themes. Dante and his guide, Virgil, come upon a band of sneering and obscene devils, who in a mock military parade deride and deceive them as they do the sinners. If the *Commedia* is like a Gothic cathedral, these are the gargoyles. "This whole passage," advises Liszt in the score, "should be understood as sardonic, blasphemous laughter and must be sharply defined as such." Again we note the lack of modulations and the low orchestral register: basses, bassoons, contrabassoon, and trombones very freely and boldly used. The composer's master stroke of literary interpretation occurs at this point as he brings back the appoggiatura motif of groans and cries, but this time, by taking them away from the mouths of the sinners, as it were, and putting them into those of the devils, he transforms them into blatant irony and a cruel mockery of the victims whom these sounds parody:

This almost suggests a triumph of the devils, as indeed even Virgil fears at that moment in the poem; an assertive forte and rising tonalities sharpen the grotesque mockery. But the downward chromatic reminder returns, and even when Dante stands in the sight of Lucifer at the very center of Hell and the defiance motif is heard again, we know that the challenge is empty and sense that gravitational pull forcing everything downward. Lucifer's flat faces produce flat, hollow chords in Liszt: a climax of winds and strings over open fifths (D and A), together with the inexorable assertion of the motto theme emphasizing the proclamation of hopelessness. One thing about Dante's *Inferno*: it is a world already judged, and judged inexorably. Liszt's finale of the first movement leaves no room to doubt this.

Liszt's tour de force in the "Inferno" movement of the *Dante Symphony* represents a highly successful musico-literary relationship in which specific description has betrayed neither the original concept of the poet nor musical form. It would be difficult to think of a more pertinent example of cohesiveness between the ethic and the aesthetic. By being eminently "musical" in the first movement, Liszt has sacrificed nothing to the literary inspiration, so that we might even go so far as to say that he has shown us the "musicality" of Dante's vision. The picturing of the outward (the program) has been kept duly sensitive to the picturing of the inward (the purely musical needs), and though he sketched according to the "spiritual moments" he chose, he has not "subordinated [musical considerations] to the action of the given subject." From beginning to end, and even through the increasingly restive tempos (4/4 to 2/2 to 5/4 to 7/4, and so on, which parallel the movement and anxiety of Dante's descent), the first movement satisfies the demands of aesthetic coherence and of that favorite theory of Berlioz's, the unity of instrumental music with poetry.

II

In the second movement of the *Dante Symphony*, Liszt abandons the "strict" one-to-one relationship between music and poem that makes possible an analytical study of the "Inferno" movement, and chooses to depict by loose analogy, allowing the listener merely to infer the literary association rather than examine it. Here his manner corresponds more with the notion of "spiritual moments"; he moves closer to his "Après une lecture de Dante" or to Tchaikowsky's *Francesca* Fantasy. In relation to what has preceded, however, his adoption of a different approach does not betray an inconsistency. On the contrary, the shift in manner is consistent with the text, and the shift becomes even more pronounced at the end, after the "Purgatorio" movement, in the brief "Paradiso" section. In other words, the evolution, like Dante's, is coherent. For the *Commedia* moves from the satanic through the human to the angelic in a mounting progression from matter through form to essence, or from the negational through the existential to the essential. Similarly, the *Dante Symphony* moves eventually from the heavy, deep, and "ugly" through the smoggy and hopeful to the airy, ethereal, and beautiful; from the specific or concrete, active *Inferno* the music climbs through the atmospheric or meditational, passive[8] *Purgatorio* to the general or rarefied, rapturous *Paradiso*. In painting, the analogous progression would range from bold oil colors to subtle aquarelles.

A canticle of meditation shaped by a liturgical atmosphere, the *Purgatorio* does not invite accurate episodic treatment. To be sure, Liszt informs us at the very beginning of the movement of the liberating sensation Dante experiences at the sight of the "Sapphire of the East":

> Dolce color d'oriental zaffiro,
>   che s'accoglieva nel sereno aspetto
>   del mezzo puro insino al primo giro,
> alli occhi miei ricominciò diletto. . . .
>
> (The gentle hue of oriental sapphire
>   gathering on heaven's face serene
>   from clear horizon to the first circle
> once again gladdened my eyes. . . .)
>   [*Purgatorio* 1.13–16]

As in the *Commedia*, the gravitational pull is greatly lessened, and the horn accordingly intones a theme of serenity followed by the oboe, then by the English horn, clarinets, violas, flutes, the second oboe, and harp:

With the introduction of the next musical idea,

the atmosphere of meditation is established. We note that the characteristic appoggiaturas are not forgotten, except that here their context changes them from sighing to striving because of the musical means adopted: ascending melodic phrases. From this point on, meditation finds its underpinning in the liturgical motive of prayer, which forces the repenter—for repentance provides the foundation for the canticle—to look into himself. The clue of humility is probably suggested by that passage in Canto 10, admired by the religious composer, which tells of our proud and twisted minds that cannot measure our own inferior reality:

> O superbi cristian, miseri lassi,
>   che, della vista della mente infermi,
>   fidanza avete nei retrosi passi,
> non v'accorgete voi che noi siam vermi
>   nati a formar l'angelica farfalla,
>   che vola alla giustizia sanza schermi?
>
> (O Christians proud, exhausted wretches,
>   sick of vision and of mind,
>   who place your trust in backward steps,
> do you not see that we are worms
>   born to form the angelic butterfly
>   that to judgement soars defenseless?)
>   [*Purgatorio* 10.121–26]

Liszt stresses throughout the sense of this kind of consciousness and of noble aspiration—a commingling of these motives—which permeates Dante's middle poem. For both Dante and Liszt, a liturgical song symbolizes the collective or societal aspect of existence, society striving as a unit for salvation. Like an organ, therefore, the orchestra led by the woodwinds brings forth the repentant yet hopeful choralelike theme

which is followed by another "spiritual moment," a sober, contemplative, low-keyed rendering, initiated by the trombones, of the idea of the missed opportunities to do good during life that forms part of the penance of Purgatory:

The theme successfully blends meditation and liturgy.

It is here that Liszt introduces a fugue to emphasize aurally what the sinners are undergoing spiritually: a profound, moral introspection, for of all the musical devices that force the listener to enter inside a composition, the fugue is the most "introspective." This quality gathers emphasis from the fact that the composer uses no fewer than five voices. Not in strict counterpoint, this *Lamentoso* flows in and out of itself, consistent musically with the intention of introspective meditation:

Interesting things happen in this fugue. The appoggiaturas stand out, and, as the spiritual gravity of the poem begins to shift,[9] a number of them start turning upward. Musically, the piece holds together with consistency as the musical ideas develop. The broader fibers are also clearly woven into the fabric, and all accumulate into a swelling of major triads, adumbrating a kind of liberation or victory, in contrast with the bondage and defeat of Hell,

along with an impressive developmental passage:

A hint of the resolution of the tritone is suggested by moving the *gemendo* G–C♯ to C♯–F♯. Then a delicate return to the meditational chorale drags matters forward. The movement is very long (before the Magnificat, the "Purgatorio" section takes close to twenty minutes in performance), one might even say dreary, for the way of penitence and renunciation of sin to redemption is slow, in some cases lasting thirty times as long as the period of disobedience. But eventually one comes into the Earthly Paradise: the triadic major chords ascend in the harp and violins

modulating continuously upward and, when three flutes and the harmonium join in the ascent, a boys' choir (or a chorus of female voices) begins the "Paradiso" section with a Magnificat:[10]

and:

A long trumpet note, then a solo voice (Beatrice?) is heard in a fine line suggesting music from the liturgy:

The sense of time that marked the *Purgatorio* is replaced, also in musical terms, by a sense of timeless rising—a direction emphasized by Dante, as he ascends from sphere to sphere toward the Godhead, with the image of a golden ladder:

> Dentro al cristallo che 'l vocabol porta,
>   cerchiando il mondo, del suo chiaro duce
>   sotto cui giacque ogni malizia morta,
> di color d'oro in che raggio traluce
>   vid'io uno scaleo eretto in suso
>   tanto, che nol seguiva la mia luce.

> (Within the crystal which bears the name,
>   circling around the world, of its famous chief
>   under whom all wickedness lay dead,
> I saw, in golden color that flashes
>   in the sun, a ladder rising high
>   so that my sight could not follow it.)
>   [*Paradiso* 21.25–30]

A *tutti* of triumph in major harmonies is followed by a Hosanna, which flows upward in seemingly endless, harp-punctuated modulations and settles ethereally in the calm ecstasy of a final Hallelujah.

Thus, as Dante's text becomes more and more rarefied, Liszt lets go of it, allowing the music merely to describe by analogy. The loosely structured

"Purgatorio" section takes only a few thematic cues from the poem, shaping moods ("spiritual moments") more than events, and the "Paradiso" *coda*, while appropriately ascending and suggesting the song and beatitude of the angels and the blessed, leaves the text aside totally (apart from the Hosannah, which, taking into account both Earthly Paradise and Paradise proper, rings five times in Dante's poem) when Latin hymns unmentioned by the poet are introduced (there is no Magnificat or Halleluja in the poem).[11] There was no better way to transform "la dolce sinfonia di paradiso" (*Paradiso* 21.59) than through a chorus of high voices. Nor was there a better way to translate Dante's epic, for whatever one's opinion of the composition as music, Liszt's literary understanding of it reveals sensitivity and sophistication: sensitivity to the poetic impulses that shape its meaning, and sophistication in the restraint he exercises in permitting the text to dictate only so much and in leaving the primary utterance to music expressed ultimately through musical means alone. Wagner was in a state of "wonder"[12] when he heard Liszt perform the symphony at the piano, and for Nietzsche the composition was a discovery. James Huneker put it aptly: in the *Dante Symphony* Liszt "gave us the best he could give . . . the summit of his creative power, and the ripest fruit of that style of progamme music that is artistically justified."[13]

(1982)

NOTES

INTRODUCTION

1. Calvin S. Brown, *Music and Literature: A Comparison of the Arts* (Athens, Ga.: University of Georgia Press, 1948). It has been reprinted by the University Press of New England (1987). The reader might also wish to consult James A. Winn, *Unsuspected Elegance: A History of the Relations Between Poetry and Music* (New Haven: Yale University Press, 1981).

2. H. Horwarth, "Eliot, Beethoven, and J. W. N. Sullivan," *Comparative Literature* (1957): 322. The reference is to John William Sullivan, *Beethoven: His Spiritual Development* (New York: A. A. Knopf, 1951).

3. C. A. Bodelsen, *T. S. Eliot's Four Quartets* (Copenhagen: Copenhagen University Publications Fund, 1958), 29.

4. See Brown, *Music and Literature*, 212–17.

1. MUSIC IN ZWIEG'S LAST YEARS: SOME UNPUBLISHED LETTERS

1. This essay was written in collaboration with Harry Zohn.

2. The correspondence was in the possession of Alfred Einstein's (died: 1952) widow, at the time of this writing a resident of El Cerrito, Calif.

3. Now deposited in the Houghton Library, Harvard University, Cambridge, Mass.

4. See Herr Hinterberger's *Catalogues* IX and XX, issued in Vienna, 1936–37.

5. See A. Einstein, "Die Sammlung Speyer," *Philobiblon* (Vienna) 8, no. 4 (1935): 155–58.

6. Another facsimile edition of this work, with an introduction by Paul Nettl, was issued by Storm Publishers (New York, 1949).

7. See Franz Trenner, *Richard Strauss: Dokumente seines Lebens und Schaffens* (Munich: Beck, 1954), 228ff., for an account of the tempestuous history of the latter work.

8. "Stefan Zweig und die Musik," *Aufbau* 1, no. 1 (New York, March 6, 1942).

9. On this collection, cf. Harry Zohn, "Stefan Zweig as a Collector of Manuscripts," *German Quarterly* 25, no. 3 (May 1952): 182–91; G. H. Thommen-Girard, "Stefan Zweig als Autographensammler," *Das Antiquariat* 10, nos. 17–18 (September 1954): 205–8.

10. Gisella Selden-Goth, "Stefan Zweig, Lover of Music," *Books Abroad* 20, no. 2 (Spring 1946): 150. Mme Selden-Goth lived in Florence; she died in the late 1970s.

2. BALZAC AND BEETHOVEN: THE GROWTH OF A CONCEPT

1. *L'Artiste* 19 (1837): 322. A detailed assessment of the general situation may be found in Leo Schrade, *Beethoven in France* (New Haven: Yale University Press, 1942).

2. *La Gazette musicale* (January 1837).

3. *La Revue musicale* 4 (1828–29): 515.

4. "Questions sur le beau," *La Revue des deux mondes* 24 (1854): 310.

5. "Charges," *La Caricature*, February 10, 1831. He called it an "admirable symphony" but little else, describing quite ingenuously a silence after a climax: "There is a moment when all the instruments stop playing in a spontaneous action. The effect is marvelous. You have no idea, unless you have heard it. It's a crescendo, crescendo, crescendo. . . . Then, suddenly, complete silence."

6. See Georges Guéroult, *Eugène Sauzay* (Mâcon: Protat frères, n.d.), 9.

7. *Lettres à l'Etrangère*, ed. Calmann-Lévy (Paris: Calmann-Lévy, 1899–1950), Nov. 7–14, 1837, I, 433; hereafter cited in the text as *Lettres*.

8. The letter continues: "I live in such a solitary way that I need not tell you about life in Paris," 443–44.

9. Honoré de Balzac, *La Comédie humaine* (Paris: Bibliothèque de la Pléiade, 1950–55), 9: 65, 76. Along with opera, Beethoven too served as a distraction: "At times I relax. My only distraction comes by way of the most extreme resources of thought, Beethoven, the Opéra." Quoted from Louis-Jules Arrigon, *Balzac et la "contessa"* (Paris: Editions des Protiques, 1932[?]), 35.

10. *L'Artiste* 8 (1834): 151.

11. Quoted from Schrade, *Beethoven in France*, 38. In addition, see Anton Schindler's references to this and similar attitudes in *Beethoven in Paris* (Münster: Aschendorff'sche Buch Handlung, 1842), 5, 7, 21, 40n.; A. Schindler, *Life of Beethoven* (London: H. Colburn, 1841), 2: 80–162.

12. Quoted from Edwin Evans, *A Critical Study of Beethoven's Nine Symphonies* (New York, 1923–24), 123 and 56, respectively (a translation of Berlioz's *A travers Chants*); also London (Reeves, 1913).

13. See, for example, d'Ortigue, *La Revue musicale*, May 11, 1833; Berlioz, in *Le Rénovateur* on the Fifth Symphony, April 27 and May 11, 1834; on the Sixth Symphony, March 2, 1834.

14. *A travers Chants* (Paris: Michel Lévy, 1862), 30–35.

15. Léon Guichard, e.g., believes that the Beethoven sections serve only the function of comparison: *La Musique et les lettres au temps du romantisme* (Paris: Presses Universitaires de France, 1955), 312. See also Hugh S. Worthington, "The Beethoven Symphony in Balzac's *César Birotteau*," *Modern Language Notes* 39 (1924):

414–19, and Maurice Serval, "Autour de Balzac: *César Birotteau,*" *Revue d'histoire littéraire de la France* (April–June 1930): 196–226.

16. The bracketed interpolations in the last sentence interpret Balzac's idea which is based on an analogy with a literary technique of Sir Walter Scott.

17. *Music in the Romantic Era* (New York: Norton, 1947), 33.

18. Guichard, *La Musique*, 106, considers 1837 a termination and rejects Mme Maurice-Amour's argument ("Balzac et la musique," *Mercure de France*, January 1, 1950) that it is a commencement, a year in which Balzac's "ignorance [was burning] to become knowledge."

19. *Correspondance*, in *Oeuvres complètes*, ed. Calmann-Lévy (Paris: Calmann-Lévy, 1869–76), 24: 343.

20. *Gambara*, 9: 430; *Lettres*, 3: 92; *César Birotteau*, 5: 463; *L'Artiste*, 8: 151; and *Lettres*, 3: 149; respectively.

21. Léon Emery, *Harmonies* (Lyon: Les Cahiers Libres, 1954), 90.

22. Thérèse Marix-Spire, *Les Romantiques et la musique: le cas George Sand* (Paris: Nouvelles Editions Latines, 1954), 38.

23. Fernand Baldensperger also remarked on this in *Orientations étrangères chez Balzac* (Paris: Champion, 1927), 221. We know from Berlioz that there had been a fine performance of *Fidelio* in Paris in 1827, but we have absolutely no indication of Balzac's having attended it.

3. REVISITING THE *CANTI CARNASCIALESCHI*

1. F. T. Perrens, *Histoire de Florence* (Paris: Hachette, 1877), 3: 394. In this essay I have attempted to fuse a number of variously expressed opinions in order to present a total picture, artistically speaking, of the famous carnivals.

2. See Nesta de Robeck, *Music of the Italian Renaissance* (London: The Medici Society 1928), 8.

3. See anthology by F. Trucchi, *Poesie italiane inedite* (Prato: Guasti, 1846–47).

4. Cited from E. J. Dent, *Music of the Renaissance in Italy* (London: British Academy Proceedings, 1933), 7. Also see F. Ghisi, *I Canti Carnascialeschi nelle fonti musicali del XV e XVI secolo* (Florence and Rome: Olschki, 1896), 11.

5. Giosuè Carducci, *Caccie in rima dei secoli XIV–XV* (Bologna: Zanichelli, 1896), 11.

6. See F. Torrefranca, "I Primordi della polifonia del cinquencento," *Nuova antologia* (November 1, 1934): 107–8. Also consult Luigia Cellesi, *Documenti per la storia musicale di Firenze* (Turin: Fratelli Bocca, 1927).

7. E. Barfucci, *Lorenzo de' Medici e la società artistica del suo tempo* (Florence: Gonelli, 1945), 90.

8. G. Vasari, "Vita di Piero di Cosimo," *Le vite* (Florence, Sansoni, 1878–1906), 4: 137.

9. See Fr. X. Haberl, "Wilhelm du Fay, Monographische Studien über dessen Leben und Werke," *Vierteljahrsschrift für Musikwissenschaft* (1885), 1: 436–37.

Concerning the Canzone, see Otto Kade, "Biographisches zu Antonio Squarcialupi," *Monatshefte für Musikgeschichte* (1885), 17: 14ff.

10. His death, between 1475 and 1480, occasioned many tributes, musical, poetical, and so on. Benedetto da Maiano sculptured the famous bust of Squarcialupi,
and Lorenzo wrote the epitaph on his tomb in the Duomo:

> Faremo insieme O Musica lamento
> Sopra il viro immortale oggi sepolto
> Morte si scusa e dice "io ve l'ho tolto
> Per far più lieto il ciel con suo concento."
>
> (So lament shall we, O Music,
> The man today interred immortal;
> Says Death, excusing herself, "I've taken him
> From you to make the heavens happier with his harmony.")

11. He wrote two imposing six-part motets "Optime Pastor" and "Virgo Pruden-
tissima"), and his is the first polyphonic treatment of the entire collection of the
Gregorian chants that make up the *Graduale*.

12. Lorenzo entrusted Isaak with composing the music for *San Giovanni e Paolo*,
the *sacra rappresentazione* which contains many of Lorenzo's social and political
ideas. Ficino too praised Isaak, and Poliziano honored him with several epigrams.
When Lorenzo died in 1492, Isaak and Poliziano collaborated in paying tribute to
Il Magnifico: *Laurentium Medicem intonata per Arrigum Isaac* (may be found in I.
Del Lungo, *Poliziano, Prose volgari e poesie latine inedite* [Florence: G. Barbera,
1867], 274).

13. Paul-Marie Masson, *Chants de carnaval florentins* (Paris: Senart, 1913).

14. As in modern jazz orchestras, the trombone was then considered a melodic
instrument (see [n.i.] Bracci, *Tutti i Trionfi, Carri, ecc.*, ed. Cosmopoli [n.d.], xxxvi–
vii).

15. V. Rossi, *Il Quattrocento* (Milan: Vallardi, 1933), 44.

16. In the following paragraphs, I have condensed a few of the more significant
critical perspectives (such as Rossi's, Perrens', and Barfucci's) on this socio-psycho-
logical dimension.

17. Paul Valéry, *L'Idée fixe* (Paris: Gallimard, 1934), 132.

4. THE EVOLUTION OF TEXT AND TONE IN THE RENAISSANCE

1. See Cecil Gray, *The History of Music* (New York: Barnes and Noble, 1968),
117–18.

2. D. G. Hughes, *A History of European Music* (New York: McGraw-Hill, 1974),
106.

3. From *De arte contrapuncti*, quoted in Friedrich Blume, *Renaissance and Baroque Music* (New York: Norton, 1967), 16. He discusses the notion of *varietas* and
suavitas on p. 17.

4. See Blume, *Renaissance and Baroque Music*, 20.

5. Ibid., 25. For other general discussions from which I have profited, the reader might consult Howard Mayer Brown, *Music in the Renaissance* (Englewood Cliffs, N.J.: Prentice-Hall, 1976); Bruce Pattison, *Music and Poetry in the English Renaissance* (London: Methuen, 1948); and, of course, the classical standby, Paul Henry Lang, *Music in Western Civilization* (New York: Norton, 1941).

5. "HOW SOUR SWEET MUSIC . . . WHEN TIME IS BROKE"

1. William Shakespeare, *Richard II*, V, 5, vv. 42–43.
2. Leonard Meyer, *Music, the Arts and Ideas* (Chicago and London: University of Chicago Press, 1967, 1970), 66.
3. "The Second Coming," vv. 3–4.
4. See my interview with Richard Strauss in *Modern Austrian Literature* 20, no. 2 (1987): 179–86.
5. Gerald Abraham, *The Tradition of Western Music* (Berkeley and Los Angeles: University of California Press, 1974), 17. The case can be made, of course, that these new styles relate to historical realities, but ultimately it cannot progress very far: see note 6.
6. Meyer, *Music, the Arts and Ideas*, 17.
7. See Julius Portnoy, *The Philosopher and Music* (New York: Humanities Press, 1954), 206.
8. Vv. 1–2.

6. EXPLORATIONS IN A NON-WESTERN CONTEXT

1. There are any number of works on the literature and the music, separately considered, of the cultures I am investigating, but—as various scholars in the field have confirmed to me—none treats substantially their actual interrelation.
2. In the case of China, I have looked into the following works written in Western languages: Bliss Wiant, *The Music of China* (Chung Chi Publications, Chung Chi College, The Chinese University of Hong Kong, 1965); Walter Kaufmann, *Musical References in Chinese Classics*, Detroit Monographs in Musicology No. 5 (Information Coordinators, 1976); M. Granet, *Fêtes et chansons anciennes de la Chine* (Paris: E. Leroux, 1929); A. Hoffmann, *Die Lieder des Li You, Herrschers der Südlichen T'ang Dynastie* (Cologne: Greven, 1950); L. C. Arlington, *The Chinese Drama from the Earlier Times Until Today* (Shanghai: Kelly and Walsh/Bronx, New York: Bloom, 1966); G. Soulié de Morant, *Théâtre et musique modernes en Chine* (Paris: Geuthner, 1926); J. R. Hightower, *Topics in Chinese Literature* (Cambridge: Harvard University Press, 1950); J. L. Levis, *Foundations of Chinese Musical Art* (Peking: French Bookstore, 1936); C. W. Luh, *On Chinese Poetry* (Peiping: Foreign Language Teaching and Research Press, 1982); and Meng Chih, *Remarks on Chinese Music and Musical Instruments* (New York: China Institute of America, 1932). For the relation between sounds and words and the pentatonic system, one would have to look into Chang Yen, *Tz'u Yuan*, the source of *tz'u* (only data available to me).

3. It is not my purpose here to go into the differences between northern and southern *tz'u*, the latter being more revolutionary or political in inspiration, nor to describe the kinds of instruments commonly used in performance: strings, such as the three-string banjo, flute, mouth organ, percussion—all of which are, of course, closely related to texture.

4. I am not mentioning the matter of comic opera, which dates back to the Sung Dynasty (eighth to thirteenth centuries) and which also invites speculation on the musico-literary level, particularly in analogy, though it may sound strange, with the works of Gilbert and Sullivan.

5. For Japan, I have consulted the following works written in Western languages: William P. Malm. *Japanese Music and Musical Instruments* (Rutland, Vermont, and Tokyo: Tuttle, 1959); Earle Ernst, *The Kabuki Theatre* (New York: Oxford University Press, 1956); Noël Péri, *Le No* (Tokyo: Maison Franco-Japonaise, 1944); Donald Keene, *No: The Classical Theatre of Japan* (Tokyo and Palo Alto, Calif.: Kodansha International, 1966); Toyochiro Nagami, *Zeami and the Treatises on Noh* (Tokyo: Tsunetaro Hinoki, Hinoki Shoten, 1973); Shigetoshi Kawatake, *Kabuki: Japanese Drama* (Tokyo: Foreign Affairs Association of Japan, 1958); P. G. O'Neill, *Early No Drama* (London: Lund Humphries, 1959); James T. Araki, *The Ballad Drama of Early Japan* (Berkeley: University of California Press, 1964); Makota Ueda, *Literature and Art Theories in Japan* (Cleveland: Press of Western Reserve University, 1967); Earl Miner, *The Japanese Tradition in British and American Literature*, (Princeton, N.J.: Princeton University Press, 1958); Armando Martins Janeira, *Japanese and Western Literature, a Comparative Study* (Rutland, Vt.: Tuttle, 1970).

6. In civilized society, the flute is Korean; rustics play on carved sticks.

7. See Malm, *Japanese Music and Japanese Instruments*, 224.

8. One need only recall Panchpakesa Bhagvatar and his twenty-four-hour changing recitals of the *Rāmāyana*.

9. In the case of India, I have consulted the following works in Western languages: Reginald Massey, *The Music of India* (New York: Crescendo, 1977); Sir William Jones, *On the Musical Modes of the Hindus* (Calcutta: Asiatic Society of Benegal, 1792); Kapila Vatsyayan, *Classical Indian Dance in Literature and the Arts* (New Delhi: Sangeet Natak Akademi, 1968); G. H. Ranade, *Hindustani Music: An Outline of Its Physics and Aesthetics* (New Delhi: Maharashtra Information Center, 1967); Peggy Holroyde, *Indian Music—A Vast Ocean of Promise* (London: Allen and Unwin, 1972); A. B. Keith, *The Sanskrit Drama* (Oxford: Clarendon Press, n.d.); L. Renou, *La Poésie religieuse de l'Inde antique* (Paris: Presses Universitaires de France, 1942); S. M. Tagore, *Hindu Music from Various Authors*, 3d ed. (Varanasi, India: Chowkhamba Sanscrit Series Office, 1965); E. J. Thompson, *Rabindranath Tagore, Poet and Dramatist*, 2d ed. (London: Oxford University Press, 1948); and Ethel Rosenthal, *The Story of Indian Music and Its Instruments* (New Delhi: Oriental Books Reprint Corp., 1970).

10. See Massey, *The Music of India*, 25.

11. Thyagaraja set his simple poetic prose to musical phrases *(sagathis)* derived

from *ragas* and also used melodies from folk *teyts* and songs. Hence, his work has broad appeal and is not limited to use in religious ritual. He also wrote three operas.

12. For Africa, I have consulted the following works available in Western languages: *Essays on Music and History in Africa*, ed. Klaus P. Wachsmann (Evanston, Ill.: Northwestern University Press, 1971); Francis Bebey, *African Music: A People's Art*, trans. Josephine Bennett (New York and Westport, Conn.: Lawrence Hill, 1975); J. H. Kwabena Nketia, *The Music of Africa* (New York: Norton, 1974); L. J. Damas, *Poètes d'expression française* (Paris: Seoul, 1974); and Roland Lebel, *Histoire de la littérature coloniale en France* (Paris: Larousse, 1931).

13. See Bebey, *African Music: A People's Art*, 132.

14. Ibid., 120.

7. ROMANTIC WRITERS AND MUSIC: THE CASE OF MAZZINI

1. Or, again, "Music is the most Romantic of all the arts, as its subject is only the Infinite, the secret Sanskrit of Nature expressed in tones which fill the human heart with endless longing, and only in music does one understand the songs of the trees, flowers, animals, stones, floods!" *Sämtliche Werke*, ed. E. Grisebach, 15 vols. (Leipzig: Universal-Edition, 1900), 1: 37.

2. *Letters, Journals and Conversations*, ed. M. Hamburger (London: Cape, 1966), 221.

3. In this sense, chapter 5 of Alfred Einstein's *Music in the Romantic Era* (New York: Norton, 1947), entitled "The Contradictions," is a misnomer. Seemingly self-contradictory values, e.g., isolation and popularity or intimacy and virtuosity—can coexist to explicate a truth.

4. We are merely "reminded" of opera, symphony, and theme and variations; Diderot's actual intention remains unspecified.

5. Samuel Taylor Coleridge, *The Inquiring Spirit*, ed. Kathleen Coburn (London: Routledge and Kegan Paul, 1951), 214.

6. See Hugo Leichtentritt, *Music, History, and Ideas* (Cambridge: Harvard University Press, 1947), 219.

7. The emphasis placed by Romantic music on nature has been noted. This was the great period of development of tone poems and of descriptive music generally: after, e.g., Beethoven's Sixth Symphony, Mendelssohn's overtures, Liszt's symphonies on Faust and Dante.

8. Immanuel Kant, *Critique and Judgement* (London: Macmillan, 1914), 217.

9. See Walter T. Stace, *The Philosophy of Hegel* (New York: Dover Publications, 1955), 475.

10. Quoted from E. F. Carritt, *Philosophies of Beauty* (New York: Oxford University Press, 1931), 156. See Eduard Hanslick, *The Beautiful in Music* (London: Novello and Co., 1891).

11. Friedrich Schelling, *Philosophie der Kunst*, in *Sämtliche Werke* (Stuttgart: J. G. Cotta, 1859), v. 369.

12. In *The Philosophy of Schopenhauer*, ed. I. Edman (New York: Modern Library, 1928), 201.

13. "On the Metaphysics of Music," in *The World as Will and Idea*, trans. Haldane and Kemp (London: Trench, Trubner, 1948–50), vol. 3, chap. 39, p. 232.

14. Friedrich Nietzsche, *The Birth of Tragedy* (New York: Modern Library, 1937), 198.

15. Ibid., 202.

16. It is noteworthy that in this respect Nietzsche refutes his original notion that art is essentially affirmation, benediction, and deification of existence.

17. Note that composers generally shunned expressing themselves philosophically or ethnically. They did not speak of producing "good" men or "perfect" states; rather, for them music was the emotion-producing movement of tones and rhythms. Such was the case of Rossini, for example, and Berlioz. But Liszt, in many ways a mystic, provides an obvious and illustrious exception.

18. Giuseppe Mazzini, *Filosofia della musica*, ed. Adriano Lualdi (Milan: Fratelli Bocca, 1943). The works referred to in this paragraph are: Andeina Biondi, *Mazzini uomo* (Bresso: Tramontana, 1969); Edyth Hinkley, *Mazzini: The Story of a Great Italian* (New York and London: Kennikat Press; reprinted, 1970); and Giovanni Cattani, *Mazzini autore romantico* (Faenza: Stab. Grafico F.lli Lega, 1972). Furthermore, *Il veltro*'s special issue on Mazzini (1973: 17, 4–6) contains not a word about the *Filosofia della musica*, despite considerable coverage of aspects of the Mazzinian personality (the issue is called "Mazzini nel mondo"). I regret the unavailability of E. Fondi, *La musica nel pensiero di Giuseppe Mazzini* (Rome, 1923). In the present study, I am indebeted also to various opinions found in L. Tomellieri, "Sulla 'Filosofia della Musica' di Giuseppe Mazzini," *Rivista musicale italiana* 42 (1938).

19. As will be noted, Mazzini's sense of music combines the fullness of aesthetic involvement with the dedication of social concern.

20. See A. Lualdi, ed., Mazzini, *Filosofia della musica*, 47.

21. See ibid., 69.

22. Mazzini declared that Beethoven was the exemplar of German harmonism, As for French music, Mazzini thought it was quite Italianate and not really original—except for the beautifully bold attempts by Berlioz and his "powerful concepts."

23. If Mazzini denied Romantic organicism in one sense, he upheld the idea of organicism itself. Rossini "concluded" a school, yes, but from his emancipation from academic authority, and from his development of melody, a European music will arise, he believed. "And no European musical school can exist except the one that will take into account all the musical elements that partial previous schools have developed."

24. "Poetry, literature, history, philosophy, are all expressions of a single phenomenon."

25. The important word in Schlegel's phrase is "again" *(wieder)*, implying the former existence of a total unity and expressing Romanticism's desire to return to it. See *Athenäum* fragment 116, in *Kritische Schriften* (Munich: Hanswer, 1964), 38.

26. Lualdi, ed., Mazzini, *Filosofia della musica*, 63.

27. Einstein, *Music in the Romantic Era*, 347.

28. Coleridge, *Inquiring Spirit*, 214. He confessed he had no ear, but did have a taste, for the art, p. 213.

29. See, e.g., Tomellieri, "Sulla 'Filosofia della musica,' " 514–15.

30. See a discussion of this in Lualdi, ed., Mazzini, *Filosofia della musica*, 80–81. For Schopenhauer see *The World as Will and Idea*, chapter "On the Metaphysics of Music."

31. Nietzsche, *The Birth of Tragedy*, 198. Mazzini considered music with words more frequently than pure music. While music expresses the ineffable and is too complex for verbalization, and while it does not translate *specific* feelings and ideas, it can, if given words, incite a mood and orient humanity along fraternal and progressive ways. As Hanslick too was to say, music can imitate the motion of a psychic process according to its various phases—presto, adagio, forte, piano, crescendo, and diminuendo (see Mariangela Dona, *Espressione e significato nella musica* (Florence: L. S. Olschki, 1968), 49, discussing Hanslick's *On Beauty in Music*). In this, Mazzini sided with Kant, Hegel, and Rousseau.

32. Nietzsche, *The Birth of Tragedy*, 202.

33. For a discussion of this view see J. Portnoy, *The Philosopher and Music* (New York: Humanities Press, 1954), 172–73.

34. J. Barzun, *Darwin, Marx, Wagner* (New York: Fawcett, 1962), 15.

35. Wilhelm Wackenroder, *Writings on Music (Scritti sulla musica)*, ed. B. Tecchi (Florence: Valecchi, 1934), 174.

36. Humanity can function (let alone survive) only through civility, and civility functions only through generosity, particularly in its most extreme expression, sacrifice. In this sense, music is both a civilizing agent and a religious experience.

37. Quoted from Bianca Magnino, *Storia del Romanticismo* (Mazara: Società Editrice Siciliana, 1950), 226.

38. Quoted from Portnoy, *The Philosopher and Music*, 179.

39. The *Fantasia and Fugue*, incidentally, is written for the organ, the instrument favored by the Romantics as the "whole" or "complete" instrument, hence the instrument of Totality.

40. In applied terms, "[the art to which] belongs the initiative of a concept that the other arts will come to translate and develop successively."

8. A CASE OF LITERARY DIPLOMACY: BALZAC AND MEYERBEER

1. Translated from the French by Alain Veylit.

2. R. Montalée, *En lisant Balzac* (Paris: Eugène Figuière Editeur, 1925), 36.

3. Mme Maurice-Amour, "La Musique," *Balzac: le livre du centenaire* (Paris: Flammarion, 1952), 207.

4. Léon Guichard, *La Musique et les lettres au temps du romantisme* (Paris: Presses Universitaires de France, 1955), 329.

5. Thérèse Marix-Spire, *Les Romantiques et la musique: le cas George Sand* (Paris: Nouvelles Editions Latines, 1954), 38.

6. See Maurice Regard, "Balzac est-il l'auteur de 'Gambara'?" *Revue d'histoire littéraire* (October–December 1953), 498.

7. Let me note in passing that, aside from some early and less significant dramatic works, Meyerbeer's production was limited to these two well-known operas at the time *Gambara* appeared.

8. See Thérèse Marix, "Histoire d'une amitié: Fr. Liszt et H. de Balzac," *Bibliothèque de la revue des études hongroises* 10 (January–June 1934): 36–68.

9. *Gambara's* date is 1837 and *Massimilla Doni's* 1839, but Balzac was working on both of them in 1837.

10. Herbert J. Hunt, *Balzac's Comédie Humaine* (London: Athlone Press, 1959), 143.

11. As for the opinion that *Robert le Diable* expresses ideas while *Don Giovanni* excites sensations, we should see in it, in light of Balzac's comments on Mozart's opera in *Le Cabinet des antiques*, nothing more than a circumstantial utterance.

12. Italics are mine.

13. F. Schiller, *Die Raüber*, I, 2.

14. Guichard, *La Musique et les lettres*, 326–27, and Léon Emery, *Balzac en sa création* (Lyon: Les Cahiers Libres, n.d.), 59, advise—one directly and the other indirectly—not to identify Gambara's point of view with Balzac's; the issue was debated in the press of that time. Supposedly, Balzac had no opinion on the matter. I cannot accept this notion. First of all, *Robert le Diable* was triumphantly received by the public, by the press, and by other composers (Berlioz, Liszt, Chopin, and later even Wagner); the opinions in favor were far more numerous than the opinions against. Second, Rossini and Beethoven were also the subject of debates with reference to their relative merits, and on this issue Balzac leaves no doubt as to the esteem in which he held both of them. Whether mistakenly or not, he definitely had fixed opinions on both music and composers. Therefore, to deny him his judgment only in the case of Meyerbeer seems to me to be arbitrary and inconsistent.

9. MUSIC AND THE STRUCTURE OF DIDEROT'S *LE NEVEU DE RAMEAU*

1. "This admirable satire of manners, in which we will always go searching for the author's final word about music." Adolphe Jullien, *La Musique et les philosophes au dix-huitième siècle* (Paris: J. Baur, 1873), 200.

2. Herbert Dieckmann, "Zur Interpretation Diderots," *Romanische Forschungen* (1939), 53: 71.

3. Rudolf Schlösser, *Rameaus Neffe* (Geneva: Slatkine Reprints, 1971), 69 (facsimile of original Berlin edition).

4. N. David, *Le Neveu de Rameau par Diderot précédé d'une étude de Goethe sur Diderot* (Paris: Dubuisson, 1863), xi. For Goethe's original see "Anmerkungen," *Goethes Werke* (Weimar: H. Böhlau, 1900), 45: 206–13.

5. Lester G. Crocker, *The Embattled Philosopher* (East Lansing: Michigan State College Press, 1954), 270.

6. Melchior Grimm, *Correspondance littéraire* (Paris: Garnier frères, 1877–82), 202.

7. Pascal Boyer, *Lettre à M. Diderot sur le projet de l'unité de clef dans la musique* (Paris: Chez Vente, 1767). As for Bemetzrieder, he was indebted to Diderot for the popularity he gained in Paris around 1770.

8. Charles Burney, *The Present State of Music in France and Italy* (London: T. Becket, 1771), 391–92.

9. *Oeuvres complètes de Diderot*, Assézat edition (Paris: Garnier, 1875/1876), 7: 162. All further references to works by Diderot are taken from this edition.

10. Paul H. Meyer, "Unity and Structure of Diderot's 'Le Neveu de Rameau,' " *Criticism* 2 (1960): 374.

11. Leo Spitzer, *Linguistics and Literary History* (Princeton: Princeton University Press, 1948), 187.

12. "Sur l'origine et la nature du Beau," *Oeuvres complètes*, 10: 26.

13. Jean Benjamin de la Borde, *Essais sur la musique ancienne et moderne* (Paris: Chez E. Onfroy, 1780), 3: 615–17.

14. Jean Fabre, ed., *Le Neveu de Rameau* (Geneva: Droz, 1950), Introduction, xci.

15. Georges May, *Quatre visages de Diderot* (Paris: Boivin, 1951), 182.

16. Yvon Belaval, *L'Esthétique sans paradoxe de Diderot* (Paris: Gallimard, 1950), 295.

17. "Leçons de clavecin et principes d'harmonie par M. Bemetzrieder" (1771), *Oeuvres complètes*, 12: 184.

18. In 1754, Louis de Cahusac had published *La Danse ancienne et moderne, ou, Traité historique de la danse*, in three volumes. It was the master Noverre, however, who actively put to work Diderot's ideas contained in the *Entretiens sur Le Fils naturel* (cf. Alfred Richard Oliver, *The Encyclopedists as Critics of Music* [New York: Columbia University Press, 1947], 71ff.).

19. *Oeuvres complètes*, 7: 161.

20. "Leçons de clavecin," *Oeuvres complètes*, 12: 238.

21. "Troisième entretien," *Oeuvres complètes*, 7: 159.

22. Alice Green Fredman, *Diderot and Sterne* (New York: Columbia University Press, 1955), 116.

23. Pierre Mesnard, *Le Cas Diderot* (Paris: Presses Universitaires de France, 1952), 210. The intimate opposition has been studied also by Daniel Mornet, "La véritable signification du *Neveu de Rameau*," *Revue des deux mondes*, August 15, 1927 (40), and by Carl Becker, "The Dilemma of Diderot," *Philosophical Review* 24 (1915).

24. Fabre, *Le Neveu de Rameau*, xlvi. The thesis was strengthened earlier (p. lxxxviii), where he said: "If to become himself the character Rameau was in search of an author, Diderot's aesthetic, on the other hand, was in search of such a character, and the success of the work stems from this encounter."

25. Ralph H. Bowen and Jacques Barzun, *Rameau's Nephew and Other Works* (New York: Doubleday, 1956), Preface, 2.

26. Mesnard, *Le Cas Diderot*, 211.

27. Fabre, *Le Neveu de Rameau*, liii.

28. "Lettres à mademoiselle Volland," October 20, 1760, *Oeuvres complètes*, 18: 514. Diderot saw fit to allude to this technique in the "Leçons de clavecin," *Oeuvres complètes*, 12: 415: "begin a progression, interrupt it to begin a second, which I'll leave to begin a third, and not finish one of them . . . ," to which he added modestly, as if looking back on his dialogues, "I don't know whether this method adds to the interest of a work of literature."

29. Diderot echoed Rameau's theories variously, as, for example, in the "Leçons de clavecin," *Oeuvres complètes*, 12: 428, where he says: "you must . . . prepare each consonance with a dissonant harmony that calls for it."

30. Otto Engelmayer, "Romantische Tendenzen im Künstlerischen, Kritischen und Kunstphilosophischen Werke Denis Diderots" (Memmingen: diss. [Munich], 1933), 65.

31. "Troisième entretien," *Oeuvres complètes*, 7: 147.

32. It is interesting to note that Belaval, *L'Estétique*, 300–301, in his concluding remarks on Diderot's aesthetics, couches a similar idea, without direct reference to music, in these terms: "all that Associationism can do to take newness into account beginning with the past comes down to uniting elements that one does not normally see together, and uniting them nonetheless normally to insure their cohesion. Now, all action is based on stimuli that are most directly useful to it and it neglects the harmonies, variables according to the experimental context, that accompany them, preserve themselves, reverberate too easily to be noticed. Therefore, one must suspend that action or, better still, be diverted by them in order to allow those harmonies to play more freely and reveal themselves clearly. And this is why, already for Diderot, a good, fruitful observation takes place in a state of semi-distraction: it hears without listening and sees without looking."

33. "Leçons de clavecin," *Oeuvres complètes*, 12: 520–21.

10. FROM THE SUBLIME TO THE SUBLIMINAL: THE PROUST-BALZAC MUSICAL CONNECTION

1. The only full study on Balzac and music happens to be my dissertation, "Balzac and Music: Its Place and Meaning in His Life and Works" (Harvard University, 1953). In her dissertation, Anna Maria Schneiderbauer takes up some aspects of the question in relation to the demonic: *Das Element des Daemonischen in Honoré de Balzacs Comédie Humaine* (University of Munich, 1967). Then there are a number of articles, around two dozen, from among which I might single out for the purposes of this essay: Louis de Fourcand, "La Musique dans Balzac," *Universal Review* 1 (May 1888), and "Le Musicien de Balzac," *L'Echo de Paris*, September 30, 1910; Auguste Getteman, "Balzac et la musique," *Revue musicale*, June 1, 1922; Olin Downes, "Balzac and Music," *Harvard Musical Review* 1 (July 1913); Paul Edmond, "Wagner et Balzac," *L'Intermédiaire des chercheurs et des curieux*, December

20–30, 1919, and January 10, 1920; L. Maurice-Amour, "Balzac et la musique," *Mercure de France*, January 1, 1950; D. C. Parker, "Balzac the Musician," *Musical Quarterly* 5 (April 1919). A fine study on *Balzac et la musique religieuse* (Paris: Naert, 1929) was written by Philippe Bertault, and a revealing one by Julien Tiersot on "Balzac et la chanson populaire" (*Revue des traditions populaires*, 10). Not to be omitted are the introductions to the editions of *Gambara* by Maurice Regard and of *Massimilla Doni* by Max Milner, both Paris: José Corti, 1964. In comparison with these meager pickings, there are scores of studies on Proust and music, some of them full-length books and with significant bibliographies (see Claude-Henry Joubert, *Le Fil d'or: Etude sur la musique dans "A la recherche du temps perdu"* [Paris: Corti, 1984]). Many, of course, relate to the question of style. Though I must touch on it, especially in the context of D'Annunzio, in this chapter I am not concerned with language and with what might be called stylistic musicality (e.g., syntactic suppleness, images, metaphors)—or, for that matter, with another debated problem that has concerned many critics: the identification of Vinteuil's music (a useless debate, in my opinion)—but simply with comparing the idea of music each author fashioned for himself.

2. Unlike Balzac, Proust played the piano, albeit modestly: four-hands, opera and symphony reductions, and some chamber music and vocal accompaniment. He came from a musical family (his mother and maternal grandmother were pianists), and the desire to make use of the keyboard came naturally. Balzac, on the other hand, had to labor to get a small piano into his garret room as he set out to conquer the world of letters, but his stubby fingers and general lack of ability never permitted him to progress beyond a ditty like Cramer's "Le Songe de Rousseau."

3. Getteman, "Balzac et la musique," 220.

4. Respectively, letters of July 1, 1834; July 13, 1834; *La Duchesse de Langeais*; *La Peau de chagrin*; *Massimilla Doni*.

5. Bertault, *Balzac et la musique religieuse*, 34.

6. Just a few phrases suffice. Swedenborg: "The musical art is skilled to express various kinds of affections" (*Heaven and Hell*); "Musical sounds express affections, and produce them with joy" (*Apocalypse Explained*); "Love is spiritual conjunction, whence is heavenly harmony" (*Arcana Coelestia*); "In order that spiritual gladness or happiness may be understood, an idea may be conceived of them from the harmonies of sounds, and also from the harmonies of visual things. The harmonies of sounds belong to spiritual harmony; and the gladness thence resulting is spiritual gladness; hence the music of the ancient Church is so delightful" (*Spiritual Diary*). Saint-Martin (to dissipate the "disharmonic" influences that surround us): "[Music] is a regulating instrument of life; it opens up for us the region of God" (*L'Esprit des choses*).

7. Various critics have stressed this. See, e.g., André Coeuroy, *Musique et littérature* (Paris: Librairie Bloud & Gay, 1932), "La Musique dans l'oeuvre de Marcel Proust," 228–62, and Luigi Magnani, *La musica, il tempo, l'eterno nella "Recherche" di Proust* (Milan: Ricciardi, 1967).

8. Magnani, *La musica*, 94.

9. Charles Baudelaire, "Lettre à Wagner," *L'Art romantique* (Paris: Garnier, 1962), 689.

10. For the *Cahiers*, see Karuyoschi Yoshikawa, "Vinteuil ou la genèse du sep-tuor," *Cahiers Marcel Proust* (Paris: Gallimard, 1979), 9: 298. For the woodwinds, see Sybil de Souza, "Pourquoi le 'Septuor' de Vinteuil," *Bulletin de la Société des Amis de Marcel Proust et des amis de Combray* no. 23 (1973) 1599.

11. Philip Kolb, "La 'Petite Phrase' de la Sonate," *Bulletin de la Société des Amis de Marcel Proust et des amis de Combray* no. 18 (1968): 675. Kolb is commenting on *Jean Santeuil*, maintaining that when Swann wants to rehear the Sonata, it is, conversely, the music he wants to experience. But he wants to experience it for his feelings, not for the beauty of its structure. Primal sounds are still the psychic force.

12. Cf. Souza, "Pourquoi le 'Septuor' de Vinteuil," 1600–1.

13. Coeuroy, *Musique et littérature*, 237.

14. As we know, Giacomo Meyerbeer was an idol in the Paris of his day; Bee-thoven, a name. Yet Balzac came around to sensing the true greatness of the master from Bonn, comparing him with "titans" like Michelangelo and Dante and alluding to his work, notably the Fifth Symphony, in his novels—e.g., *César Birotteau*.

15. The Capet Quartet did much for Beethoven's chamber works during Proust's lifetime; Balzac, however, leaned more toward the symphonies, thanks largely to his conversations with Liszt and Chopin, and to his knowledge of the efforts of Berlioz and the conductor of the Concerts du Conservatoire, Habeneck.

16. Coeuroy, *Musique et littérature*, 240.

17. See Frank Sidney Alberti, "La 'Musique' d'Albertine," *Bulletin de la Société des Amis de Marcel Proust et des amis de Combray* no. 27 (1977): 423. Proust cannot accomplish this without great intricacy of detail. Indeed, Albertine becomes a work of art by virtue of an accumulation of details, among which Yoshikawa in the *cahiers* identifies her black hair, fingers, shoulders, and beautiful legs—and here again I am reminded of Balzac, this time of Frenhofer's "La belle Noiseuse" in *Le Chef-d'oeuvre inconnu*, with all the accumulation of the details of her creator's thoughts, though Marcel would see reality before the hapless painter (whose chaotic canvas, except for the beautiful detail of a foot, dismays his audience): "But alas, she very soon revealed what she was for me [Marcel]—something quite different from a work of art, some-thing rather like a great Goddess of Time" (309).

18. Alfredo Gargiulo, "Il 'Notturno,' " *Letteratura*, 3 (1939): 15.

19. G. De Robertis, "D'Annunzio," *Scrittori del novecento* (Florence, 1958), 10. I discussed the relationship in "Reciprocal Homage: D'Annunzio, Debussy, and 'Le Martyre de Saint Sébastien' "—to be published soon—in a paper for the American Association of Teachers of Italian conference, Duquesne University, April 1987.

20. See Michel Butor, *Les Oeuvres d'art imaginaires chez Proust* (London: Ath-lone Press, 1964), 15ff. The notion of the prism had appeared in *Contre Sainte-Beuve*.

21. Souza, "Pourquoi le 'Septuor' de Vinteuil," 1606.

11. MOTIF AND LEITMOTIF: MANN IN SEARCH OF WAGNER

1. This essay was written in collaboration with Cynthia Maldonado.

2. See, for example, Von Helmut Koopmann, *Die Entwicklung des "Intellectu-alen Romans" bei Thomas Mann* (Bonn: Bouvier Verlag Herbert Grundmann, 1971), 61ff. Also see Kenneth G. Wilson, "The Dance as Symbol and Leitmotiv in Thomas Mann's *Tonio Kröger*," *Germanic Review* 29 (1954): 282–87.

3. One is R. Hinton Thomas, *Thomas Mann* (Oxford: Clarendon Press, 1963). Another is T. J. Reed, *Thomas Mann: The Uses of Tradition* (Oxford: Clarendon Press, 1974), which picks up on Mann's own statement: "It is indeed not hard to detect in my 'Buddenbrooks,' that sequence of generations connected and woven through with leitmotivs, a breath of [Wagner's] 'Ring' " (75). But, unfortunately, the term is misused by his critics to mean simply motif. A quotation from the *Münchener Neuste Nachrichten* of December 24, 1901, is typical: "Specifically Wagnerian is the eminently epic effect of a rigorous use of leitmotifs, the verbal reference back, over great stretches of the book, from one generation to the other" (76). Most Mann criticism fits this inexact category when the musical term is used.

4. James R. McWilliams, *Brother Artists: A Psychological Study of Thomas Mann's Fiction* (Lanham, Md.: University Press of America, 1983), 202.

5. Calvin S. Brown, *Music and Literature: A Comparison of the Arts* (Athens, Ga.: University of Georgia Press, 1948), 211.

6. R. Peacock, *Das Leitmotiv bei Thomas Mann* (Bern: Paul Haupt, 1934). See *Sprache und Dichtung. Forschungen zur Sprach- und Literaturwissenschaft* (1934), 55: 53.

7. Ibid., 55.

8. V. H. Koopmann, *Thomas Mann*, 59.

9. See R. H. Thomas, *Thomas Mann*, 89.

12. BEETHOVENIAN OVERLAYS BY CARPENTIER AND BURGESS:
THE NINTH IN GROTESQUE JUXTAPOSITIONS

1. Michael Valdez Moses, *"The Lost Steps:* The Faustian Artist in the New World," *Latin American Literary Review* 12, no. 24 (1984): 19.

2. Thomas Mann, *Genesis of a Novel* (London: Secker and Warburg, 1961), 171 and 178.

3. Quoted from Phyllis M. Goodman, "Beethoven as the Prototype of Owen Jack," *Shaw Review* 8 (1965): 16.

4. In T. K. Scherman and L. Biancolli, *The Beethoven Companion* (Garden City, N.Y.: Doubleday, 1972), 938–39. There have been writers, of course, who have thought highly of the Ninth Symphony, enough to use it as a structural model for their works the way Carpentier and Burgess use the Third in *El acoso* and *Napoleon Symphony*, respectively: William Brown, "A Welcome"; Wallace Stevens, "Peter

Quince at the Clavier"; T. S. Eliot, "Four Quartets"; and others. For more on the use of Beethoven in literature, see the excellent dissertation by Donna Ann Beckage, "Beethoven in Western Literature," University of California at Riverside, 1977. An account of the question of the Ninth has been made by Juan Barroso in "The Ninth Symphony of Beethoven in Alejo Carpentier's *The Lost Steps*" (Innsbruck: Proceedings of the Ninth Congress of the International Comparative Literature Association), vol. 3: *Literature and the Other Arts* (1981), 283–87. On Carpentier's use of the Third Symphony in *El acoso*, the reader might consult the convincing piece by Emil Volek, "Análisis del sistema de estructuras musicales e interpretación de 'El acoso' de Alejo Carpentier," and the less convincing one by Helmy F. Giacoman, "La relación músico-literaria entre la Tercera Sinfonía 'Eroica' de Beethoven y la novela 'El acoso' de Alejo Carpentier," both in H. F. Giacoman, *Homenaje a Alejo Carpentier* (New York: Las Americas Publishing, 1970), 385–438 and 439–65, respectively.

5. J. B. Priestley, Introduction to A. Carpentier, *The Lost Steps* (New York: Knopf, 1967), x.

6. The first critic is Donald L. Shaw, *Alejo Carpentier* (Boston: Twayne, 1985), 48. The second is Ian R. Macdonald, "Magical Eclecticism: *Los pasos perdidos* and Jean-Paul Sartre," *Contemporary Latin-American Fiction*, ed. S. Bacarisse (Edinburgh, 1980), 4.

7. See Karen Taylor's premise as put forth in her "La creación musical en *Los pasos perdidos*," *Revista de Filología Hispánica* 26, no. 4 (1977): 141–53.

8. See Roberto Echevarría, *Alejo Carpentier: The Pilgrim at Home* (Ithaca and London: Cornell University Press, 1977), 154.

9. Ibid.

10. See Shaw, *Alejo Carpentier*, 51.

11. See Beckage, "Beethoven in Western Literature," 114–15.

12. Emil Ludwig, *Three Titans*, trans. E. C. Mayne (London and New York: Putnam, 1930), 265.

13. Robert K. Morris, *The Consolations of Ambiguity* (Columbia, Mo.: University of Missouri Press, 1971), 1.

14. Ibid., 69.

15. Both Burgess and Carpentier place symbolic meaning in the number 7—the seven days of Creation—Carpentier through his narrator's six "days" plus the Sunday that never comes; Burgess, through his narrator's three sections, each of seven days.

16. Burgess, in his *Paris Review* interview, as quoted in Richard Mathews, *The Clockwork Universe of Anthony Burgess* (San Bernardino, Calif.: Burgo Press, 1978), 42–43.

17. The allusion is to Christ. Critics have brought out the sin–penance–resurrection analogy relating to the three parts of this complex novel.

18. Stanley Kubrick's film *A Clockwork Orange*, which brought Burgess's novel to worldwide consciousness, visually exploits this cruelty. For comments, see Samuel Coale, *Anthony Burgess* (New York: Frederick Ungar, 1981), 94–97.

19. See A. A. Devitis, *Anthony Burgess* (New York: Twayne, 1972), 107.
20. Morris, *The Consolation of Ambiguity*, 57.

13. ROMANTIC IRONY IN MUSIC

1. For example, the *Athenäum*'s variously expressed point of view was that Romantic irony is a distinct relation of the artist to his material and to the act of creation, a special literary structure as a result of this relation, and a particular relation between the ironic work and some larger world view as exemplified by the opposition of what is *Endlich* to what is *Unendlich*. Among the best studies, I should like to note Ingrid Strohschneider-Kohrs, *Die romantische Ironie im Theorie und Gestaltung* (Tübingen: Max Niemeyer, 1960); Douglas C. Muecke, *The Critical Idiom: Irony* (London: Methuen, 1970); Ernst Behler, *Klassische Ironie, Romantische Ironie, Tragische Ironie* (Darmstadt: Wissenschaftliche Buchgesellschaft, 1972); Rudolf Haym, *Die romantische Schule* (Berlin: Weidmannsche Buchhhandlung, 1914); Raymond Immerwahr, "The Subjectivity or Objectivity of F. Schlegel's Poetic Irony," *Germanic Review* 26 (1951): 173–91; Helmut Prang, *Die Romantische Ironie* (Darmstadt: Wissenschaftliche Buchgesellschaft, 1972); and Peter Szondi, "F. Schlegel und die romantische Ironie," *Euphorion* 48 (1954): 397–411. I am indebted to my friend and colleague, Dr. George Slusser, for all the profitable conversations we had on the elusive subject of this essay.
2. Friedrich Schlegel, *Kritische Schriften* (Munich: Carl Hansor, 1964), Lyceum Fragment no. 48, p. 12.
3. Ibid., Lyceum Fragment no. 108, p. 20.
4. Ibid., Lyceum Fragment no. 42, p. 10.
5. Ibid., Athenäum Fragment no. 116, pp. 38–39.
6. D. C. Muecke, *The Critical Idiom: Irony*, 199.
7. Alfred Einstein, *Music in the Romantic Era* (New York: Norton, 1947), 39.
8. Rey M. Longyear, "Beethoven and Romantic Irony," *Musical Quarterly* 56, no. 4 (October 1970) 647–64.
9. Ibid., 664.
10. My discussion is limited mainly to Romantic irony in instrumental music, since the sense of irony injected into music by words, the external literary factor (e.g., an operatic or an art song text), is not relevant to the immediate subject.
11. Longyear, "Beethoven and Romantic Irony," 655, 658–59, and 655, respectively.
12. Ibid., 660–61, 661–62, and 663, respectively. Similarly, Longyear refers to the Rondo Finale of Violin Sonata, opus 30, no. 3, and a "false recapitulation" in the minor mediant and "abrupt" tonal shifts, emphasized in the coda, as "jokes" which destroy a listener's illusion "through deliberate playing with the key, the form, and his sense of tonal stability" (656–57). He also claims Romantic irony in Beethoven's "exuberant delight in displaying his contrapuntal skill" (e.g., the fugal Finale of Piano Sonata, opus 106 and the *Grosse Fugue*, even in titles: "Fuga a tre voce [sic], con alcuna licenza," and "Grande Fugue, tantôt libre, tantôt recherchée"

[656]. I fail to see the ironic intent or the self-mocking direction. I might note that another critic, Arnold Schering, in *Beethoven und die Dichtung* (Hildesheim and New York: G. Olms, 1973), sees unquestionable irony in the first movement of String Quartet, opus 59, no. 3, in the way the violin "with breakneck daring attains in the forte the highest register, in order to plunge immediately piano into fathomless depths and to cadence harmlessly" (297). Again, I remain somewhat skeptical. More often than not, I feel that Longyear confuses Romantic irony with humor.

13. Longyear, "Beethoven and Romantic Irony," 658 and 655–56, respectively. Again, this critic points to the final movement of Cello Sonata, op. 102, no. 1—"can't the musicians get together?" and "a fugato that cannot get under way until the two performers know what they are going to do"—as containing "practical jokes," including "sustained open fifths in the cello" (658).

14. Aldous Huxley, *Point Counter Point* (New York: Watts, 1947), 293–94.

15. Schering, *Beethoven und die Dichtung*, 487 and 489.

16. Ibid., 488.

17. See Luigi Magnani, "Beethoven, das philosophische Denken und die Ästetik seiner Zeit," *Beethoven-Symposium* (Vienna: H. Böhlaus Nachf., 1971), 204. Magnani, speaking of the fugue in Piano Sonata op. 106, and of the *Grosse Fugue* op. 133, sees the *Licenze* this way: "an unprecedented, an unheard of [thing], which seems to dissolve the usual form and order, but in reality imposes a new order."

18. Longyear, "Beethoven and Romantic Irony," 654. For example: the first movement of Piano Sonata op. 10, no. 2; the introduction to the Finale of the First Symphony; the Trio of the Scherzo of Violin Sonata op. 30, no. 2; the third movement of Piano Sonata op. 78 (cf. see 654–55).

19. Alfred Einstein, "Opus Ultimum," *Essays in Music* (New York: Norton, 1956), 80.

20. *Doktor Faustus*, trans. H. T. Lowe-Porter (New York: Knopf, 1948), 54.

21. Behler, *Klassische Ironie*, 44.

22. The piano contradicts the voice's emotion with offbeat accents. See André Boucourechliev, *Schumann* (New York: Grove, 1959), 110. As Paul Dukas noted, Schumann understood the comic ability of music ("Comedy in Music," *Composers on Music* [New York: Pantheon, 1961]). Once more, I should emphasize that more often than not Schumann's humor (see his "portraits" of Chopin and Clara Wieck in *Carnaval*, or the four-note-based [A-S-C-H, the name of a town, or A-E♭-C-B] short pieces) remains descriptive, more in the nature of *Spass* than of sarcasm. Similarly, in Elgar's *Enigma Variations* where the composer musically portrays his wife (variation I) and his publisher (variation IX), the two most important influences in his life, and then brings them thematically together in his concluding self-portrait, we are again facing straight humor, mild at that, rather than ironic wit. If it may be argued that the music thereby calls attention to itself, was the intention ironical?

23. Noted by Longyear, "Beethoven and Romantic Irony," 648, footnote 6.

24. Jean-Paul Richter, "Vorschule der Aesthetik," *Werke* I: 2 (Munich: Piper, 1963), 31.

25. See Hans Sedlmayr, *Die Revolution der modernen Kunst* (Hamburg: Herold, 1955).

26. See Paul Bekker, *Gustav Mahlers Sinfonien* (Berlin: Schuster u. Loeffler, 1921), or Zoltan Roman, "Connotative Irony in Mahler's Totenmarsch in 'Callot's Manier,' " *Musical Quarterly* 59, no. 2 (April 1973): 207–22.

27. Mahler reveals his intention in his indication: "Ironical in the sense of Aristotle's *eironeia*," though in my opinion the composer goes beyond the Greek philosopher's objective irony.

28. Works like *Till Eulenspiegel* and the *Domestic Symphony*, with all their humorous ingredients, remain just that: humorous, not ironical.

29. Alberto Ghislanzoni, "La genesi storica della Fuga," *Rivista Musicale Italiana*, 53, nos. 1 and 2 (1951): 97.

30. Leonard B. Meyer, *Music, the Arts, and Ideas* (Chicago and London: University of Chicago Press, 1967), 195–96.

14. MUSIC AS FANTASY

1. Richard Wagner, *Beethoven* (Boston: Lee, 1872), 23.

2. The Schopenhauer reference is obviously from his *Die Welt als Wille und Vorstellung*. The Spengler quotation is from his *Der Untergang des Abendlandes*, 2 vols. (Munich: C. H. Beck'sche Verlagsbuchhandlung, 1929), 2: 10.

3. Friedrich Zelter to Friedrich Schiller, Berlin, February 20, 1798, in *Sitzungsberichte*: 229. Band, Österreichische Akademie der Wissenschaften (Vienna: Rudolf M. Rohrer, 1955), 72–73.

4. I recall how the sounds of a Mozart symphony, in preference to gifts and trinkets, allowed a team of explorer-anthropologists to communicate with a deadly tribe of Amazon head hunters in the 1940s. To substantiate these generalities of mine, a good essay to read might be François Berthier, "Ecoute de Mozart," *La Musique souvent . . . —Essais sur l'imaginaire musical* (Grenoble: Recherches et Travaux, University of Grenoble III, 1984).

5. Patrick A. Heelan, "Music as Basic Metaphor and Deep Structure in Plato and in Ancient Cultures," *Journal of Social Biological Structures* (London: Academic Press, 1979), 2: 279. Heelan refers to Ernest McClain's works, *The Myth of Invariance* (London: Heelan, 1976), and *The Pythagorean Plato* (Stoneybrook, N.Y.: N. Hays Boulder, 1978).

6. Nelson Goodman, *Languages of Art* (Indianapolis and Cambridge: Hackett Publishing, 1976), 189.

7. Giuseppe Mazzini, *Filosofia della musica* (Milan: Fratelli Bocca, 1943), 149.

8. Marcel Proust, "La prisonnière," *A la recherche du temps perdu*, 2 vols. (Paris: Gallimard, 1939), 2: 76. Even before Proust, E. T. A. Hoffmann, in *Kreisleriana*, had referred to music as the mysterious language of a distant kingdom of spirits.

9. François Le Lionnais, *The Orion Book of Time*, trans. William D. O'Gorman, Jr. (New York: Orion, 1966), 108, quoted by Howard Nemerov, "On Poetry and

Painting, With a Thought of Music," *The Language of Images*, ed. W. J. T. Mitchell (Chicago and London: The University of Chicago Press, 1980), 13. Again, E. T. A. Hoffmann in *Kreisleriana* had called the "hieroglyphs" of music the Sanskrit of Nature.

10. Tzvetan Todorov, *The Fantastic* (Cleveland: Case Western Reserve University Press, 1973), 25.

11. See Heinrich Schenker, *Der freie Satz* (Vienna, 1935; rev. ed., University Edition A.G., 1956), though in all fairness Schenker himself never commits himself to a static interpretation of the musical process.

12. Robert P. Morgan, "Musical Time/Musical Space," *The Language of Images*, ed. W. J. T. Mithcell (Chicago and London: The University of Chicago Press, 1980) 261–62.

13. Bruce Morrissette, "The New Novel in France," *Chicago Review* 15 (Winter–Spring 1962): 18.

14. John Cage, *Silence* (Middletown, Conn.: Wesleyan University Press, 1961), 10.

15. Henri Bergson, *La Pensée et le mouvement* (Paris: Alcan, 1934), 164.

16. Since poetic mysticism eventually took over all Plato's ulterior speculations—his Pythagorianism notwithstanding—his line of argument, which only falsely suggests anticipations of modern scientific thinking, acquires metaphorical value—not exactly what he, in his necessarily rational posture, thought best for man to rely upon. When Balzac, in *Gambara*, says that music is the ensemble of sounds harmonized by Number, he may come closer to modern "scientific" thinking than the more mathematical Plato. The above quotation, pp. 172–73, is Heelan's 2:279.

17. Heelan, "Music as Basic Metaphor," 284 and 281.

18. My saying "reduced" would never be acceptable to Plato, in whose acoustical numerology the musical scale internalizes the cosmos—not an unusual practice, in the last analysis, among many ancient thinkers of the West whose auditory mythology can be matched by their counterparts in Han China.

19. Kathryn Hume, "Critical Approaches to Fantasy," *Fantasy and Mimesis: Responses to Reality in Western Literature* (New York and London: Methuen, 1984), 5.

20. See Julius Portnoy, *The Philosopher and Music* (New York: Humanities Press, 1954), 20.

21. See Hume, "Critical Approaches to Fantasy," 5.

22. Ibid., 12. The critics' quotations that follow may be found on pages 13–17 of her essay.

23. André Breton, *Les Manifestes du surréalisme* (Paris: Panvert, 1972), 22.

24. Leonard B. Meyer, *Music, the Arts, and Ideas* (Chicago and London: The University of Chicago Press, 1967), 12.

25. Morgan, "Musical Time/Musical Space," 261.

26. Roland Barthes, *Image, Music, Text* (New York: Hill and Wang, 1977), 152.

27. See Hume, "Critical Approaches to Fantasy," 24.

28. I am borrowing some terms from Mikel Dufrenne, *The Phenomenology of Aesthetic Experience* (Evanston, Ill.: Northwestern University Press, 1973), 251.

29. Ibid., 253.

30. Michael Valdez Moses, "The Lost Steps: *The Faustian Artist in the New World*," *Latin American Literary Review* 12, no. 24 (Spring–Summer 1984): 16.

31. Adapted from Hume, "Critical Approaches to Fantasy," 20.

32. Meyer, *Music, the Arts, and Ideas*, 15. The Bach quotation comes from his (C. P. E. Bach's) *Versuch über die wahre Art das Clavier zu spielen* (Berlin, 1762), trans. as *Essays on the True Art of Playing Keyboard Instruments* by W. Mitchell (New York: Norton, 1949), 84.

33. Barthes, *Image, Music, Text*, 152.

34. See *Izvestia*, February 11, 1948.

35. Along these lines, the greatest influence on Liszt was the thirty-year older Paganini, who gave his first concert in Paris in 1831, not only by the extraordinary way he performed the classics, but also through the astounding imagination that developed his own compositions.

36. Cf. Wilfrid Mellers, *Man & His Music* (New York: Schocken, 1969), 4: 224.

37. Anthony Burgess, "Music and Literature," *Wilson Quarterly* (Winter 1983): 93.

38. Barthes, *Image, Music, Text*, pp. 151–52.

39. Robert Scholes, *Structural Fabulation* (South Bend, Ind.: University of Notre Dame Press, 1975), 7.

40. Luciano Berio, "Form," *The Modern Composer and His World*, ed. J. Beckwith and U. Kasemets (Toronto: University of Toronto Press, 1961), 140.

41. Jonathan Cullar, *The Pursuit of Signs: Semiotics, Literature, Deconstruction* (Ithaca, N.Y.: Cornell University Press, 1981), 34.

42. See Justis Buchler, ed., *Philosophical Writings of Peirce* (1940; reprinted, New York: Dover, 1955), 115.

43. Cage, *Silence*, 84.

44. Mellers, *Man and His Music* 4: 222.

45. Freeman Tilden, "Not by Truth Alone," *Science*, 148 (June 11, 1965): 1416.

46. The reason may be fairly obvious. Writers and critics of literature are up on the social sciences, but the arts, *especially* music, fare less well in their range of familiarities. Note the short shrift music gets in commentaries on Mann's *Doktor Faustus* and, in fact, how relatively few novels actually deal with music in any concentrated way. Similarly, writers of science fiction are up on the same social sciences and, if anything, turn their energies in the direction of science but hardly of music. I am aware of attempts made here and there, of course, like Anne McCaffrey's in *Crystal Singer* where diamond crystals are cut by musical sounds, and the instances in her short story collection, *The Ship Who Sang*, which uses Bob Dylan and where music attunes one mentally to specific moods. What I am looking for, however, is a more fundamental, pervasive, and integrated use of music as in *Doktor Faustus*. I am indebted to Dr. George Slusser, Curator of the J. Lloyd Eaton

Collection of Fantasy and Science Fiction at the University of California at River-side, for having called to my attention several titles still worthy of investigation: Lloyd Biggle, Jr.'s *The Metallic Muse* (1974), seven short stories about what could happen in the world of music, among other things, if certain practices continue; Jack Vance's *Space Opera* (1979), about a possible musical work originating in outer space; conceivably Philip K. Dick's *The Preserving Machine* (1969); and Samuel R. Delany's *Nova* (1969)—Mouse's instrument of sensor projection; and quite likely Robert A. Heinlein's *Time Enough for Love*, in whose Table of Contents appear repeatedly the words Prelude, Counterpoint, Variations on a Theme, Intermission, Da Capo—the latter complete with bars of musical notation.

47. Mazzini, *Filosofia della musica*, 149.

48. See Ferruccio Busoni, *Entwurf einer neuen Aesthetik der Tonkunst* (Leipzig: Insel Verlag, 1916).

49. Spengler, *Der Untergang des Abendlandes*, 1: 375–76.

50. Giacomo Leopardi, *Zibaldone* (2 vols.), in *Tutte le opere di Giacomo Leopardi*, ed. F. Flora, (Milan: Mondadori, 1949), 2: 55 and 329–30 respectively.

15. PERCEPT AND CONCEPT: ON HUGO'S *HERNANI* AND VERDI'S *ERNANI*

1. Review of November 2, 1892, in *Shaw's Music*, ed. Dan H. Laurence (New York: Dodd, Mead, 1981), 2: 724–25. In my opinion, there are ultimately two true masters of characterization in the world of opera, Mozart and Verdi. Wagner and Puccini both came close in *Die Meistersinger* and *La Bohème*, but legendary and fierce passions otherwise precluded a faithful musical rendering of human conduct. The Baroque heaviness of Monteverdi and Rameau staidly aimed at expressive solidity, and modern atonalism, however adroitly conceived, tends to discard the human in favor of the technical. Comedy (say, Rossini's) is necessarily hyperbolic, and the Impressionistic aesthetic (say, Debussy's) likes mysticism. Character delineation through music—the portrayal of psychological motives without violating the principles of composition—first requires a literary sensibility, since the libretto precedes the scoring, and both Mozart and Verdi had it. Then it requires that uncanny ability to make the music say the human things the libretto says, even if there were no libretto. It is here that Mozart and Verdi surpass all other composers of opera, and it is on these grounds that Verdi's special appreciation of Mozart lies. Shaw would not disagree.

2. Ibid., review of May 30, 1894, 3: 227.

3. Ibid.

4. P. Conrad, *Romantic Opera and Literary Form* (Berkeley–Los Angeles–London: University of California Press, 1977), 51. Conrad continues: "and Verdi employs it with Shakespearean generosity, allowing characters condemned by the drama to save themselves by singing. Much is forgiven Marguerite in Dumas's *La Dame aux camélias* because she has loved greatly; all is forgiven Violetta in *La Traviata*

because she has sung beautifully. Music grants her a way of revealing her goodness in seraphic singing which is denied her literary prototype."

5. Gary Schmidgall, *Literature as Opera* (New York: Oxford University Press, 1977), 10. Another fine source to consult is Herbert Lindenberger, *Opera: The Extravagant Art* (Ithaca and London: Cornell University Press, 1984), particularly chapter 1, "Opera or Drama," 25–74.

6. Quoted from Pierre Richard, Introduction to *Hernani* (Paris: Librairie Larousse, 1951).

7. Ibid.

8. David R. B. Kimbell, *Verdi in the Age of Italian Romanticism* (Cambridge: Cambridge University Press, 1981), 461.

9. Ibid., 463.

10. We should remember, too, that Hugo wrote his play at age twenty-eight, and Verdi his opera at age thirty-one.

11. Eduard Hanslick, *Die moderne Oper* (Berlin: A. Hofmann and Co., 1875), 222.

12. See W. D. Horwarth, *Sublime and Grotesque: A Study of French Romantic Drama* (London: Harrap, 1975), 164–65.

13. F. Busoni, "The Essence and Oneness of Music" (1921), in *The Essence of Music and Other Papers*, trans. Rosamond Ley (London: Salisbury Square, 1957), 12.

14. See Conrad, *Romantic Opera*, 50.

15. Letter of September 5, 1843, in F. Abbiati, *Giuseppe Verdi*, 4 vols. (Milan: Ricordi, 1959), 1: 473.

16. Sandro Della Libera, ed., "*Ernani* di G. Verdi, Cronologia," Archive of the Teatro La Fenice, Venice, September 22, 1843.

17. Letter of October 2, 1843, in Abbiati, *Verdi*, 1: 475.

18. C. Gatti, *Verdi: The Man and His Music*, trans. Elisabeth Abbott, (New York: Putnam's, 1955), 71.

19. Michael M. Harrison, "Composers as Political Artists," *Opera Quarterly* 2, no. 1 (Spring 1984): 95.

20. W. H. Auden, "Some Reflections on Music and Opera," *Partisan Review* 19 (1952): 15.

21. M. Mila, *Giuseppe Verdi* (Bari: Laterza, 1958), 151–52.

22. Charles Osborne, *The Complete Operas of Verdi* (New York: Knopf, 1970), 90.

23. We should recall that Hugo's democratic ideology did not take shape until 1848.

24. Hugo also took umbrage at the opera's high melodrama (!) and at the omission, in the process of compression, of credible details (!).

25. Gaetano Donizetti produced it in Vienna; Hans von Bülow praised it in Germany; and in England even the harsh critic who was not in the ranks of Verdi admirers, Henry Chorley, was forced to say good things.

26. Kimbell, *Verdi*, 469. Indeed, Hugo had had trouble constructing the tomb–

conspiratorial scene and had left much up to the stage directions. Verdi, through his music and a chorus that Hugo did not have, was able to thicken the scene's texture dramatically and create one of the opera's most stirring moments.

27. Massimo Mila, *Il melodramma di Verdi* (Milan: Feltrinelli, 1960), 46.

28. Conrad, *Romantic Opera*, 53.

29. Kimbell, *Verdi*, 482. On the next page, the critic continues: "Set to music, the pledge becomes something dramatically three-dimensional: it still carries the conceptual [for me, aesthetic] force of Hugo's pledge, but it is expressive and symbolic too. Our sense that it will have tragic consequences is intensified by the grim and solemn harmonies, and the brassy colouring of the chords makes of them a tonal symbol perfectly analogous to the visual symbol of the horn."

30. Osborne, *The Complete Operas*, 91. Writes Osborne: "He had heard no Wagner in 1844. *Der fliegende Holländer* was new, had not yet been published, and had not been performed in Italy. *Tannhäuser* was composed and awaiting production, which it achieved in Dresden in 1845. There is really no Wagner influence anywhere in Verdi, and no such influence would even have been possible at this stage of the Italian composer's career."

31. Busoni, "The Essence and Oneness," 7.

16. A MATTER OF INCOMPATIBILITY: PUSHKIN AND TCHAIKOWSKY

1. See my "Counterpoint of the Snapping String: Chekhov's *The Cherry Orchard*," *California Slavic Studies* 10 (1977): 121–36.

2. Quoted from Roman Jakobson, "Marginal Notes on *Eugene Onegin*," *Pushkin: Eugene Onegin*, ed. Walter Arndt (New York: Dutton, 1981), xi.

3. See A. D. P. Briggs, *Alexander Pushkin* (Totowa, N.J.: Barnes and Noble, 1983), 190.

4. Gary Schmidgall, *Opera as Literature* (New York: Oxford University Press, 1977), 219.

5. Ibid., 219 –43. Schmidgall, in fairness, acknowledges the "good" renderings by Tchaikowsky: the way in which the pleas in Onegin's letter are blended with Tatiana's rejection, the use of musical moments suggested by Pushkin's poem, the expansion of Triquet's song at the Larin ball, and the festive scenes (237).

6. See Gerald Abraham, *Tchaikowsky* (London: Lindsay Drummond, 1946), 151. He considers this "a fusion of emotional expression with graphic tone-painting."

7. Schmidgall, *Opera as Literature*, 241.

8. See Herbert Lindenberger, "Opera as Drama," *Opera: The Extravagant Art* (Ithaca and London: Cornell University Press, 1984). chap. 1.

9. Schmidgall, *Opera as Literature*, pp. 225–26.

10. In my examples, I have stayed within the Romantic tradition, Tchaikowsky's own, with the exception of the Busoni opera, which could not contain a more complete roster of musical ironies.

11. Its elusiveness, however, demands great caution by the composer.

12. V. Shklovsky, *Teoriya prozy* and *Pushkin i Sterne* 6 (Prague: Volya Rossii, 1922).

13. John Bayley, *Pushkin: A Comparative Commentary* (Cambridge: Cambridge University Press, 1971), 245.

14. See the discussion in A. D. P. Briggs, *Alexander Pushkin*, 221–22.

15 Wilfrid Mellers, *Man & His Music* (New York: Schocken Books, 1969), 4: 64.

16. S. L. Frank, "Svetlaya pechal," *Etyudy o Pushkine* (Munich: Prideaux Press, Letchworth, Herts, 1957), 125–26.

17. Briggs, *Alexander Pushkin*, 239. The Shestov reference is to "A. S. Pushkin," *Russian Views of Pushkin* (Oxford: Meeuws, 1976), 110–11.

17. FROM *OTHELLO* TO *OTELLO: IRA OVER GELOSIA*

1. This essay was written in collaboration with Terri Frongia.

2. Joseph Kerman, *Opera as Drama* (New York: Vantage, 1956), 7.

3. Ibid., 13.

4. Herbert Lindenberger, *Opera: The Extravagant Art* (Ithaca and London: Cornell University Press, 1984), 26.

5. Gary Schmidgall, *Literature as Opera* (New York: Oxford University Press, 1977), 8.

6. Kerman, in *Opera as Drama*, for example, points to the "imagery and poetic music" of Othello's words when he enters with the candle in the last scene before he kills Desdemona and the corresponding music's dramatic, emotional depth (9–12); Schmidgall, in *Literature as Drama*, to how *Othello* "required the style of the late Verdi"—the Moor's despairing renunciation (III, 3), the operatic set pieces (drinking song, love duet, vengeance duet, prayer), including the "Willow Song" (6); Lindenberger to Jago's "Credo" (34).

7. Quoted from Dan H. Laurence, *Shaw's Music* (New York: Dodd, Mead, 1981, 3: 579.

8. See Lindenberger, *Opera: The Extravagant Art*, 34.

9. Letter to Boïto, 21 January 1886, *Carteggio Verdi-Boïto*, 99–100, quoted from Julian Budden, *The Operas of Verdi*, 3 vols. (London: Cassell, 1981), 3: 319.

10. Budden, *The Operas of Verdi*, 3: 328.

11. Citations are from the Bantam edition of *Othello*, ed. Oscar Campbell, Alfred Rothschild, and Stuart Vaughan (New York: Bantam Books, 1962). Kerman's comments in *Opera as Drama* have been helpful.

12. Spike Hughes (Patrick Cairns), *Famous Verdi Operas* (London: Robert Hale, 1968), 454.

13. Budden, *The Operas of Verdi*, 3: 366.

14. Ibid., 3: 381.

18. THE *KALEVALA*, SIBELIUS, AND THE MEANING OF INWARDNESS

1. See Francis Peabody Magoun, Jr., Foreword, *The Kalevala* (Cambridge: Harvard University Press, 1963), xiii. All translations from the *Kalevala* in this chapter are his.

2. Domenico Comparetti, *The Traditional Poetry of the Finns*, trans. I. M. Anderton, (London: Longmans, Green, 1898), 341. Like Comparetti, we continue to recognize today the *Kalevala* as a powerfully beautiful poem, replete with folk realism and artistic symbolism, balancing pathos with lyricism, with an unobtrusive yet significant moral philosophy. It is small wonder that Henry Wadsworth Longfellow was so attracted to it for his *Song of Hiawatha*.

3. Ibid., 229.

4. For a study of Väinämöinen see Martti Haavio, *Väinämöinen, Eternal Sage* (Helsinki: Finnish Academy of Sciences, 1952).

5. Comparetti, *Traditional Poetry of the Finns*, 246.

6. One of the causes to which Sibelius lent himself was the Press Celebrations, ostensibly to raise money for journalistic pensions, but actually for the freedom of the press. In this vein, he wrote his *Scènes historiques I* (1889).

7. For more on Sibelius and the epos see Robin Gregory, "Sibelius and the Kalevala," *The Monthly Musical Record* 81 (1951): 59–62.

8. Veikko Helasvuo, *Sibelius and the Music of Finland* (Helsinki: Otava, 1952), 19.

9. Translation is mine, derived from other—for me less satisfactory—renderings.

10. Critics have justly pointed to the affinities between Sibelius's tone poems and his symphonies. Accordingly, I would suggest that the same affirmative character imposes itself in the symphonic category. The gauntly tragic rhapsody called the Symphony no. 4 yields to the minor-keyed but energetic first, the luminous sixth, to say nothing of the major-keyed grandiose second, classical third, perorative fifth, and especially noble sixth.

11. See Angel Records 35002 (Symphony no. 5 and *Finlandia*), notes by Andrew Porter. The first visitor was Rose Newmarch (*A Short Story of a Long Friendship*, Boston [1939 and 1945]); the second, Bengt de Törne (*Sibelius: A Close-up* [London, 1937]).

12. Cecil Gray, *Sibelius: The Symphonies* (Freeport, N.Y.: Books for Libraries Press, 1935 and 1970), 18. In this passage, Gray is speaking of Sibelius's symphonies, but the musical design he describes easily applies to all his works.

13. *New York Times*, December 21, 1947.

14. Quoted from Helasvuo, *Sibelius and the Music of Finland*, 20.

15. See Robert L. Jacobs, "Sibelius, *Lemminkäinen and the Maidens of Saari*," *Musical Review* 24 (May 1963): 149–50.

19. THE AMBIGUOUS FAUNS OF MALLARMÉ AND DEBUSSY

1. Verses on a copy of "L'Après-midi d'un faune," illustration by Edouard Manet and sent to Debussy by Mallarmé.

2. To avoid misunderstanding, allow me to clarify at the outset that the occasional grammatical terminology in this essay, like "rhetoric" and "syntax," serves simply as a metaphor, with definitions provided by any dictionary (nothing more). When I gave a talk on this subject a few years ago at the University of California at

Davis, a band of semiotic structuralists assaulted me with terms like "sign," "signifier," "referent," "deconstructive process," "communicant subject," "underlying mode," "subjacent pattern," and so on, in an attempt to coerce the subject into a casserole I do not cook with. Theirs was simply old-hat formalism with a new vocabulary, but the jargon kept pointing to critical theory rather than to aesthetic substance, and Mallarmé and Debussy disappeared in the process. My intention in this essay is quite modest: to relate one work of art to another without the benefit of a stylish glossary stemming from a "nouvelle cuisine théorique."

3. Stéphane Mallarmé, "La Musique et les lettres," in *Oeuvres complètes*, Pléïade edition, ed. Henri Mondor and G. Jean-Aubry (Paris: Gallimard, 1945), 645.

4. See Henri Mondor, *Histoire d'un faune* (Paris: Gallimard, 1948), 74.

5. T. Munro, "L'Après-midi d'un faune et les relations entre les arts, "*Revue d'esthétique* (1952): 232; later, in *Toward Science in Aesthetic* (New York: Liberal Arts Press, 1956).

6. Leonard Bernstein, *The Unanswered Question* (Cambridge, Mass., and London: Harvard University Press, 1976), 239. However, for better or for worse, Bernstein, to whose views I am indebted because I find them very pertinent, attempts a linguistic analysis along "structuralist" lines, which is not my intention here.

7. These are elements of a summary found in Charles Mauron, *Stéphane Mallarmé: Poems*, trans. Roger Fry (New York: New Directions, 1951), 193–97.

8. Ibid., 30. We ought never forget, however, that Mallarmé intended his poetry to receive close, thoughtful scrutiny in addition to reception of its immediate impression.

9. March 7, 1885. Mallarmé always felt that music was an incomplete art, inferior to poetry in that it lacked the access to idea which only a verbal art can enjoy; poetry can name immediate reality and, starting from that, arrive at any degree of abstraction or ideality, and even fuse the two. Mallarmé, it is known, had no knowledge of music technically.

10. *Divagations*, "Richard Wagner: Rêverie d'un poète français," *Oeuvres complètes*, 541 and 543.

11. See, e.g., Mauron and Fry, *Stéphane Mallarmé: Poems*, 23.

12. *Divagations*, "Théodore de Banville," *Oeuvres complètes*, 522.

13. Charles Mauron, *Mallarmé l'obscur*, (Paris: Editions Denoel, 1941), 71.

14. *Divagations*, "Crise de vers," *Oeuvres complètes*, 368.

15. Mauron, *Mallarmé l'obscur*, 74–75.

16. A. R. Chisholm, *L'Après-midi d'un faune: An Exegetical and Critical Study* (Carlton Victoria: Melbourne University Press, 1958). Paul Valéry ("Ecrits divers sur Stéphane Mallarmé," *Nouvelle revue française* [1950]: 86) identified three: Sensuality (the rape of the nymph); Musicality (remembrance and dream); and Art (the flute), which makes dream an artistic reality.

17. Mallarmé, "Réponse à l'enquête de J. Huret sur L'Evolution littéraire" (1891), *Oeuvres complètes*, 867.

18. Ibid., 870.

19. Valéry, "Ecrits divers," 86.

20. Thibaudet, *La Poésie de Stéphane Mallarmé*, 2d ed. *(Paris: Gallimard [1913],* 1926, 2: 398.

21. The interrelation has been variously commented on. Apart from the studies already mentioned, I might also mention: Lloyd James Austin, "Mallarmé on Music and Letters," *Bulletin of The John Ryland Library* 42 (1959–60): 19–39; Helga Böhmer, "Alchimie der Töne: Die Mallarmé-Vertonungen von Debussy und Ravel," *Musica* 22 (1968): 83–85; Marianne Kesting, "Mallarmé and die Musik," *Melos* 35 (1968): 45–56; Joyce Mitchell, "Symbolism in Music and Poetry" (diss.), Philadelphia, 1944; Henri Mondor, "Stéphane Mallarmé et Claude Debussy," *Journal musical français* 1 (September 25, 1951), 8; Helmut Schmidt-Garre, "Rimbaud-Mallarmé-Debussy: Parallelen zwischen Dichtung und Musik," *Neue Zeitschrift für Musik* 130 (1969): 512–19; Vincenzo Terenzio, "Debussy e Mallarmé," *Rassegna musicale* 17 (1947): 132–36; and especially Suzanne Bernard, *Mallarmé et la musique* (Paris: Librairie Nizet, 1959), and Arthur B. Wenk, *Claude Debussy and the Poets* (Berkeley–Los Angeles–London: University of California Press, 1976). A study entitled "Mallarmé et Debussy," in *Les Cahiers de marottes et violons d'Ingres*, (September–October 1954), was unavailable to me. A recent study, not yet published at the time of this writing, deserves attention: David M. Hertz, *The Tuning of the Word* (Carbondale and Edwardsville: Southern Illinois University Press, 1987). It is a study of the Symbolist movement.

22. C. Debussy, *Lettres à deux amis* (Paris: José Corti, 1942), 121.

23. The resulting analogy, however, is not purely inferential; it may be assessed—if not actually measured—analytically by experiencing the "Prélude" with the Elegy from outset to finish.

24. See Léon Vallas, *Achille-Claude Debussy* (Paris: Presses Universitaires de France, 1944), 170–71.

25. C. S. Brown, *Music and Literature* (Athens, Ga.: University of Georgia Press, 1948), 253.

26. Quoted from ibid., 254.

27. Mauron, *Mallarmé l'obscur*, 115: "Debussy, they say, proudly claimed that when he wrote his admirable *Prélude à 'L'Après-midi d'un faune,'* he followed the poem verse by verse."

28. Wenk, *Claude Debussy and the Poets*, 152. He also notes that since the middle section of Mallarmé's poem comprises a mere twenty lines (42–61) while that of Debussy forty-two measures (37–38), Debussy has increased the importance of the section, making of Pan's casual pipe-playing a "rapturous melody which escapes for a few moments the vagueness of rhythm and tonal sense" which accompanies his earlier, troubled musings (167).

29. I cannot go along with Wenk when he interprets Mallarmé's reaction to the "Prélude," that is, "[establishing] the setting more earnestly than the color" (from Mallarmé's letter, *Oeuvres complètes*, 1465) as meaning that the composer was "more attentive to articulating changing settings than to painting in music the faun's colorful dreams" (167). If ever there was a score that could paint dreams, the "Prélude" is it. The problem with the statement by Mallarmé, who thought of music as intel-

lectual metaphor rather than as abstract language or as system in its own right, is that it is simply incorrect.

30. This is not to attempt the kind of reverse gloss attempted by V. Emm. C. Lombardi in 1887—to "follow [the poem] faithfully"—which amounted to little because it aimed at a literal transposition (key words placed in the score, which is then dominated by the text [see Bernard, *Mallarmé et la musique,* 166–67]). But, given the close association of the eclogue with the idea of music, Lombardi's essay betrayed a logical notion of interrelation whose possibilities Debussy did not overlook.

31. Letter to Willy (Henry Gautier-Villars, a critic), October 10, 1895.

32. *Correspondance de Claude Debussy et Pierre Louÿs,* ed. Henri Bourgeaud (Paris: José Corti, 1945), 63.

33. Quoted from André Fontinas, *Mes souvenirs du Symbolisme* (Paris: Editions de la Nouvelle Revue Critique, 1928), 93.

34. I owe this association to Bernard, *Mallarmé et la musique,* 169.

35. See ibid., 111.

36. See H. Mondor, "Stéphane Mallarmé et Claude Debussy"; quoted in Wenk, *Claude Debussy and the Poets,* 149.

37. With reference to the changes in typography Mallarmé uses (three fonts: small caps, roman, and italic), Bernstein, in *The Unanswered Question,* believes that the episodes concerned, "curiously enough, are analogous to similar episodes in Debussy's musical counterpart" (255), but he does not say how. In my opinion, his belief is unfounded and, if pursued, would force us to read into the music episodic correspondences which just are not there. An explanation of the problematic typography is in order here to understand my reservation about Bernstein's statement, and I owe this typographical elucidation to my friend and colleague, Dr. Keith Macfarlane. Each font reflects a different level of reality and marks out the cognitive structure of the poem. *Small caps:* two imperatives (CONTEZ [NARRATE], SOUVENIRS [MEMORIES]), both in small caps, preceding the italicized narratives. In both cases something exterior to the faun (characters ["nymphes," nymphs], setting ["bords siciliens," Sicilian shores]) is called upon to bear witness to the veracity of the narrative or to be the faun's accomplices in fabulating. The nature of the two words thus written is such that it underlines the ambiguity of the process at work in the poem: "tale" as verbalized fiction, "memory" as immaterial representation of something purportedly real. They are mirror images of each other. *Italics:* the "narrative," ostensibly, what really happened, giving rise to all this reflection, but of problematic reality. So, what seems most real (the narrative, a succession of deeds and events uninterrupted by reflection or meditation) is in fact the most problematical. *Roman:* the faun's reflection on the narrative. Taken by itself, the cogitation is the least affirmative, the most hesitant; yet the only certainty in the poem is that the faun is perplexed and, because of that, is trying to make sense out of the events of the narrative. The italics represent a problematic objectivity; the roman, a believable subjectivity; and the two words in small caps, an attempted fusion of the objective and the subjective. So typography is a key to cognitive structure and a counter to the ambiguity which the poem's theme dictates. To claim, then, that Debussy's music transposes this involuted pro-

cess of varying psychological moments is somewhat far-fetched, and I am glad that the composer stuck to "the general impression of the poem."

38. In *Claude Debussy and the Poets*, Wenk's symmetrical dissection of the "Prélude" in sections and subsections and more, neatly balancing each other off (not just the four parts but the ingredients of the four parts as well—see pp. 161–63), strikes me as ingenious but not corresponding to Debussy's disciplined yet flexible creative process. While I strongly believe that each note is in place, as it were, to find such a strictly balanced symmetry suggests a doubtful degree of conscious calculation. What calculation there is in the creative process—and assuredly there is—is always more instinctive than analysts, by the very nature of their science, care to make it. Ultimately, the greater artist has the finer instincts. As I conclude, Debussy's "Prélude" is definitely calculated, or willed, but I find it more proper to stay on this side of such a scalpeled dissection.

39. See Debussy's letter in "Claude Debussy et Ernest Chausson," *Revue musicale* 7 (1926): 118. It is interesting that Debussy, who advised Chausson not to be concerned with "undertones," should have proven to be such a skilled "undertonalist" himself (see J.-P. Barricelli and Leo Weinstein, *Ernest Chausson: His Life and Works* [Norman, Okla.: University of Oklahoma Press, 1955], 66).

40. Ruth Moser, *L'Impressionisme français* (Paris: Droz, 1942), 197.

41. Italics mine.

42. Bernstein, *The Unanswered Question*, 241.

43. See Wenk, *Claude Debussy and the Poets*, 68.

44. Bernstein, *The Unanswered Question*, 243. Debussy uses the identical tritone, for not unsimilar purposes, in *L'Isle joyeuse*.

45. Letter to Willy, quoted from Vallas, *Achille-Claude Debussy*, 181. Mallarmé appreciated the correspondence between his poem and Debussy's music when he wrote to the composer: "Your illustration would sound dissonant from my text only if it went further, really, into nostalgia and light with finesse, uneasiness, and richness" (*Oeuvres complètes*, 1465). Bernard (*Mallarmé et la musique*, 170–71) quotes J. Rivière's comparison of the two works: "I find Debussy marvelously adequate to Mallarmé in the *Prélude*. I was rereading the poem. What is beautiful in it is not its exact meaning but those thrusts of desire, those élans that immediately drop, overcome by too much thickness, those gestures to get up and those relapses. Even the jagged rhythm of the verses translates this admirably. And Debussy felt that quite well. The music is a continuous undulation of heat with short leaps, swellings that deflate, passionate appeals and collapses" (Rivière's letter to Alain Fournier, March 31, 1907, *Correspondance* 2, *Nouvelle revue française* [1926]: 60).

46. *Oeuvres complètes* (1965 ed.), 1465.

20. FAUST AND THE MUSIC OF EVIL

1. Goethe had, in fact, thought of Meyerbeer as the only living composer possibly up to the task, but he would have felt more confident with Mozart, the composer of *Die Zauberflöte* and *Don Giovanni*.

2. *Faust* (review), no. 1 (1921): 30–31.

3. In the ranks, we identify such examples in the nineteenth century as: Peter J. von Lindpaiter's *Ouvertüre zu Faust*, Julius Rietz's Singspiel *Faust*, Henry R. Bishop's Romantic drama *Faustus*, Gaetano Donizetti's opera *Fausta*, Adolphe Adam's orchestral score for a *Faust* ballet, Mikhail Glinka's "Margarita's Song for Goethe's Tragedy *Faust*," Giovanni Battista Gordigiani's opera *Fausto*, Pietro Raimondi's opera *Il Fausto arrivo*, Florimon Hervé's opera buffa parody in fifteen tableaux *Le petit Faust*, Alexander Winterberger's *Faust-Szenen* for piano, Alexey N. Verstiwsky's Singspiel *Pan Twardowsky*, Louise Bertin's opera *Faust*, Wilhelm Fritze's musical scenes, Maurice Béjart's ballet on Hector Berlioz's *La Damnation de Faust*, Carl Loewe's songs *Sieben Gesänge zu Faust*, Modest Mussorgsky's "Mephistopheles' Song of the Flea" and "Mephistopheles' Song in Auerbach's Cellar," Joseph Bohuslav Foerster's melodrama with piano *Faustulus*, Max Zenger's stage music, Franz Schubert's various songs like "Gretchen am Spinnrade" in *Szenen aus Goethes Faust*, J. von Zaitz's Singspiel *Twardowsky*, Eduard Lassen's opera *Faust* (I and II), not to mention Louis Spohr's opera *Faust*, Franz Liszt's *Zwei Episoden aus Lenaus Faust für grosses Orchester* and his *Eine Faust Symphonie* along with his piano transcriptions on Faust subjects, Berlioz's dramatic oratorio *La Damnation de Faust*, Richard Wagner's "Six Pieces for Goethe's *Faust*" and his *Faust-Ouvertüre*, Arrigo Boïto's grand opera *Mefistofele*, Robert Schumann's operatic oratorio *Szenen aus Goethes Faust*, Charles Gounod's opera *Faust*, and later, in the twentieth century, Moritz Moszkowski's Faust-based "Prelude and Fugue" (op. 85) and his opera on Christian D. Grabbe's *Don Juan und Faust*, C. Kistler's musical drama *Faust*, Max Richard Albrecht's incidental music, Leopold Reichwein's stage music, Sergei Rachmaninoff's piano *Sonata on Faust*, Charles Tournemire's trilogy *Faust-Don Quichotte-St. François d'Assise*, August Bungert's musical scenes for Parts I and II for Max Grube's adaptation of Goethe's work, Anton Rubinstein's symphonic poem *Faust Symphonie* or *Faust: ein musikalisches Charakterbild nach Goethe*, Felix Weingartner's musical scenes, C. Urbini's *Faust on the Sabbath*, H. Ambrosius's *Faust, Symphonische Dichtung*, M. Moreau's operetta parody *Faust 1944*, H. Kirsova's ballet *Faust*, F. Skvor's ballet *Doktor Faust*, G. Adenis's cantata *Faust et Hélène*, R. Ducasse's symphonic poem *Au jardin de Marguerite*, H. U. Engelmann's burlesque opera *Dr. Faust's Höllenfahrt*, J. L. Saenz de Heredia's comic opera *Si Fausto fuera Faustina*, H. Vogel's ballet *Mephisto*, Alfredo Ginastera's *Obertura para el Fausto criollo de E. Campo*, even Richard Adler's and Jerry Ross's Broadway musical comedy *Damn Yankees* and the score of the recent movie *Mephisto*, like that of *Bedazzled*, not to mention Gustav Mahler's second movement to his *Symphonie der Tausend* (no. 8) and Busoni's opera *Doktor Faust*. The list, already copious, could be lengthened.

4. Alfred Rosenberg, *Der Mythus des XX Jahrhunderts* (Munich: Hoheneichneu Verlag, 1930), p. 434.

5. Paul Valéry, "Notre destin et les lettres," *Conferencia* 2 (1937): 343.

6. A text lends a focus of meaning to the musical passage, for music, as we know, does not communicate concrete ideas. But it does have its own strategies and de-

vices, without which a given musical passage would not adequately fit the dramatic meaning. It is the strategies and devices that interest me here, not the text.

7. Spohr's *Faust* was written in Vienna in 1813, to a poor libretto, and produced in Frankfurt in 1818. For a while, it was popular on the German, English, and especially French stages, but despite a fine orchestral adagio before Faust enters in Act II, some good choral writing with harmonic vocal effects, Act I's popular tempo di minuetto, and the equally popular Polonnaise during the nuptial banquet, all that has survived outside of Germany is the aria "Die stille Nacht entweicht." Most of the opera, even in its 1852 revision when recitatives were added, shows a rigid, studied construction which even its technical instrumental richness cannot alleviate.

8. The *Faust-Ouvertüre* dates from January 1840, and its performance came in 1844. For almost eleven years, Wagner kept revising it. In fact, Liszt, who repeatedly urged the composer to bring it into final form, retrieved it from oblivion around 1852, but it never enjoyed much success. It is not one of Wagner's best efforts.

9. The work, on a J. Barbier and M. Carré libretto, was written in 1859, with recitatives and ballet added three years later. It owes its prominence in the repertoire of opera to many beautifully flowing passages and scenes, like the chorus of peasants in Act I (though Berlioz deemed it a bad substitute for Goethe's Easter Song); Act II's choruses, waltz, and Faust's "Ne permettrez-vous pas, ma belle demoiselle"; Act III's cavatina "Salut, demeure chaste et pure," the King of Thule song, the Garden quartet, Faust's "Laisse-moi . . . ô nuit d'amour" and the duet following it, Marguerite's ecstasy at the window, her "Spinning Wheel" song in Act IV in which we hear Valentin's "Ce qui doit arriver . . ." and the "Church Scene" music, and the inspired religious music, including the duet, the final trio, and the chorus of apotheosis of Act V. Other sections occasionally fall into blandness, like Siebel's aria and the Soldier's Chorus. But the opera shows advancement over previous operatic styles— cadences blending music with recitative, fluid ensembles, intimate cooperation between orchestra and voice, and an unmistakable melodic elegance for expressing emotions of religion or love.

10. The oratorio interested Schumann from 1832 to 1853; he wrote sections of it at different times those years and the work as a whole received its first performance in 1862. The style changes, from his earlier manner (Part III) under the influence of Felix Mendelssohn, to his later manner (Parts I and II) under the influence of Wagner. Gretchen's lines are lyrically free, good examples of continuous melody, encompassing all shades of feeling, from the flower-plucking "Er liebt mich, liebt mich nicht . . ." to the operatic "Hilf! Rette mich von Schmach und Tod!" Fancifully scored, the opening of Part II follows the opening of Goethe's Part II, including Ariel's Song with aeolian harps and the later choruses, as indicated by growing self-awareness in "Die Nacht scheint tiefer" and his resurgence of hope in "Lasst glücklich schauen . . ." are remarkable numbers in oratorio style. His death after the last avowal of his dream is set forth in a dramatic flow of Wagnerian "endless melody." In Part III, Goethe's very last scene, seven sections grow out of each other, often due to the symmetrical nature of the melodies, from the holy chorus and the statements by the Pater Ecstaticus, the Pater Profundus, and the Pater Seraphicus,

to the Apostrophe to the Virgin ("Freudig empfangen wir diesen in Puppenstand"), Dr. Marianus's hymn and the intercession for Gretchen (who intercedes for Faust) by the Women Penitents (one sings an effective "Neige, neige") following an orchestral Mater Gloriosa, her moving "Komm, hebe dich zu höhern Sphären! Wenn [Faust] dich abnet, folgt er nach," and the final Chorus Mysticus on Goethe's "Alles Vergängliche. . . ." Schumann also wrote a longer, less Classical, and more continuous ending, leaving the choice to the musical director. Both are profoundly mystical.

11. Lemures are ghosts of the wicked dead who wander at night as skeletons or animated mummies and whose minds are as imperfect as their bodies. They are brought by Mephistopheles to dig Faust's grave.

12. The Symphony no. 8, written in 1906, was first performed in 1908. It is orchestrated with power and color: 4 flutes, 2 piccolos, 4 oboes, 1 English horn, 3 clarinets, 2 E♭ clarinets, 1 bass clarinet, 4 bassoons, 1 contrabassoon, 8 horns, 8 trumpets (4 offstage), 7 trombones (3 offstage), 1 bass tuba, tympani, bass drum, cymbals, gong, triangle, deep bells, glockenspiel, celesta, piano, harmonium, organ, 2 harps, 1 mandolin, and strings. And it requires two mixed choruses and a boys' chorus plus eight solo voices. With the text built into the symphonic structure, the sense of tonal unity is complete. The first movement is in sonata form, the second progressing from a long introductory poco adagio (whose theme relates to the first movement), to a scene of anchorites in a mountain gorge (Montserrat, where hermits' cells are one over the other, symbolically suggesting an upward direction toward perfection), to a Chorus of Angels, which becomes an extended finale-allegro, including a short scherzando given to a chorus of young angels, finally to the hushed entry of the Chorus Mysticus, which eventually rises to a powerful climax. The emphasis on the final movement is consistent with Mahler's practice of shifting attention from the beginning or center of a symphony to the way it ends. Hence the prominence of his "Faust" movement.

13. *La Damnation de Faust*, on a libretto by Almire Gendonnière and Berlioz himself, was suggested to the composer by a Gérard de Nerval translation of Goethe (1827), and his first musical settings are of 1829, with the final version coming in 1846. The four acts, or tableaux, include a ronde and the rousing Rákóczy March in the first; Faust's meditation; the Easter Chorus; songs of the Flea and the Mouse; the Amen fugato, "Voici les roses" and Dance of the Sylphs, followed by the Soldiers' and Students' choruses (Scene 8) in the second; Méphistophélès's serenade, the Wills-o'-the-Wisp dance, King of Thule song, and Marguerite's lament in the third; and the romance, wood hunt, dash to the abyss, infernal dance, and ascension of Marguerite in the fourth. Berlioz wrote to give every idea its own setting, according to the literary, pictorial, or suggestive content of the story. Of these, the literary was the most binding, since he viewed music and literature as identical. Music, for him, is not autonomous; it has meaning outside itself, and for this reason the two arts suggest each other in a single expression of the human soul.

14. Berlioz changes the significance of a theme by varying its color, adjusting its pace, meter, pitch, and instrumentation.

15. *Two Episodes from Lenau's Faust* are from 1859–60. The Waltz describes drunken dancing at a wedding which Mephistopheles, with diabolical cunning, persuades Faust to join; the fiend plays a vehement, sensuous violin, bringing his prey to dance madly with a black-eyed maiden whom he then seduces in the woods under the sinister twittering of a nightingale. "Ein wunderlich Geschlecht fürwahr, die Brut vom ersten Sünderpaar." Mephistopheles's music is sarcastically merry (theme 1); polyphonic writing with syncopations and appoggiaturas mark the erratic pursuit (theme 2); and the variants of themes 1 and 2 combine with the nightingale's twitter (theme 3). Liszt wrote alternative endings from which a conductor may choose. The *Procession* describes a parade of children, nuns, and aged priests. Flute trills recall nightingales and a pizzicato the slow tramp of Faust's horse (Section 1). Fragments of a plainsong ("Pange lingua gloriosi") for horns makes for a choralelike theme (Section 2) in F♯ (this key had religious associations for Liszt). After a climax, the procession disappears; the material derives from Section 1. On the whole, the music is intended to show Faust's lonely despair and his vision of faith.

16. This comparison has been variously noted by critics; Liszt ultimately preferred Goethe's greater subtlety to Lenau's directness.

17. Liszt worked on the *Faust-Symphonie* many years. It was published in 1861, after concentrated work from 1854 to 1857, but he had started it as far back as 1830 and continued it as late as 1880. The three movements—Faust, Gretchen, and Mephistopheles—end with a male Chorus Mysticus on Goethe's last verses, "Alles Vergängliche . . . Das Ewig-Weibliche zieht uns hinan," when the tenor solo intones the Gretchen theme, rising higher and higher with fortissimo fanfares and ending in triumph.

18. As an example of an analysis of the symphony followed with text in hand, fashionable a century ago, see Richard Pohl, *Franz Liszt: Studien und Errinnerungen* (Leipzig: B. Schlicke, 1883), 247–320.

19. Norman Treigle's comments in Susan Regan's notes to the recording, Angel SCLX 3806. In writing this chapter I found very useful—of course—Grove's *Dictionary*, and less traditional sources (recordings) such as the following: for Berlioz's *Damnation*, Deutsche Grammophon Gesellschaft, Georges Auric's notes; for Boïto's *Mefistofele*, London OSA 1307, Richard Law's comments; for Gounod's *Faust*, London OSA 1433, Ray Minshull's notes; for Schumann's *Faust*, London OSA 12100, the commentary by Joan Chissell, Keith Pollard, and G. Bramall; for Liszt's *Faust Symphony*, Urania URLP 606, notes by B. B. B.; and for Liszt again and Wagner's *Faust* Overture, Vox Twins VUX 2029/SVUX 52029, Michael Sonino's notes.

20. Everyone awaited the five-and-a-half-hour premiere of Boïto's *Mefistofele* in 1867, but it was disastrous, eliciting the composer's humorous written report to a friend: "Pim, Poum, Patatrac!" It was "too symphonic," "too intellectual," "too Wagnerian, Germanic," "futuristic," even in that age of Scapigliati. The arguments raged; they even provoked a duel. One of Boïto's projects was to bring into Italian a Greek system of versification: Elena sings in Classical meters, seeking of Faust the secret of "rhyme" (unknown to the Greeks), the *eco ineffabile* learning which she falls in love with Faust—an intellectualization of myth, in other words, metaphori-

cally suggesting the union, through Elena-Faust, of Classical-Romantic art, Greek-German beauty, and producing the ideal poesy. Though Boïto did not discard this Classical Sabbath, he did revamp the opera, and some contend that the final libretto is not as good as the first, which remained closer to Goethe. But it is close enough. In any event, the composer removed a symphonic interlude and a scene in the Imperial Palace, changed Faust from baritone to tenor, and added a range of numbers, including "Lontano . . . ," "Spunta l'aurora," and a Fuga Infernale. The Prologue shows the pact between God and His rival for Faust's soul. Act I is Easter evening when Mefistofele makes his other pact with Faust. Act II brings forth the love of Margherita and Faust, after which Mefistofele leads his victim to a romantic Sabbath in Schirk Valley near Brocken, where the vision of Margherita in chains appears. Act III finds her in prison (accused of killing her mother) and refusing to leave with Faust when she recognizes Satan under Mefistofele's garb—hence her salvation. Act IV takes place in Greece, near the Penejo River, where the Elena episode occurs. And in the Epilogue, Faust, old again, thinks of the vanity of all his adventures. Mefistofele wonders, concerned, why his prey has still not found the supreme moment. Faust will not fly off with him again; instead, he pronounces the fatal (blessed) words "Arrestati . . ." fixed upon a heavenly vision of rapture. Mefistofele's angry "Torci lo sguardo" does not succeed. Faust is redeemed, and Mefistofele whistles and sinks, buried under flowers while the Celestial Chorus sings praise, in one of the most powerful endings in the operatic repertoire. The music almost throughout is unforgettable.

21. *Star*, 29 May 1889.

22. Busoni did not finish his opera; it was completed by his pupil, Philipp Jahrnach, and performed in Dresden in 1925. It consists of a poet's Prologue, an Overture, two Vorspiele, a Hauptspiel, and various interludes (for orchestra, or organ) in between, before the final poet's Epilogue. Mephistopheles is conjured up in Faust's study, the pact is signed. Valentino is killed; Faust performs magic acts at the Court, then flees with the Duchess of Parma; the students discuss philosophy; Mephistopheles—bearing the child of Faust's and the Duchess's love—reports the latter's death; the heathen sets fire to the child (actually a bundle of straw); the image of Helena rises from it; Faust gives alms to a beggar (actually the Duchess, the voice of the Eternal Feminine) who gives Faust their child before disappearing; Faust turns to the Church and performs a final magic act before dying, leaving his life and soul to the child: from the little cadaver rises a youth with a blossoming branch, symbol of the human Ideal that cannot be destroyed. Busoni sought novelty, "a Leonardo [da Vinci] who would be an Italian Faust" (*Brief an seine Frau* [Erlenbach-Zürich: Rotapfel Verlag, 23 June 1913]). He went to the Puppenspiel, or puppet play, as the beginning, the Parma episode and the last scene indicate, but from Goethe, if not the Euphorion episode, he got the Prologue, Wagner's manner, Valentino's murder, the drinking with students, and other events and ideas, like the Faustian dream "Die and become" (*Stirb und Werde*). He also added elements of his own. So Busoni goes beyond the puppet theater from his personal dejection over mankind's barbarism into Goethe's idealism. As for the opera's characters, they basically reflect Busoni,

the searcher after spirituality, power, and fame. Among Faust's demands of Mephistopheles, he adds "genius" as a desire: "Beschaffe mir für meines Lebens Rest die unbedingte Erfüllung jeden Wünches, mache mich frei, lass mich die Welt umfassen, . . . gib mir Genie und gib mir auch sein Leiden auf das ich glücklich werde wie kein andrer." Says one critic: "Faust speaks with Busoni's own voice" (E. J. Dent, *F. Busoni* [London: Oxford University Press, H. Milford, 1933], p. 308), something Jahrnach had put slightly differently to his teacher: "You will never be happy; you are Faust and Mephistopheles in one" (quoted from ibid., 309).

23. It was published under the title "Über Partitur des *Doktor Faust.*"

24. Quoted from the *Enciclopedia dello spettacolo* (Rome: Casa editrice Le Maschere, 1954), 2: 1403.

21. LISZT'S JOURNEY THROUGH DANTE'S HEREAFTER

1. Tchaikowsky's *Francesca da Rimini*, opus 32, was inspired in the summer of 1876 when he attended the first Wagner festival in Bayreuth, where he read *Inferno* 5 in the original. It became the piece he conducted most frequently. The opening and the ending of the composition portray the storm:

> Io venni in luogo d'ogni luce muto,
>   che mugghia come fa mar per tempesta,
>   se da contrari venti è combattuto.
> La bufera infernal, che mai non resta,
>   mena li spirti con la sua rapina:
>   voltando e percotendo li molesta.
>
> (I came to where all light is still,
>   a place that moaned like sea in tempest,
>   if it's struck by adverse winds.
> The infernal storm, that never quiets,
>   drives the spirits on with violence:
>   wheeling and pounding it harasses them.)
>   [Dante, *Inferno* 5.28–33]

And in the slow, middle section is Francesca's story—given initially to the solo flute—a nostalgic tune that seems to depict the same words Liszt wrote into his Francesca part: "Nessun maggior dolore." Being generally descriptive, the *Francesca Fantasy* makes no attempt to render Dante specifically.

2. The Fantasia has a presto lamentoso of noble tragedy and gloom, followed by a precipitato in F♯, a loveful andante, and a dramatic, orgiastic development leading to a massive allegro in D and culminating in an excited allegro vivace and presto. But, for purposes of musico-literary analysis, the composition merely bespeaks a mood; it does not "say," any more than Tchaikowsky's Overture does, more than that.

3. Few have written about the *Dante Symphony*, though it is mentioned in most music histories and accounts of the Romantic period. I have located only the following brief analyses, usually little more than descriptions: Walter Beckett, *Liszt* (Lon-

don: Dent, 1956), 112–13; Arthur Hahn, "Liszt's Dante Symphonie" ("Eine Symphonie zu Dante's [sic] 'Divina Commedia' "), *Musikführer* no. 145 (1898): 2–21; James Huneker, *Franz Liszt* (New York: Scribner's, 1927), 146–53; Edith V. Eastman, "Liszt's 'Dante' Symphony," in W. S. B. Matthers, *Music* [n.d.], 3: 304–13; Humphrey Searle, *The Music of Liszt* (London: Williams and Norgate, 1954), 80–82; Sacheverell Sitwell, *Liszt* (London: Cassell, 1955), 166–69; and Felix Weingartner, *Die Symphonie nach Beethoven* (Leipzig: Breitkopf and Härtel, 1926), 87–88.

4. Herbert Westerby, *Liszt: Composer, and His Piano Works* (Westpoint, Conn.: Greenwood Press, 1970), 146.

5. Quoted from Frederick Niecks, "Literature: F. Liszt," *Monthly Musical Review*, London, no. 1 (July 1916): 306.

6. Frederick Niecks, *Programme Music in the Last Four Centuries* (London: Novello, 1906), 280–81.

7. The shiver of Hell at the end of *Don Giovanni*, for example, is caused mainly by the protagonist's fall and his horrifying scream, not by the sounds of the score.

8. Passive only in the external sense. In the *Inferno* there is a frenzy of activity (physical movement), but it is purposeless; in the *Purgatorio* the action is primarily internal (psychological) and only appears passive: it has a goal, hence the significant difference in the very "motion" of the music between Liszt's "Inferno" and "Purgatorio"—not to mention the still more profound difference in his "Paradiso".

9. For the souls in Hell, the center of gravity is this world, and their concerns remain directed toward it; for the souls in Heaven, "home" is "up there" where God is. Gravity begins to shift in Purgatory from home down here to home up there.

10. Liszt's Paradise is joined to Purgatory much as Dante's Eden is situated at the top of the mountain of purgation, from which the transition to Heaven is far less perceptible, let alone dramatic, than that from Hell to Purgatory.

11. A Magnificat, however, is the hymn of the Virgin Mary, and St. Bernard's prayer at the end of the pilgrim's journey is to her. The choice, therefore, is fitting, even implied by the text.

12. See Peter Raabe, *Liszts Leben* (Jutzing: Hans Schneider, 1968), 176.

13. J. Huneker, *Franz Liszt* (New York: Scribner's, 1927), 155.

INDEX

ABOUT THE AUTHOR

Born in 1924 in Cleveland, Ohio, Jean-Pierre Barricelli is Professor of Humanities and Comparative Literature at the University of California at Riverside. His B.A., M.A., and Ph.D. degrees are all from Harvard University. He has been the recipient of many honors and awards, including Phi Beta Kappa, a Harvard Humanities Award, two Fulbright awards, two University of California Humanities Institute awards, an Outstanding Educator of America designation, his campus's Distinguished Teaching Award, and has been appointed to the one-year prestigious Kenan Distinguished Professor of Humanities chair at the College of William and Mary.

Apart from the essays and the many writers and composers included in this volume, he has published other studies on Balzac, Blake, Boccaccio, Botticelli, Calderón, Chausson, Chekhov, Dalí, Dante, Doré, Gandhi, Leopardi (his book has been nominated for the MLA H. Marraro Prize), Machiavelli, Mann, Manzoni, Nattini, Plato, Pound, Rauschenberg, Rojas, Rulfo, Turgenev, Virgil, and Wergeland. His specialities lie in the areas of Romanticism, Renaissance, and the interrelations of literature, especially with law, the visual arts, and, of course, music. Some of his oil paintings have been exhibited.

He is simultaneously a professional musician: composer, musicologist, pianist, and conductor; he has performed and has been performed in Europe and the United States. He now serves as music reviewer for the Riverside Press/Enterprise. During the occupation of Germany after World War II, he was Music Director of Radio Munich, a city for the reconstitution of whose three main orchestras he was responsible. His compositions (for orchestra, solo instruments, solo voices, and chorus) have received favorable reception on both sides of the Atlantic.